Masterful Women

Masterful Women

Slaveholding Widows
from the American Revolution
through the Civil War

KIRSTEN E. WOOD

The University of North Carolina Press

Chapel Hill and London

Designed by April Leidig-Higgins
Set in Ehrhardt by Copperline Book Services, Inc.
Manufactured in the United States of America

The paper in this book meets the guidelines for
permanence and durability of the Committee on
Production Guidelines for Book Longevity of
the Council on Library Resources.

Library of Congress Cataloging-in-Publication Data
Wood, Kirsten E.
Masterful women: slaveholding widows from the American Revolution through the Civil War / Kirsten E. Wood.
p. cm.—(Gender & American culture)
Includes bibliographical references and index.
ISBN 0-8078-2859-9 (cloth: alk. paper)
ISBN 0-8078-5528-6 (pbk.: alk. paper)
1. Slaveholders—Southern States—History.
2. Widows—Southern States—Social conditions.
3. Widows—Southern States—Economic
conditions.   4. Slavery—Southern States—
History.   5. Widowhood—Southern States—
History.   6. Sex role—Southern States—History.
7. Plantation life—Southern States—History.
8. Southern States—History—1775–1865.   9. Southern States—Social conditions.   10. Southern States
—Race relations. I. Title. II. Series.
E443.W666   2004   975'.03'08621—dc22
2003024971

cloth   08 07 06 05 04   5 4 3 2 1
paper   08 07 06 05 04   5 4 3 2 1

For Mary B. Wood

CONTENTS

ILLUSTRATIONS

ACKNOWLEDGMENTS

Widowhood and slavery were both legal constructs in the early nineteenth-century Southeast, but *Masterful Women* is not primarily a legal (or quantitative) study grounded in statutes, court records, and will books. Instead, it explores the evolving relationship between widowhood, slaveholding, and mastery from the Revolution through the Civil War in Virginia, the Carolinas, and Georgia. In particular, it focuses on occasions and places in which slaveholding women's and men's roles in the Old South intersected, and it situates slaveholding widows' distinctive blend of ladyhood and mastery within the larger political and economic history of the region and period.

I have relied on many different institutions and people for help along the way. For a decade now I have shared research, writing, teaching dilemmas, professional concerns, and food with a large circle of friends and mentors. Early on, I was blessed in my graduate school advisers. Drew Faust inspired me even before I began graduate school. Admittedly I did not pay her the ultimate compliment of dressing as her at a "Come as Your Adviser" party many years ago—other, taller friends took on the charge—but I respect and admire her more than I can say. Richard Dunn helped me recognize—and I hope reconcile—many of the project's early problems, and his encouragement stood me in good stead on many occasions. Kathleen Brown came to Penn in time for me to benefit from her many insights about research, writing, and life in the profession. Each of them sets a formidable (even intimidating) standard for personal and professional achievement. But they are also great people to talk with over a coffee or a beer, which is equally important.

My friends deserve much of the credit for helping me conceive and complete this project. Beth Clement helped me articulate its central concept, and Allison Sneider has consistently forced me to stick to my guns in defending it. I owe Tony Iaccarino a debt of friendship for reading my first stabs at that frightening first chapter. Allison, Jason McGill, Jennifer Ritterhouse, and Serena Zabin helped me throughout the dissertation-writing process. At different times in graduate school, Ellen Amster, Ed Baptist, Valentijn Byvanck, Seth Cotlar, Konstantin Dierks, Tom Humphrey, Hannah Joyner, Sarah Knott, Roderick McDonald, Seth Rockman, Mark Santow, Randolph Scully, and Mark Wilkens prompted me to rethink, redefine, rewrite, and retrench. I have also received penetrating feedback at seminars and conference panels from many people, including Anne Firor Scott, Douglas Egerton, Catherine Clinton, Elizabeth Fox-Genovese, Eugene Genovese, Mike Zuckerman, Jane Turner Censer, John Boles, Dallett Hemphill, Patricia Cline Cohen, Mark Smith, Jeff Young, Stephanie McCurry, James Roark, and Lorri Glover. (Conferences also provide opportunities to catch up with old friends and make new ones, and I must particularly mention Dan Kilbride and Chris Olsen in that regard.)

Since moving to Miami, I have been nurtured, encouraged, and well-meaningly mocked by my entire department, but especially by Darden Pyron, Mark Szuchman, Nina Caputo, Hugh Elton, Mitch Hart, Lara Kriegel, and Rebecca Friedman. I have also learned much from Peter Craumer, Carl Craver, Maureen Donnelly, Keith Dougherty, Mary Beth Melchior, Ken Rogerson, Robin Sheriff, and especially Margaret Kovera. Mark and Peter deserve special thanks for all their computing help. Elena Maubrey, Hayat Kassab-Gresham, Carmen Evans de Jesus, Camilla Samqua, and Vanessa Peterson have helped in many small but crucial ways with the daily business of academic life. Ed and Stephanie Baptist, Guy and Lois Bailey, David Chatfield, Camilla Cochrane, Bonnell Denton, Thomasine Morris, Wes Walker, Willie Allen-Faella, and my fellow choristers at St. Stephen's have helped me look beyond the academy. Most recently, Tom Leness has enriched my life by introducing me to Jack Aubrey and Steven Maturin, and in several other ways besides. Even with all this local talent, I have depended upon the long-distance support of Bonnie Gordon, who deserves a medal for reading so many drafts and for being available for 7:00 A.M. consultations.

During a semester of course release from Florida International University, I squatted at the McNeil Center for Early American Studies in Philadelphia, where Niki Eustace, Matt Hale, Brooke Hunter, Brendon McConville, Randolph Scully, John Smolenski, Colleen Terrell, and Mark Thompson provided the camaraderie and hard questions that I have come to expect from that institution. I owe its director, Dan Richter, a great debt for allowing me to return to my former intellectual home. Lynn Lees offered me visiting scholar status at Penn, and Hannah Poole and Amy Baxter helped me get that all-important resource: a library card. Best of all, I got to spend six months in the company of old friends, Beth, Ellen, Mark, Randolph, Laurie Drummond, Michele Zelinsky, and Ann Greene.

I have had nearly as many sources of institutional support as friends and mentors. A Ben Franklin fellowship and a Chimicles teaching fellowship supported me during graduate school at the University of Pennsylvania. I have also received financial support from Duke University's Women's Studies Research Grant, the Mary Lily Research Fund, the Virginia Historical Society, as well as from the Provost's Office, the College of Arts and Sciences, and my own department at FIU. Like every researcher, I relied on archivists and archival staff, especially those at the Southern Historical Collection at the University of North Carolina at Chapel Hill, the Special Collections Library at Duke University, the Virginia Historical Society, the South Caroliniana Library at the University of South Carolina, the Library Company of Philadelphia, the Rare Books and Manuscripts Library at Columbia University, and the Mormon Family History Research Center in Broomhall, Pennsylvania. I remember the folks at the Southern Historical Collection with particular fondness for spontaneously resurrecting the barter system: photocopies for cookies. I owe a great debt to the anonymous readers for the UNC Press and to my editor, Chuck Grench. Amanda McMillan, Pamela Upton, and Eric Combest also helped in many ways to bring this project to completion.

My family has sustained me the longest, in both emotional and material ways. They have listened patiently—usually with interest—as I raved or fretted about my sources and arguments. Whenever I doubted that staying in school "until the twenty-second grade" was worth it, their pride and faith helped me stay the course. My sister in particular has done yeoman service in reading drafts, and she has also provided great support and many laughs along the way. Yes, Karin, you are funny.

Notwithstanding all the help I have received over so many years from so many sources, this project's shortcomings and errors are, of course, entirely my own responsibility. I can only thank my friends, mentors, editors, readers, and family that they are not more numerous.

Masterful Women

Introduction

Ask people in the United States today to name a famous woman in early American history, and many if not most will mention Martha Washington, who in fact owed her fame to her husband. Thanks to George Washington, Martha played a small role in the Revolutionary War, became the nation's first First Lady, and helped set the tone of national politics in the 1790s. In both our time and her own, Martha Washington's prominence reflected her husband's. Martha was hardly unusual in this way; in her day and age, most adult women's social position derived largely from their husbands. This book asks what happened to women like Martha Washington after their husbands died.[1]

In the decades after the American Revolution, widowhood made most women socially marginal and even destitute. Some widows, however, retained considerable economic, social, and political privilege; they lost their husbands but not all of their husbands' reflected glory. In Martha Washington's case, her lofty position owed much to being a president's widow, but it owed something as well to owning over one hundred slaves. Being slaveholders—and especially planters—made widows independent and powerful to a degree usually thought impossible for women in the early United States, especially in notoriously conservative Virginia, North and South Carolina, and Georgia. More important, slaveholding placed widows squarely among the ranks of the masters, a group usually associated with white men.

BETWEEN THE Revolution and the Civil War, few whites in the Southeast questioned that God and nature had made woman subordinate to and dependent on man. What followed from this basic assumption, however, varied considerably. Many believed that woman's natural weakness made her emotionally and morally sensitive, but the agricultural press, for example, praised women not for these qualities but for industrious housewifery.[2] Proslavery ministers and politicians penned some of the narrowest—and best known—interpretations. Openly endorsing slavery, they posited that dramatic inequality formed the basis of all stable and healthy social orders. In some strands of proslavery thought, moreover, marriage enjoyed functional parity with slavery: both were benevolent institutions which linked the strong and the weak in relations of mutual obligation and dependence. Specifically, husbands and owners governed, while wives and slaves obeyed, faring better in subordination than they could possibly do alone.[3] Therefore, moralist Virginia Cary admonished her readers, "women should never brood over the imaginary advantages of independence." Freedom suited men, in contrast, because they were strong, rational, forceful, and energetic— in short, everything women were not.[4] In practice, many supposedly mild, self-abnegating wives had trouble learning "to submit without a murmur (as every good wife should do)." As one woman complained, "I belong to that degraded race called woman—who whether her lot be cast among Jew, or Turk, heathen or Christian is yet a *Slave*." Yet even as they grumbled, slaveholding wives made a real effort to accept their lot with the proper submission. If they failed, the consequences could be severe: social ostracism and even outright coercion by husbands or legal authorities awaited the unruly.[5]

In the nineteenth-century Southeast, husbands' traditional prerogative of governing their wives merged with old ideas about servitude and new ones about representative government to form the construct of mastery. Mastery originated in English laws governing the relations of indentured servants and apprentices with their "masters." In the colonial South, it incorporated the new category of hereditary, race-based slavery. By the 1800s, slaveholders routinely referred to themselves as masters—not simply owners—of their slaves. Mastery thus meant slaveholding, but it also became a virtual synonym for "household head." Slaveholders defined the household in part as a place: for most, it encompassed a residence, outbuildings, slave quarters, and fields. But a household also comprised the "domestic relations" contained within its physical space, namely marriage, parenthood, and servitude. Householding, or household mastery, entailed two major functions: governing domestic dependents and household property, and representing the household's collective interests (as defined from the top down) in the wider world. In this sense, any free white adult could head a household, but household mastery had a further implication: white southerners associated householding with the specifically masculine authority of husbands and fathers.[6]

In the early nineteenth century, mastery acquired an explicitly political meaning, which posed a further barrier to female participation. In the solidly republican political culture of the new nation, someone who mastered a household was economically independent: that is, he supposedly possessed the means to support himself and his family and did not depend on others for his livelihood. And, as even the most elitist of republicans agreed, economic independence undergirded political independence, which in turn made an individual competent to participate in representative government. (More democratic Americans came to believe that any person with the capacity for self-governance, usually defined as a white male, was entitled to political rights regardless of his financial condition.) Thus, anyone who headed a household was entitled to political rights, such as suffrage. In some interpretations, the relationship between mastery and political rights also worked the other way: only someone with political rights could really claim to be a master, and anyone denied a vote could not. This definition excluded all white women (and most blacks) from mastery, regardless of whether they actually headed households. At the same time, an expanding suffrage meant that white men who owned little but their votes could claim to be masters. Thus, for white men, mastery was or became democratic. Throughout the early United States, Americans came to associate not just mastery but freedom itself with the franchise, but the linkage had particular meaning in the Southeast, where slavery provided a stark counterpoint to freedom, and where political democracy expanded more slowly than anywhere else in the new nation.[7]

The rhetoric of male mastery and female submission left little ideological room for widows. In fact, proslavery theorists likened slavery to marriage precisely because the analogy suggested permanence: wives, like slaves, were not supposed to outgrow their need for manly protection. In reality, however, death often intervened. In the South, married white women stood nearly an even chance of widowhood, especially if they married men older than themselves, as many slaveholders did. When slaveholders did acknowledge the existence of widowhood, they typically considered it devastating to the "defenseless sex."[8] Slaveholders described their widowed friends and relatives as "of course in great trouble," "very much distressed," or, most dramatically, "borne down by the unrelenting hand of Fate, to the very dust." Newspapers and novelists reinforced these sentiments with fictional characters who lost their minds, were "turned to stone," or had "violent convulsions" when their husbands died. Charitable institutions belabored "the suffering condition of the poor widow and the destitute orphan," while obituaries occasionally described a husband as "the only earthly dependence of an afflicted wife." Georgia slaveholder Eliza Schley put the problems in the simplest of terms: "I do not know what his wife will do without him."[9]

Yet while popular culture highlighted widows' forlorn dependence, the law insisted that widows take financial and legal responsibility for themselves. Under early American law, widowhood turned a wife bound by coverture into a free and legally independent woman. Among other things, this meant that she had to pay her own debts and taxes and that she could freely enter into contracts and be sued. Legal codes also required that a widow receive one-third of her husband's real estate, known as dower. A widow had to support herself on the basis of this dower (often supplemented by her own labor and whatever help she derived from family, friends, or charities).[10] In theory, then, widows were their own people both legally and economically, but in practice, their freedoms varied substantially. Free black widows (like all free blacks) had to be able to prove their status or risk enslavement, and some southern states required free blacks to have a white sponsor. Most black women in the South who survived their husbands were not technically widows in any case because they were slaves, and Anglo-American law did not sanction slave marriages.[11] Poor white widows fared only somewhat better. Like most free black women, they struggled with poverty and with county courts, which often indentured orphaned children on the assumption that their mothers could not support them. While that assumption reflected judicial prejudice against the poor, it also had some merit because, while the right to control property came with widowhood, property itself did not. For most American women, dower rights provided a very uncertain security, because a third of most men's estates could not provide a comfortable living.[12] For the Southeast's slaveholding women, legal widowhood had quite different implications. Slaveholding widows needed no guardians, sponsors, or patrons. They had all of the legal rights concerning their own property that white men possessed. In addition, judges were far more likely to respect these women's maternal claims, presuming that propertied white widows could decently maintain and raise children. Most important, because slaveholding men's wealth remained tied up in individual ownership of slaves and farmland, these men's widows often became the heads of productive households—virtual family-owned businesses—with authority over space, capital, and labor.[13]

In the first days of widowhood, however, most slaveholding women confirmed cultural expectations of desolation. While Martha Washington's particular circumstances were unique, her misery at her husband's death was not. Writing to another widow, she lamented that "words are inadequate to convey" her "distresses."[14] A dozen years later, a much younger Virginia widow expressed her misery at her husband's unexpected death in similar terms. In plaintive letters to her sister, Martha Cocke insisted that "you can form no adequate idea of the anguish, of feelings produced by a loss like mine." Her widowhood induced a physical and emotional collapse. Being "deprived, for ever in this world" of her much-loved husband had destroyed her "peace of mind." Wracked with grief, she declined "dayly," prompting her doctor to point out "the horrors" of passive suicide.[15]

Yet despite their initial incapacitating grief, most slaveholding women adjusted to the new demands of widowhood. They had little choice. They had to support themselves, manage their dower shares, including slaves, and sometimes also raise children and settle their husbands' estates. Long-term prostration was a luxury even the wealthiest could ill afford. It took Martha Cocke longer than some to shoulder her burdens. Ten years after her husband died, she decided on an "experiment": renting a farm and managing "my Negros & other business" herself. By getting rid of agents who had "scattered & deranged" her affairs, Cocke hoped to "get my affairs in better train than they have been for some years." While some of her friends worried that "as she is one of the fairer, I will not say weaker, sex, she will lack capacity, industry, &c," a kinswoman predicted "she will be quite a Manager." In the end, even the skeptical supported Martha Cocke's endeavor, perhaps in part because they concluded she could do no worse than a hired overseer or manager who, many thought, "seldom prove faithful." Most important, Cocke already possessed a labor force—her slaves—and had no need to hire field workers, as nonslaveholding or northern farm widows did.[16]

THROUGH WILLS AND intestacy law, male slaveholders routinely left women in charge of households, yet whether this made women into masters is a matter of perspective and definition. Because of the term's patriarchal roots and republican foliage, historians have generally doubted women's ability to master the household's power relations: if white manhood was the essence of mastery, then no widow could qualify, no matter how many slaves and acres she owned. Yet throughout the period, mastery retained a variety of connotations, such that the "master class" could still signify slaveholders in general or even the entire white population. This book argues that slaveholding widows developed a distinctive version of mastery, which harnessed ladyhood to householding and privileged both over mere white manhood.[17]

One obvious difference between slaveholding widows' and white men's mastery involved language. On the eve of the Civil War, South Carolina planter Ada Bacot encapsulated the specifically feminine nature of her position. One February day, Bacot discovered that some of the "young negroes" on her upcountry cotton plantation had been "found away from home with out a pass." Although disheartened by their truancy, she expected to show them "that I am Mistress & will be obeyed."[18] In slaveholders' writings, the word "mistress" usually denoted a master's wife, while it connoted her simultaneous authority over slaves and children and subordination to her husband. As a result of this combination of inferiority and power, slaveholders concluded that "master's eye and voice are much more potent than mistress," as Catherine Edmonston phrased it.[19] Widowhood might end a woman's direct subordination to any particular man, but it did not reverse the society-wide assumption of female inferiority. Equally important, widows, because of their sex, could not participate in many components of male mastery, such as voting, mustering, serving on juries, and holding public office.[20] Sex also barred widows from affairs of honor, which many slaveholding men considered an essential means to defend their claims to mastery. (Since the code of honor could result in lethal violence, however, widows' exclusion might well be seen as an exemption.) And finally, as Bacot's and Edmonston's words reveal, most slaveholding women saw "master" as a masculine identity.[21] Yet when used by a widowed planter like Ada Bacot, "mistress" melded a feminine gender role with the assertiveness and duties of mastery. Bacot intended to make her slaves obey her, and like many an arrogant male master, she expected to do so "without much trouble."[22] Slaveholding widows lacked the political privileges which white men came to see as their God-given right, but their version of mastery had teeth all the same. Widowed slaveholders bought, sold, and punished slaves. They hired overseers—sometimes drafting contracts that severely limited these men's autonomy—and fired them. They stood security for others' debts, foreclosed on mortgages, raised rents, and patronized local shopkeepers and artisans. They brought charges against people who traded illegally with their slaves or trespassed on their lands. In all of these ways, slaveholding widows intervened for good or ill in the lives of people within and beyond their households.

Within the cohort, individual widows' ability to shape their own and others' circumstances varied considerably. Their managerial "capacity, industry, &c" hinged in large part on their resilience and their age. Emotionally or physically brittle women had great difficulty adapting to their expanded role, which perhaps explains why it took Martha Cocke ten years to begin managing her own affairs, and why Martha Washington delegated many responsibilities to her kinsmen and to Mount Vernon's steward.[23] At least as important in shaping slaveholding widows' mastery were their material resources. Planters like Ada Bacot and Martha Washington wielded enormous coercive power over their many slaves. They also had great potential economic and social power over other whites. Because of her wealth, Bacot could afford an overseer, whom she could fire at will—and whose daughter she used as a surrogate child. Women like Bacot were also important clients for their tobacco and cotton factors, as well as potential sources of employment and patronage to less wealthy whites in their neighborhoods.[24] In contrast, widows with only a handful of slaves had less power beyond and even within their households. Catherine Lewis was born in the first years of the new century, lost her husband in 1842, and died after the Civil War. She spent her life in North Carolina, where she had a large family of siblings and in-laws. Her husband left her four young sons, an infant daughter, and a handful of slaves. During her widowhood, Lewis kept a boardinghouse, a business which supported her family but left her constantly worried about "poverty and privation and a life of toil."[25] Women in her position played a subordinate role in some of their most important relationships. As a boardinghouse keeper, she had to act deferentially with current and potential boarders and maintain good relations with her domestic slaves. Lewis also had to cultivate her in-laws' emotional support and occasional financial assistance. As a result, her manner typically suggested vulnerability rather than forcefulness, even though she headed her own household and routinely used violence to discipline her children and slaves.

Slaveholding widows' experiences also varied with their location in the Southeast. Particularly important was their proximity to kin and other useful connections. Martha Washington lived in Virginia, a state thick with influential, wealthy Washington and Dandridge connections. Catherine Lewis's connections were considerably less prominent, but she made good use of them all the same. In the early 1850s, her brother William H. Battle was teaching law for the University of North Carolina. His presence likely influenced her decision to come to Chapel Hill and helped her attract a desirable class of boarders. In contrast, Lucy Freeman found that migration to Tennessee with her husband left her dangerously isolated after his death in 1835; her siblings had remained in Virginia, which placed her at a distinct disadvantage in soliciting their help.[26] Geography also inflected widowed mastery, creating subtle differences between the Chesapeake and the Deep South, the cotton uplands and the coastal swamps. The tobacco planters of Virginia, for example, frequently divided their land and slaves into several farms, each managed by an overseer. This system typically removed planter widows from the immediate supervision of field work but could increase their clout as employers and patrons of less wealthy whites. In the cotton belt, planters typically had larger, single plantations, and they reinforced their rule over slaves and overseers by riding out to inspect progress in the fields. Different again were the coastal rice and long-staple cotton planters, who left their disease-ridden plantations seasonally or even lived full-time in Charleston or Savannah. These planters rarely visited their fields, especially not the rice swamps. Their slaves cultivated the land by the task, a labor system that gave planters the luxury of a hands-off management style while still producing great wealth. For their part, slaves liked the task system because it afforded greater autonomy than the more common and heavily supervised gang system: slaves working under the task system performed a set "task" at their own pace and then were usually free to rest, hunt, or cultivate their own produce.[27]

For the minor slaveholders, the greatest differences concerned living in a wealthy, heavily slaveholding area, a poor area with few slaveholders, or a town. In heavily slaveholding regions of the Southeast, widows could number among the richest planters, but most widows in these areas owned considerably less property than did men. As Victoria Bynum has shown, in prosperous Granville County, North Carolina, female householders' per capita wealth was 80 percent of men's shortly before the Civil War. Poor widows living among wealthy slaveholders might receive their patronage, but charity and employment often made widows dependent. While this dependence meshed well with conventional feminine gender roles, it undercut widows' authority in their own households. In generally poorer areas, however, widowed householders were economically more equal to their male counterparts; in 1860, the per capita wealth of female householders in Montgomery County, North Carolina, for instance, was 96 percent of men's.[28] Near-equality with men had some advantages but did not make it easier for poor widows to make a living, especially in rural areas where employment for women was scarce. For this reason, poor white widows tended to congregate in the Southeast's towns and small cities, which offered more chances to find paying work.[29]

Further complicating generalizations about widows' mastery, both the Southeast and the cohort changed over time. While eastern and Upper South counties stagnated or even lost population, western areas were often still growing. For example, by 1790, whites had been living in the western North Carolina county of Rowan for only a few decades. According to the federal census of that year, only 17 percent of Rowan County's households had slaves, and two-thirds had three or fewer. In that year, 10 percent of Rowan's slaveholders and 5 percent of its householders were white women.[30] By the end of the antebellum era, Rowan's white and black populations had grown significantly, and the county had subdivided twice, sluffing off its less prosperous areas. In 1860, the female proportion of Rowan County's slaveholders and householders approached 20 percent, and the average female slaveholder had five slaves. The rising proportion and wealth of propertied widows was not confined to growing western counties like Rowan. In many different areas, improvements in women's life expectancy increased the chance of widowhood and its duration, which in turn enhanced widows' likelihood both of appearing in the census and of accumulating property over time. This growth made widows more noteworthy in their neighborhoods and diluted the taint of desolation associated with their status.[31]

Despite these differences, widows' versions of mastery had common elements that distinguished them from men's, above and beyond their shared exclusion from voting, mustering, and dueling. These commonalities stemmed primarily from the construct of ladyhood which, when wedded to mastery, gave widows a potent way to justify and assert their authority. For most white southern men, and most of their historians, masters were white men, and mastery meant the patriarchal privilege of dominating everyone else. In theory, slaveholding widows acknowledged this principle of white men's dominance. In practice, they rejected the notion that as women they must defer to any and all white men. Most slaveholding widows considered themselves not just women but ladies, a label that suggested genteel white womanhood. Southern whites sometimes spoke as if all women were equally cherished and respected. Addressing an Alabama girls' school in 1845, Rev. W. T. Hamilton used "the word *woman*, in preference to ladies, or females; because I deem it more appropriate, and more consistent with true delicacy."[32] However, only certain women could aspire to be ladies; most southern whites found the idea of a black lady simply ridiculous, and while a semiliterate farmwife with work-roughened hands might command somewhat greater respect than a black woman, she too was no lady. Even if they had aspired to ladyhood, poor whites and most yeoman farmwives simply could not afford it: they lacked the education,[33] the disposable income for fashionable clothing and comfortable surroundings, and, perhaps most important, freedom from regular field work. (In the nineteenth-century Southeast, ladies not only managed domestic slaves but often worked alongside them. If her husband's absence, poverty, or widowhood required, a lady could also manage a farm, teach school, or run a boardinghouse. Some ladies even tended vegetable gardens, but only under exceptional circumstances would they be found performing field work associated with cash crops.)[34] Ladyhood constituted a social armor; it bolstered slaveholding women's authority within and beyond their households. As ladies, slaveholding women believed they were superior to most of their sex. They also considered themselves superior to many white men in manners, morals, gentility, and piety, qualities that popular opinion deemed white women's special province.[35] Supposedly character-based, these assessments invariably reflected class and race privilege.

Ladyhood mattered to widows in particular because they had no husbands to defend them, and widowhood gave slaveholding women new opportunities to assert themselves as ladies. When combined with legal independence and property, ladyhood helped widows stand up to men within and beyond their own families. In conflicts with sons, brothers, overseers, and neighbors, slaveholding widows repeatedly defended their interests and actions in terms of their prerogatives as ladies and their duties as loyal wives and devoted mothers. Widows evicted tenants, fired overseers, and sold slaves, all in the name of obeying (dead) husbands and protecting children. The posture of dependent ladyhood, meanwhile, often encouraged white men to decide that assisting a widow served their own financial interests, familial honor, or personal reputation for chivalry. Slaveholding widows' mastery thus illuminates the broader study of class among southern whites. Many of the historians who have studied white men in the Old

South can be placed in one of two camps: those who see southern whites as "inevitably divided" into slaveowners and nonslaveowners (and white society as "essentially hierarchical"), and those who see southern whites as "fundamentally united."[36] Eugene Genovese and Elizabeth Fox-Genovese have argued that planters dominated the rest of the South through a hegemonic ideology of paternalism, which cast inequality and their own power as reasonable and natural.[37] Qualifying this argument considerably, J. William Harris posits that while planters and ordinary whites in the area around Augusta, Georgia, agreed on most fundamentals, their alliance remained "precarious" because "political equality did not translate into economic equality." Others maintain that racism, white man's democracy, honor, republicanism, agriculture, or some combination produced shared values and interests among southern whites.[38] Thus Lacy Ford, for example, maintains that a shared investment in whiteness and republican independence united upcountry South Carolina planters and yeomen and prevented political domination by planters.[39] Scholars who attend to gender and women have generally supported the "essentially hierarchical" argument. Stephanie McCurry shows that South Carolina's lowcountry yeomen assumed that the privileges of manhood created an irreducible equality between themselves and the planters, despite the vast difference in their wealth. Many wealthier men agreed with this democratic application of patriarchy, although sometimes only because they feared the consequences of bullying men who could vote. However, she maintains, planters and yeomen remained "thoroughly unequal" masters. Elizabeth Fox-Genovese suggests that white women's interactions tended to reaffirm "class distance among free white families." Going further, McCurry proposes that "the signification of class boundaries was one of planter women's central political roles."[40]

Widowhood provided slaveholding women with new and distinctive opportunities to uphold those boundaries. Throughout their interactions with other whites—and especially with white men—slaveholding widows acted not only as women in a patriarchal society, but also as owners in a slave society and wealthy individuals in a profoundly unequal economy. Consequently, they provided a conservative counterpoint to the patriarchal and potentially democratic mastery espoused by yeomen and male planters. When slaveholding widows successfully defended their claims—primarily to and over property—they helped keep the region's balance of power tilted toward property and away from substantive democracy, even for the politically favored class of enfranchised white men. Yet doing so as widows, in the name of ladyhood, made it difficult for the white men they disgruntled to formulate an effective response, even one that mobilized latent class resentments in the increasingly stratified Southeast.[41]

WHILE GENDER ROLES ensured that slaveholding widows' mastery differed from slaveholding men's, the two carved parallel courses in the historical landscape. Both insisted on the prerogatives of whiteness and the necessity of slavery in a multiracial society. Both recognized that in the face of mounting moral and political criticism, slavery's future depended on a vigorous ideological defense, on slaves' constantly renewed subordination, and on continued profitability. Finally, and perhaps most important, both men's and women's mastery were ultimately founded on a myth: the myth of perfect control.[42] As every slaveholder knew—or soon learned—power did not flow automatically from property titles and slave codes. Nor did it inhere in whiteness or maleness, *pace* the proslavery politicians and theologians. Slaveholders had distinct statutory, ideological, and material advantages, but these had to be constantly asserted, defended, and if possible extended. Anyone who took the legal fact of slave ownership for granted would quickly find him or herself beset with work stoppages, truancy, theft, perhaps even arson or murder. Indeed, slaves resisted domination on the most and the least aggressively managed plantations and farms. As a result, throughout the Old South, every human encounter involved contingency, and every negotiation the potential to reverse the normal polarity, if only for a moment.

On the eve of the war that would decimate her class, Ada Bacot's words about truancy suggested her awareness of this tension: "I find some of my young negroes have been disobeying my orders. . . . I have never had any trouble with them until now. Even now I dont apprehend much." Like Bacot, most slaveholders assumed they could dominate their slaves "without much trouble." At the extreme, their "design for mastery" included the hope of completely dominating their subordinates in both will and body. No slaveholders ever achieved such perfect control, even over themselves.[43] All so-called masters—male or female, inept or clever, timid or cruel—faced resistance. Through open rebellion, covert resistance, collaboration, and other means, slaves materially shaped both mastery and slavery. Yeomen likewise shaped planters' mastery. Those who lived among planters might rely on their patronage, yet they struggled to truncate the deferential relations that some employers and benefactors sought to impose. Throughout the region, planters found that they could not consistently and openly degrade yeomen farmers' mastery without jeopardizing either their political position or the sanctity of property rights on which their own power depended.[44] Outside the febrile imaginations of proslavery ideologues, mastery could never be fully secure. This book uses the term "fictive" to encapsulate the truncated, contingent nature of all mastery, male and female. Yet while mastery rested on a series of interlocking fictions, slavery was no myth. The fiction of mastery obfuscated its violent core and naturalized its origins, but slavery remained tragically concrete. Whether slaveholders performed mastery well or poorly, they literally and metaphorically mutilated others' lives, whites as well as blacks.[45]

MASTERFUL WOMEN's first three chapters begin to unravel slaveholding widows' tangled history by focusing on households and families. Chapter 1 examines how the warp of law, demography, and economics and the weft of individual choice together shaped widowhood. Beginning in the late eighteenth century, it looks at both widows' share of and authority over their husbands' estates and women's experiences with the duties of householding before their husbands' deaths. The second chapter explores widows' relations with slaves, undoubtedly the most steadily contested aspect of any slaveholder's mastery. Slaveholding widows managed slaves much like men did, sometimes preaching disinterested benevolence, but usually privileging their own convenience and the bottom line. Gender did make a difference in some areas of slaveholders' behavior, including their recourse to violence, but slaves were not necessarily better off with widowed owners. In fact, the transition from a male to a female master often reduced slaves' negotiating room, for the simple reason that a master's death drastically increased slaves' risk of being sold or separated from kin. As a result, slave resistance persisted but rarely exploded under female masters.[46] Like slaveholding itself, widows' kinship networks both buttressed and challenged their authority. Widows placed family at the center of their identities and leaned on their kin for help with householding and planting. Chapter 3 argues that while this reliance might suggest a distinctively feminine dependence, widows ordinarily couched their requests in terms of familial reciprocity. Even when widows fought with kin—especially sons and sons-in-law—the ethos of mutualism gave widows powerful ethical weapons, complementing the authority that property conferred.

Chapters 4 and 5 consider the public consequences of widows' household mastery, and Chapter 6 the personal implications of widowhood for slaveholding women themselves. The fourth chapter uses widows' involvement with commerce to rethink notions of public and private space in the South. Widows' commercial responsibilities led them into spaces supposedly hostile to women, such as shops, banks, and court houses. Throughout the period, however, widows' economic relationships regularly intersected with sociability and kinship in ways that facilitated their transactions and their forays into public places. As widows exchanged with men and other women in and beyond the household, they blurred the already unstable distinction between male and female "spheres." Chapter 5 explores three distinct aspects of slaveholding widows' public activity: organized benevolence, formal politics and party patronage, and contests for mastery. In all three arenas, slaveholding widows asserted a vision of strictly hierarchical social relations among whites, one which afforded them considerable moral and even instrumental power. And yet, as Chapter 6 explains, widows adopted the garb of mastery without ever becoming entirely comfortable in it. Reluctant yet determined, they illustrated the difference between being and feeling powerful.

The seventh and final chapter explores the Civil War's devastating impact on slaveholding widows' mastery. Although many widows—and wives —weathered the early years of war quite well, over time the picture became exceedingly bleak. Poverty, relocation, conscription, and newly explosive class conflict and slave resistance severely undercut every would-be master. Historian Drew Faust has argued that wartime difficulties show southern women's unpreparedness for householding, suggesting that they could not become "everyday" slave managers "without in some measure failing to be what they understood as female." Yet slaveholding widows had done this work for generations, without ever losing their feminine sense of self.[47] Confederate women's defeat thus reflected not the logical outcome of antebellum gender roles, but rather unprecedented material deprivation, foreign invasion, and domestic insurgency.

Broken Reeds

In the early nineteenth-century Southeast, published and private texts advised that man's genius was to rule and woman's to yield. In her popular 1828 advice book, Virginia Cary praised women for their greater facility at "submission." A decade later, moral philosopher Jasper Adams admonished women that they must "give way" if ever they disagreed with their husbands.[1] Although pliancy was sometimes considered a strength of the sex, it also suggested weakness. In 1812, Virginian Charles Cocke believed that widowhood had desolated a "tender" and "meek" kinswoman, who was now "like the broken reed, bending before the strong blast of adversity." In Aesop's fable, a possible source for Cocke's metaphor, a reed wins a contest of strength with a tree because the reed bends before the wind, while the tree is uprooted. In the context of widowhood, the image harkened back to the discourse of feminine strength and resilience. Cocke may have had the Bible rather than Aesop in mind, however: the broken reed collapses under pressure, and Cocke described his widowed cousin as reduced "to the very dust."[2]

Such images of womanly weakness obscure slaveholding men's faith in and reliance on both wives and widows. Colonial historians have long known that southern widows' share in and authority over their husbands' estates declined over time. Less appreciated, however, is the fact that slaveholding widows' resources and duties remained substantial despite that decline. In their laws and wills, slaveholding men continued to give widows access to and authority over property. During marriage, they also relied on wives to act as seconds-in-command, giving women experience with managing property in the process. In the largely rural communities of the Southeast, wives' obligation to fill their husbands' shoes changed relatively little from the mid-eighteenth through the mid-nineteenth centuries. These two continuities—between marriage and widowhood, and between the late colonial and early national periods—help explain both how widows incurred the obligations of household mastery and how they managed to fulfill them.

THE ROOTS OF nineteenth-century southern widowhood stretched back to English precedents which accompanied the colonists.[3] English common law deemed widows legally independent individuals. Consequently, widows were judged competent to settle their husbands' estates and were granted the first claim to administer intestate estates. Every widow was also legally responsible for managing her own property. That property usually took the form of dower, or a life estate in one-third of her husband's lands. A widow could claim dower whether her husband died intestate or wrote a will. If the will allotted her less than dower, she could contest the legacy and be awarded her thirds. In real terms, the meaning of a dower share varied considerably. Among rural landowners, dower typically included all or part of a house plus farm land. Widows could use or sell whatever crops were produced from their dower land, but they could not sell or bequeath the land itself, and they had to protect its value. This meant, for example, that they could not raze timber stands and had to maintain fences and outbuildings.[4]

All of the southern colonies followed England in acknowledging widows' dower thirds, legal personhood, and claim to administer intestate estates. They differed, however, in the shares of personal property they assigned to widows, a category that included furniture, tools, livestock, foodstuffs, and bedding. Virginia and North Carolina required that widowed mothers divide the personalty equally with their children, while the widows of childless men received one-third of their husbands' personal property. In Georgia, widowed mothers also received a child's share, but childless widows took one half. South Carolina decreed that widows should take one-third whether or not their husbands had children.[5] The tendency to treat widows somewhat less generously in the Upper South also shaped the distribution of slaves. Under Virginia's intestacy law, widows received slaves only for life, on the premise that slaves should descend on the same terms as land. In North Carolina, widows also took slaves for life only, unless their husbands had no descendants. In South Carolina and Georgia, however, widows received absolute title to their slaves. This included the right to sell or devise them, and it made widows the owners of female slaves' future offspring. Upper South widows were thus at a comparative disadvantage in their share of their husbands' estates, although the day-to-day demands of slave management and agriculture loomed as large for widows who held slaves for life as for those who owned slaves outright.[6]

In the southern colonies, the statutes that undergirded widowhood changed little from the seventeenth century to the Revolutionary era, but their application shifted.[7] The best known case concerns the Chesapeake. Through the first several decades of settlement, husbands in Virginia and Maryland favored widows over other heirs: nearly three-fourths of those who wrote wills bequeathed their widows more than their statutory thirds. A considerable proportion gave widows their entire estates for life or even outright,[8] and the vast majority made their widows sole or joint executors.[9] Over time, however, both widows' legacies and their access to executorship declined markedly. By the Revolutionary era, far fewer husbands bequeathed their wives more than dower law required, and increasing numbers excluded widows from executing their estates. Before mid-century, nearly two-thirds of Amelia County, Virginia, husbands named their widows as executors—either sole or joint—but thirty years later, that proportion had slipped to 43 percent. In South Carolina, the proportion of widows named as sole executors declined by 50 percent during the eighteenth century.[10]

Yet while widows' access to property and authority contracted, the responsibilities of widowed householders remained as substantial as ever. They had to order and pay for slaves' provisions, keep an eye on field work, collect and pay debts, and sell whatever crops they raised. For slaveholders, this often entailed trans-Atlantic commerce. After Gawin Corbin died in 1760, his widow Hannah managed Peckatone plantation in Westmoreland County, Virginia, for many years. Corbin sold her tobacco through several London concerns, and she conducted an extensive business correspondence with these Londoners and fellow Virginians. Her contemporary Martha Custis ran a tobacco plantation between her first husband's death and her remarriage in 1759. Custis had help from her husband's former manager, but she personally negotiated terms with her London factors, sternly directing them in their duty "to get me a good price."[11] Mid-eighteenth century widows were less likely to receive managerial authority over non-agricultural businesses, but those who did were also involved in complex commercial and legal transactions. When Elizabeth Timothy's husband died in 1738, she supported herself and her children by running the family print shop in Charleston. Timothy printed broadsides, pamphlets, and blank legal forms, published the *South Carolina Gazette*, and served as the official printer to the colony. In the mid-1740s, she diversified into books and stationery. According to the Timothys' business partner, Benjamin Franklin, Elizabeth Timothy was an exemplary business woman, while her husband had been "ignorant in Matters of Account." Franklin recalled that Elizabeth sent him accounts "with the greatest Regularity & Exactitude every Quarter." She even managed "to purchase of me the Printing-house and establish her Son in it." By the time she died, this enterprising widow owned at least six slaves, a house, and a small parcel of land, as well as books, silverware, and furniture.[12]

Critical in the managerial successes of slaveholding widows like Hannah Corbin and Elizabeth Timothy was their previous experience with productive and commercial endeavors. Timothy apparently learned accounting as a girl in the Netherlands, where formal education in such matters was not uncommon. Benjamin Franklin's admiration for Elizabeth Timothy prompted him to recommend that parents include accounting in their daughters' education, since that was "likely to be of more Use" to young women "than either Music or Dancing."[13] Genteel American families almost universally ignored this sound advice. Most slaveholding women learned about business in a more fragmentary fashion, by acting as agents for friends, relatives, and husbands. Slaveholding women routinely shopped for each other, for example, and they could also make agreements to buy or sell goods on their husbands' behalf. If her husband was away, a wife could make a contract that would be legally binding upon him as long as it involved routine business and unless he contested her actions on his return: she could buy essential supplies, but she could not sell off the back forty.[14] Wives also substituted for their husbands in supervisory capacities, overseeing slaves and other workers. Some wives spent only the occasional day as "deputy husbands," but others managed for weeks or even months, in their husbands' absence.[15]

Slaveholding wives' ability to act as deputies hinged on the day-to-day mingling of domestic and business concerns within their households. According to the increasingly popular texts that instructed wealthy colonists in gentility — some of which Elizabeth Timothy herself may have published — the home should be a haven of elegance and leisure, not a site of labor and commerce. In reality, however, both productive and commercial activities occurred in slaveholders' living spaces. Bed chambers and parlors were sites of business, not just testaments to wealth and good taste. Consequently, wives had the opportunity to witness transactions and decision-making. This passive education gave them at least some preparation for acting as their husbands' deputies, which in turn provided women with some understanding of what might await them in widowhood.[16]

Also important to late colonial widows' householding were their connections to well-placed and well-disposed men. Elizabeth Timothy's success depended in part on conserving her ties to her husband's business partner, Franklin, an enormous asset to anyone in the printing or bookselling trade. Planter widows similarly adopted their husbands' commercial networks, selling tobacco to the same factors in London and relying on the same agents for more local business. Kinsmen made perhaps the most useful connections, particularly if they were themselves wealthy or politically prominent. A letter that Martha Custis's cousin Mary Campbell wrote to the governor of Virginia provides a particularly clear example of how well-placed widows sought to manipulate their ties to even more powerful men. During Lord Dunmore's brief tenure in the governor's palace (1771–75), Mary Campbell asked him to halt an execution on her property, ordered by the General Court to settle her second husband's debts. In her petition, Campbell appealed not only to justice, but also to her wealth and connections. As she reminded Dunmore, she possessed "a fortune that set me on a level with the foremost in the colony." Equally significant, "both Birth & Marriage" connected her "to some of the best familys in Virginia." Dunmore probably knew that she was a Dandridge by birth, and he would surely have remembered that her first husband had been John Spotswood, son of Governor Alexander Spotswood. As for her children—Alexander, John, Anne, and Mary Spotswood—their "names alone, methinks[,] should endear them to Virginia." Campbell's money and connections did not entirely exempt her from the law, but they loaned considerable force to her request for special treatment after the fact.[17]

The eighteenth century undoubtedly witnessed a pronounced contraction in widows' access to property and managerial authority in their husbands' wills, and the last quarter of the century did not reverse this decline. However, slaveholding widows continued to manage land, slaves, and often entire households up to the outbreak of the Revolution. The war years dramatically increased the number of female householders and the breadth of their responsibilities. Independence and revolution also altered long-standing patterns of thought and behavior, prompting at least some women to claim the rights of liberty and representation.

SLAVEHOLDING WIDOWS participated directly and indirectly in the Revolutionary struggle. Some became fierce partisans, many lost kinsmen to the war, and others fled violence or became its victims themselves. All encountered some economic disruption, from boycotting imported goods to losing property to American or British military forces. These challenging circumstances bested some women, but others developed new confidence, especially in their dealings with public authority. More generally, the war years confirmed that declining legacies and decreased access to estate management in the late colonial period had not caused a definitive female retirement from householding.

Some widows articulated political commitments well before independence. In the summer of 1767, Hannah Corbin participated in a response to the Stamp Act crisis, contributing £5 to a subscription honoring Lord Camden for his opposition to the Act. The funds were destined to commission a portrait of Camden to hang in the Westmoreland County courthouse, so that "all future Judges may be induced . . . to recollect those virtues the possession of which procures Lord Camden the love of his Country." Because the Camden portrait was never painted, this political gesture was short-lived, but the subscription identified which Westmoreland notables —male and female—supported the American cause. It also suggests the thicket of relations that united them. In addition to Hannah Corbin, the contributors included four of Corbin's brothers, her future sister-in-law Elizabeth Steptoe, and Elizabeth's sister, Anne Washington.[18]

By 1774, both the imperial crisis and women's interest in it had heightened considerably. In that year, a group of wealthy women from Edenton, North Carolina, made a joint public statement of their politics. To illustrate their support for patriot leaders in the colony, they jointly pledged "to do everything as far as lies in our power, to testify our sincere adherence" to the new boycott of British goods. The Edenton declaration involved an equally elite and interconnected group as the Camden subscription: among the signatories were Penelope Dawson and Jean Blair, close kin to a former and a future governor, as well as several of their kinswomen and close friends. This statement exposed its authors to public scorn in England, provoking a satirical cartoon and at least one letter likening the

Edenton ladies to Amazons. North Carolinians, by contrast, received the Edenton ladies' act far more favorably.[19] More typical than the Edenton statement were the political sentiments that appeared in personal letters, especially after the fighting began. In the spring of 1778, North Carolina widow Elizabeth Steele reminded her brother-in-law in Pennsylvania "to pass no opportunity of giving us the news." She also thanked him for sending her "the Crisis No. 5." As she observed, this publication served "to brace our minds, long relaxed by the Inaction of the armies thro the winter season."[20] When the fighting later shifted to the South, Steele provided regular reports of battles and armies and begged for "northern intelligence" in return, reminding him that "you know I am a great politician."[21]

Some widows found that the war spilled over from newspaper reports and battlefields into their neighborhoods and households.[22] In May 1779, a rumor that "the British troops will certain be here by Wednesday night" set the women of Edenton, North Carolina, to frantically packing "every thing yesterday even to the Pictures and looking glasses." That rumor proved unfounded, but two years later the town was less lucky. In mid-April 1781, "a certain account" of an English advance prompted Jean Blair and others to evacuate. Blair and her large household relocated to Windsor, some twenty miles west across the Chowan River from Edenton. Blair's family spent several months in Windsor, which she concluded "is as safe as any where else" for herself and her daughters.[23] From Windsor, Jean Blair agonized over her kinswomen's safety. As the British approached Edenton, she urged her cousin Penelope Dawson to come to Windsor as well, if only "on account of the continual dread and uneasiness."[24] Jean worried even more about her young daughters. "You may think," she observed to her sister Hannah Iredell, "that such as Peggy might be safe any where but children of her age were treated in a most shocking manner near about Hillsborough. Their parents tied and the Girls abused in their sight." The Blair girls escaped such outrages, but a month after moving to Windsor, Jean recorded that "the British have abused" some married women of her acquaintance. Memories of wartime abuse lingered for decades. Fifty-five years after the fact, William Gipson recalled that Tories had tied up and whipped his mother in 1777 for urging "the cause of American liberty."[25]

Far more widespread than death or assault were wartime economic losses. Countless widows lost livestock, buildings, fields, and other property. When Tories assaulted William Gipson's mother, they also torched her house.[26] Lord Cornwallis's troops ransacked Elizabeth Steele's corner of North Carolina early in 1781: "In February last the British were so kind as to pay us a visit, at a time when my little family were ill with the smallpox, in which my little youngest granddaughter died—the rest have all happily recovered. I was plundered of all my horses, dry cattle, horse forage, liquors, and family provisions, and thought I escaped well with my house, furniture and milk cattle. Some in this county were stript of all these things."[27] Other women lost property to American troops. Loyalist Henrietta Wragg claimed that rebels destroyed all of her crops, leaving her slaves without provisions. Even staunch patriots sometimes lost property to the militia or the Continental Army. Widowed Elizabeth Elliott blamed the militiamen quartered on her property for destroying her warehouse.[28] General Benjamin Lincoln ordered William Taggart to burn down his house and outbuildings outside of Charleston to prevent their use by the advancing British. Taggart complied, at great cost to his soon-to-be-orphaned family.[29] Planters often lost a great deal of property simply because they made such obvious targets. By 1783, Mary Byrd had lost several dozen slaves, cattle, two small ferry boats, and £200 worth of other "articles" to the British. Wealth made planters targets of opportunity in another way as well: location. Byrd's Westover plantation, for example, was advantageously situated on the James River, a site that had facilitated her tobacco exports in peacetime but made her vulnerable during the war. Penelope Dawson's location on the Albemarle Sound left her similarly exposed.[30]

Perhaps the most grievous economic consequence of the Revolution for wealthy southerners was its ability to disrupt bondage. As early as the Stamp Act crisis of 1765, a group of slaves paraded around Charleston, "crying out 'Liberty.'"[31] Once the war began, thousands of enslaved Africans and African Americans headed to the free states, the frontier, Spanish Florida, the coast, or the British lines. Others stayed put but refused to work. In 1779, Eliza Lucas Pinkney's slaves took advantage of the chaos to do "what they please every where." Somewhat later, she remarked that "the Crops made this year" throughout lowcountry South Carolina "must be very small by the desertion of the Negroes in planting and hoeing time." She attributed this "deplorable state" to the presence of "two armies . . . for near two years." Another lowcountry planter, Mrs. Graeme, discovered that her driver, Andrew, had made himself the leader of her defecting slaves. They eventually returned, but only after she "made terms with Andrew," a remarkable shift in the balance of power between owner and slave.[32] Jean Blair faced similar resistance from her house slave Sarah throughout their sojourn in Windsor. According to Blair, Sarah fancied herself "ill used" by the relocation to lesser quarters in Windsor. Blair warned, "If she gives herself many more airs she shall never see Edenton again. Very little more will provoke me to sell her." In this case, while wartime disruption inspired Sarah to assert herself more forcefully, Blair retained the upper hand as long as she could credibly threaten a sale. In contrast, slaveowners had great difficulty regaining slaves who absconded or were stolen by the British. Mary Byrd lost forty-nine slaves when the British visited Westover plantation. She never recovered them even though the British agreed to return them, because her slaves "hid themselves" when sought and "could not be found." Even more troubling than these examples of disobedience and truancy was the prospect of slaves' being armed by the British. In July 1781, the Edenton "Vollunteers" turned out "to surprise six hundred Negroes who were sent out by L Cornwallis to plunder and get provisions." The slaves had "no Arms but what they find," but even haphazardly armed, they greatly frightened the white women sheltering in Windsor.[33]

During and after the war, economic need forced unprecedented numbers of widows to petition their state legislatures for relief or restitution. In the twenty-five years before 1776, the South Carolina legislature received thirty-two petitions from women. In the same period, North Carolina received only eleven. Between independence and 1800, however, those numbers more than quintupled.[34] Legislatures quickly satisfied some demands but delayed or rejected others for myriad technical reasons. Mary Taggart received compensation for the buildings her husband destroyed at General Lincoln's orders only after two decades and multiple petitions to the South Carolina legislature and Congress.[35] Widows' petitions suggest that the war expanded the cohort of women who believed they had a claim on public consideration well beyond the ranks of governors' daughters and legislators' widows. When Mary Davidson petitioned the North Carolina legislature, she suggested that her dead husband's services "are still in the Memory of her Country" and gave him "a Claim on the Patriotism the Honor and the justice of his Fellow Citizens." Another widow suggested that "all the Friends of America" in Guilford County, North Carolina, knew that her husband had "distinguished himself as a true friend to the American Cause" before being mortally wounded in battle.[36]

As the war dragged on, some slaveholding widows stretched the boundaries of female politics still further. The wives and widows of public officials sometimes found that their traditional work as deputy husbands had expanded dramatically. When the Sheriff of Rowan County, North Carolina, was taken prisoner and died in British custody, for example, his widow "proceeded to make the Collection of Taxes for the year."[37] A handful of widows went further, claiming their own rights as revolutionary citizens. In 1778, eleven years after subscribing to the Camden portrait, Hannah Corbin identified her own status as a disenfranchised taxpayer as a form of taxation without representation. Her brother, Richard Henry Lee, disagreed with Hannah's characterization of the property taxes in question, but he accepted her claims about voting rights: "representation . . . ought to be extended as far as wisdom and policy can allow; nor do I see that either of these forbid widows having property from voting, notwithstanding it has never been the practice." Regarding widowed and single women of property, he proclaimed he "would at any time give my consent to establish their right of voting," a remarkable promise even if he calculated he would never have to keep it.[38]

Fellow Virginian Mary Byrd seized on republican arguments for another purpose: to protest ill treatment at the hands of some Continental soldiers. Before dawn on February 21, 1781, she complained, soldiers commanded by Major George Lee Turberville searched her house, seized some of her papers, and held her and her daughters at swordpoint. Rather like Hannah Corbin, Byrd protested that she had "paid taxes, during a tedious War; and now am not protected by my Countrymen." She complained to Thomas Jefferson, then governor of Virginia, that the invasion of her house "cannot be called *Liberty*."[39] To Baron Steuben, she described her treatment as "Liberty that Savages would have blushed at." With her appeals to liberty, Byrd was not merely seeking protection as a "defenseless Woman," she was also demanding her rights as a taxpaying citizen. In a later missive to Jefferson's successor, Byrd claimed the right of redress "as a female, as the parent of eight children, as a virtuous citizen, as a friend to my Country, and as a person, who never violated the laws of her Country."[40]

In the short run, the Revolutionary War provided a few women with a new language for articulating individual appeals for justice. In the long run, similar language would help groups of women organize collective appeals for gender equity.[41] However, women's public, ideological patriotism soon faced competition from a postwar print culture which rhetorically confined women to their homes. Public authorities benefited from women's demonstrable ability to govern themselves and their property, but they neither granted widows the vote nor extended married women's property rights. Even women's financial contributions received only partial recognition; some women received some remuneration, but far fewer than had actually suffered financial losses during the war.[42] Yet the postwar picture for slaveholding widows was not entirely bleak, although they did not re-

BROKEN REEDS

coup the long-term decline in their legacies and their executorial authority. Women who had survived years of occupation or guerrilla warfare had
experience with juggling tight finances and tighter supplies. Those who
had encountered hostile soldiers might well find disagreeable neighbors
comparatively less intimidating. More generally, the ideology of republican womanhood conferred new honor on women's traditional responsibilities: as wives and mothers, they helped guarantee the life, liberty, and property of the next generation of citizens. Yet widowed mothers could not
rest on their republican laurels; they had their hands full getting debts paid,
fields plowed, and crops planted and sold. For the next seven decades, they,
their daughters, and their granddaughters would shoulder the myriad
burdens of household mastery.[43]

IN THE NINETEENTH CENTURY, southern print culture and popular opinion increasingly limited respectable white women to domestic concerns. At
the same time, they defined masculinity as one—if not the only—essential prerequisite for heading households and participating in civic affairs.
Despite these new ideas, slaveholding men still relied on their wives to help
manage the household. As a result, many slaveholding women had experience with agricultural operations and financial transactions by the time
they entered widowhood. Slaveholding husbands also endowed their widows with considerable property and responsibility, albeit less so than their
colonial forefathers. Widows retained their right to at least their dower thirds,
and a sizable minority of men named their wives as executors. Many more
widows administered intestate estates. Even slaveholding women who acted
in neither capacity generally received charge of a household—a dwelling,
often several outbuildings, and some land—for the duration of their widowhood, if not longer.

Slaveholding women's ability to act as their husbands' agents in the post-
Revolutionary Southeast depended on what their husbands did for a living. In addition to assisting with agricultural enterprises, white southern
women could help their husbands run schools, boarding houses, or dry-
goods stores. In Petersburg, Virginia, Caroline Kennedy assisted in her husband's millinery and mantua-making business and succeeded him when
he died.[44] In some trades, wives even became the family breadwinners.
Virginia Cary's married sister Mary Randolph supported her family by
running a successful Richmond boardinghouse and publishing a popular
cookbook, *The Virginia Housewife*.[45] In contrast, women married to pro-

fessionals and merchants had little or no opportunity to assist their husbands during marriage or to pick up the reins in widowhood. Susan Hutchison could not take over her husband's job at a bank in Augusta, Georgia; Mary Steele could not assume her husband's duties as an agent for North Carolina's Cape Fear Bank; and Martha Jackson could not succeed her husband as a professor at Franklin College (later the University of Georgia). Instead, these widows had to support themselves by other means— Hutchison by teaching, and Jackson and Steele by farming.[46]

Susan Hutchison's diary illustrates the difficulties of women married to men in commerce or the professions. In its pages, this former teacher frequently mentioned her uncertainty about her husband's business and finances. In January 1828, Susan observed that Adam had, most unusually, spoken "freely of his affairs mentioning without reserve things of which I was quite ignorant." This forthrightness was only temporary, however; later that year, Susan learned that Adam had mortgaged their household goods without her knowledge. Although Adam's secretiveness worried Susan, she rarely pressed him, perhaps because of his "violent temper." Adam was so cruel that the couple's church formally censured his conduct toward his "injured and persecuted wife." One source of Adam Hutchison's anger and secretiveness alike must have been his repeated economic failures: his cotton speculations invariably went wrong; land he won in a state lottery of Indian territory proved all but worthless; his job at an Augusta bank cost him when he had to pay for a substitute during an illness.[47] Some of Susan Hutchison's ignorance had a structural cause, however. When Adam went to the office, she could not overhear his business dealings. When he fell ill or left town, she could not take his place at the bank, and she likely could not assist him in his cotton speculations either. Yet Susan still assumed more than a conventional middle-class wife's part in the household economy; as Adam's fortunes sank, she offered to resume teaching to "support her family." Once widowed, she continued to teach, eventually starting a school in Salisbury, the seat of Rowan County, North Carolina.[48]

Women whose husbands made their livings from agriculture often knew more about their husbands' business than did women like Susan Hutchison.[49] A careful observer could learn a great deal simply by noticing whom her husband did business with and how he reacted to what he saw in the fields. Wives also learned by acting in their husbands' stead when men left to conduct business, visit kin, attend militia musters, or sit on a jury.[50] Land speculation often required men to travel far from home. When Henry

Jackson went to visit his absentee plantation in Alabama, he left his wife Martha in charge of their Georgia farm for months at a time. Men's tendency to name each other as their executors—in preference to widows—often had the ironic consequence of requiring an executor to rely on his own wife to manage the household in his absence: Sophia Watson spent nine months managing her husband's plantation while he was away settling his father's estate. Stints as deputy husband sometimes lasted even longer. Virginia slaveholder Paulina Pollard coped without her husband for more than five years. Although so long an absence was by no means routine, she described it simply as "an additional responsibility." Fellow Virginian Ruth Hairston might have chosen saltier language, but then the circumstances of her husband's lengthy absence were quite different. Robert Hairston's departure from Virginia in 1841 reflected a permanent estrangement between husband and wife, cause or effect of his relationship with an enslaved woman and their illegitimate daughter, Chrillis. Until Robert's death in 1852, Ruth supervised his and her vast properties in Virginia and North Carolina with help from Robert's brother Samuel. While acting a man's part could brand a woman as transgressive or unseemly, it carried no such implications in these cases when a wife acted as her husband's deputy with his consent and for her family's benefit.[51]

Although leaving a wife in charge expressed a certain confidence in her abilities, many traveling husbands wrote detailed letters home, seeking to govern from afar. John Steele's letters to his wife Mary reveal both his efforts and his inability to command from a distance. In the 1790s and early 1800s, John Steele held a variety of offices in state and federal government. While serving as a state legislator, U.S. Congressman, and Treasury Department official, John spent at least thirty-seven months away from his home in Rowan County, North Carolina.[52] The political calendar ensured that these absences often occurred during the critical harvesting, plowing, and planting seasons. In his letters, John Steele sketched improvements for his plantations, from routine operations like repairing fences to innovations like growing cotton. Each of those improvements required Mary's active participation. In 1792, for example, John instructed Mary to determine if the groom was neglecting the horses, to direct a tenant about building a stable, and to inquire after some misplaced goods. Some years later, he suggested that she hire a particular overseer, but he left the decision and the negotiations to her. When he decided to grow cotton, he asked her to consult with the overseer about how much to plant. John even gave her some authority over his treasured racehorses.[53] Completing her husband's instructions required Mary Steele to negotiate with a variety of men, from slaves and overseers to neighbors, tradesmen, and artisans. John asked her to buy cattle, hire overseers and other laborers, amend agreements with his tenants, and acquire rights of first refusal on land. Yet when Mary reported that his debtors had not paid their obligations, he balked at sending her to press them. This decision may have reflected his political sensibilities as much as any desire to spare his wife. Sending her to dun their friends and neighbors for money when he had no urgent need for cash would hardly burnish his reputation among local voters.[54]

John Steele's reliance on Mary facilitated his political career, but his correspondence suggests that her surrogate mastery had mixed consequences for his self-image. In praising her arrangements for renting some properties, he observed that "everything is exactly as I would have done it myself."[55] On other occasions, he concluded that "every thing is done for the best, as if I were present."[56] At times, however, John admitted that he was "to[o] far off to direct" and that Mary acted on her own recognizance, writing that "in respect to our private affairs I need say nothing. You will do for the best, and to your discretion I leave the mannagement of every thing." In January 1802, he acknowledged that he did not "know enough of our farming business to give any positive directions." Six months later, however, after trusting his property to Mary for so many years (and despite his own mother's example as a widowed business woman), he remarked that she and their daughters were "helpless" because they were "females." The timing is suggestive: within four months, John would decide to resign from the Treasury and return home. Perhaps he imagined a need to reassert himself in a ménage that had coped without him for so much of the preceding decade.[57] At one point casting himself as the indispensable guarantor of his family's future, at others giving Mary credit for performing his work, John Steele nicely illustrates how slaveholding men struggled to reconcile their reliance on their wives with their own need to be masters.

The Steele marriage illustrates the chief reason why slaveholding wives acted as deputy masters: for white men to enjoy their privileges fully, wives simply had to act a manly part when men left their enclosures. If slaveholding men had been utterly consistent in enforcing women's subordination and inferiority, they could hardly have left the house for fear their wives might have to make decisions in their absence. The functional substitution of women for men did not fundamentally challenge male preeminence in marriage, however, since wives' surrogate mastery generally encompassed only those tasks needed to keep a household running. In any case, despite their clear reliance on their wives' competence and initiative, slaveholding men persisted in regarding them as extensions of their will. And yet, wives could not meet their responsibilities without making choices on their own and casting some doubt on men's supposedly unique capacity for domestic governance.

THE COLONIAL PATTERN of wives acting as their husbands' agents survived the turn of the century. This persistence helps explain why post-Revolutionary slaveholding men felt comfortable bequeathing their wives substantial amounts of property and authority, even as print culture increasingly enclosed white women in ideological gilded cages. Men's wills powerfully illuminate this matrix of independence and constraint.[58] Samples of wills written between the Revolution and the Civil War suggest that southeastern slaveholders rarely allotted their wives exactly their dower "according to law."[59] Instead, they seized the opportunity to depart from the statutory defaults for dower, but not, for the most part, in ways that seriously injured their widows' interests. In fact, most of the wills sampled left slightly more than a dower share to widows. The primary exception concerned the wealthiest husbands, who tended either to leave less than dower or to restrict legacies to widowhood. Even so, a small share of a vast fortune left most planters' widows better off than the average widow who received a larger proportional share.[60]

Whether they met or exceeded dower minimums, southeastern husbands assigned to widows some of their most valuable forms of property. Men who owned slaves usually allotted one or more to their widows. Most also gave widows possession of the "home place"—the farm or plantation where the family lived—or a house and some fields, a town lot, or other realty. Slaveholding widows also acquired a range of goods for housekeeping such as spinning wheels, cookware, and, for the wealthy, imported tea sets, and silver candlesticks. Widows often obtained livestock, especially cattle and pigs, and farming tools, such as hoes, plows, and wagon gears. In contrast, slaveholding men frequently excluded their daughters from real estate and farming utensils, bequeathing them furniture, slaves, and sometimes money instead. This difference reflected men's expectation that their daughters would rely on husbands to maintain them, while widows had to support themselves. In the Southeast, slaveholding widows rarely received only their maintenance and the right to occupy a room in the house, which was common practice elsewhere.[61]

Slaveholders' widows typically received the use of land (and sometimes slaves) for their lifetimes or for the duration of their widowhoods, as opposed to gaining outright ownership. In Rowan County, North Carolina, for example, less than one half held their realty for life or outright. Throughout the Southeast, widows were most likely to get less than dower if their tenures were for life or longer. Conversely, the shorter her tenure, the more likely a widow was to get more than dower. (The most important exception to this pattern involved the small number of men—almost invariably childless—who gave their widows most or all of their estates outright.) The time-limited nature of most legacies reduced widows' control over property but did not prevent their involvement with day-to-day management. In practice, a woman who held a farm for her lifetime might well manage the place for a decade or more. Even legacies for widowhood could make women into householders for years on end since most never remarried.[62]

Two important factors shaping provisions for widows were their age and the presence of children. Childless husbands almost always gave more than a dower share to their widows and were most likely to give fee simple legacies. A widowed mother left with a houseful of little children also stood a good chance of being given more than dower. These widowed mothers often bore the weighty responsibility of managing the entire estate for the benefit of their young children. Often, however, their legacies expired (or at least shrank) when the children reached adulthood. Young mothers might also hold their legacies for widowhood only, a provision that fathers thought would protect their offspring from the vagaries of being stepchildren. Widows with grandchildren, meanwhile, tended to hold their shares for life because they were almost certain not to remarry (and perhaps to die quickly). They also were much more likely than other widows to receive less than dower, on the theory that they had only themselves to support.[63]

Men's disposition of their property profoundly shaped widows' relationships with children.[64] Children usually had to wait until their mothers died, remarried, or voluntarily gave up their dower to claim what was typically a significant share of their inheritances. This choice made children at least somewhat dependent on their mothers.[65] Tying his children even more closely to their mother, a testator could also empower his wife to decide when and how their children should receive their inheritances, particularly when some or all were still minors. Under her husband's will,

Margaret Anderson had the right to decide which of her children should inherit a female slave. John Irvin instructed his wife Rachel to distribute property to her sons Joseph and John "as she thinks fit." In devising the legacies for his children, Willis Alston of Halifax County, North Carolina, left one of his sons whatever livestock "his mother sees fit." Sarah Alston also got the power "to use and manage" her underage children's estates "as to her seems best."[66] Still, not many men gave their wives such concrete economic power over their children. Most specified exactly what their children should inherit, and when. Some even felt the need to justify a division of property that favored their wives. When David Fraley gave Ellen his entire estate for her lifetime, he explained that his only intent was "to make due provision for the comfortable support and maintenance of my wife." James Graham bluntly informed his children that "if I had made my will in any other way, your mother could not have got along."[67]

The few slaveholding widows who received their maintenance without direct control of a house and lands had the least power over their children. Indeed, they depended on their children's willingness and ability to supply them with food, shelter, and fuel. In such cases, testators rarely imposed conditions on the child (almost always a son) charged with maintaining his mother. Abel Armstrong simply directed his son to provide his mother, Mary, with "a reasonable support," while George Bost called for an "ample" maintenance for his widow, and Matthias Garner ordered that Catherine receive provisions "suitable for an old woman." In contrast, Richard Gillespie directed that if his wife Nancy and son James could not cooperate in managing his plantation, they must divide it in two and run their halves separately.[68] Of course, even the most careful testator could not ensure that his children would treat their mother considerately. If moral suasion failed, a widow whose children stinted her had no recourse other than embarrassing and costly lawsuits.

Men's wills further shaped familial authority after their deaths by designating executors. While early colonial husbands had relied overwhelmingly on their wives to execute their estates, either alone or with the help of a son or friend, nineteenth-century husbands chose their wives much less often. One interpretation of widows' exclusion from executorship is that husbands no longer thought their wives competent to handle the position. Fears of female incompetence cannot entirely explain trends in executorship, however, because husbands who named others as executors still entrusted their widows with large portions of their estate. If they truly doubted widows' ability to manage property—the key to executing an estate—they surely would have hesitated to bequeath generous dowers and to rely on the uncertain protection of legal strictures against wasting dower shares. Men's faith in their own wives explains why women named as joint executors and an overwhelming majority of sole executors received more than dower. Widows who were sole executors were also unusually likely to get their share in fee simple.[69]

Returning from the aggregate to the particular further illuminates slaveholding men's reflections on women's capacities. At his death, John Steele was one of Rowan County's largest slaveholders.[70] In his will written in 1810 and revised in 1815, he left a poignant record of his hopes and fears. John gave Mary "the use of my Mansion House" together with its outbuildings and 860 acres along Grants Creek.[71] Daughters Eliza and Margaret shared the rest of his real estate and their mother's portion after her death. Each woman also received a third of John's personal property. John charged Mary with "the safe Keeping and management of my whole estate." He also hoped to minimize any disruption to his household: "My next concern is to provide for the accommodation and welfar of my family in a manner that will be Satisfactory to each one of them if possible, and at the same time by rendering no immediate change necessary in their manner of living, it may seem after my decease that the head of the house is only absent on a Journey, and not as is too frequently the case that the house itself is divided and fallen by the introduction of new views and Interests." This long sentence expressed Steele's hope of shaping his family long after his death, revealing how deeply he valued being "the head of the house." Despite his desire to ward off change, however, Steele spared his wife an elaborate array of limitations on her management.[72]

Considered by itself, John Steele's last testament suggests some equivocation about how his widow should behave. On the one hand, he gave her complete discretion to manage his estate, but on the other, he suggested that she and his daughters should act as if he were still alive. Placed in the context of his marriage, the meanings of his will become clearer. In 1802, he had fretted that his family was "helpless because it consists solely of females."[73] In 1810, when he wrote his will and considered how those females would fare without him, he surely remembered the times his wife had proved herself not so much helpless lady as indispensable, albeit unequal, partner. Loathe to imagine his family without himself at its head, he nonetheless granted Mary the authority to take his place as she had done on his previous, temporary journeys.

Knowledge of Thomas Burge's marriage similarly clarifies his will.

Like John Steele, this Newton County, Georgia, planter recognized his wife's managerial skills. When he drafted his will shortly before his death in 1858, Thomas had adult male blood relations living nearby to whom he could have left property, authority, or both. Instead, he left Dolly "sole and entire control" of the whole estate, "with as free powers concerning the same" as Thomas himself had. Thomas had good reason to trust his wife. Even when he was at home and healthy, she kept a careful eye on the plantation, recording in her diary the slaves' progress in the corn, wheat, and cotton fields. She also accompanied her husband when he went to town to sell cotton, so she had some familiarity with formal commerce as well as planting. Finally, Thomas knew that Dolly had been widowed once before and had coped on her own for over six years.[74]

As the Burge and Steele families suggest, nineteenth-century marriages and wills provide a mixed picture of slaveholding widows' access to and control over property. Most continued to receive at least a dower share, but they held it for restricted periods. Widows' access to estate execution continued to decline in some places but recovered in others. However, even when they did not execute or administer estates, they still had to manage their own shares. In the slaveholding class, this customarily included a household of their own, which they had to keep in good order for their own sake and their children's future benefit. In addition, widowed mothers often managed their minor children's property as well. In their wills, men like John Steele often tried to minimize the effect of their deaths by shaping relations among their survivors. But after they were gone, it was largely up to widows themselves to decide how—and sometimes whether—to implement their husbands' wishes.

EXPERIENCE WITH resolute deputy husbands prompted slaveholders to expect widows to manage land, slaves, and other property competently, even though early nineteenth-century culture typically associated slaveholding women with "delicacy, dependence, and retirement." Ideologically, these qualities served to distinguish slaveholding women simultaneously from white men and from enslaved and poor white women. A lady's acute moral perceptions—the source of her great influence in the family—stemmed from her subordinate position: "their state of dependence on man, makes them peculiarly sensitive." Yet while slaveholders praised their womenfolk for "those little feminine offices, and those homely domestic virtues, which fall exclusively within the province of woman," they also expected women to rise to the occasion when disaster struck. As the *Southern Cultivator* proclaimed in the summer of 1843, "Nothing can be more touching than to behold a soft and tender female, who had been all meekness and dependence, and alive to every roughness, while treading the prosperous paths of life, suddenly rising in mental force to be the comforter and supporter of her husband under misfortune, abiding with unshrinking firmness the bitterest blasts of adversity." These attitudes made slaveholding widowhood far more complicated than Charles Cocke's image of the "broken reed" initially suggests.[75] Moreover, the fact of slaveholding widowhood bore a direct relationship to slaveholders' understanding of their peculiar institution. Most slaveholders agreed that white women lacked men's vigor and forcefulness and therefore had to rely on influence and persuasion to make their way. In this context, white women's ability to manage slaveholding households could be read as evidence that a gentle hand and a quiet voice could mold bondspeople as well as husbands and children, which in turn implied that slavery was natural, harmonious, and orderly. In the Southeast, that politically useful fiction grew ever more important over time, as the recently united states began to line up and ultimately fracture along the axis of bondage.[76]

CHAPTER 2

The Management of Negroes

homas Burge died in December 1858 at his plantation in Newton County, Georgia. For the first month after his death, Dolly Burge used her diary to describe his last days and record her thankfulness that she had the "privillage" of serving him "until the very last moment of his life." By the middle of February 1859, however, she began making very different entries, noting the weather and the slaves' preparations for the next growing season, such as "hauling out manure & bedding cotton land."[1] Dolly and her widowed peers might have preferred to do what Savannah planter Martha Richardson recommended to her sister-in-law: sell off the slaves and "be done with the trouble."[2] But most slaveholding widows did not have that option, while those who could have sold off or freed their slaves almost never did. Few white women raised with slaves could imagine a future without them, and for most widows, having slaves meant managing them. Few widows could rely on relatives to manage everything for them, and only the richest could afford to be fully absentee planters. Consequently, new widows had little choice but to attend to slave management, especially the critical matters of labor, provisions, health, and discipline.

Widows like Dolly Burge worked hard at supervising both house and field slaves. In the process, they conformed but sporadically and unevenly to the ideals of charity and kindness that increasingly dominated southern prescriptions for slaveholding women. Even in the antebellum decades, when benevolent ideals had their greatest currency, slaveholding widows routinely pursued their financial interests and personal comforts at the expense of slaves. Most imposed heavy workloads, often while economizing on rations. When slaves failed to live up to their expectations, widows rarely caviled at corporal punishment, and they expected the state and law enforcement to uphold their rights in human property. In all of these ways, slaveholding widows closely resembled their male peers.

Within this basic pattern, how a widow managed slaves varied with the size of her household and her financial condition. Widows with limited means and only a few slaves had a distinctive (if less well documented) experience of slave management. These widows often had to do remunerative work as well as manage slaves. Yet white southern women had few employment choices that were both reasonably profitable and respectable; needlework, teaching, and boardinghouse keeping were among the most important. Some widows made a living by taking over their husbands' businesses, such as a dry goods store, tavern, or millinery shop. The majority of small slaveholding widows, however, had been married to yeomen farmers, and they had great difficulty filling their husbands' shoes. For both sets of widows, slave labor had the potential to make their own work both more ladylike and more lucrative. Planter widows had less physically demanding work than yeoman widows. Whereas yeoman farmers might have to work the fields alongside slaves, planters ordered that fields be plowed and crops planted, hoed, harvested, and sent to market. They decided how and whether to make capital improvements. They also determined whether and how to give slaves incentives for working well. In all of these areas, planter widows focused on moneymaking staple crops, although they did not always allocate labor efficiently, read markets accurately, or invest wisely. Like their male peers, most stuck with farming methods and staples that they knew instead of experimenting with scientific agriculture or new crops.[3]

Despite the many similarities of widows' slave management to men's, gender distinguished widows' actions and attitudes in certain key areas. While widows paid close attention to profits and losses in the fields, they often measured their personal success or failure more in terms of house slaves' performance. Widows also differed from men in their willingness to assert their power over slaves in raw physical terms. Planter and yeoman widows alike were less likely than men to whip slaves themselves, and sexual domination or its threat did not commonly figure in their mastery. Widows' ambivalent relationship to sexual and other violence against slaves might suggest that their slaves experienced a moderate form of slavery and could resist their bondage more openly than those managed by men, but the evidence points in another direction. Rather than benefiting from a widow's management, slaves often fared no better or even worse than before, for three simple reasons. First, estate settlement made slaveholders into misers, because few estates could fully settle debts and satisfy legacies with the cash on hand. Second, the death of a slaveholder increased slaves' risk of losing kin, either through sale or through distribution among heirs. As many fugitive and former slaves testified, separation from family members could hurt more than a whipping. Finally, slaves discovered that even if some widows were inclined to ignore all sorts of truancy, others were not, to say nothing of the state and other whites who assisted widows in policing their slaves. On the whole, therefore, slaves had little reason to look forward to life under a widow's rule. As former slave Nancy Williams remembered, "de real trouble start for us when ole marsa died."[4]

WHILE EVEN SMALL slaveholders were wealthy compared to most widows, they often had serious trouble making their income match their expenses. When a slaveholding husband died, he deprived his household of his labor, a particular problem for those with only a few slaves. His death also meant that his debts had to be repaid. Although yeomen farmers generally avoided the staggering debts that ruined some planters, some debt was almost inevitable, and their widows could rarely settle all such claims out of pocket. Simply sorting out the tangle of indebtedness could take years. In the meantime, widows had to produce the income needed to feed and clothe themselves and often an entire household. They also had to pay taxes, and those who served as executors or administrators had to pay estate debts and fulfill legacies. In many yeoman widows' households, the income for all these purposes came from their own as well as their slaves' labor.[5]

After her husband's unexpected death in November 1835, Virginia-born Lucy Freeman found herself with a household of young children to support. The family's comparative poverty required that she jealously manage the scant resources of their small Tennessee farm.[6] Making matters worse, her husband had died intestate, and she did not qualify as the estate's administrator, in part for want of timely advice from kinsmen in Virginia. When the administrator hired out the estate's slaves to pay her husband's debts, the "boys" hired for sixty dollars apiece for the year, which suggests they were old enough for serious work. Lucy could afford to hire back only "the woman and children," whose price—"their victuals and cloths"—indicates their low value. Lucy thus had several slaves in her house but little useful labor. She could not rely on her own children because they were either too young for hard work or in school, which she saw as essential to their futures. With so many mouths to feed, Freeman likely had to do double duty, working in the fields as well as the house. Among small slaveholders, such a combination was not unusual. While planter widows might shrink from the sun and the soil, yeomen families generally accepted that their womenfolk had to work in the fields from time to time. Yeomen did not boast of the pattern, but necessity readily justified the woman—especially the widow—who did both field and house work.[7]

A gender role that allowed widows to do both indoor and outdoor work was a limited advantage. On the one hand, it gave them a certain flexibility in deciding how best to use their own labor. On the other, a widow could not do all her own work and her husband's as well; there simply were not enough hours in the day. Making up the labor deficit proved difficult for rural widows unless they owned or could hire prime field hands. Hiring a cheaper younger slave might fit a yeoman widow's budget, but such a hire would not likely spare her from all heavy outdoor work. In contrast, widowers could more easily make up for the loss of their wives's labor, even though their gender role virtually banned them from housework. Widowers remarried more often than widows, perhaps because marriage threatened neither their legal personhood nor their property, while a remarried widow certainly lost the one and possibly the other. A widower also found it comparatively cheap to replace his wife's labor by hiring a housekeeper or coaxing a single kinswoman to live with him.[8]

Despite the difficulty of running a farm without adequate labor, Lucy Freeman managed. After four years of struggle, she happily reported that "by the present state of crops it will be seen that we never had a more flourishing year so fare." She noted in particular that "I have this year a verry fine crop of weat and corn and some oats," crops she could both sell and feed to her household.[9] Freeman also boasted that "I run two ploughs," which suggests that her field labor force had expanded by one if not two people, even though her children remained in school. Perhaps one of the slave children she had hired in 1835 had matured enough to plow; perhaps, since she had paid off her debts, she could afford to hire more expensive and profitable labor.[10]

A decade later and hundreds of miles to the south, Caroline Burke struggled to make a living on an Alabama farm. Burke had moved herself, her son, two daughters, and two handfuls of slaves from South Carolina to Alabama in the early 1840s, hoping that her children would enjoy greater

THE MANAGEMENT OF NEGROES

health than they had in Charleston. While the Burke children thrived in Alabama, Caroline Burke's slaves did not. Sickness repeatedly left Caroline with "not force enough to work" the farm. By 1854, eight slaves had died, leaving the Burkes with a slave man, a "sickly" woman, and seven children under ten years old, at least four of them orphans. Like Lucy Freeman, the Burkes had more slaves than labor. Caroline Burke took it "very hard" when her slave Isaac died in 1844, because her son John had hoped to plant a "heavy crop" that year. Without Isaac's labor, John Burke had to scale down his plans or see cotton rotting in the fields at harvest. Six years later, the slaves Margaret and Betsey died, "taken in the spring with a cough . . . altho constantly attended by two Eminent Doctors." Caroline mourned them as links to her mother, from whom she had inherited them. But she also lamented their loss because of her daughters: as her son observed, "It will be a difficult matter for them to get the education that we once hoped to give them." What Margaret and Betsey had hoped for their now-orphaned children apparently never entered the Burkes' minds.[11]

With a slave force of infants and sickly or dying adults, Caroline Burke had to do a substantial amount of physical work herself. Family letters give no indication that she worked in the cotton fields, however, surely the result of her son's presence. Instead, she grew vegetables and raised poultry, work that even planter ladies might do. In these tasks, Caroline likely drew on the labor of the slave children who were too young for serious field work. Gardening and poultry-raising were not simply make-work for ladies and children. Caroline's produce supplemented the diet of corn and pork that her son raised, reducing the need to buy food, and it also brought in cash. In 1854, Caroline's son-in-law, James Marlow, urged her to move nearer to Selma where her garden could fetch "from two to three hundred dollars" a year. The family dearly needed the money by that time since drought, the death of three horses, and renewed sickness among the slaves had blighted the previous year's cotton and corn crops.[12]

Widows who worked for wages faced a different set of challenges. This work could be less strenuous than farming, but underemployment was a constant threat. Caroline Burke's widowed daughter Rebecca Younge did "all that she can to assist herself and child, but it is only at times that she can get any work to do." (Better employment opportunities were yet another incentive for the Burke family to move closer to Selma.) Even educated widows had problems with underemployment. Boardinghouse keepers struggled to find enough lodgers, and teachers enough students.[13] They were able, however, to make good use of the sort of slaves they owned or could hire for reasonable terms: children and women trained in basic domestic work.[14] In a boardinghouse or school, slaves' domestic work was essential to the business. Without reliable laundry, cooking, and cleaning, a widow could not expect paying lodgers. In Catherine Lewis's Raleigh establishment, Martha and Alana did "all my washing and ironing," while Lucy "attend[ed] to the dining room." Their labor freed Lewis to attend to her five young children and her boarders. It also ensured that her hands remained clean. Lewis had several other slaves whom she hired out to avoid the costs of maintaining them. She hired out Eliza for her keep and "put out old Venus for her victuals and she finds her own clothes." Old Bob, "a faithful old servant," worked "wherever he can get a job at 25 cts a day and find him one meal." In her circumstances, Lewis remarked, saving the price of even one slave's meal "helps me to live too."[15] Domestic slaves also assisted schoolteachers, particularly those with boarding students. Susan Hutchison hired female slaves to sweep the schoolroom, wash clothes, "scour the parlor," prepare dinner, and "get tea" for her students, mostly the daughters of wealthy North Carolina slaveholders. She also hired Ned to look after her young son Adam, who was subject to fits. For Hutchison, Ned's labor was less a luxury than a necessity; she could not tend her son while teaching all day long. Hutchison remarked that she "would gladly have bought" Ned if she could. Like Ned's care of Adam, the female domestics' work highlighted the non-manual and thus more respectable nature of Hutchison's own labors.[16]

The slaves whom Catherine Lewis owned and whom Susan Hutchison hired were the sort of slaves who kept Lucy Freeman and Caroline Burke struggling to make ends meet: the young, the elderly, and the infirm. In urban settings, even these slaves could help widows to earn their livings, while any slaves able to work helped both rural and urban widows maintain a claim to ladyhood. The presence of slaves gave widows some freedom to choose what they would and would not do, and like Catherine Lewis, whose slaves labored in the kitchen and laundry, they chose to have slaves do the heaviest, dirtiest labor. Equally important, slaves' social and legal degradation served to elevate their white owners and hirers by comparison.[17]

UNLIKE MOST yeoman widows, planter widows had the means to be ladies in a far fuller sense of the word. Most obviously, planter widows did not do field or wage work. Instead, their efforts were more narrowly managerial, although most remained involved in the domestic production of food and clothes. Planters also had the financial means to pursue a high standard of gentility, domesticity, and benevolence, all of which were key to southern ladyhood after the Revolution.[18] The nineteenth century's proliferating print culture provided lady planters with explicit models to follow. George Tucker's romantic novel of the Grayson family, *Valley of the Shenandoah* (1824), for example, offered up an idealized plantation mistress in the character of even-tempered, pious, generous Mrs Grayson. According to the narrator, her behavior toward the family's slaves created a "moral picture of genuine benevolence." A few years later, Virginia Cary wrote more honestly than Tucker about the vexations that plantation mistresses often experienced, but she invented an equally idealized model for their conduct. Her fictional widow, Emilia, cared for her slaves as she would for her own children, combining salutary firmness with infinite patience and sincere concern. As a result, Emilia owned "the most moral and correct set" of slaves "in the country." Critically important to this ideal lady planter was her utter unconcern with moneymaking. Totally ignoring the role of slaves in the household economy, Cary's epistolary narrator credited Emilia's daughter for relieving her widowed mother's "embarrassed" finances by teaching painting, as if Emilia's slaves did nothing but receive her bounty.[19]

Widowhood gave slaveholding women new opportunities to act on these benevolent ideals, without interference from their husbands. Most continued to act on Emilia-like motivations only sporadically. Natalie Sumter's efforts to catechize her slaves' children and Marion Deveaux's quest to hire a preacher for her plantation, for example, suggest that these South Carolina cotton planters felt a Christian obligation to their slaves. Planter widows also expressed some commitment to the ideal of "Lady Bountiful" when they distributed gifts and privileges. When Georgia widow Mary Downs visited her fields, she brought treats such as gingerbread for the slave children. Fellow Georgian Martha Jackson gave occasional gratuities to favored house slaves: twelve and a half cents "to Polly in Athens for sleeping in Martha's room" and twenty-five cents "to Emma to purchase a little present for [her] children." Natalie Sumter also gave little gifts from time to time. "Old soldier Tom" received some of her husband's old clothes, Old Venus a "new cotton flanel gown," and Priscilla a new frock and black apron. Once Sumter treated the old slaves to a "good dinner" of "soup & meat & baked apples & peaches," and she allowed her favorites to attend weddings on other plantations.[20] Many widowed planters gave some kind of Christmas treat to their slaves: extra food, whiskey, or a holiday from work. Sylvia Cannon recalled that her owner would "kill hogs en a cow every Christmas an give us all de eggnong en liquor we want dat day." Slaves often came to see such treats as rights, not privileges, but planters typically viewed them as testaments to their own enlightened stewardship.[21]

Some favors gave widows a way to micromanage slaves' family lives. Former slave Fannie Berry recalled that, on her Virginia plantation, "if you wanted to marry one on 'nother plantation, Miss Sarah Ann would fust fin' out" whether the other slave "was a good nigger." If so, Abbott "would try to buy him so husband an' wife could be together." While slaves often preferred "abroad" spouses, for those who wanted to live together, Abbott's practice provided a real incentive to get her approval.[22] Other favors, such as permitting slaves to grow and sell garden crops, chickens, and eggs, benefited planters as well as slaves. These schemes reduced slaveholders' expenses and gave slaves a reason to stay put and busy during their few leisure hours. Letting slaves grow cotton on their own time, as both Martha Jackson and Dolly Burge did, was less common because it competed more directly with slaves' care for their owners' cotton.[23]

Micromanaging slaves' marriages was one manifestation of widows' paternalism; linking gifts to productivity was another. During the 1851 cotton harvest, Martha Jackson concocted a variety of schemes to motivate her slaves. In one six-day picking "race," every slave who gathered over four hundred pounds received fifteen cents. Slaves who picked eight hundred pounds got forty cents, with additional incentives for picking over one thousand pounds. During this week, most of Jackson's field hands picked over one hundred pounds a day, while three picked well over 1,000 pounds apiece over six days. Over the course of five weeks, the top pickers, William Hooker, Bob, Mary, and William Hart, earned between $3.92 ½ and $2.70 apiece. Overall, Martha Jackson disbursed almost thirty dollars to her cotton pickers. That year, short-staple cotton earned slaveholders on average 9.8 cents per pound, while Jackson's slaves made roughly one-sixth to one-half of a penny for each pound they picked. Several of the slaves put their money toward dresses, which they bought at a local store on Jackson's account. As a result, a few of the slaves became indebted to Jackson, even as the cotton they picked helped pay off her debts.[24]

The irony of slaves' receiving as gifts or prizes what their labor paid for reappears in the theatricality with which some planters distributed provisions. On her plantation near Columbia, South Carolina, Natalie Sumter made a point of handing out provisions in person; she "went to the

plantation to see negro children . . . had the allowances given to all the Negroes [and] spoke to them."[25] These events encapsulated key themes in the
plantation drama as slaveholders saw it: slaves' dependence, owners' care-
taking, and the vertical power relations that bound them. On July 4, 1840,
Sumter also allotted tools to the field hands and "wrote down all their new
hoes." By assigning each slave to a particular hoe, Sumter could hold individuals responsible for mishandling tools, a common problem on plantations. The scene also insinuated a profit-minded quid pro quo into the
drama of paternalistic care: Sumter's slaves owed her cotton as well as
gratitude in exchange for their sustenance.[26]

Sumter's provisioning ritual and Jackson's incentive scheme resemble
what Jeffrey R. Young calls corporate individualism. By holding each slave
accountable for his or her own conduct, Sumter and Jackson implicitly
recognized their slaves' moral agency. These planters also acknowledged
differences among their slaves when they rewarded and punished according to each individual's merits or faults (real or imputed). At the same
time, they measured slaves by a narrow compass, noticing only those acts
that affected the welfare of the household (especially its financial welfare)
as defined from the top down. In contrast, planters did not generally reward slaves for helping each other, and they punished slaves for fighting
among themselves for the harm slaves did, not to each other, but to planters'
interests.[27] The self-justifying and racist assumptions embedded in widowed planters' paternalism can be no surprise. Slaveholding wives who
bothered with benevolence shared them, and widowhood brought no ma-
gical conversion to altruism—quite the contrary. Although money matters played scant role in prescriptions for the planter lady, widowhood implicated female planters in the financial aspects of slave management as
profoundly as it did the more needy yeoman women, particularly in terms
of weighing what slaves earned against what they cost in provisions and
medical care. In most planter widows' papers, moments of apparent benevolence were rare counterpoints to the steady rhythm of cotton bales harvested, corn milled, payments received, and slaves beaten.[28]

PLANTER WIDOWS had many reasons to think self-interestedly about slaves'
labor, provisions, and medical care.[29] Most obviously, they rarely encountered Africans and African Americans except as chattel, and their husbands' deaths only highlighted the slave's degraded status. When a slaveowner died, his slaves were appraised, sold on the block, divided by lot, or

bequeathed. The very language of sales and divisions bespoke the fungible nature of human chattel: slaveowners would put slaves in their pockets or "put 'the niggeres in a hat' and draw for them." These sales and divisions privileged heirs' and creditors' interests well above any concern for preserving slaves' families.[30] Even being bequeathed by name to a new owner was a very ambiguous recognition of personhood.[31] None of this encouraged slaveholding widows to empathize with slaves. Finally, even planters' widows often discovered that "*economy* should now be the order" for their households.[32] With this in mind, widows could be quite aggressive in their efforts to increase profits by improving production, cutting operating expenses, or both. Their economies typically meant hard work and short rations for slaves, especially during the depressions following the Panics of 1819 and 1837.

Like their male counterparts, planter widows knew the importance of personally inspecting outbuildings, fences, and fields. Just two weeks after her husband's death in June 1840, Natalie Sumter toured the fields of his central South Carolina plantation. While there, she closely observed the cotton and corn, noting crop diseases and weather conditions. She also issued "tous les ordres" for the house and the hands, visited the sick and the slave children, and inspected the mill. During the next year, this transplanted French aristocrat[33] made at least thirty separate visits to fields and outbuildings. Most of them occurred during the fall of 1840 when she employed no overseer and needed to secure the cotton harvest. Many years later, former slaves remembered seeing other widows inspecting their fields. North Carolinian Clara Cotton McCoy described how Maria Cotton rode her horse "'bout de fields like an overseer, seein' after de cotton an' cawn' and taters." Evoking her years of bondage in Georgia, Dosia Harris recalled that after George Downs died, Mary Downs rode out to inspect the plantation "evvy mornin'" to check on her slaves and overseer.[34]

Based on these inspections and on consultations with kinsmen or overseers, slaveholding widows decided where and how to employ their slaves. Most slaves spent most of their working hours in the fields, but planters had to apportion slave labor among cash crops, food crops, capital improvements, and maintenance. In the winter months, when there was little field work to do, planters might make slaves clear timber stands to prepare new fields and provide wood for buildings and fences.[35] Many tasks competed for attention during the busy summer and fall. In September 1839, Paulina Legrand had the slaves at her Charlotte County, Virginia, plantation digging a well, tending the vegetable garden, picking cotton, digging and storing Irish potatoes, and hauling sand.[36] Weather also forced planters to jigger work assignments. A summer rainstorm prompted Natalie Sumter "to stop the people from working," perhaps fearing they would get chilled or even struck by lightning.[37] When a storm damaged fences and buildings at Martha Jackson's Alabama plantation, she ordered that slaves stop working on her new house and devote their efforts to repairs and the cotton crop.[38]

Unlike the many widows who wanted for laborers, planter widows sometimes had to cope with surplus labor. Unwilling to leave slaves idle for long, these widows hired out, sold, or moved slaves from place to place. In the Upper South after the Revolution, these moves were often local. In 1787, for example, Susannah Wilcox of Buckingham County, Virginia, directed her overseer to reapportion the slaves between her two tobacco farms.[39] As the Upper South's tobacco economy stagnated and its expanding grain economy demanded fewer slaves, many planters sent slaves farther south and west. Virginia widows Jane Cocke and her daughter Mary Archer sent some slaves to Tennessee and Mississippi in the 1810s and 1820s. By the 1850s, North Carolina's Sarah Alston had divided her slaves between her home and her children's plantations in Texas, in part for want of "responsible" local hirers.[40] Even in the Deep South, soil exhaustion and other factors sometimes left planters with more slaves than they could productively use, and they too moved or sold slaves to Alabama, Mississippi, and beyond. In the 1840s and 1850s, meanwhile, the nascent railroad industry provided some planters with an alternative use for their excess slave labor. Natalie Sumter, fellow South Carolinian Marion Deveaux, and Virginia's Sarah Ann Abbott each hired out male slaves to railway construction projects. For these planters, hiring out even a substantial number of their strongest men did not mean abandoning staple-crop agriculture; a year after sending hands to the railroad, for example, Deveaux made a very respectable eighty-plus bale cotton crop.[41]

Despite their willingness to move and hire out slaves, most slaveholding widows did not take the next step: hire out all their slaves and "be done with the trouble."[42] Instead, they focused their efforts on making slaves produce whatever cash crop their subregion supported. In Charleston, Eliza Flinn and her daughter Eliza Wilkins counted bushels of rice; in Virginia, Susannah Wilcox and Ruth Hairston numbered hogsheads of tobacco, while Georgia's Martha Jackson dreamed in bales of cotton. While these staples made many fortunes, a sudden decline in price could spell disaster. The plight of cotton farmers after the Panic of 1837 is a case in point. In 1836, when Henry Jackson bought Cookshay plantation, the average price of short-staple cotton was 16.8 cents. The year he died, it had fallen to just over eight cents, and it continued to drop, exceeding the 1840 price only in 1847. In those years, Martha Jackson's response was invariably to produce more cotton, even when local prices fell to three and four cents, as they did in 1846. Since she could not afford more hands, making more cotton meant working her slaves more intensively. During the 1840 harvest, her overseer advised her to send any "spare hands" in Georgia "to help to save the crop" in Alabama. Having none to spare, Jackson attempted to increase output in another way—changing her overseer's pay from a flat salary of $500 to a per-bale rate, thereby giving him a strong incentive to drive slaves even harder. Not incidentally, under this scheme he could only match his "*enormously* great" salary if he made the 100 bales of cotton that Jackson thought Cookshay should produce.[43] Even after Henry Smith refused these terms and left her employ, Martha Jackson continued to aim for one hundred bales with his replacement. He had an even tougher job because Jackson had settled Smith's past-due wages by giving him one of her few adult male slaves. By the end of 1844, Vincent Pierson complained that "I hav made such exertions . . . I am nearly broke down my health." Pierson's records of slaves' illnesses and deaths show that overwork took a far greater toll on the Jackson work force.[44]

At the same time that Martha Jackson was trying to get more work out of her slaves, she was also attempting to save money on their provisions. Shortly after her husband died, she decided that her overseer, Henry Smith, should butcher some old cows to feed the slaves instead of buying bacon, their usual meat. When Smith dissented, she debated making a slave churn the cows' milk into butter for sale. But because low cotton prices made large harvests seem especially urgent, she would not divert any hand who was "able to work" from the fields, "not even a small one." Jackson concluded that her house slave Patty—who had a "Rheumatic affection" in her shoulder—should add churning to her existing duties. Any remaining milk would go to the slave children, to "save something in meat, by lessening their allowance." Varying this plan slightly, in 1847 Jackson proposed that Fanny and Patty should both churn. By that point, Fanny was fifty-seven and Patty fifty-two, and both were deemed "old" in the estate appraisal of that year. They could churn without interfering with other moneymaking work, and as before, the slave children would consume the sweet milk and buttermilk and receive less meat. By slaveholding standards, these choices were not particularly unusual or harsh. In this era, slaveholders generally assumed that their slaves could thrive on fare they could not imagine eating themselves. Jackson could even interpret her scrimping as being in her slaves' best interest; by economizing, she avoided bankruptcy, which would have required her to sell off her slaves and destroy their families in the process.[45]

Yet even in good financial times, slaves still suffered ill health and high infant mortality. Most planters had a very imperfect understanding of the relationship of overwork and poor diet to fetal death and infant mortality. In considering slaves' sickness, widows often spent less time thinking about causes than about the impact on the harvest. In a 1789 letter describing Susannah Wilcox's "prasent affares," overseer James Wills reported that while most of the hands had been sick with "this Enfluency cof," they were now "all geting wel and fit for Bisness," namely cleaning the wheat crop.[46] Widows complained mightily about lost labor, but in fact they rarely excused the sick from all work. Martha Cocke cheerfully reported that while young Eliza "has been sick almost ever since she came up," she was "notwithstanding very useful for one of her size and I think in time will become very valuable."[47] One of Martha Jackson's slaves suffered from epilepsy and another had a crippled foot, but both had to work in the fields or the yard.[48]

While slaveholders often presumed that slaves faked illness—one reason to keep the sick and lame busy—they agreed that some complaints needed medical attention. A small number were willing to spend substantial sums on doctors' bills. In 1847, a doctor in Columbia County, Georgia, made seventy-eight visits to Mrs. E. F. Lamkin's plantation. Dr. Neeson's remedies included bleeding, cupping, cathartics, and blisters, the typical therapies of contemporary white medicine. He also set a broken arm, attended a pregnant slave during childbirth, and performed an unspecified surgery on another female slave. For these and other services, Lamkin shelled out nearly $340, an amount that could have paid an overseer for a year or bought a young slave.[49] Even Martha Jackson believed slaves deserved a doctor's care, notwithstanding her efforts to save money on their rations (surely a false economy). In June 1840, overseer Henry Smith described a litany of ailments among the Jackson slaves. John had "a Rheumatick affection in his shoulder" which "became inflamatory." "A severe attack of the Billious Chollick" left Frank bedridden for two days. James "hurt his eye some three days ago with corn blade," and "Daphny has been threatened with a miscarriage." In each of these cases, Smith and his wife "gave the complaint I think proper treatment." Smith explained that "no Doct has been called in" because "losing this labour is bad enough but paying Doct. Bills is worse." Smith probably calculated Jackson would be pleased to save this cost, but she was not. The next time Smith wrote about a serious illness, he assured her that "I sent for a Doct. forth with." Bringing in a doctor was no guarantee that a sick or injured slave would recover, but it had other merits: planters interpreted their willingness to bear the expense as a sign of their own good stewardship.[50]

Financial self-interest played a central role in widows' decisions about slaves, but nearly as important was the power these decisions had to reflect or distort their self-image as benevolent or hardheaded, prudent or venturesome. Widows' concern with these qualities, like their actual decisions, did not categorically distinguish them from male planters. To that extent, their gender roles and their versions of mastery overlapped. In other areas, however, particularly discipline and domestic housekeeping, male and widowed planters' gender roles diverged without making widows into either the idealized ladies or the hapless incompetents that some interpreters imagined any single slaveholding woman must be.

NOTIONS OF elite white womanhood encouraged slaveholding widows—especially planters—to invest considerable importance in genteel housekeeping despite the demands of farming. By the same token, they were far less invested than most white men in their ability to dominate their slaves physically. Indeed, most slaveholders would have said it was unseemly for ladies to beat slaves, while sexually coercing a slave—a common but taboo aspect of male slaveholders' domination—was absolutely unspeakable. Yet despite their rhetorical distance from violence, widows remained deeply implicated in the brutality at slavery's core. On the whole, the challenge of combining ladyhood with force constrained but did not eliminate widows' violence, and it certainly did not make their households more peaceable than male-headed households. Even if widows themselves used force less often than male householders, a range of other people, from overseers to slave patrollers and judges, tended to be especially free with the whip where widows' slaves were concerned. Whatever problems combining mastery and ladyhood posed for widows, their bondspeople had little hope of experiencing a less brutal form of slavery.

For women enmeshed in the masculine-identified work of farming and commerce, dressing tastefully, presiding over a clean and orderly house, and entertaining guests properly were key touchstones of femininity. In each of these areas, slave labor was indispensable, yet house slaves often could not or would not fulfill their owners' desires.[51] Natalie Sumter regularly complained that she could not go to bed when she wanted because "Priscilla was not to be found" or "priscilla kept me waiting." After Sally "forgot to get vegetables," Sumter brooded that "we had a miserable dinner," and she lamented that she did "not know what to do" when Caty reported that she could not cook.[52] Whereas Natalie Sumter admitted only to helplessness, Keziah Brevard acknowledged her anger: "A mess of a dinner this was—every thing had an odd taste—sometimes my anger rises in spite of all I can do—what is the use of so much property when I can't get one thing cooked fit to eat—such a dinner—I am mad when I think how mean my negroes serve me."[53] Brevard's anger owed much to the fact that eight guests had partaken of the ruined meal and witnessed her inability to offer seamless hospitality.

With rather less cause, widows could be equally resentful when a slave's sickness interfered with entertaining guests, visiting, and writing. Natalie Sumter felt flustered when slaves' ill health inconvenienced her guests. "My house is full & servants sick I dont know what to do—it is 12 oclock before they are all fixed for bed," she wrote—rare words of frustration from this usually phlegmatic diarist. Elizabeth Lee begrudged the days she spent nursing a slave with cholera, especially since she knew Marjory had contracted the disease after running away from her hire-master. "I have little patience," Lee sniped, "when I know she brought this trouble & expense on me by bad conduct."[54] Martha Richardson found herself unable to write "a very long letter" because of "the sickness of some of my negroes." Her kinswoman, Delia Bryan, similarly complained of being "so much engag'd with sickness & domestic employments that I really have not had the time to devote any portion of my moments to my pen."[55]

Being thwarted by slaves in these and other ways often prompted slaveholders to react violently, especially if they suspected slaves were being deliberately slow or infuriating. For slaveholding men, resorting to force seemed natural, routine, even de rigueur. For slaveholding women, violence was significantly more complicated, and widowhood only made it more so. On the one hand, self-interest dictated that widows not maim their valuable, income-producing property, whether they owned it or held it only for life. In addition, antebellum proslavery writers told them that the peculiar institution hinged not on force but on the organic hierarchy that bound master and servant. Equally important, the arbiters of ladyhood rarely approved of female violence. Virginia Cary's *Letters on Female*

Character, for instance, told readers to shrink from the sight of a young lady whipping a slave. On the other hand, as Cary herself admitted, "the trials incident to domestic life" provoked many a woman to violence.[56] Some historians have argued that this tendency to lash out in anger illustrates that slaveholding women could not personally enforce the slaveholding regime. Historian Drew Faust reasons that "rationalized, systematic, autonomous, and instrumental use of violence belonged to men."[57] Former slaves often bore out the first part of this analysis; they recalled women attacking domestic slaves and children with pokers, irons, brooms, and whatever else came handy. Also supporting the claim, some slaves described female slaveholders as too compassionate or too weak to beat slaves into submission.[58]

Even though violence played little or no role in their gender prescriptions, slaveholding women inhabited a world rife with violence and acted accordingly. In a letter to her sister-in-law, Catherine Lewis matter-of-factly recounted its place in her own household, noting that "Joel Richard and Gaston [her sons] have all tired themselves since we have been here & have done more fighting since I have been here than in two or three months down at the Falls[.] Gaston has not improved at all, since you last saw him althogh he has had at least 4 or 500 lashes I do think he is the hardest child to break from crying I ever saw[.]"[59] In a world where mothers expected whippings to teach a four-year-old not to cry (and where wives could count themselves lucky if their husbands did not beat them), we should not be surprised that slaveholding widows used force deliberately and instrumentally against slaves. In the same letter, Lewis continued, "I do not think Leah [a slave] improves either I have had her to switch twice since I have been here and intend since I have commenced to conquer her."[60] Habitual violence and the language of conquest belonged to a larger vision of physical and even emotional domination.

Numerous slaveholding widows delegated punishment to others, especially overseers, kinsmen, and agents of the state. Few bothered, however, to record what these agents did on their behalf. In an 1844 letter, Vincent Pierson made a rare reference to force on Martha Jackson's Alabama plantation, writing, "Hester is a fine girl for worke I hav not had to strike her a lick this yeare."[61] Hester had presumably been less fortunate in previous years, and other slaves at Cookshay plantation likely felt the lash as well. This sort of discipline was so routine that Pierson felt no need to seek Jackson's approval and she no need to inquire. Of course, her absenteeism made it difficult for her to intervene, but other widows had ample opportunity to observe and, if they chose, check their overseers' discipline. The overseer on Mary Downs's Georgia plantation "sho' was mean to de slaves." According to former slave Dosia Harris, "Sometimes it seemed lak he jus' beat on 'em to hear 'em holler." Downs witnessed this brutality (or its effects) during her daily visits to the plantation, but she did not restrain him. Thanks to this division of labor, the slave children learned to associate the overseer with whippings, and Downs with the treats she brought them, even though she both sponsored and benefited from his violence. By the same token, Mack Taylor of Winnsboro, South Carolina, recalled that Margaret Clark sometimes protected slaves from being thrashed by the overseers she herself had hired. While rural planters could turn to overseers for this violence at a remove, urban slaveholders had easier recourse to agents of the state. Charleston's Mary Motte sent "little Philander" to the workhouse in Charleston at least four times between 1838 and 1842. Around the same time, the plantation partnership of sisters Louisa Alexander and Dorothea Van Yeveren sent a slave to the Savannah jail for punishment. Ex-slaves themselves recalled seeing "plenty" of slaves "whipped over at the jail."[62]

Slaveholding women's decision to have someone else whip their slaves in part reflected their efforts to conform to changing gender norms. After the Revolution, few slaveholders would have thought to ask a kinswoman to punish a slave on his behalf, as one of Hannah Corbin's brothers once did.[63] This was not simply a matter of gender, however, for male planters also delegated some discipline to overseers and agents of the state. Like Mary Downs, some preferred to remain somewhat removed from discipline, the better to maintain the fiction of benevolent stewardship. At the same time, while many whites considered violence unfeminine, few proscribed it, and if ex-slaves' memories are any indication, some widows used violence much like men. North Carolinian Clara Cotton McCoy maintained that her widowed owner "handled de niggers same as a man." Annie Poore, who lived near Belton, South Carolina, was "her own whuppin' boss"; according to former slave Tom Hawkins, she "beat on 'em for most anything." While some widows relied to sheriffs and slave patrols, Poore "didn't need no jail for her slaves. She could manage 'em widout nothin' lak dat." Some slaveholding women even wielded the whip despite the presence of white men competent for the work. Jerry Hill recalled a Spartanburg, South Carolina, woman who carried a bullwhip while touring her brother's fields and used it on "any slave she thought needed it." These examples all come from the Civil War years, when the extraordinary military mobilization reduced the numbers of white men available for domestic policing. During this period, slaveholding widows had the greatest responsibility for personally maintaining control over slaves by force and the least chance of success. In peacetime, more widows had the luxury of deploying systematic violence at a remove.[64]

Slaveholding widows' efforts to distance themselves from violence reflected their desire to wed ladyhood and mastery. In 1799, Lucy Thornton of Virginia witnessed her drunken overseer brutally beating one of her slaves. The beating horrified Thornton; "Indeed I feared it might be attended with fatal consequences as the Wounds were on his head and the blood gushed out of his eyes, attended with great swelling." Yet as she related the event to a kinswoman, the story shifted from a tale of a slave's near death into one of her own financial loss and outraged sensibilities. Describing the slave's gruesome injuries quickly gave way to the cheerful news that he recovered "with only the loss of three or four days work." Once the slave could work, Thornton apparently could not imagine that he suffered any lingering ill effects. For herself, however, the wounds of witness lingered. "My apprehensions are so great," she wrote, "that my life is a burden to me." Thornton may have been genuinely moved by the sight of the battered slave, but she rapidly converted his suffering into her financial and emotional self-interest. And despite her expressions of fear and powerlessness, Thornton acted very much like a male master in making herself the center of this drama while displacing the moral responsibility for her agent's abuses onto his shoulders.[65]

In a very different time and place, Keziah Brevard similarly danced around her own power over her slaves. In September 1860 she wrote, "I wish to be kind to my negroes—but I receive little but impudence from Rosanna & Sylvia—it is a truth if I am compelled to speak harshly to them —after bearing every thing from them I get impudence—Oh my God give me fortitude to do what is right to these then give me firmness to go no farther."[66] In praying for "fortitude," Brevard sought not the courage to use violence but the "firmness" to control it. Her concern that she might lose control tends to bear out Drew Faust's conclusions about women's tendency toward frenzied rather than instrumental violence. Yet Brevard's musings illustrate that neither piety nor ladyhood barred women from calculating how best to use force. And when calculation gave way to rage, they could pray for more restraint in the future while blaming the objects of their wrath for provoking them in the first place. Whether any slaveholders really tried to moderate their violence or not, their claims of attempting restraint helped preserve the myth of Christian stewardship.

When widows deferred violence to men, they also protected their self-image as gentlewomen without, critically, sacrificing violence as a tool of racial control. When they delegated to men whom they considered their social inferiors, such as overseers, it worked a deeper magic: reinforcing class distinctions. Just as a widow might take pride in rebuking an overseer for his mingy reluctance to bring in a doctor, delegating whippings to an overseer or jailer confirmed her refinement and his coarseness.

Keziah Brevard's reflections reveal a further factor that diminished the importance of widows' capacity for systematic violence: the possibility of sale. After dwelling on her slaves' misbehavior and its effects on her own temper, she wrote, "At my death it is my solemn desire that Tama—Sylvia—Mack—Maria & Rosanna be sold—I cannot think of imposing such servants on any one of my heirs."[67] Slaveholding widows understood the power of the slave market: it served as a deterrent, and if that failed, it converted slaves into cash and sent a potent lesson to the remaining slaves.[68] In the fall of 1849, for example, Charleston planter Eliza Wilkins resorted to the market to deal with her slave Billy. As her brother observed, "She had borne his insolence and neglect of duty a long time, but at length they became intolerable, and he was sold for $600." This sale's conditions demonstrated that Wilkins intended not only to be quit of Billy but to punish him as well: she "insisted" that the buyer take Billy "out of the State." Following Walter Johnson's analysis of the slave market, we might speculate that Billy had been angling to be sold, but the condition of being taken outside of South Carolina suggests Wilkins had the final word. If nothing else, transportation beyond the state symbolically linked this sale with the punishment commonly meted out to alleged rebels.[69]

While the most important weapons in slaveholding men's arsenal of domination—violence and the marketplace—were more or less compatible with ladyhood, a third, sexual coercion, absolutely was not. Yet this vexed subject did not vanish in widowhood. On the one hand, vengeful widows sometimes seized the opportunity to sell off their husbands' former concubines or rape victims. Virginia planter Ruth Hairston's decision to sell everything she inherited from her husband's Mississippi holdings likely had something to do with his having abandoned her to live in Mississippi with his enslaved mistress and child.[70] On the other hand, slave men sometimes became newly vulnerable to sexual predation. While legal proceedings sometimes created highly public knowledge of sexual liaisons between white women and black men, these cases usually involved socially marginal women charged with bastardy and fornication. In contrast, all but total silence greeted elite women's sexual exploitation of black men. Information about the practice is thus fragmentary at best, and it permits only speculative conclusions about patterns of interracial sex among slave-holding widows. Anecdotal testimony gathered by the American Freedmen's Inquiry Commission during the Civil War suggests that some slaveholding women—married, single, and widowed—sexually coerced enslaved men. One former slave related that his owner "'ordered him to sleep with her . . . regularly'" after she had been widowed for almost a year. Since many slaveholding widows never remarried and spent at least some of their widowhoods in households without other adult whites around, slave men's vulnerability to sexual exploitation likely increased after slaveholding husbands died.[71] With their large households, planter widows had greater opportunities for privacy than yeoman widows, and they were more likely to have male domestics, whose appearance and manners many whites preferred to field hands'. Planters also had the security of knowing their social status afforded some protection against gossip and prosecution, notwithstanding the considerable risk of bearing an illegitimate, mixed-race child.[72] In contrast, while yeoman widows had less privacy and less protection against public outrage, their small households often fostered a certain familiarity between owners and slaves. For the poorest widows, meanwhile, forming a relationship with another owner's slave (or a free black man) could provide labor as well as sexual companionship. Already on the fringes of survival and respectability, these women had relatively little to lose and perhaps a good deal to gain from such a connection.[73] Regardless, if slaveholding widows seized every opportunity for sex with male slaves—and thus did so far more often than the surviving evidence can prove—the practice still meant something rather different from slaveholding men's sex with slave women. Most obviously, slaveholding women could neither boast of their conquests nor view them as rites of passage. For slaveholding men and boys, sex with slaves was simultaneously illicit and accepted; it confirmed essential qualities of white manhood, including physical vigor and patriarchal rights over women. In contrast, both interracial sex and female sexual aggression jarred violently with normative understandings of white womanhood. Even so, however, both found expression during some widowhoods, in addition to the more commonplace and—to whites—more acceptable expressions of power inherent in whipping and selling slaves.[74]

THE MANAGEMENT OF NEGROES

UNDERSTANDING THE potential—and pitfalls—of combining ladyhood with mastery involves considering the matter from slaves' point of view. In the eyes of slaves as well as whites, slaveholding widows' authority did not look exactly like white men's, and to the extent that slaves shared the belief in white women's weakness, they likely disrespected widows' orders more than white men's. However, as slaves well knew, their bondage depended not on any individual slaveholder's forcefulness but on the collective power of the state and the white population. Moreover, a slaveholding husband's death often divided slaves' communities and families and subjected them to more work on smaller rations. As a result, while slaves routinely undermined widows' mastery, they typically behaved much as they did in male-headed households, and many found themselves in no position to ratchet up their resistance when a widow took over.

The picture of slaves' conduct on widows' farms and plantations closely resembles that painted by historians of slave resistance throughout the United States. Especially common forms of willful disobedience were stealing and malingering. Natalie Sumter eventually figured out, for example, that her slaves were leaving the cow house open at night "so they could climb in the stable & steal the Horses corn[.]" She also learned "that my house doors were left open every night" so her enslaved domestics could slip out while she slept.[75] Sumter's house slaves Delia and Priscilla were skilled at another form of subversion: working slowly and misunderstanding orders to provide as much annoyance as service. In a classic example, Sumter instructed Delia "not to let Priscilla wake me up and to tell Hampton I would not go out." But Delia said nothing until "the carriage was at the door & Priscilla woke me up—so I could not go to sleep again." Sumter may have realized that her slaves deliberately were annoying her, but more often than not, slaveholders refused to recognize such actions as a form of protest. Instead, they described resistance as misbehavior and chalked it up to racial inferiority. In this way, they diminished its significance and perhaps made themselves feel more secure.[76]

Another popular but riskier form of protest was running away. When Elizabeth Lee's slave Marjory ran away from her hire-master, she remained at liberty for three weeks, which perhaps made her bout of cholera seem worth the trouble. Sometimes slaves ran not just to escape but to strike back at their owners. When Elizabeth Cromwell's Tom ran away from her North Carolina farm in 1813, he remained in the neighborhood, killing her "cattle, hogs, sheep, &c." Further south, Natalie Sumter's household witnessed a range of runaway attempts. One August night, Sumter reported that "it is 11 o'clock & I cannot go to bed every body is looking for prescilla." Not absent for long, Priscilla disappeared again in mid-September, and again Sumter complained that she "could not get to bed early" because her slave "was not to be found." Other Sumter slaves vanished for longer periods. On July 4, 1840, Sumter recorded that Milly was missing and "has *not been found*." Milly reappeared in an August list of sick slaves. At the end of November, meanwhile, Richard absconded. Perhaps on the assumption that a male slave would make a permanent bid for freedom, Sumter wrote: "Richard has run away." A month later, however, he too reappeared in her diary.[77]

Why slaves ran away is relatively easy to deduce. Slaves ran from widows for the same reasons that they did from men: to avoid work or punishment, visit distant relatives or friends, or, most ambitiously, reach freedom. Whether slaves ran from widows with special frequency is far more difficult to determine. Runaway slave advertisements can provide a profile of slaves who ran, for example, and even of the advertisers, but the relationship between that population and the slaveholding class more generally is difficult to determine. Why, for example, did women post less than 5 percent of the runaway notices in Virginia newspapers between 1801 and 1820, when they made up roughly 10 percent of the slaveowners? One answer may be that Virginia widows often held slaves for life because of that state's intestacy law, and thus someone else took responsibility for placing advertisements, such as their husbands' administrators and heirs. Another piece of the answer may be found in the sorts of slaves widows held. Young and female slaves typically made up a high proportion of women's slaveholdings. Although slaves of all ages and both sexes did run away, as John Hope Franklin and Loren Schweninger have recently demonstrated, children, women, and especially women with young children were less likely to reach freedom than men. As a consequence, widows may have treated these slaves' disappearances as self-appointed holidays rather than serious bids for freedom, and thus have seen no need to advertise their flight. In addition, young runaways and mothers with small children were especially likely to get caught before their owners bothered to incur the cost of advertising for them.[78]

In addition to protesting and trying to escape bondage, slaves occasionally struck directly at their oppressors. Historian Philip Schwarz argues that widows and single white women looked particularly vulnerable to slaves, yet widows rarely expressed any fear of being attacked. Of course, the rare insurrection or conspiracy scare left them—as well as other whites—feeling panicky, and their level of alarm also increased markedly just before and during the Civil War. In more ordinary times, however, slaveholding widows generally saw unruliness or stupidity rather than vengefulness when they looked at their slaves and thus lived among them with great complacence. And widows had reason to feel safe because the state and the white population at large devoted considerable resources to keeping slaves in check.[79]

During the early nineteenth century, judges, legislators, sheriffs, slave patrols, and militias all worked to hem in slaves. Their control was far from perfect, but they helped give real meaning to the name of slave. In addition to defining slaveholders' legal rights and responsibilities, the state assisted in day-to-day enforcement. Sheriffs and jailors helped discipline slaves, and they also assisted in capturing runaways. When Eliza Ruffin's slave Nelson absconded, the Goochland County, Virginia, sheriff caught, jailed, and then returned him to her plantation.[80] Intervening more decisively in the owner-slave relationship, the state occasionally prosecuted slaves for crimes. As these examples suggest, beyond the household, upholding slavery was largely a white man's job. In most jurisdictions, all owners of "settled plantations"—male and female—had to contribute to the "security of that district where their interests lie," but only men served on the slave patrol and held offices with the responsibility for apprehending and prosecuting slave criminals.[81] The all-male composition of the South's police power reinforced the assumption that women would be lax in enforcing slavery, a logic no less compelling for its circularity. That assumption created an incentive to intervene in widows' slave management, but it also made it easy for widows to rely on the state's coercive power. If widows feared to act firmly, or simply thought it incompatible with their gender role, judges, slave patrollers, sheriffs, and others had every reason to suspect, convict, and harshly punish slaves for them. Such appears to have been the pattern in eighteenth-century Virginia, where slaves owned by women were disproportionately likely to be prosecuted, convicted, and sentenced to death.[82] Similarly, among the slaves accused of conspiring to rebel in Charleston in 1822, those owned by women were more likely to be convicted and executed than those owned by men.[83] Because upholding slavery was a collective as well as an individual duty, being owned or managed by a woman did not mean a less onerous bondage for slaves. Instead, as Nancy Williams recalled, it often brought them "real trouble."[84]

MANY FACTORS prevented slaveholding widows from realizing the idealized mastery of novels and advice manuals, and their ability even to approximate it varied over time. At the beginning of widowhood, many women felt unsure of themselves or were simply too grief-stricken to think much about mastery. Some actively denied their authority even as they began to wield it. When widows first took farm and plantation affairs into their own hands, they regularly claimed that they were only acting on their husbands' wishes. In recording one of her first decisions after her husband's death, Natalie Sumter deftly camouflaged her agency. In her diary, she wrote that she demoted Dennis from his position as slave driver because "he desobeyed us having made the Negros work in the Heat of the day though I had told him it was his master's last order's they should not work when it was hot." By writing "us," Sumter suggested that the plantation's management remained essentially unchanged, that there was still a "we" in charge when in fact there was only her. Equally, by defining the slaves' midday rest period as "his master's last order," she elided the fact that the instruction Dennis had ignored actually had come from her mouth.[85]

Over time, widows began taking credit and dispensing blame, punishment, and favors much like any slaveholding man. When several of Natalie Sumter's slaves got into a fight a year after her husband's death, she reacted much like Ada Bacot, who expected to rein in some disobedient slaves "without much trouble." After the fracas, Sumter sent for a doctor to tend to James, who "got his head broke by Anna." She did not, however, send for anyone to discipline the brawlers. She assumed that she "soon could put them to rights," and instead of castigating herself for failing to suppress the fight, she blamed the slaves.[86] Relatedly, experienced widows rarely gave slaves due credit for good outcomes, appropriating their labor verbally as well as materially. When Lucy Freeman bragged that "I run two ploughs," she wasted no ink on the obvious: slaves had done some or more likely all of the work. Dolly Burge similarly elided enslaved workers from her diary: "laid by all of the corn looks very well but had a bad time getting a stand," and, later, "got a bag of cotton out." At one level, this ellipsis was utterly typical: slaveholding men regularly wrote as if they themselves had done the slaves' plowing, planting, and picking, while their wives took credit for slaves' sewing, gardening, and scrubbing. At another level, widows' usage was distinctive; unlike other women, they appropriated both domestic and field labor, expressing a sense of possession over the entire slaveholding household.[87]

However comfortable they became with juggling mastery and ladyhood, widows still struggled with the economics of slavery, sometimes losing property from year to year. The problem was particularly acute early in widowhood. After her husband died, Martha Jackson spent years trying to get out of debt and succeeded only by selling up in Alabama and buying a Georgia farm in partnership with her younger daughter. Other factors also interfered with making money. Caroline Burke's prospects slumped as her slaves sickened and died; even with her son's help, she barely scraped a living from her Alabama farm. These financial shortcomings were not, however, a distinctively feminine failure. Even in flush times, male slaveholders left estates encumbered with debts, and many teetered on the brink of ruin at one point or another. Women widowed during an economic contraction could hardly expect to escape the foreclosures and bankruptcies that snared so many male slaveholders.[88] When not undone by their husbands' debts, the business cycle, and other factors equally beyond their control, determined widows could make their economizing pay. Lucy Freeman's ability to run two plows by no means made her rich, but it represented a step toward financial security and meant she could keep her children in school. At the other end of the scale was South Carolina's Keziah Brevard. In 1850, she managed two farms valued at $22,500 on which 180 slaves produced 190 bales of cotton, as well as substantial amounts of corn, oats, hay, sweet potatoes, and domestic manufactures. Ten years later, she had more than doubled her acreage, and her slave force had grown by 16 percent.[89]

As slave managers, widows were not fully successful masters, but neither were they benevolent ladies or hapless incompetents. Gender did not guarantee that a widow would fail any more than it ensured her kindness. Gender did, however, profoundly shape how widows responded to the endless struggle to master slaves. Widows assessed their mastery in terms of their entire households, but they judged themselves as women through their domestic management and, as we will see, their relationships with other whites, especially kin. For men, however, their manhood and their mastery were typically one and the same. Drew Faust suggests that South Carolina planter, senator, and governor James Henry Hammond spent his life trying to become the ideal southern master—a man of implacable will who extracted obedience from subordinates and respect from peers. Hammond's ambition exceeded other men's in intensity but not in substance, and it was a specifically male ambition. Despite a lifetime of effort, Hammond himself fell short of his goal, learning instead to cultivate what Faust calls "the art of the possible." Where Hammond failed, no slaveholding woman could reasonably hope to succeed. But then slaveholding women never expected to achieve the autonomy and power that Hammond considered the essence of southern manhood. Raised to place the interests of their families above their own, slaveholding women grew up knowing that they did not determine their own destinies. While they *wanted* to get their way and often acted petulantly, or worse, when they did not, they never expected to dominate their own little corners of the universe.[90] As a result, when slaveholding women added the duties of master to those of mistress, they did not assume the same psychological burdens that white masculinity entailed. They more readily eschewed the impossible goal of perfect mastery for the reachable compromises—the "art of the possible"—of fictive mastery.[91]

CHAPTER 3

The Strongest Ties That Bind
Poor Mortals

While slaves provided slaveholders with most of their income and much of their social standing, most slaveholding widows would have identified their relatives as their greatest sources of practical as well as emotional support. That this would happen was not immediately obvious from some renderings of kinship in the early nineteenth century. In this period, slaveholders had two primary models of family to draw upon. The conjugal or nuclear family was a hierarchical institution based on patriarchal right. Even though prescriptive literature increasingly romanticized marital love, the legal system and popular opinion continued to give men almost untrammeled power over their wives and minor children. As historian Suzanne Lebsock has observed, a marriage was "only as companionate as the husband allowed it to be."[1] Widowhood profoundly disrupted the premises of this conjugal relationship. By predeceasing his dependents, a patriarch left them supposedly defenseless and alone. According to some obituaries, a husband's death not only jeopardized a wife and children's material survival but also their bonds to each other; it "severed the strongest ties that bind poor mortals together." Authors like George Fitzhugh described women and children as equally unable to forge their survival in the rough-and-tumble world. Without their husband and father, a mother and her children were not quite a family, and the law deemed fatherless children orphans.[2]

Yet whatever else slaveholders said and wrote about familial hierarchy

and the indispensable paterfamilias, they did not demand that widows remarry or become the wards of male in-laws, brothers, uncles, fathers, or
other patriarchal figures. Instead, slaveholders situated widows within a
different set of familial relationships. For siblings, cousins, and other extended kin, family suggested bonds of affection, cooperation, and mutual
assistance. These often intragenerational bonds cut across the rigid gender roles of patriarchal marriage: older sisters advised younger brothers,
for example, and influential relatives of both sexes mediated wives' dependence on their husbands. Slaveholders of both sexes also acted as agents
for their kin, loaned each other slaves and household supplies, and generally promoted familial interests. Depending on relatives in this way facilitated householding, and strong family connections promoted success in
business, politics, law, and courtship as well.[3] Slaveholding widows leaned
particularly heavily on their extended kinship networks to cope with their
expansive responsibilities. This reliance was not, however, simply another
form of women's dependence on men because most widows were benefactors as well as beneficiaries. Equally important, the help widows extended
and received crossed lines of generation and gender, blurring the distinct
roles and spheres associated with the patriarchal household.[4]

The implications of familial networks became most clear not when they
functioned smoothly but when relatives came into conflict. Sometimes,
slaveholders quarreled because one person felt another was not acting with
the "affectionate kindness" and "anxious solicitude" appropriate to "near
relations." The most contentious disputes, however, typically concerned
property. Charges of embezzlement, fraud, or simple mismanagement
could divide families for years. When men—especially sons and sons-in-
law—disagreed with the way a widow was handling her husband's property, conflict over material goods easily expanded to include gender roles.
While some slaveholding men displayed nothing but affection for their
widowed mothers and mothers-in-law, others saw them as threats to their
independence and manhood, especially in the decades immediately following the Revolution. According to historian Carol Karlsen, disputes over
widows' role in transferring property between generations in colonial
Massachusetts sometimes yielded deadly witchcraft accusations, but in
the nineteenth-century Southeast, such conflicts typically had more pro-
saic consequences: suits in equity or chancery courts. As a rule, the southeastern judiciary opposed female independence, but the nature of equity,
which was designed to provide remedies that the law could not, lent itself
to judicial paternalism. This in turn proved beneficial to widows because

judges often saw female plaintiffs and defendants as needing protection. Even when judges did not intervene in their favor, however, widows had other resources in their conflicts with overbearing kinsmen, from the practical fact of controlling property to the ideological expectation of familial and gentlemanly assistance to distressed widows.[5]

FAMILIAL AID TO widows depended on their resources and changed over time. For many families, the first months of widowhood were often the most demanding because grief left some widows too stupefied to take in the practical details of getting a will probated, having the estate appraised, and sorting out their husbands' papers. This was a particular problem for widows of young men and mothers of young children. To the newly widowed, kins*women* typically offered sympathy and kins*men* practical help. That gendered split did not characterize all familial aid, however; men also attended to widows' emotional needs, and women assisted each other with legal, financial, and planting matters. After several years of widowhood, and especially after their husbands' estates were settled, many slaveholding widows extended a helping hand in return.

In addition to condoling with the bereaved, relatives offered financial assistance and advice. In 1829, Fredericksburg widow Elizabeth Rootes turned to her husband's siblings for help because his estate was still tied up in chancery court. Her sisters-in-law, Martha Jackson and Sarah Cobb, sent "twenty dollars for the immediate relief of the family," and each offered to take in one of Rootes's children to save her the cost of raising them.[6] Outside the planter elite, slaveholding women relied on their relations' material help throughout widowhood. In the 1850s and early 1860s, Ann Wheeler of Salisbury, North Carolina, was unable to support herself solely by sewing and leaned heavily on her sons, whom she hoped would one day be able to buy her a home of her own. Wheeler also depended upon her rich cousin, Ruth Hairston (previously Ruth Wilson). Ruth paid to educate one of Ann's sons and sent small sums of money for Ann's other children.[7] Instead of providing cash, however, most slaveholding women helped widows by offering their labor or handmade goods. Catherine Lewis's kinswomen, for example, made clothes for her children and gave her foodstuffs like lard and butter. One sister lived with Catherine as a paying boarder. While this sort of help never assuaged Catherine's anxiety about "coming to poverty by slow and certain degrees," it helped her pay some debts, replenish her larder, and keep up her boardinghouse.[8]

Rich widows typically needed advice rather than cash. When she was widowed in 1813 at the age of thirty, Ruth Wilson received her husband's southside Virginia plantation as her dower. As she began to manage it, she wrote regularly to her father, Peter Hairston, asking him for "derections in every thing." In addition to advising Ruth about agricultural affairs and her daughter's education, he also assumed the significant task of executing his son-in-law's estate, but far from urging Ruth to shed her duties as a planter, Peter Hairston helped her carry them out. As this father-daughter relationship suggests, reliance on a kinsman need not confine a widow to "woman's sphere."[9] Timely advice from a kinsman could save new widows from costly mistakes. In the early 1840s, lowcountry planter John Berkeley Grimball protected Eliza Wilkins's interests in his capacity as her only brother and co-trustee of her separate estate. Like Ruth Wilson, Charlestonian Eliza Wilkins was a substantial property-holder. Her trust estate included dozens of slaves, and she stood to inherit more from her mother, Eliza Flinn. Her husband's estate, however, was a mess. Martin Wilkins had died significantly indebted, and there was some question whether his wife or his brother and partner, Gouverneur, was liable for his debts. (Martin's will instructed that his estate be kept together until either his plantation's profits or his wife paid off his debts.) After consulting his co-trustee James L. Petigru, Grimball informed his sister that Gouverneur was "undoubtedly liable" for the partnership's debts. As a result, he "certainly could not undertake to advise" that she satisfy her husband's debts out of her own property. Eliza accepted an arrangement that protected her, but out of concern for her brother-in-law, she claimed no dower against her husband's estate. She also asked Gouverneur to "retain a parental interest" in his nephew and namesake and "give him the advantage of your advice and protection." Once her financial situation had been sorted out, Eliza Wilkins no longer needed her brother's counsel quite so urgently. Over the next two decades, the siblings settled into a more equitable give-and-take of favors, such as endorsing each others' notes and loaning each other money. In this and many other slaveholding families, widows gave as well as received aid.[10]

Another aspect of familial assistance involved doing business with kin. Transacting with retailers and factors who were also their relatives meant keeping money and connections in the family. In the 1820s in Mecklenburg County, Virginia, Lucy Burwell bought many of her plantation supplies from a brother-in-law.[11] At the same time in Georgia, Annabella Porter patronized a cotton factor who was also her son-in-law. This relationship served Porter well because Henry Cook was even more helpful than factors generally were. If ever he could not meet one of Porter's requests, he felt doubly obliged to "make it up in some way to you." When she asked that he reduce his firm's commission, for example, he had to refuse, but he instructed her to consider him her agent for "any business" she had in Augusta, "without regard to any trouble it may impose upon me."[12] This was by no means a useless or trivial offer, as reliable agents in market centers greatly facilitated a rural slaveholder's ability to do business at a remove.[13]

For the richest and poorest widows alike, the most intensive sort of familial assistance involved co-residence. When widows joined someone else's household, whether they retained any independence hinged on their financial condition and their life cycle. Impoverished widows had little weight to throw around. For Rebecca Younge, living with her mother, Caroline Burke, was her best and perhaps her only recourse since her husband had left her almost no property. Yet Rebecca remained legally and morally responsible for herself and struggled to find work even though, as her brother noted, their part of Alabama was "a poor country for a female to get along in."[14] In wealthier families, widows usually shared their households for companionship more than need. Eliza Wilkins regularly brought her children to live in her mother's Charleston house during the unhealthy summer seasons. After spending many years in small-town Georgia, Louisa Alexander moved to Savannah and shared a home with her sister. With no plantation responsibilities, the pair devoted themselves to the tasks they liked best; Louisa sewed, Dorothea gardened, and domestic slaves did whatever housework the two widows found unpalatable. Martha Richardson similarly enjoyed her residence with her sister and brother-in-law in Savannah although in this case the situation was less equitable; Martha tended to overshadow her milder-tempered sister.[15] Even living with a male relative did not make a widow truly dependent unless utter destitution or crippling illness prevented her from contributing to the household economy. Age and a truncated labor force made Caroline Burke (and eventually her daughter, Rebecca Younge) reliant on her son, John, a responsibility he took seriously. Although he dreamed of lighting out to Texas, he would neither abandon Caroline nor make her brave "the hardships of a new country." Yet his sacrifice and labor did not make him the undisputed boss of the household. Instead, Caroline shared with him the burden of supporting it, both through her own labor and through the income she continued to receive from a trust estate her mother had arranged.[16]

In some families, however, bringing a son into the household permitted a widow to relinquish many of her responsibilities. In the early 1820s, Sarah Hillhouse invited her son, David, and his wife to move into the house she had built in Washington, the seat of Wilkes County, Georgia. Sarah found this arrangement delightful, marveling that "I did not think I could ever be so comfortably situated." To her, the essence of comfort was to spend most of the day in her room, free to read, knit, or do "whatever work presents itself." This return to domesticity followed an extraordinary career; she had edited a newspaper, managed a print shop, and published the state's official records for a decade after her husband died. After her daughter's death in 1808, she had also raised a granddaughter. By 1823, with her son long-since grown up and her granddaughter finally married, Sarah was ready to enjoy some "indulgence."[17] Far away in rural Amelia County, Virginia, Jane Cocke ended her widowhood in another sort of retirement. For many years, she shared her plantation home with her son and daughter-in-law, James Powell (called Powell) and Caroline Cocke. Jane Cocke's early widowhood was more conventional than Sarah Hillhouse's, but it had its share of responsibilities. When her husband died in 1794, Jane had five children under the age of twenty. Her husband's will named her co-executor and empowered her to manage his entire estate throughout her widowhood. From its profits, she was to support herself, educate the children, and pay specified legacies. Jane managed the home plantation for at least ten years while her sons were at school, coming of age, and getting married. After Powell married Caroline Lewis, the couple moved onto the plantation that he would inherit when Jane died, whereupon Powell took over the plantation management from Jane. Powell's many absences, however, ensured that Jane retained some responsibilities for the place since her daughter-in-law was often too sick from repeated pregnancies, childbirth, or miscarriages to act as a deputy husband. In addition, Jane Cocke retained control over her own finances, and unlike most wives, she traveled when she pleased. She and Sarah Hillhouse, in short, were more liberated than confined by living with their sons.[18]

Kin's assistance often reflected the gendered division of labor among slaveholders: men advised on law, commerce, and agriculture while women assisted with child-rearing, domestic production, and housekeeping. But because women's and men's expertise overlapped, and because slaveholders recognized no rigid distinction between business and family, there were many exceptions to this pattern. Family letters moved swiftly between intimate matters of health, for example, and concerns about finances. Martha Cocke's correspondence with her sister Caroline is a case in point. She confided both her feelings and her practical managerial problems to Caroline, using her as a sounding board for all of her concerns. When Martha finally decided to rent a farm, for example, she described the details to Caroline and hoped "to get your opinion," as Caroline was "so *fond* of every thing of the *kind*." When Martha sought her brother-in-law Powell's help hiring out a slave, she made the request through Caroline. In many other slaveholding households, anything that touched on family welfare, from births to debts, concerned both women and men. Women typically had more insight into childbirth and men into debt, but these distinctions were more relative than absolute, and where widows were concerned, they all but disappeared.[19]

WHETHER THEY HAD thousands of dollars at their disposal or only a lifetime of practical experience, slaveholding widows tried to help their families much as they were helped. Control over property enabled some widows to send children to school, launch men in business, and finance the purchase of slaves. Widows usually extended the most help to their own children or to their siblings' children, thus reinforcing their generation's authority over the next. At the same time, many recognized the special importance of property to women—who had so few chances to earn it—and were especially generous to daughters and nieces.

During her widowhood, Jane Cocke sought to assist both her sons and her daughters. By the early 1830s her son Powell had become substantially indebted to his three surviving sisters. Shortly before her death, Jane assumed his $1,000 debt to his widowed sister Judith. According to one grandson, Jane "would willingly have made any disposition of her money" that would do Powell "real service." Another grandson agreed that Jane would do anything for "the wellfare of those for whom she should feel the greatest solicitude," but he pointed out that "you cannot but admit that Aunt Judy"—not Powell—was "in a condition to claim her most anxious concern."[20] A decade later, Eliza Flinn acted similarly in her efforts to help both of her children. In 1837, for example, Eliza helped her son by selling a plantation to a Mrs. Rivers in an arrangement that "extinguished" a debt Berkeley owed to Mrs. Rivers's late husband. On other occasions, Eliza endorsed the renewal of notes he had drawn on the state bank. Yet when her son-in-law died, she rewrote her will to favor her daughter Eliza, giving her control over her children's inheritance and an additional legacy of $4,000.[21]

Wealthy and childless widows often patronized their nephews and nieces. Martha Richardson claimed that all her money was merely "trash" unless it could be used in the service of those she loved. Living up to her boast, she informed her favorite nephew that she was "happy to be your Banker" to the sum of $1,000 if he wanted to extend his European tour. If this offer was purely altruistic, other gifts to the Screven family more clearly reflected Martha's disposition to meddle. When her niece Emily wanted to marry a man of whom her father disapproved, for example, Martha "almost forgot my prudence" and offered to share her income with the couple, so they could afford to wed without parental approval. Although she doubted that "an old Woman" could find a "better use . . . for money than to make her children happy," she eventually opted against this rash course, fearing that she would be "called officious." Her willingness to intervene may, however, have prompted John Screven to forgive the pair. Martha Richardson further inscribed herself in the Screven family economy when she gave another of John's children thirteen slaves in trust, on the condition that he pay her a $250 annuity.[22]

Even without significant economic power, slaveholding widows could make a profound impression on their families. During lengthy visits to her adult children, North Carolina's Polly Battle passed along invaluable advice. When her eldest son, William Horn Battle, moved to a new house in Raleigh, she showed "how to fit up his lot for it was very much out of repair." Polly's daughter Catherine Lewis felt "truly thankful" when her mother "consented to stay" with her and her husband in 1838. "She knows all about farming and every thing else, her health is very good and she finds enjoyment a plenty in putting in window glasses and all such jobs you would laugh to see her," Catherine wrote. "How I do wish Mother [Lewis] could do about like her, she goes down to the spring has it cleared out does all kinds of jobs[.] I think she would earn her board anywhere learning one to save and by saving herself but she will pay her board in some way or other every where she stays long enough." Polly had been only sixteen when she married Joel Battle, and if she was like most planters' daughters, she had had little prior experience performing the serious work that awaited her as a wife, deputy husband, and widow. Thirty years of marriage and a decade of widowhood later, however, she knew how to make herself indispensable to those on whom she relied.[23]

Many of the situations that forced married men to make their wives into deputies, such as travel and illness, also prompted them to look to widowed kinswomen for assistance. During an extended trip to the North with his wife, James Screven asked his aunt Martha Richardson to keep an eye on his plantation. She took the charge seriously and worried over occasional reports of weather-related damage to the crops. After a slave told her that spring rains had left a low-lying cornfield in need of replanting and the rice fields "covered with water," she asked one of her nephew's in-laws to give her "a correct account of the state of your fields." She reported to James that other slaves "tell me that you have not suffered as yet." Thanks to this diligence, James Screven could be confident that his plantations remained in good hands during his travels in the North.[24]

In such day-to-day matters of planting and householding, it little mattered whether the helpful kinswoman was a wife or a widow, provided she knew what she was doing. In matters of law, however, widows and other single women could help their kin in ways a wife could not. Because few slaveholders kept very systematic records, they sometimes had to rely on their womenfolk's memories to establish the history of particular transactions, but only an unmarried woman had the capacity to testify in case of a formal dispute.[25] In the mid-1840s, Martha Jackson's memory and legal personhood played a key role in staving off a financial disaster that threatened her sister and brother-in-law, Serena and Henry Lea. Sometime after marrying Serena in 1828, Henry Lea had created a trust estate which reserved to her and their children the slaves she had brought to their marriage. When Henry fell into debt after the Panic of 1837—like many of his peers, he had stood security to too many friends—his creditors claimed that the trust was fraudulent, hoping that they would be allowed to take the slaves as payment. Because this separate estate was created after the marriage, Henry needed to prove that he had not created it after becoming indebted in order to defraud his creditors. To do so, he sought testimony from Serena's family to the effect that they had insisted upon his creating the trust. In this effort, Martha Jackson in particular was "absolutely *essential*" because she was the only one of Serena's relatives who could speak directly to the trust's origins. The other two who had pressed the trust upon Henry could not speak; Serena's widowed aunt, Lucy Thornton, had died, and her sister, Sarah, was married and thus could not testify on her own account (although her husband did so on her behalf). In two separate depositions, Martha attested that she, Sarah, and their aunt had all wanted Serena's property reserved to her before the wedding. She further affirmed that "it gave Mrs Lea's Relatives great satisfaction to hear that it was afterwards carried into effect by a settlement of the property upon the children." As a respectable, property-owning widow, Jackson carried significant weight, not just in her own household, but also in her extended family and in the courtrooms that adjudicated her kinsmen's suits. Years later, her Lea nephews and nieces attested to her importance in their own lives with their opinion that "whatever Aunt Patsy says is right."[26]

None of the parties concerned with the Lea trust seemed to find Martha Jackson's role surprising. To many other southeastern slaveholders, such favors in the family seemed so routine that they rarely commented on the practice even when it blurred supposedly rigid gender boundaries between men's and women's concerns. As a result, it can be difficult to determine how a series of favors developed, how ideals of family and gender shaped their exchange, or even how the practice of mutual assistance changed over time. Conflict within families, however, made the routine contested, exposing how slaveholders weighed the obligations of kinship against self-interest on the one hand and patriarchal prerogatives on the other.

THROUGHOUT THE Southeast, slaveholders' understanding of kinship and widows' control over property intersected to create mutually beneficial networks of advice and assistance. Yet slaveholders did not always agree on how to handle either their relations or their property. A characteristic problem for widows involved situations where they sought more help than their relatives could or wanted to give. When the dispute concerned not property per se but affection and consideration, slaveholding widows typically favored moral suasion as the means of getting their way. Between the Revolution and the antebellum decades, however, the specific manner in which slaveholding widows tried to extract emotional support and even material assistance from balky relatives changed in ways that reflect the slow transition from predominantly hierarchical to increasingly companionate understandings of extended familial relationships.

Coming out of the Revolution, many older slaveholders retained a comparatively authoritarian understanding of kinship. Especially important were children's duties to their parents. Even as adults, children owed their parents deference and obedience. The younger generation, however, often had different ideas. Before the Revolution, Mary Campbell had expected her sons' distinguished names to assist her in convincing Lord Dunmore to halt an execution against her property. After the war, she expected those sons to come to her aid. The elder, Alexander, fell well short of her hopes. In 1791, for example, she groused that "he knows & sees my sufferings" but it was "no use to ask any thing of him." A winter of "sevear weather" left her with "scarcely fire to warm us," but when she told him that "we very near experienced Hunger as well as cold," he insinuated that she had mismanaged her larder. His eventual offer to send her more bacon did not mend matters: "had I been his menist servant he could not have offerd his favor with more Indignity than he did, I Told him I would lay under no obligations to him. . . . Indeed I dont wish any connection with him or his unhappy family they act unsincear parts." At least, that was how she related the incident to her other son, John, whom she found far more satisfactory. "I cannot sufficiently make my acknowledgement to my dearest son," she wrote; "god only knows what would become of me had I not such a child." These words suggest that Mary Campbell recognized she could not simply command her sons' help as a prerogative, but rather she had to ask for it and give thanks in return. Thus far, a more companionate form of reciprocity had made its impression. Yet while she nodded to the voluntarism of grown children's aid to their parents, she continued to uphold a more coercive, hierarchical model of parent-children relations. After abusing Alexander and extolling John, she issued John an ultimatum: "I wish you have not the least dealings with him." Mary Campbell presumed the right not only to judge an adult son who failed in his duty, but also to make her displeasure binding upon her other, more obliging son.[27]

Twenty years later, slaveholders were still negotiating the obligations of children to parents. A pair of cases involving two Virginia planting families in the early 1810s suggests this flux. In February 1810, Buckingham County planter Linnaeus Bolling wrote his mother to tell her of his daughter's birth and to congratulate her on her recovery from a recent illness. In addition to asking her to lend him some rum and wine, he also promised to "pay my personal duty" as soon as he could leave his wife "with safety." Bolling's sense that he had to leave his newborn child and wife in order to visit his mother suggests that he accepted a certain formality in their relations.[28] Other Virginians were less punctilious, twitting their relations about their "ceremonious" social demands. James Powell and Charles Cocke challenged their mother's refusal to write until she received a response to previous letters. While she insisted on her right to an answer—a question of manners and filial duty—they criticized her "upbraiding letters" and reminded her of her own duty as a mother, which apparently included expressing boundless love while demanding little or nothing in return.[29] Another twenty years later, slaveholders were still wrestling with new expectations for sentimental affection, and many more individuals had discovered it could be a demanding standard. Certainly John Berkeley Grimball felt the none-too-hidden coercion that lurked within the ideal of affection. In 1836, he was "grieved" to learn that his mother "thinks I have neglected her." Although he maintained that her perception "really does me, as far as intention goes, great injustice," he hurried nonetheless to "do all I can" to reassure her. His haste suggests that both his mother's feelings and his own image as a dutiful, loving son were at stake. Wealthy widows Mary Campbell, Susannah Wilcox, Jane Cocke, and Eliza Flinn all measured their relations' love in terms of what kin did for them, but their specific expectations for demeanor were changing. While Mary Campbell and Susannah Wilcox required a degree of deference from the younger generation, Jane Cocke and Eliza Flinn (and their sons) looked more for emotive assurances of affection.[30]

Moving into the antebellum period, slaveholding widows grew ever more likely to combine the language of sentimentality with chivalrous ideas of how gentlemen should treat damsels in distress. After her husband died in 1835, Virginia-born Lucy Freeman asked her brothers to move to Tennessee, or at least visit her there, insisting that "the ondley distant hope I have is my connection." She also told her brother Jessie Vaughan that "it always seamed to be the wish of my husband that brother Jesse should manage the estate." When her siblings proved unresponsive, she wrote again, complaining that she was "in a great deal of trouble at this time for want of a friend." The long-suffering and neglected persona that Freeman crafted was profoundly strategic in two ways. Even as Lucy played the hapless dependent in an effort to make her brothers act the generous patriarchs, she recognized the need to appear self-reliant. Whatever financial disaster lurked in the future, she wrote, she would "be found a trying." In addition, far from being alone in Tennessee, she had several relations in the area. Mentioning them, however, could only have helped her brothers decide that coming to see her was above and beyond the call of kindred.[31]

Much as expressions of feminine dependence coexisted uneasily with widows' active efforts to cope on their own, the rhetoric of sentimental love could undermine widows' long-standing expectations of tangible assistance. Colonial historian Kathleen Brown has argued that the ideal of loving affection, which she dates to the mid-eighteenth century among the Virginia gentry, benefited men most because it provided "authority on a silver platter to men who need never raise their voices in anger or lift the lash." Expectations of familial affection and domestic harmony certainly had the potential to silence complaint by making it seem unloving or even deviant. By the same token, they could also force needy widows into endless protestations of loyalty and love. Catherine Lewis showered her in-laws with just such pledges throughout her widowhood precisely because she needed their help yet often felt neglected by them. Seeking to trigger a reciprocal reaction, she assured them repeatedly that "it is my most earnest wish that my dear Husbands family should treat me as they do each other." Perhaps even more hazardous to widows' interests, however, was the possibility that an emotion-centered understanding of family would de-emphasize tangible support as a familial obligation, something which widows in particular had every reason to fear. One of Catherine Lewis's brothers-in-law, for example, suggested that sincere affection and financial demands were incompatible when he complained that she and his other relatives were "very affectionate" when "they wanted *money*." Anxious to reverse this equation, Catherine charged in turn that Kenelm Lewis had "always stood aloof from us" and claimed that she had often "wept bitterly" at his neglect. Moreover, she had no intention of disavowing a financial interest in his affection; in that very letter, she asked him to send some money for his niece. Kenelm Lewis obliged because for him, and indeed for most slaveholders of his day, emotional and material support in fact remained two sides of one coin. Consequently, slaveholding widows continued to reap the benefit of carefully cultivated kinship networks even as changing notions of family constrained their freedom to protest mistreatment.[32]

IF TRYING TO EXTRACT attention and favors from unwilling relatives was an unpleasant and even humiliating experience, disputes over estate management and family property were far worse. These conflicts were especially dangerous because quarrels that began in private with persuasion could easily end up before judges with the power to hand down coercive solutions.[33] In general, nineteenth-century women found courts unfamiliar, unfriendly places, even the equity courts which had jurisdiction over estate settlement, guardianship, and married women's property. Yet for slaveholding widows, succeeding in a dispute over family property did not depend solely on their comfort with the law or the physical space of a courthouse. Instead, it hinged as well on the merits of the case and their ability to recruit talented men to handle the motions, pleas, and other legal arcana. Moreover, while women could never negotiate as equals with men at law, the essence of equity was to craft "fair" solutions, and southern judges readily believed that women needed protecting. In addition, since equity proceedings were expensive, the widows involved were almost by definition women of property and thus unlikely to receive the disrespectful hearing judges accorded to women charged with offenses against social order (such as bastardy and fornication). In this context, judicial paternalism could simultaneously enshrine the principle of female inferiority and protect individual widows' interests. Finally, property disputes were not only handled through legal formulae. Even as a particular complaint worked its way through the legal system, kinsfolk also negotiated informally with each other, and in this context, widows operated on more equal terms with men. Throughout, widows sought to appeal to judicial and familial sympathies, often by turning norms for familial and womanly behavior to their own advantage.[34]

Perhaps the most explosive conflicts pitted widowed executors and administrators against the younger generation of men. In a pair of illustrative cases during and after the American Revolution, sons-in-law identified widows as bad mothers and accused them of usurping masculine authority. In his 1760 will, Gawin Corbin directed that his executors (his widow, Hannah, and her brother) provide for his underage daughter, Martha.[35] Nine years later, Martha married George Turberville,[36] and five years after that, George accused Hannah Corbin of wasting timber on his wife's land. In 1783, he made the far more serious charge that "Mrs. Corbin has imbasel'd a great part" of Gawin Corbin's estate. Turberville claimed that while Martha was still a minor, her mother had spent only a "mean and Trifeling" amount on her, essentially reducing her to poverty. Indeed, it was only with the "utmost Frugality" that Martha had managed to "appear tolerably decent when she went into company, and she really could not be warm in the Winter." Insisting that this was not the "genteel Maintenance" that Gawin Corbin's will had stipulated, George claimed that Hannah's actions proved "she had not Love or regard for her daughter." He threatened to bring an action against her in chancery court in right of his wife, a remedy that, under the rules of coverture, would make him the beneficiary of any award to Martha.[37]

Some twenty years later, James Thruston Hubard made strikingly similar charges against Susannah Wilcox, who was his mother-in-law and the executor of her second husband's estate. Like George Turberville, Hubard accused his mother-in-law of using her daughter's inheritance for her "own purposes." To cover her tracks, he alleged, Susannah Wilcox "intends charging extravagantly for the board & expenses of her daughter & ward." Hubard believed that because Edmund Wilcox had left Susannah a very wealthy widow, she had no right "to charge his only child for board, & the expenses of dressing, and resorting or going to places of amusement." And even if she had the legal right, it was "certainly extremely unnatural." Seeking relief in chancery court, James Hubard accused Wilcox of trying to "controul" the funds "belonging to my dear Wife." As far as he was concerned, managing his wife's property was his exclusive prerogative, and Wilcox's actions were "highly absurd & unjust." According to him, she was an unnatural mother and faithless executor.[38]

In neither case is there incontrovertible evidence of executorial malfeasance although it is certainly possible that Susannah Wilcox and Hannah Corbin willfully stinted their daughters and abused their authority. In both cases, however, the family letters make it abundantly clear that James Thruston Hubard and George Turberville accused their mothers-in-law of malfeasance at least in part because they resented these women's lingering control over property their wives would eventually inherit. Educated men, they must have known that their wives' property would ordinarily augment their own authority and wealth. Yet this property remained tantalizingly out of reach as long as their widowed mothers-in-law controlled it. Hubard and Turberville were not simply motivated by the reasonable fear that this property might lose value in the interim; they also felt improperly subjected to their widowed mothers-in-law. Hubard admitted as much when he charged that Wilcox was trying to use her daughter's marriage contract to dominate him, asking, "Can you suppose for one moment that I would submit to your control or direction or to that of such men as Mr. West or Mr. Rootes or Mr. Allen? It appears that you have believed so, but I now beg leave to assure you that I never shall—no earthly power can ever make me so far degrade myself, unless I have so stupidly committed myself in your marriage contract as to make me a slave—which I know I have not done."[39] Such heated language, especially the reference to enslavement, suggests that this generation of young slaveholding men felt threatened when their wives' property remained under another's control, as in a separate estate, and they may have felt both more unhappy and more free to complain when mothers-in-law held the purse strings. This reaction is very much in keeping with a broader pattern of backlash against the Revolutionary era's potential to redefine women's status. Yet men's anger at particular women's power over them did not always translate into a categorical opposition to female authority over property; George Turberville even named his wife as his executor.[40]

For their part, Hannah Corbin and Susannah Wilcox could neither laugh off nor ignore these accusations of "unnatural" and "unjust" behavior toward their daughters because these charges had serious legal consequences, to say nothing of the scandal. Nor did they surrender. Instead, Corbin and Wilcox counterattacked, returning each accusation tit-for-tat. In a "long and scurilous letter" to her lawyer, Hannah Corbin detailed her son-in-law's failings so pointedly that she reduced him to whining, "She has use'd me so ungenteel." Susannah Wilcox challenged her son-in-law in court and subverted his authority at home. On one occasion, she ordered his confused overseer "not to attend to [Hubard's] directions any further." She may also have tried to turn her daughter against him in addition to rallying her son and other kinsmen to her side.[41]

Such open hostility appears to have plagued more families in the period before 1820 than after it. Explicit personal insults on both sides and overt masculine hostility to widows became somewhat less common in antebellum families. In legal fights as in informal quarrels, more measured reproaches and references to hurt feelings slowly replaced the invective that characterized Wilcox's and Corbin's fights with their sons-in-law. By the 1850s, even the bitterest disputes with the largest stakes produced comparatively little acrimonious prose.[42] This shift reflected a broader trend toward manufacturing the appearance of unanimity and consent by stifling protest among and against slaveholders. It did not, however, result in widows' disempowerment. Rather, antebellum widows continued to resist family members' assaults on their property rights, but they did so in ways that conformed to—and extended—changing norms of familial interaction.

In the 1810s, Martha Richardson's campaign to protect her property in a dispute with her brothers suggests how widows could navigate the sentimental idioms of companionate families and dependent females. Even for a planter, Richardson was unusually forceful and self-righteous. Few of her female peers would ever have asserted, as she did, "I am glad I received no help—I have been the carver of my own fortune let it be more or less." Richardson expressed herself even more strongly when she learned her brothers had questioned her husband's will. In a letter to her favorite nephew, she snarled, "What *right* have they to a reason?—I reply it was his *Will* to will it as he did and it is my will that his will remains in force!!" Claiming that they were doing what their husbands would have wanted was a common means for slaveholding widows to justify their actions. Most felt more comfortable claiming authority as their husbands' delegates and agents than in their own names. In equating her own will (a question of individual agency) with her husband's last will (a legally enforceable document), however, Richardson took this formula to an extreme. While her determination stood her in good stead, she occasionally had to put a damper on her stridency. In her letters, her tone changed from vinegar to honey as she shifted between confidences to her reader and comments for a broader audience. In the same letter where she boasted of making her own destiny, she also painted a pitiful self-portrait; she was "distressed with lawsuits and struggling hard to save her property from the Sheriff." Worse, she was abandoned by siblings who showed no "Brotherly love" in her hour of need.[43] Two years later, she continued to blend delicate femininity with bravado. In words destined solely for her nephew's eye, she adopted a tone that Hannah Corbin could have applauded: "every plan will be pursued to cross and vex me, but my resolution is equal to the contest." Those who had "invaded" her "rights" and shown "no delicacy" for her "feelings" would learn to their cost "that a woman is their equal." Yet in a text "which I gave Mr DeSaussure to use in Court," Richardson represented herself quite differently. Here, she endorsed the notion that even the merest whisper of scandal—however unwarranted—stained a lady's honor: "Last, but not least, is my Brothers allusion respecting my marriage. . . . had he considered the business properly, he ought to have know that any circumstance which could bring blushes to a sisters cheek, ought in like manner to affect her Brother —lost must that heart be to manly feeling, who to gain a paltry sum would descend to calumny and subterfuge even with men & strangers, but when used towards a sister who asked only for her rights, and who would have given up half her claim to avoid a lawsuit, I think the conduct disgraceful and beneath the conduct of *Man*." Bold to the point of arrogance in private, Richardson wreathed herself in feminine fragility as she crafted an image for public consumption. This approach served her well. Perhaps she triumphed in court purely because, as she claimed, "it was so plain a case" that the judge "was surprised it could be disputed." Yet it is more than likely that her careful self-fashioning encouraged the judge to decide that equity meant ruling in her favor.[44]

More than thirty years after Martha Richardson won her case, Virginia planter Ruth Hairston became embroiled in a series of claims against her dower and the property she inherited from her father. Like Richardson's dispute, their outcome hinged not only on the actual facts and jurisprudential expertise but also on the ways that family members represented themselves and each other in personal and official papers. The quarrel began with the attempt to settle Robert Hairston's vast estate, which sprawled across Virginia, North Carolina, Mississippi, and Tennessee. Its course depended on lawyers, judges, court hearings, and binding settlements: in other words, on people and places that slaveholding women encountered on the most unequal of terms. Involving three sets of state laws and multiple courts, the matter proved so complex that trained lawyers could not easily unravel it, to say nothing of an old woman whose schooling had ended some fifty years earlier. Yet by carefully cultivating her blood kin and insisting that her in-laws were trying to defraud and defame her, Ruth emerged from the conflict with her property holdings vastly enhanced and her blood kin more committed to her than ever before.[45]

As he lay dying in the spring of 1852, Robert Hairston wrote a brief will in which he revoked all previous testaments, emancipated his only child, a slave girl named Chrillis, and left her his entire estate. This document flouted contemporary standards of both law and propriety in Mississippi, where he wrote it. The Lowndes County probate court quickly invalidated its key provisions—Chrillis's emancipation and her inheritance—because such bequests were strictly illegal. With Chrillis's claim dismissed, Robert's siblings and their children scrambled to establish their own rights to the vast estate. To the various white Hairstons, the critical question was whether Robert's last will was entirely void, or only the specific provisions concerning Chrillis. If the entire will was void, then a previous will would govern the estate. If, however, the last will had nullified all previous wills, then the estate would be divided as if Robert had died intestate. This was a critical question for Robert's blood kin because previous wills gave a few favorite nephews the bulk of the property, leaving the rest of the family with nothing. If, however, Robert died intestate, then his property would be divided equally among his many siblings and their heirs. Under Mississippi law, each sibling had an equal right in the estate, and the children of his deceased siblings would divide their parents' shares equally. Ruth Hairston was not an heir under any of these circumstances, but she had a dog in the fight nonetheless. Her only child was Agnes Wilson, born during her marriage to Peter Wilson. Shortly after Ruth married Robert Hairston, Agnes married Robert's brother Samuel, who was not only her uncle by marriage but also a distant cousin. Robert's original will favored Agnes and Samuel's sons, who were Robert's nephews and Ruth's grandsons. Ruth Hairston, her daughter, and her brother/son-in-law Samuel Hairston all hoped that

Ruth's grandsons would inherit under one of the early wills, but most of Ruth's in-laws hoped the estate would be deemed intestate.[46]

The estate squabble had another element of more immediate import to Ruth Hairston—her dower. None of Robert Hairston's wills had made any provision for Ruth's dower although she was entitled to it under the laws of every state in which Robert owned property (Mississippi, North Carolina, Virginia, and Tennessee). Because her dower right did not depend on what the probate court ruled about Robert's various wills, one of Ruth's grandsons predicted that "there will be no difficulty about your rights as I believe all the family concur in them." Events quickly proved him wrong, however, because it made an enormous difference which state's laws determined her actual dower share. Robert's siblings hoped to limit Ruth's dower by settling the estate in Virginia, where she was entitled to one-third of the estate for her lifetime only. Ruth wanted her dower laid off under Mississippi's more generous provisions: in addition to one-third of the realty for life, that state allotted a childless man's widow one half of the personalty, including slaves, in fee simple.[47] All of Ruth's in-laws except Samuel "most strenuously resisted" this possibility. In one North Carolina hearing, for example, their lawyer "laboured much to maintain that Robert Hairston had died a citizen of Va." At this, however, "the Court laughed" and informed Ruth's lawyer that "we need give us no further trouble on that."[48]

Yet Ruth Hairston's troubles persisted even after the Lowndes County probate court ruled in her favor on the matter of dower. For starters, her in-laws immediately appealed to the Mississippi Court of Errors and Appeals although they eventually agreed to a settlement that preserved most of Ruth's dower rights. Still, they were not ready to accept defeat, and they tried to claim property Ruth had owned before and acquired during her marriage to Robert. The Hairston siblings had clear rights to any personalty Ruth brought to her marriage because that property became Robert's absolutely since it was not protected by a separate estate or similar document. In addition, Ruth's own lawyer feared her in-laws might have far greater rights in Ruth's paternal inheritance than they supposed, and he warned her grandsons to keep quiet so as not to give them "any such idea." But the Hairston in-laws quickly discovered the possibility for themselves and vigorously pursued it in multiple lawsuits in three different states. Because Peter Hairston's will had been poorly worded, there was a chance that any of a number of courts could have decided that, under coverture, the property that Peter had bequeathed to Ruth actually passed into her husband's hands and thus became part of his estate after his death. It took years for a court in North Carolina (where Peter Hairston had lived) to decide that Robert's heirs "get nothing that belongs to the Estate of your father."[49]

The entire process of settling Robert Hairston's estate was deeply troubling and insulting to his widow. Already humiliated by her husband's behavior, she faced further outrages from her in-laws. Yet the surviving family papers suggest that Ruth never responded to her in-laws' actions with the acerbity of a Susannah Wilcox or a Martha Richardson. Instead, she found quieter means to defend her reputation and fortune. Soon after Robert's death, Ruth warned her grandsons that her in-laws (their uncles and cousins) were up to no good. Fearing that her grandsons did not appreciate the threat, she consistently assigned the worst possible interpretation to the other Hairstons' conduct. Her eldest grandson, Peter Wilson Hairston, at first resisted her warnings, urging her to compromise for the sake of "peace and quiet." Over time, however, he realized that Ruth's "views of the whole matter throughout have been correct with regard to the family."[50] Critical in changing Peter Wilson Hairston's mind were the personal hostilities that motivated his uncles and cousins. In January 1853 he decided that the more he knew of his cousin George, "the less I like him." The same month, he learned that his cousin Robert was determined "to keep Uncle Marshall out of the property" simply on account of something, "I know not what," that Marshall had allegedly said about Robert. Still worse in Peter Wilson Hairston's mind were the aspersions cast at Ruth herself. He heard that his uncle Hardin and cousin George "have exerted themselves to keep her out of her dower" in Mississippi and that "Uncle Hardin spoke of her in the matter with great bitterness." To Peter Wilson Hairston, that sort of behavior toward female kin was beyond the pale. As he swore to his brother-in-law back in Virginia, "Had I known this sooner, I never would have gone to his house except when compelled to do so on business."[51]

These scenes deeply wounded Ruth Hairston, but her in-laws' malicious efforts "to disturb & perplex" her had one positive consequence: they encouraged her grandsons to interpret the dispute as something more than a squabble over property. Personal insults and grudges turned the property grab into a question of honor, which in turn made it all but impossible for her grandsons to advocate compromise solely for the sake of "peace and quiet." Ruth's grief at the attacks on her "integrity" thus superceded the younger generation's desire to frame the problem in the less personal terms of legal right and negotiated settlement. At the same time, her woeful demeanor implicitly reminded her grandchildren of their duty to make her feel cared for and protected. Hardin Hairston had, in effect, done her a favor when he smeared her name.[52] Yet Ruth's response to the scandalous situation was not simply to adopt a suffer-in-silence attitude. From the first, she moved adroitly to secure the help she correctly imagined she would need. Mere weeks after she heard of Robert's death, she commissioned Peter Wilson Hairston to secure her legal representation first in Mississippi and later in Virginia and North Carolina. (She needed these agents because at sixty-nine she could not make the trek herself—even her thirty-something grandson found it exhausting—and in any case, no single person could oversee the entire business.) Acting as Ruth's agent, Peter Wilson Hairston negotiated with his uncles and cousins, consulted with Ruth's lawyers in three states, and regularly sent updates back to his grandmother's plantation. To ensure his diligence, Ruth contracted to pay him 5 percent of all the money she received from her husband's estate in Mississippi. Since he also stood to inherit from her once she died, he had a double incentive to act vigorously. In this light, his initial willingness to "sacrifice something" to compromise with his cousins suggests his deep attachment to familial harmony. At the same time, because he believed so strongly in the obligations of kinship, he was all the more shocked by his cousins' and uncles' behavior.[53]

As the Hairston rumpus so richly demonstrates, property both pitted relatives against each other and glued families together. Yet monetary self-interest alone does not explain why slaveholders assisted their widowed kinswomen. Long before the battle over her husband's estate, Ruth Hairston and her descendants had created an interdependent family in which the younger generation learned to interpret their aid to Ruth as a matter of self-interest, obligation, and affection. Before becoming his grandmother's agent, for example, Peter Wilson Hairston helped her manage her plantations. He and his brothers also wrote letters for her and negotiated with her factors and overseers. Ruth's daughter and granddaughters were less involved in planting and business, but they kept in close contact as well, providing family news, housekeeping advice, and emotional support. In times of crisis, the support that widows got—and sometimes did not get—from their relatives owed as much to past practices as to current expectations of proper gender and familial behavior. As long as most slaveholders considered good relations with extended kin a useful resource, a moral obligation, and a reflection on themselves, slaveholding widows stood a very good chance of realizing their claims on familial assistance.[54]

DURING THE United States' first seven decades, southeastern slaveholding widows consistently manipulated familial relationships in order to critique others, demand help, and justify themselves. In this, they were by no means unique. As a class, slaveholders routinely relied on their relatives to help them master their households, their slaves, and their futures. Concealed within this consistency, however, lay important variations and changes in the expression of family. Though late-eighteenth-century widows like Mary Campbell still employed a relatively formal rhetoric of duty, this more patriarchal conception of generational hierarchy was already being challenged by more companionate visions of extended kinship. Thanks in part to this sentimental and voluntaristic rendition of family, antebellum widows were more likely to represent themselves as dependent and distressed ladies than as spirited defenders of their own or their husbands' will. But even for them, womanly dependence usually represented either an unaffordable luxury or a strategy of last resort.[55] While the iconic southern lady of antebellum print culture was profoundly confined, slaveholding women had some choice about which threads in the tapestry of gender to pull. They had particularly wide possibilities as widows because that status made them simultaneously instrumental and reliant. That widows' actions sometimes wore the clothes of feminine dependence should not be surprising, for that part of their gender role bound them tightly indeed. Conduct books and novels urged southern ladies to suffer "meekly" and bear their burdens "with grace, courage, and silence." But widows like Mary Campbell, Lucy Freeman, and Ruth Hairston could not afford to remain mute in their own causes. Instead of cleaving exclusively to the passive and helpless strands of ladyhood, slaveholding widows drew on endurance, resignation, and determined struggle as well, qualities equally a part of their gender role. What historian Bertram Wyatt-Brown calls an "implicit" emphasis on "feminine grit" in southern gender ideology became explicit in this cohort. As they well knew, their culture honored women who confronted "the bitterest blasts of adversity" with "unshrinking firmness." And when adversity struck, slaveholders' habits of familial interdependence provided a key resource, ensuring that this subset of women escaped the one-dimensional fate of the "broken reeds" so common in popular fiction and poetry.[56]

CHAPTER 4

A Very Public Road

Negotiating with slaves and kin constituted the domestic face of slaveholding widows' mastery. Their responsibilities also had a more public face which entailed representing their own and their households' interests in the wider world. This posed some problems for widows because of the solidly masculine character of mastery in the public sphere. In the early nineteenth-century Southeast, exercising the franchise became the quintessential public assertion of mastery, a process which markedly excluded white women. The slave patrol, the militia, the jury, and the duel—other highly visible aspects of mastery—similarly debarred widows. Far more common than duels or elections, however, was a more understated activity in which widows regularly participated: representing the household through commercial exchange. Through commerce, slaveholders found markets for their crops, supplied their dependents with food and clothes, secured essential services, and met their legal obligations. Buying and selling helped individuals meet their responsibilities as slave- and householders, and it could confirm or refute their reputation as individuals competent to act in their own and others' interests. Trade also reinforced both the socioeconomic ties between households and the stratification of white southern society writ large.[1]

The standard narrative of southern women's history suggests that in the early nineteenth century, white women had little firsthand contact with commercial exchange despite their functions as consumers and producers.

As wives, they rarely marketed their own domestic produce, for example, and their husbands or fathers often procured their consumer goods. Even wives with separate estates rarely managed their own property.[2] Reasons for this exclusion can be found not only in coverture but in location. In the Southeast, commercial transactions occurred in factors' offices, courthouses, taverns, banks, and country stores, and none of these places, according to most scholars, were particularly congenial to white women. Neither were the roads and public conveyances that connected them. And yet, despite these handicaps, slaveholding widows marketed crops, bought provisions, and acted a masterly part with people beyond their immediate households.[3]

The patterns of slaveholders' commerce explain how widows could participate and what their involvement meant for their blend of ladyhood and mastery. Like their male peers, slaveholding widows did much of their business by letter, through agents, or at home. These practices spared widows from leaving their homes, but they also made the home less a private sphere than a commercial venue. In addition, slaveholding widows ventured beyond their enclosures, further weakening the rhetorical association of women with domestic confinement. Within this basic similarity among widows' commercial activities, however, lay an essential difference—their transactions also reflected and reinforced individual widows' unequal access to money, property, and influence.

SLAVEHOLDING WOMEN relied on the market throughout widowhood because their households were rarely self-sufficient even in simple foodstuffs such as corn and bacon. Widows also purchased a wide range of goods they could not produce domestically, such as thread, pins, molasses, bagging, and rope. Thanks to their limited rights in their husbands' property, many even had to buy beds, cookware, and other basic furnishings. For all these reasons, widowhood quickly ushered slaveholding women into the world of commerce and ensured that they remained regular participants.

From the beginning of widowhood, slaveholding women participated in exchange as both consumers and producers. Death itself determined many of widows' first transactions, such as paying for their husbands' funerals and coffins.[4] Also quick to appear in widows' accounts were the black fabric and accessories that indicated bereavement. Lucy Burwell bought black bonnets for herself and her daughters shortly after her husband died. Thirty years later, Ruth Hairston ordered an entire wardrobe of merino, bombazine, thread, ribbon, and dress buttons, all in black.[5] She might not have mourned Robert very deeply, but she dressed the part. Agricultural production brought many widows into the marketplace equally quickly. Six weeks after her husband's death, Mary Steele began making inquiries about cotton prices and instructed a Petersburg factor to "look out for a market" for the eighty-four bales of cotton she planned to deliver.[6] At her husband's estate sale in the early 1830s, fellow Rowan County widow Mrs. Click bought hoes, a plow and its gears, axes, a flax hackle, hay, straw, ten bushels of wheat, raw flax, beef, and a shoat, all essential farming supplies. In 1849, North Carolina planter Caroline Foscue spent over four hundred dollars on livestock, tools, and foodstuffs from her husband's estate, and half as much again on furniture and housewares.[7]

Considered as transactions, surprisingly little distinguished luxury and personal consumption from agricultural purchases. The same kind of contracts, bills, and receipts covered all manner of movable goods. (Slaves were an exception, with their own logic and paperwork.)[8] The merchant who supplied Susannah Wilcox with sealskin slippers, cherry wine, and elegant long gloves also sent her nails, iron bars, and rough osnaburg cloth for her slaves. Along with her bonnets, Lucy Burwell received salt, herring, bagging, and rope. Virginia retailer Archibald Vaughan sent Paulina Legrand fine French merino at $2.25 per yard, as well as blistered steel, canvas, and a spade. The Virginia merchants who supplied Ruth Hairston's mourning wardrobe also delivered kegs of blasting powder, rough slave shoes, and whiskey.[9]

Although widows secured a wide range of goods through single retailers, they usually did business with several different merchants or shopkeepers. Planters in particular transacted regularly with a range of men, from merchants located in distant ports to their own neighbors and local artisans. In the spring of 1821, Lucy Burwell bought foodstuffs and metal goods from three different merchants in addition to her Petersburg factor. The following year, she made significant purchases both in Petersburg and at home in Mecklenburg County. A few years later, Annabella Porter of Morgan County, Georgia, had accounts with at least five different retailers, not including her cotton factor. Over a period of ten years, Ruth Hairston did business with three different factors and the Sandy River grist mill. She also ordered a substantial amount of lumber from a nearby sawmill: twelve hundred feet of plank in 1854; door frames, shutters, blinds, flooring, weatherboarding, and shingles in 1857; and staves, fencing, and oak logs in 1859. Doing business with several retailers multiplied widows' appearances on the economic stage in the process. It also increased the number of commercial men who had a stake in widows' financial success.[10]

Further extending their economic reach, slaveholding widows did business on a smaller scale with many of their neighbors. Some householders hired local weavers to supplement the cloth they bought from northern mills or wove at home. In 1840, for example, Natalie Sumter commissioned Mrs. Eveleigh to sew shirts and weave hundreds of yards of cloth.[11] If they lacked slave artisans, widows also contracted with skilled white men to sharpen blades, replace saw teeth, and mend cotton gins and presses. In 1795, North Carolinian Elizabeth Steele paid blacksmith Absalom Taylor for mending traces, sharpening various tools, shoeing horses, and "hooping a churn." Thirty years later in Georgia, Annabella Porter commissioned one man to repair her carding machine and another to craft a spindle, harrow teeth, and a gun lock. As her husband's executor, Porter paid debts to some thirty people in 1825 and nineteen people in 1826. Many of these creditors were relatives by marriage, but the majority were white men unrelated to Annabella but with an interest in her actions, thanks to their past economic relationships with her husband.[12]

Viewed in their entirety, widows' individual transactions added up to a steady flow of goods, services, and money. Natalie Sumter's thirteen-month diary provides an especially vivid record of one woman's extensive local economic connections, mentioning dozens of exchanges and nearly one hundred individuals with whom she transacted. Other sources suggest the intensive nature of widows' economic relationships. Over the course of twenty years, Ruth Hairston received at least a hundred letters from her factors. Virginia retailer Archibald Vaughan's accounts similarly indicate Paulina Legrand's frequent entries into the marketplace. In 1835 alone, Vaughan noted purchases against Legrand's account on seventy-nine different days, or an average of once every five days.[13] This degree of commercial interaction was admittedly typical only of planters. With their substantial plantations and many slaves, women like Legrand, Sumter, and Hairston engaged in more regular and more substantial commercial transactions than did either yeoman farm widows or self-supporting townswomen.[14]

WHATEVER THE SCOPE of their business, slaveholding widows employed similar means to conduct their exchanges. These patterns were, in fact, as potent an indicator of their masterful responsibilities as what they bought and sold. Whenever possible, they did business with people they knew personally, and they relied heavily on letters and agents. Transacting with kin kept money in the family, one likely reason why Annabella Porter did business with Henry Cook, Mary Ann Hendrick with A. G. Boyd, and Lucy Burwell with Alexander Boyd, all related by marriage.[15] Doing business with connections also helped ease widows into the world of commerce. When Mary Steele had to size up the cotton market in the fall of 1815, she automatically turned to an old family friend and to her husband's factors with whom he had a long-standing business relationship. Writing to Walker and Atkinson, a Petersburg firm, she asked them to "continue as accommodating in transacting the business as you have always been."[16] If John Steele had died in debt to his factors, then Mary likely had little choice about selling her cotton to them, but even so, working with men who had known her wealthy and politically prominent husband did her no harm. Relying on their husbands' associates served the interests of ladyhood by reducing widows' interactions with strangers, especially strange men. The common practice of transacting by letter and by proxy, meanwhile, enabled slaveholding widows to meet their commercial obligations without leaving their households. This pattern simultaneously permitted them to keep an eye on their slaves and other dependents, one reason that slaveholding men also relied heavily on letters and proxies. Yet widows' mediated transactions meant something different for women than for men: they served the demands of ladyhood as well as mastery, helping to reconcile two seemingly contradictory paradigms.

The rural Southeast's dispersed settlements made commercial letters and proxies indispensable for any household doing business above the level of bare subsistence.[17] Business by letter and proxy characterized the trade in staple crops destined for distant markets in the North, Europe, and the Caribbean. Merchants who dealt in cotton, tobacco, rice, or wheat congregated in towns and cities along the region's coasts, waterways, and railroads. In contrast, farmers and planters sprawled out in the hinterlands, separated by miles of fields, woods, and swamps from each other and from the men who would buy their crops. More than two hundred miles separated Rowan County's Mary Steele from her Petersburg factors, and another hundred miles lay between her and her connections in Fayetteville. When she wanted to inform Walker and Atkinson of her husband's death and consult with a family friend about cotton prices, she did not trek those long distances. Instead, she wrote letters. From Hugh Campbell, she learned current prices in Fayetteville, Wilmington, and New York, information that he likely gathered from other correspondents and newspapers. Armed with his advice, she wrote to Walker and Atkinson, authorizing them to sell the cotton "on a short credit" if that garnered a better price.[18]

Like letters, agents allowed widows to do business without leaving their own homes. When Eliza Flinn sold a plantation in 1837, she stayed at home while her son Berkeley brought the bond and mortgage to the buyer to sign and then delivered the papers to his sister for safekeeping. On other occasions, Eliza directed Berkeley to collect her dividends from her shares in the Bank of the United States and bring them to his sister. Thomas Smith similarly served as his mother's agent in Gloucester County, Virginia, traversing the neighborhood to pay her creditors and bring her their receipts. In central Georgia, William Porter provided the same services to his sister-in-law, Annabella Porter. Transferring money from hand to hand was a family affair for Catherine Lewis as well. When one of her brothers-in-law decided to give her fifty dollars "to fit out" her daughter for school, he "handed" the money to William Battle, Catherine's brother, to send to her. William in turn enclosed a check to Catherine in a letter to his wife, instructing her to have it "safely delivered to her." If Catherine could not use the check, he promised to "send her the money itself next week," entrusting its safe carriage to his brother-in-law, Samuel Phillips.[19]

Agents provided far more than safe conduits for goods, money, and letters, however; they also conducted negotiations and made purchases in widows' names. In 1801, Colonel Varick obtained several barrels of apples for Martha Washington, both selecting and paying for them. In 1811, Mary Archer had her brother James Powell Cocke buy cloth, spades, and salt when he visited Richmond. Also in Richmond, William H. Cabell performed a series of commissions for his cousin Paulina Legrand, buying lamps, ordering a table, and hiring an upholsterer.[20] Factors were particularly useful in this regard because of their urban locations. They could easily make purchases in planters' names from the retailers who likewise clustered in towns and cities. Their control over planters' funds also enabled them to settle debts. Before the Revolution, Martha Custis sent extensive lists of items to London for her factors to obtain, while Hannah Corbin's factors paid out money to her London creditors. Eighty years later and much closer to home, Ingraham and Webb, a South Carolina concern, settled Marion Deveaux's debts with local retailers.[21] Most agents who were not factors had comparatively informal authorizations to act for their principals. A widow might mention in a personal letter, for example, that she needed a paper of pins or a gallon of molasses. At times, however, agents needed more definitive imprimaturs. Mary Steele gave her half-brother, Robert Cochran, a general power of attorney so he could collect "'Dividends & Moneys'" from her bank shares. Decades later, Ruth Hairston gave her eldest grandson one power to collect from her debtors and another to "ask, demand, sue for[,] recover and receive for me, my interest in the Estate of Robert Hairston." In 1853, she made an additional contract with John M. Withers in which he agreed to supervise her affairs in Mississippi and forward monthly accounts to her. In this case, the ill feeling surrounding her husband's estate and the sizable sums involved made explicit legal arrangements highly desirable for Hairston and her agents.[22]

Through writing letters and acting as proxies, slaveholding men spared widows the necessity of leaving their homes to conduct business. At the extreme, they did the thinking as well as the acting, instructing widows what to do and how to do it. While this pattern suggests that the Southeast perhaps contained a private realm for white women and a public one for men, other trends point in quite a different direction. Slaveholding widows did rely heavily on agents, but some of their agents were women, and sometimes widows acted as agents for men. In the 1790s, Penelope Dawson asked her cousin Helen Iredell to research and acquire a range of goods, from shawls and carpeting to "good black mode for a bonnet." Two decades later, Susan Hubard looked to her sister-in-law in Richmond to buy a bombazine dress "of the first quality" for her "dress Mourning." While William Cabell arranged to ship window glass and putty to Paulina Legrand, his wife commissioned a dress. Around the same time, Polly Townes and Jane Cocke traded information about local prices, grousing that goods and money alike were "almost as scarce as Hens teeth."[23] Slaveholding women prided themselves on their ability to determine both the quality of cloth and similar goods and the fairness of the price. By the antebellum decades, female customers had become so important that dry goods retailers increasingly considered the ladies in crafting their image. By the 1830s in Virginia and by the 1850s in the rest of the South, merchants were adopting letterhead stationery for their correspondence. The more elaborate examples included drawings of shopfronts with well-dressed women promenading alongside. Such images implied that merchants desired female consumers, that women did their own shopping, and that women would now find retail stores comfortable and pleasant. These images reflected real practices, not mere advertising; antebellum shopkeepers actively sought to bring female consumers into their stores, and slaveholding women and girls made shopping into a form of entertainment.[24]

Alongside distinctively feminine consumer experiences, women continued to participate in legal, land, and agricultural transactions. In 1777, Walter Lindsay of Rowan County, North Carolina, designated Elizabeth Steele as "my true and Lawfull Attorney . . . to sell or otherwise dispose of" his Black Creek plantation and "execute" any necessary legal agreements. Forty years later, Elizabeth's daughter-in-law Mary Steele gave her own daughter Margaret a power of attorney to collect bank dividends. (Mary turned to Robert Cochran after Margaret married.) Sometime after 1827, Philadelphia's Zaccheus Collins "Authorized and empowered" his widowed sister Elizabeth Lee to buy a lot in Washington, D.C., for him and "to contract for the erection of a dwelling house thereon."[25] In the 1840s, Martha Jackson interceded for a nephew with the trustees of a familial estate.[26] Acting as agents for men and women, in agricultural and legal as well as millinery matters, slaveholding widows virtually collapsed any distinctions between male and female spheres of knowledge and activity.

IN THE EARLY nineteenth century, American writers regularly envisioned the home as a sacred domestic space. Set apart from the "dissipation" and "manifold temptations" of the rough-and-tumble world, the home was supposedly woman's special sphere of influence. Like other middle-class and elite people of their era, slaveholders consumed these ideas and reproduced them in their own writings.[27] Yet their use of proxies and letters to do business within their own homes complicated their allegiance to domestic privacy. Other aspects of widows' commercial transactions further challenged the illusion. While widows often bought and sold indirectly, they also did business face-to-face within their own homes. Estate settlement attracted a variety of outsiders and had the potential to turn the household into a public spectacle. Less theatrical but more common were the many occasions when people visited widows at home to make a purchase or settle a debt, instead of dispatching an agent or letter.[28]

The barriers between slaveholders' households and the wider world were rarely more frail than in the immediate aftermath of a householder's death. The process of settling an estate almost inevitably turned family affairs into matters of public record, and estate sales offered up the household and its contents for public consumption. When an estate went to probate, a local court appointed a trio of commissioners to inventory and value every article of property. Court-appointed commissioners also laid out the widow's portion of her husband's estate, including provisions for the first year. After probate, the executor or administrator had to apply for permission to sell any portion of an estate. Once the appropriate court authorized the sale, he or she then had to notify the public by publishing an announcement in a newspaper or posting one on the door of the county court house and several other public locations.[29] Estate sale records typically provide little information about the social dynamics at play, but a fictional account in George Tucker's *Valley of the Shenandoah* illustrates how estate sales corroded the patina of domesticity. In the novel, Colonel Grayson's reputation and the size of his estate attract much of the neighborhood to the sale. Some come in search of bargains, and a subset sees the event as a spectator sport. Most are men, but "among the company, were a few females." Before the sale, Mrs. Grayson sends her unmarried daughter away to spare her the sight of strangers tramping through the house and fingering its contents. She herself, however, is present at the sale. She participates indirectly when her agent Mr. Trueheart bids on various articles of "household furniture" on her behalf. (Most of her neighbors refuse to bid against him out of "respect" for her.) She is also more directly involved—as each item is sold, the buyer goes to her to formalize the transaction. Throughout the sale, she sits "quietly signing receipts, or receiving bonds."[30] Not every widow played such a public role in her husband's estate sale, but the proceedings almost invariably opened up the household to a wide range of people and transactions, nor did the end of the sale mark a widow's seclusion.

After the estate sale, a widow who acted as executor or administrator had further obligations. The law demanded that the estate's representative return an account of the sale to the court and swear to its accuracy, usually in person. Local courts also expected sworn annual accounts of disbursements and collections for as long as the estate remained unsettled, again usually in person. In fact, the law's demand for accountability and transparency trumped any contrary wishes of both the dead and the living. Two generations of Crenshaw men and women in Hanover County, Virginia, for example, stipulated in their wills that no inventory or appraisal be made of their estates. But as another Virginian observed in a similar case, "The will abjures but the law requires a just inventory & appraisal."[31] Survivors also lamented having their "private affairs" made public through legal administration. After Martha Smith's death, her son Thomas longed for a private division of his mother's and father's estates: "I cannot reconcile it to myself to have exposed to sale those articles of furniture &c which has cost our Parents so much time & labour to collect together." Similarly, in 1858, one C. A. Brown hoped that her mother's estate could be divided "in a pleasant manner," to avoid having "to resort to the courthouse and . . . make all our family affairs public."[32]

While slaveholders sometimes complained that estate settlement involved "useless and unnecessary exposure," they readily accepted outsiders in their homes on business on other occasions. In part because writing letters and sending agents enabled slaveholders to remain at home, others who had business with them often sought them there. In 1797, a Mr. Lumpkin arranged to call on Susannah Wilcox to collect a judgment against her. On another occasion, a merchant apologized to Wilcox for not coming in person to collect a debt. In 1810, Wilcox invited lawyer Archibald Austin to visit her plantation so they could discuss her suit against her son-in-law then pending in chancery court. Other houses witnessed similar traffic. James Bullock sent an agent to Wilcox's daughter Susan Hubard to collect a debt, and Richard Theweate planned to come to buy a horse. Martha Turberville requested Joseph Jones Monroe (brother of the future President) to come to Peckatone "to advise me," and in 1806, one James Dishman "waited on Mrs. Marshall" to inquire about the possibility of buying some of her dead husband's land. In one week in September 1840, Natalie Sumter's house witnessed a range of transactions: two of Natalie's sons came to discuss estate finances, Dr. Anderson treated her sick slaves, and Parson Graham and Mr. McDonald negotiated real estate transactions.[33] Who stayed at home and who ventured out depended on personal circumstances and the nature of the transaction. The preceding examples all involve men calling on women, but gender was often not the deciding factor. Health and age also played a role. In January 1823, George H. Wethers suggested to Mary Steele that they meet at her son-in-law's house to conclude their business "as I cant venter far from hom this cole weather." People who lived in towns sometimes took advantage of their town's gravitational pull on rural residents. When Joseph Hampton of Salisbury, North Carolina, hoped to hire a slave from Mary Steele, he presumed she would come to him; if she called "when you come to town again," he would offer her "a fair price." As a general rule, however, buyers called on sellers, and creditors on debtors. When Dolly Burge needed to settle up with one Mr. Graves, for instance, neither her gender nor the miserable March rains kept her ensconced at home. She made the trek to his house, did her business, and came home the next day.[34]

Notwithstanding the evidence that slaveholding widows transacted much like men and used their homes for commerce, slaveholders continued to pledge their allegiance to a special domestic sphere for women. Virginia Cary is a case in point. Her *Letters on Female Character* insisted that when a woman "undertakes masculine duties, she resigns her own appropriate sphere, . . . bursts the bonds imposed on her by divine authority, and thereby forfeits divine protection." Yet this widow could not practice what she preached. Cary earned her living as a writer, an unusual career for a woman, and one which put her squarely in the public eye. Other widows made themselves visible beyond their own homes as they tried to drum up pupils, boarders, or customers. Those who ran farms and plantations had a different but no less real visibility. Farming and planting widows found it congenial to do business quietly at home, but they did not strain a point to remain within their households. Instead, like their male peers, they left their enclosures to fulfill their myriad commercial responsibilities.[35]

ENGAGING IN commerce through letters, proxies, and housecalls was a fairly simply matter for literate slaveholding widows with some money. Leaving their home was practically and ideologically more complicated, especially when they ventured further than their closest neighbors. The Southeast's long settlement and dense social networks had neither eliminated significant distances between rural households nor guaranteed an adequate infrastructure. Plantation agriculture placed a premium on moving crops from plantations to ports, so southern transportation networks often served producers better than passengers. Travelers in the South regularly complained of expense, discomfort, and danger. Ann Swann's family confronted a range of travel-related hazards in 1855; one son took a bad fall from a horse, another nearly died at sea, she narrowly escaped injury during a trip to visit family in Jackson, Mississippi. On her way home, a steamboat on the Mississippi River burned up and a tunnel near the Cumberland Gap collapsed shortly after her train passed through.[36] Exploding steam-engines and similar catastrophes were far from the only dangers threatening female travelers. As Patricia Cline Cohen has observed in studying northern travel, women faced greater moral and physical risks on public conveyances than men did.[37] White women's vulnerability beyond their own homes formed a persistent subtheme in southern literature, suggesting that as soon as women left their homes, they faced danger from nearly every masculine quarter: gentlemen, poor whites, and slaves.[38]

Virginia Cary, portrait by Charles Crowell Ingram. A cap like Cary's signified that a woman was or had been married, while her dark clothes suggest a widow's mourning dress. (Virginia Historical Society, Richmond)

Certain women were indeed vulnerable, namely enslaved and poor white women, but prosperous slaveholding widows traveled with comparative impunity, with or without chaperones.[39]

When slaveholding women left their homes, they usually remained within their own neighborhoods. They dropped in on neighbors, attended church, and perhaps went to town. Widowhood created new occasions and new destinations for slaveholding women's excursions. During her first widowhood, schoolteacher Dolly Lewis "went down town" and "called at most of the stores," but without either a household to manage or an estate to settle, she needed to do little more. As planter Dolly Burge, however, she "went to town" to pay her taxes, to buy "meat & groceries," to attend a session of the court, and to consult with a judge. Until her final illness, Natalie Sumter left her house regularly. Her most common destinations were her church and her friends' houses, but she also went to the post office and to Statesburg "to swear to my accts." In a typical week, she toured her fields, went to church, took her grandchildren to school, visited her daughter Brasilia, and went to Mr. Hood's for cloth.[40]

Such episodic, casual errands helped knit communities together. They inscribed circles of some five, ten, or even twenty miles in diameter, loosely defined areas in which an individual knew many of the inhabitants and the social relations that connected them.[41] Slaveholding widows could not always remain within this familiar territory, however. Legal proceedings could demand their presence in a distant location. In the 1810s, Martha Richardson's lawsuit with her brother required her to attend a court hearing in Charleston. Some forty years later, Gabriella Butler made the reverse trip after receiving word "that her presence at Savannah . . . is indispensable, in connection with the business of the Butler Estate." Shortly before the Civil War, South Carolina planter Louisa McCord traveled from her plantation to Charleston to be deposed before the Equity Court of Appeals. Financial needs such as securing bank loans also required travel. Natalie Sumter traveled twenty-five and one hundred miles, respectively, to visit banks in Camden and Charleston. Absentee planters also moved with some frequency. In 1840, Martha Jackson calculated that she would make "a yearly visit" to the family plantation in central Alabama where she would stay for a month or more. Eliza Flinn and her daughter Eliza Wilkins moved between plantation and town residence in accordance with the seasons. A combination of personal and financial concerns took Dolly Burge from her plantation east of Atlanta to Macon in 1859; her stepdaughter Lou was a student at Macon Female College, and Dolly herself had bills to pay.[42]

Even on these longer trips, slaveholding widows traveled unmolested and often unchaperoned. Martha Jackson hoped her son would be able to accompany her on the trek from Athens, Georgia, to Alabama, but she "would even undertake the journey without him." Dolly Burge made at least one of her trips to Macon primarily alone. On this occasion, she set out by carriage with a married couple from her church to meet the train at Social Circle. From there, she took the Georgia Railroad to Atlanta, some forty-five miles west, and then boarded the train bound for Macon, eighty-five miles to the southeast. On her return, she left Macon at midnight, when the streets and the train depot were both "very lonely." A friend put her on the train and "introduced the conductor to me." (Her phrasing was exact: men were introduced to ladies, not the other way around, and to be strictly correct, one first had to ask the lady's permission.)[43] Once safely on the cars, Burge found "a few gentlemen all sleeping," but "not a single lady aboard." Arriving safely in Atlanta the next morning, she had time for breakfast and some shopping before boarding her next train. Two and a half hours later she reached Social Circle where she found her sister-in-law and daughter waiting to take her the rest of the way home in the carriage. The strictly proper Louisa McCord would have had no quarrel with Dolly Burge's movements. She vouched for the safety of southern train travel—and the politeness of southern conductors—in a letter to a northern kinswoman, writing, "The conductors on our road are the civillest people in the world, and we know them almost all personally." Mary Dulles needed simply to get "Mr. Holmes or any other gentleman accompanying you to introduce you to the conductor of the Columbia train at the Charleston depot." McCord was far less impressed with northern trains, whose passengers she found markedly less "civil" than her fellow southerners.[44]

Dolly Burge's and Louisa McCord's experiences with train travel had everything to do with their generation and location. Trains came slowly if at all to most parts of the Old South. Equally critical was their own obvious standing as ladies. McCord believed her name was enough to guarantee Mary Dulles a comfortable trip. Tell them "who you are, and to whom you are coming," McCord wrote. "I will answer for your being well taken care of."[45] Even when they were not known by name, planter widows had visible advantages as they traveled. For starters, they enjoyed more comfort and safety than the average female traveler. The risks of travel declined significantly for those who brought servants or slaves, used first-class public conveyances, and stayed in the better hotels. A widow in those circumstances might be in public and unchaperoned, but others could tell she possessed money and likely had influential connections as well. Riding in a private carriage—like the one Dolly Burge rode to Social Circle —was a similar mark of distinction. Compared to the utilitarian farm wagon, even the plainest carriage was a readily legible sign of wealth. Mary Campbell traveled in style in her husband's "coach and six hourses

Dolly Sumner Lunt Burge. Taken shortly after Thomas Burge's death in 1858, this photograph shows Dolly Burge wearing mourning clothes and holding her husband's daguerrotype. Though severe, Dolly's mourning was also richly ornamented and made from elegant fabrics, as befit a planter's widow. (Special Collections and Archives, Robert W. Woodruff Library, Emory University)

with coachman and postillions." Martha Turberville had a coach, chariot, and riding chair at her disposal. Other planter widows spent sizable sums to acquire new carriages. Susan Hubard paid $600 and Mary Steele $700 on theirs, amounts that exceeded a year's wages for most overseers, to say nothing of widowed teachers or boardinghouse keepers.[46]

Dress further distinguished the planter widow from the yeoman or poor widow. Custom prescribed that new widows dress from head to toe in black and that their clothes be made of matte cloth, particularly crepe or bombazine (a mix of silk and wool). Over time, widows could don more lustrous fabrics and lighter colors, but many could not afford to observe these gradations. While humbler widows dyed old dresses black, planters bought new wardrobes in a variety of fabrics, from relatively cheap wool and cotton blends to silk, silk satin, and velvet.[47] Planter widows could afford bonnets and shoes "in the height of the fashion," and they invested in mourning jewelry. A year after John Steele died, Mary Steele commissioned a "most fashionable" mourning ring. Two pairs of bracelets, perhaps for her daughters, were also "to be the newest fashion."[48] In contrast, strapped Catherine Lewis rarely mentioned fashion, except to say that she no longer went out "fashionable visiting in the summer." This choice may have reflected the discomfort of wearing black in the North Carolina heat, but it likely stemmed from a lack either of stylish mourning or of adequate transportation. Widows' clothing thus bespoke far more than their gender and marital status. While mourning was their garments' most obvious message, attire also indicated socioeconomic position. For wealthier widows, dress became less a badge of weakness than a shield.[49]

Slaveholding widows' ability to travel reflected more than the social protections of ladyhood, however; it also stemmed from the demands and prerogatives of mastery. On the one hand, they often left home to fulfill their duties as householders, slaveowners, guardians, and executors. On the other, the freedom to travel reflected mastery. Even the most privileged of wives needed implicit if not express permission to move beyond their own households. To go further than their own feet could carry them, they also needed the means—such as trainfare or a horse and saddle—which they rarely controlled. Masters, by contrast, needed no one's permission and could allocate their resources as they chose.[50]

ALL SLAVEHOLDING widows engaged in commerce at some point and in similar ways, but they did so on far from equal terms. They could do business by letter, for example, only if they could pay the postage or find private carriers, and, of course, write. Thanks to overall improvements in women's education, white southern women born after 1800 were more likely than their foremothers to read and write well enough to keep accounts and transact business by letter. Yet literacy remained a badge of class: only quite well-off families bothered to educate their daughters beyond a minimal standard, such that differences in spelling, handwriting, style, and even content continued to distinguish the compositions of the humble from those of the grand. The scope of widows' business also reflected their position. The Paulina Legrands and Natalie Sumters operated on a much larger scale, fiscally, socially, and geographically, than the Catherine Lewises and Lucy Freemans. The great planters brought thousands of dollars' worth of staple crops to their factors, who in return steadily carried out a wide range of commissions. Catherine Lewis fretted about spending "three cents" for postage.[51]

By the same token, whether a widow had commercially useful networks of kin and friends depended in large part on wealth and the closely related factor of geographic persistence. As Charles Bolton has argued, in long-settled antebellum eastern communities, the poorer sort increasingly found landownership or even leaseholds out of their reach and were forced to move, often repeatedly.[52] Geographically persistent planter widows, by contrast, had influence well beyond their own families. In 1810, Susannah Wilcox tapped her connections to protect her interests in a lawsuit in another county. At the time, her suit "vs John C. Pike now depending in the Superior Court of P George's County" had been delayed, because Pike had told the court that a material witness, "Mr Joseph Cabell Sen of Buckm. County," was sick: "his Health is so impaired & in so low a state, as to render it out of his power to attend in person as a Witness." Suspicious by nature, and perhaps with cause, Wilcox did not take Pike's word for it. Instead, she contacted friends who lived near Joseph Cabell. Briefly relating the relevant facts, she asked them to determine whether Cabell was indeed in poor health. In reply, Edward and Samuel Jones informed her that the supposed invalid "rode about to transact his business as other men."[53] Between the Revolution and the Civil War, having connections to tap as agents, sources of information, and advisers remained a distinct asset, and one that tended to track the distribution of wealth.

Changes in the pattern of southern economic life in the early nineteenth century only somewhat mitigated the lack of wealthy and influential connections. Over time, southerners came to rely more on formal written instruments rather than informal arrangements for their transactions. In the Northeast, the trend toward formal written instruments—associated with the spread of capitalist modes of production and exchange—tended to make personal acquaintance less important in commerce, and it facilitated business over longer distances.[54] In the South, slaveholders themselves generally continued to keep spotty financial records, but retailers began providing more regular and legible accounts, sometimes using printed stationary, lined paper, fine-pointed pens, and a "clerical" hand. Arguably more important to financial transparency was the proliferation of printed forms. Some transactions had involved blank forms even before the Revolution. In 1778, for example, the Entry Officer for land claims in Rowan County used a printed form to instruct the county surveyor to lay off one hundred acres for Elizabeth Steele.[55] Printed forms became significantly more common after the Revolution, expanding beyond public business to private exchange. In 1813, for example, James Powell Cocke bound himself to pay $63 to his sister-in-law Martha Cocke using a printed form. While slaveholders continued to write out many agreements by hand, using a form had the distinct advantage of standardizing transactions. Since forms used legally acceptable language, they reduced the risk that slaveholders untrained in the law would find themselves bound to something they had not intended simply because of a misused phrase.[56] The impersonality of the printed form did not, however, make contracting parties equal, any more than the legal theory of freedom of contract neutralized inequalities of wealth and power between landlords and tenants, or employers and employees.

The growth of banking, meanwhile, increasingly enabled wealthy slaveholders to pay their bills by check. Savvy widows used these new financial instruments as readily as traditional promissory notes. In 1816 and 1817, Mary Steele wrote dozens of checks to satisfy her husband's creditors; her husband's years as an agent for the Bank of Cape Fear assuredly explain her comfort with this device. A few years later, Martha Richardson and Sarah Screven drew on the Bank of the United States and the Georgia state bank as a secure means to send funds to kin traveling in the North. By the 1840s, the wealthier slaveholders throughout the Southeast routinely used both checks and notes to pay each other and their commercial creditors. Using banks in this way was largely a prerogative of the wealthy and the well connected because many banks were semiprivate institutions that catered to particular cliques or factions of planters.[57] Relatedly, the proliferation of commercial print increased the quality and range of information available to literate people who chose to avail themselves of it. Access to print culture was only somewhat more democratic than banking. For the most part, only the more prosperous households subscribed to newspapers specializing in agricultural and commercial concerns and received "prices current" bulletins that enabled them to track distant markets.[58] These new sources typically complemented rather than replaced more personal channels of information and influence. On the eve of the Civil War, for example, Peter S. Bacot could admonish his factors that they were "not *quite up* with Charleston prices" on the basis of information learned from his daughter and fellow planter Ada Bacot. Then as now, access to multiple streams of information had advantages, and that access usually followed wealth and connections.[59]

SCHOLARS WHO DRAW sharp lines between slaveholding women's and men's roles in the nineteenth-century Southeast have some excellent reasons for doing so, yet the two groups found fundamentally similar means of fulfilling the commercial aspects of household mastery and estate management. Widows and men both did business by letter, by proxy, within their households, and beyond them. They transacted with a similar range of people: fellow slaveholders, artisans, postmasters, shopkeepers, and factors. Slaveholding men indubitably had more frequent contact with formal commerce than most women, but widows steadily acted as consumers and producers, creditors and debtors. The extent and nature of their commercial activities owed much to widows' legal status, but they owed at least as much to the southern household, whose multiple functions of production, reproduction, and consumption confounded the ideological separation between the private home and the public world beyond. And yet, similar modes of commerce had different implications for women and men. Doing business at home benefited any slaveholder, and those without a spouse or overseer to share in surveillance had particular cause to remain at home. But for widows, staying within their households also created an appearance of domestic seclusion that their travel did not entirely eliminate and that matched the prescriptions for respectable women, especially those in mourning. In this case, adopting their male peers' practices probably made slaveholding widows look more womanly, not less.

In ideological terms, southern ladyhood and mastery were essentially antithetical. In daily life, they enjoyed a more complex relationship: sometimes contradictory, sometimes supportive. The tension is evident in the differences among slaveholding widows. Both Paulina Legrand and Catherine Lewis managed households, raised children, supervised slaves, and handled money. Their shared reliance on agents, letters, and connections to do so did not, however, make them equally ladies or equally masters. The circulation of goods and services in and out of their households not only reinforced existing networks of kinship, friendship, and credit, but also tended to augment the differences between Legrand's connections and Lewis's. Relatedly, the commodities these widows bought did not disappear into a private realm but became signs of their wealth and aspirations, visible to anyone who saw them either at home or abroad. The roles they filled in their transactions—agent and principal, debtor and creditor, employer and employee—also bespoke their social and economic position. White southerners may not have been able to tell at a glance whether an individual belonged to the "best sort" of "gentry," as some claimed, but the differences between the lady planter and the farmer, teacher, or boardinghouse keeper were generally obvious. Equally important, many wealthy white southerners believed they were and should be unmistakable.[60]

The general contention that wealth conferred privilege upon women as well as men in the Old South—and that planter women could be snobs—is nothing new, but the specific implications of female privilege require further explanation. Slaveholding widows' involvement in the world beyond their households extended their claim to mastery and merged masculine and feminine "spheres." It also created a special challenge to the increasingly democratic culture of white masculinity. The convention of woman's vulnerability and subordination served both the patriarchal premises of white men's mastery and its democratic promise. Despite vast differences in wealth, rich and poor white men were supposedly equal in their superiority to and power over wives, children, and slaves. But legally independent widows who acted like masters and demanded to be treated like ladies confounded this quasi-egalitarian masculinity. Scholars of class in the Old South have long used the visual cues of dress and the economic relationships of credit, employment, and patronage in their arguments for the region's essential democracy, planter hegemony, or latent class strife. Adding the variable of widowhood to this debate is the work of the next chapter.

CHAPTER 5

The Leading Men and Women

laveholding widows' involvement in the southern public
sphere extended well beyond
commerce to include formal and informal politics. While the wives of politicians lost their primary link to the world of government, parties, and elections, they and other widows continued to take an interest in political
events and partisan affairs. In part, this was self-interested: widows used
political connections for their own benefit. But widows also promoted their
sons' political careers and their dead husbands' partisan causes.[1] These
political activities typically involved cultivating ties to people widows considered their social and economic peers, in relationships that implicitly set
them apart from less privileged whites. When widows relied on their connections to secure patronage for their sons, for example, they reinforced
antidemocratic tendencies in southern politics. That implication became
explicit in the ways widowhood transformed slaveholding women's relationship to informal politics.

As householders, slaveholding widows became involved in the defense
of mastery, a constant undercurrent to both sociable and political relationships in the Southeast. Defending mastery often implied patriarchal domination of women and white unanimity against threats to or from slaves,
but it also involved competition among whites. All masters had to protect
their households from outside interference, such as theft and trespass. They
also had to insist on being treated as equals by other masters because the
lack of this endorsement jeopardized both individual self-respect and au-

thority over dependents. Accordingly, any man who fancied himself a master struggled to make a subordinate position, such as being a richer man's overseer, tenant, or client, compatible with mastery. In this context, differences in wealth and connections had a real impact on any individual's ability to sustain the appearance of mastery. While a yeoman farmer's claim to mastery never evaporated in the presence of a planter's riches and connections, planters had more ways to convince or compel others to honor their mastery. This had important implications for slaveholding widows; while mastery's patriarchal basis created an obvious challenge for them, its roots in property rights created an opportunity for those widows in southern society's upper stratum. Stephanie McCurry suggests that planters' wives had to "grin and bear" the social consequence that male planters bestowed on socially inferior but enfranchised white men. Planter widows had other choices. They asserted rights and obligations not usually associated with their sex, including that of protecting the household against outsiders. In the process, their vaunted hauteur leaped the boundary of sex to impinge directly on white men's claims to be masters. What's more, the region's economic and political evolution in the antebellum decades tended to bolster planter widows' position, a pattern that bespoke the enormous political power of the slaveholding regime, but simultaneously boded ill for the years of war on the horizon.[2]

IN RECENT YEARS, the study of early American politics has increasingly reflected the influence of gender and women's history, although not in ways that would obviously include slaveholding widows. On the one hand, much of the research has focused on the intersection between sociability and politics in the nation's capital towns and cities. Living in a town or city significantly increased widows' chances of observing mass partisan gatherings, even when they were not eager partisans. In 1817, Martha Richardson had little interest in attending festivities celebrating James Monroe's inauguration, "as I am no party woman," but she was well aware of the plans; "A dinner for the Men a Concert in the evening for the Ladies—no doubt all will be very brilliant or endeavor to be so."[3] Living in Richmond gave Caroline Marx the opportunity to attend Virginia's Constitutional Convention in 1829, while her friend Eliza Ruffin, who lived in rural Hanover County, could only read about it in letters and newspapers.[4] In August 1843, Savannah's Louisa Alexander could hardly help but notice the activities of the local Whigs who "meet every evening" in the nearby "Lysium

Hall." "Such yelling and screaming you never heard," Alexander grumped. Even more disruptive were the parties' nightly marches through the city "with fife and drum and a half dozen lanterns as big as a barrel." Tired of the regular brawling that erupted between Whigs and Democrats, "which ends in demolishing each others lanterns," Alexander longed for the election to be over, when "we would be quiet enough in town." Notwithstanding her disapproval, Alexander was an acute observer. She noted that the Whigs raised a "large liberty pole" and "three flags flying in fine stile." She also knew that a neighbor, Mr. Holt, was "on their ticket for City Counsel."[5] Disapproval clearly did not mean inattention for these urban women. Yet while urban widows had the advantage of location, rural widows also had political opportunities, in part because in rural areas, political activities served multiple functions. Since rallies, political barbecues, and elections themselves assembled much of the community, widows sometimes treated them as opportunities to do business. In 1817, for example, Elizabeth Oldham promised to repay Peter Hairston for some wheat and corn at the upcoming Henry County election.[6] Politics also afforded social opportunities. In 1844, Serena Lea thought her husband's trip to the Whig Convention in Montgomery, Alabama, would allow her to visit her sister. Four years later, Ruth Hairston anticipated a visit from a cousin who planned to pass through her neighborhood en route to the Whig convention in Philadelphia.[7] Location did not, in short, prevent the rural widows with whom this book is most concerned from observing and even participating in political activities.

The second theme in studies of women and party politics in this period —their entrée through husbands in particular—equally cannot be taken as a categorical barrier to widows' participation. On the surface, women's involvement in politics through husbands' careers and in sociable settings such as dinner parties and salons would seem to pose an obvious barrier to widows' participation—their husbands were dead, and mourning and managing left little time or, perhaps, inclination for socializing.[8] Yet the widows of political men did not automatically vanish into obscurity when the first clods of earth hit their husbands' coffins. Nor were husbands women's only means (or reason) for following elections and tapping patronage networks. Instead, formal politics implicated slaveholding widows both through their dead politician-husbands and living, politically active kinsmen.

Condolence letters provide one means of tracking whether and how the wider world took note of politicians' widows. Not surprisingly, the more distinguished the dead man, the more prominent those who wrote to condole with his widow. Presidential widows Martha Washington and Dolley Madison are the most extreme cases in point. After George Washington died in December 1799, Martha's condolence letters were a who's who of early American politics: she received letters from John and Abigail Adams, Alexander Hamilton, Jonathan Trumbull, Henry Knox, Timothy Pickering, the Marquis de Lafayette and his son, Gouverneur Morris, Henry Lee, and Elias Boudinot, to name just a few. In addition to these at least partially personal tokens of regard, various associations corresponded with Martha. Masonic Lodges and Societies of Cincinnati from around the nation sent their respects, and numerous divines wrote as well, enclosing copies of some of the 300-plus public addresses delivered in Washington's memory.[9]

In 1836, James Madison's death also provoked considerable public notice even though he had left the presidency twenty years earlier. The notice from the American Colonization Society that its members would wear mourning bands for a month could not have surprised Dolley Madison, considering that her husband had been its president and left it a legacy in his will. Also predictable were the regards of the Franklin Literary Society at Randolph Macon College, of which James had been an honorary member. The Society planned to deliver a suitable address, send copies to James's friends, and publish its respects in the *Southern Advocate*, *Virginia Conference Sentinel*, and *Richmond Whig*. The Independent Highlanders of Nashville and the Democratic Young Men's Convention from Harrisburg, Pennsylvania, also saw fit to write to Dolley, and letters came from several communities near the Madison home, Montpelier. The citizens from the nearby town of Madison pledged to wear crepe for thirty days and to publish their resolutions of respect. Those of Petersburg and the members of the Louisa County Court informed Dolley that they, too, would don mourning bands. A letter from the Fluvanna Court House, by contrast, disdained such trivial devices; its authors required no visual reminder to mourn the "illustrious Patriot and Statesman."[10]

In addition to their respects for the dead and their widows, these letters shared an expectation that a husband's public service imposed certain civic obligations on his widow, as they had on his wife. When Congress asked that George Washington's body be interred in the capital, with a monument commemorating "the great events of his political and military life," Martha Washington replied that she "must consent to the request" even though it required a considerable "sacrifice of individual feeling . . . to public duty." After all, her husband's example had taught her "never to oppose my private wishes to the public will." Nor was this the only request Martha felt obliged to grant. Private individuals and organizations asked for locks of George's (and sometimes her) hair. The Grand Lodge of Massachusetts promised to place the lock in a specially prepared golden urn. Three women from Providence, Rhode Island, who styled themselves "A Society of Females" pledged to wear the hair "as a charm to deter us from ill."[11] Condolence letters to presidential widows constituted a demand in themselves. They required an answer, with words from the widow recognizing that the public, too, had suffered a loss. For the most prominent widows, this was by no means an easy burden. Elderly Martha Washington found the volume of correspondence quite overwhelming. An uncertain writer at the best of times, she relied on her husband's former secretary, Tobias Lear (who was also a niece's husband), to draft letters for her.[12]

Even far less prominent political widows received some public recognition for their losses. After Henry Jackson died in the summer of 1840, for example, most of Martha's letters came from friends and family, such as Eliza Schley, who wrote to "truly sympathize" with her aunt's loss. Martha also received a formal condolence from the Demosthenian Society of Athens, Georgia. This letter informed her that the society's members planned to wear mourning badges in honor of one of Georgia's "most distinguished citizens." Henry Jackson had last held a high-ranking office in the 1810s, when he was chargé d'affaires in France, and he had long since stopped teaching at Franklin College as well due to ill health. Even long-ago public service, however, counted for something in the Southeast's political culture of mourning.[13]

Occasionally, political widows served not simply as symbols of the past but rallying points for their husbands' allies. During her brief widowhood, Martha Washington was one such figure although she doubtless would have preferred a more retired life. The factional acrimony of the 1790s ensured that George Washington did not remain the widely loved figure he had been when his presidency began, but when he died, the nation mourned. Even those who despised Federalist policies could remember Washington fondly in his earlier incarnation as the hero of the Revolution. Still, Martha herself became something of a Federalist magnet. A substantial proportion of those who wrote condolence letters to her were avowed Federalists, such as Fisher Ames and Harvard's president, Joseph Willard. Many had benefited from Washington's patronage. Washington had appointed Henry Knox as Secretary of War, Jonathan Trumbull Jr. as his secretary, Richard

Varick as his military secretary, Colonel William Stephens Smith (John Adams's son-in-law) to several government posts, and Timothy Pickering as Postmaster and Secretary of War. Before being recalled by Thomas Jefferson, Colonel David Humphreys served as ambassador to Spain, whence he wrote Martha long, personal letters after George died.[14] In contrast, leading Democratic-Republicans were vanishingly scarce among Washington's mourners. Thomas Jefferson himself did not attend the Congressional memorial for the dead president, and when he visited Martha Washington at Mount Vernon in 1800, the two prudently confined their conversation to family matters.[15]

When fellow Federalists such as Chief Justice John Marshall and Reverend Manasseh Cutler came to Mount Vernon, however, the conversation took a more political turn. Both men observed that Martha seemed older and sadder than previously, which was hardly surprisingly under the circumstances. But Cutler also recalled something else of his visit in January 1802. "We were all federalists, which evidently gave her particular pleasure," he remembered. "Her remarks were frequently pointed and sometimes very sarcastic on the new order of things and present administration."[16] A few months later, Martha Washington's reply to yet another condolence letter provides a further hint of how mourning her husband and mourning the Jeffersonian ascendancy might mesh. In this missive, she thanked Winthrop Sargent for his "expressions of respect," writing, "Nothing can be more soothing to my mind that *those* testimonies of respect and veneration paid to my deceased and ever regretted Friend, particularly by those who knew him well, and whom he considered with esteem and regard." The connotation here was probably as "pointed" as her remarks to Cutler; Jefferson had recently denied Sargent reappointment as governor of the Mississippi Territory, a post the staunch Federalist had received during the Adams administration.[17]

A more indirect partisanship characterized Lucy Barbour's widowhood. Shortly after the 1844 election, Barbour launched a campaign to honor Henry Clay, recently defeated in his third presidential run. Two years before, Lucy had buried her husband, James Barbour, a substantial Orange County, Virginia, planter, former governor of Virginia, secretary of war, and minister to England. In a letter to the *Richmond Whig*, Lucy Barbour encouraged her fellow "Whig women of Virginia" to create "some token of respect" for Clay. Partisan convictions and prior experience with public benevolence prompted some two thousand Virginia women to subscribe to the Virginia Association of Ladies for Erecting a Statue to Henry

Clay. Their efforts excited considerable Democratic derision. One pseudonymous writer disparaged the "political amazons," while the *Lynchburg Republican* wondered that such infamous partisans could consider themselves ladies. Yet the Clay Association ladies found staunch defenders in the state's Whig newspapers, which both asserted the Whig women's right to articulate political opinions and insisted that ladies were above base partisan demagoguery. For their part, as Elizabeth Varon observes, many benevolent Virginia women found the Whig party a logical fit with their interest in improving society by promoting leaders of "property and talents." For the woman who started the campaign, however, the Association surely meant something more personal as well. In honoring Clay, Lucy Barbour honored her husband and extended his political legacy. James Barbour had been a personal friend of Henry Clay and had helped found Virginia's Whig Party, which in turn defended his widow's initiative in its newspapers and speeches. Lucy Barbour's trebly privileged position as a lady, a planter, and the widow of a prominent political figure did not immunize her from Democratic taunts, but it significantly limited the personal risk she incurred in making her politics public.[18]

Another hint of how dead public servants and their widows continued to figure in popular politics comes from the research of political historian Christopher Olsen. Looking at election procedures throughout the South, he has found that elections sometimes took place at the houses of prominent men's widows. This entailed an even broader publicization of a widow's house than an estate sale: polling locations were prominently published in newspapers, and on election day, they gathered a particularly wide cross section of the white male population. In addition, when questions arose about an individual's right to vote—whether he owned enough property, for example—women sometimes testified about men's qualifications.[19] While the overall significance of widows' place in election-day proceedings awaits fuller elaboration, it serves as a reminder that slaveholding widows intersected the political realm through the living, not just the dead. Martha Jackson's connections to public service, for example, were not confined to her husband's time in the diplomatic corps, nor to his older brother's turn-of-the-century career as a U.S. senator and Georgia governor.[20] In the years following Henry's death, the next generation of Jacksons and Cobbs (Martha's nephews) built their own political careers. Her son, Henry Rootes, became a U.S. district attorney four years after Henry died, and he later served on the Georgia Supreme Court. Her nephew, Howell Cobb, became a U.S. congressman, Speaker of the House, and governor of

Georgia. His brother, Thomas R. R. Cobb, served as the state Supreme Court reporter and compiled the Georgia criminal code in the late 1840s and 1850s. Catherine Lewis also had links to the world of government and patronage, primarily through her brothers, sons, and nephews. William Horn Battle served on the North Carolina Superior and Supreme Courts, her son Gaston secured a position in the U.S. Survey Corps, several of her nephews were lawyers, and one went on to be president of the University of North Carolina.[21]

Slaveholding widows sought benefits from their connections to both dead and living public figures. Political widows sometimes solicited from the public rather more than the emotional comfort of knowing their husbands were remembered. Before the Revolution, for example, Mary Campbell had tried to make her place in Virginia's past political genealogy count in her favor in her petition to Lord Dunmore. Some privileges came unsought. In the new nation, for example, Congress granted presidential widows a franking privilege for the mail they sent and received. As Virginia's Henry Lee explained to Martha Washington, "as soon as we understood that the postage of letters to you had become immoderate," Congress unanimously passed a bill giving "the right of franking" as a "testimonial of respect to yourself." Years later, Dolley Madison received the same privilege, and the House of Representatives promised her "a seat within the Hall" (as opposed to the public gallery) whenever "it shall be her pleasure to visit the House."[22] Dolley also made more lucrative use of her husband's reputation. Shortly after James Madison died, she tried to get his papers published privately to help defray his enormous debts. When that failed, Congress appropriated $30,000 to purchase his papers from the Constitutional period. When Dolley faced renewed financial troubles (thanks in part to her spendthrift son Payne Todd), Congress appropriated a further $25,000 to purchase the balance of James Madison's papers. This time, they placed most of the money in trust for Dolley so her son could not squander it.[23] At a much lower rung on the political ladder, Martha Jackson tried to convince Franklin College to purchase her husbands' books and minerals for $500. (The Trustees approved the purchase, but the Faculty did not pursue it.)[24] Finally, many widows of Revolutionary and 1812 veterans sought military pensions based on their husbands' service to the nation. Some widows sought pensions even though their husbands had never served in the military. Richmond's Hope Mulford claimed a pension on the grounds that her husband had died in the line of duty during a yellow fever epidemic. As a health officer for Richmond, she maintained, his "'strict attention to the public Interest'" during an 1800 outbreak had brought "'much safety & tranquillity to the State,'" at the cost of his own life.[25]

In addition to conjuring with the names and public records of the dead, widows sought help from the living. Men's public service created myriad serendipitous opportunities for them to help their kin. Serving in a state legislature or on a court, for example, required slaveholding men to travel from rural residences to county, state, and national capitals. In the process, they might rely on their own wives to manage in their absence, but they were also well placed to fulfill their relations' commissions. While James Powell Cocke was in Richmond, for example, he looked to his widowed mother and his wife to oversee the family plantation, and he in turn ran errands for his widowed sister Polly Archer and her sons.[26] Widows also benefited from the ability to tap the legal knowledge of their political kin and connections. When it came time to draft her will, Martha Washington summoned the assistance of Charles Lee, one of her husband's appointees and a devoted Federalist. On completing the job, Lee assured Martha he would carry out her complicated wishes in "the most convenient perfect and advantageous manner," and he had reason to know: he was the U.S. attorney general.[27]

Slaveholding widows' interest in politics was not solely a matter of pursuing personal advantage. Widows also took a keen interest in politics when their relations' interests were at stake. As Georgia's political leaders geared up for the presidential election of 1848, future governor Howell Cobb informed his aunt, Martha Jackson, that he was "going to our Convention at Milledgeville to make an effort to save our party from the disgrace of nominat[ing] a Whig for the Presidency." He also asked her to deliver a message, requesting that she "tell Cousin Henry that I honestly hope that he has not been carried away by the popular clamor in favor of Genl Taylor. I love victory but I love my principles more." For her part, Jackson paid attention to Hezekiah Erwin's principles when he came to court her elder daughter; she reported that while he was "a democrat in politicks," at least he did not "express himself, like a *hot* party man." International affairs, meanwhile, attracted Martha Jackson's interest in a different regard. Because her only son led a regiment during the Mexican War, she and her sister, Sarah Cobb, hoped that the election of a new Mexican president, "who is called the peace president," might produce a speedy end to the "dreadfull war."[28]

In times of peace, widows' most immediate political concern might be their relatives' fate at the polls. When Jane Cocke's son, Charles, lost an election in 1822, for example, he expected that she would be mortified.[29] Widows' stake in their children's success was particularly high when they became involved in the effort to get them appointed or elected. The year after Martha Jackson lost her husband, her son sought a position as solicitor on the Chatahoochie circuit court. Seeking to improve his chances, young Henry solicited support from several men in the area. Colonel J. H. Watson declined to take sides, but Wilson Lumpkin agreed to promote Henry, and George R. Gilman promised his support if he were present when the legislature made its choice. Extending the campaign, his cousin, Joseph Jackson, canvased several other men, and so too did Martha herself. One of her contacts was Charles Jenkins, whom she knew was a force in Democratic politics. Presuming on their acquaintance during his schooling at Franklin College, she pointed out that if the Democrats won a majority of the legislature in the upcoming elections, her son would be a candidate for the solicitor's office. In his reply, Jenkins fondly remembered his student days and promised to support Henry. Martha also contacted a Mr. Bullock. Here, she relied not on the ties of alma mater but on the influence of her brother-in-law, Colonel John Addison Cobb. Following the conventions of political name-dropping, she wrote, "Col. Cobb allows me to say, that any favors done by yourself or Mr McCallister for my son, will be esteemed by him, as a personal attention to himself."[30]

Martha Jackson's efforts to promote her son's political career suggest a need to rethink whether widowed mothers were usually a burden to their politically and economically ambitious sons, as some prominent examples might suggest. According to George Washington biographer Douglas Southall Freeman, for example, Washington profoundly resented his mother's demands upon him. During his youth, Mary Washington expected him to heed her wishes about his career; in 1755, she resisted his career-making opportunity to serve as an aide to General Braddock. Throughout her later years, Mary Washington also repeatedly borrowed small sums of money from George. Far more significant, financially, was her refusal to relinquish Ferry Farm to George when he came of age, as her husband's will had stipulated. "Filial duty" prevented George both from evicting her from his farm and from ignoring her requests. While one could hardly claim that Mary's intervention stunted George's political career, this evidence suggests that he succeeded despite and even in defiance of his mother.[31] Family papers provide less information about Thomas Jefferson's relationship with his mother, Jane Randolph Jefferson, widowed circa 1757, but surviving financial records reveal that he took over much of the book-keeping when he came of age. She presumably served as a continued connection to the influential Randolph clan and her husband's friends, but Dumas Malone concludes that "he probably did not value her counsel very highly."[32]

James Henry Hammond's mother, Catherine, provides another example: Carol Bleser and Drew Faust maintain that Hammond found her a burdensome responsibility. James's father, Elisha, died in 1829 when the young James was just beginning his legal and political career. Because his father left barely enough to settle his debts, James himself assumed the burden of maintaining his mother and his orphaned younger siblings. In fact, according to James, his mother depended on him throughout forty-five years of widowhood. In 1841, he claimed that she and "her family"—his younger siblings—had already "cost me $10,000, not counting interest." It was in 1841 that James finally broke his great-uncle's will, which enabled his mother to inherit some $20,000, a sum he imagined would "make her comfortable and relieve me of all expense." Yet, in fact, James still felt obliged to render financial assistance until her death, including providing a home and paying for a companion. After all these services, James felt betrayed to learn in 1864 that she had left her estate not to him or his children but to a granddaughter whom he disliked. Whether these particularly illustrious sons and their apparently tedious mothers are ripe for reinterpretation is a question best left to their biographers. However, it is worth noting, for example, that in the summer of 1829, young James Hammond did not drop all his own affairs to attend to his father's estate. Instead, his mother remained on his father's small farm outside of Macon, Georgia, where she harvested the year's crop and saw to the estate's local concerns until she was able to sell the farm and return to Augusta. There, she took in boarders to support herself and her three younger children. Her efforts in this period (1829–31) spared James the full burden of replacing his father at a critical moment in his early adulthood. During this time, he was selected to edit the antitariff *Southern Times*, which quickly advanced him to prominence among South Carolina's nullifiers. He also finally convinced a rich Charleston widow to let him marry her daughter, the young heiress Catherine Fitzsimons—without a marriage settlement. Counterfactual speculation is always a risky business, but it is at least entertaining to consider whether, if his mother had not managed the Macon farm and taken in those Augusta boarders, the problems of Elisha's estate might have so preoccupied James as to have prevented him from making one or both of those connections, which provided so critical to his future career.[33]

Widowed mothers could also serve their sons as symbols, as in the case of Andrew Jackson. Throughout his life, Jackson attributed his sense of honor to his mother. He claimed, for example, that she taught him to defend himself calmly, but to fight rather than resort to law to avenge an insult. (In an age that considered mothers crucial in their children's development as good little republicans, it only added to the story's symbolism that Elizabeth Jackson could be called a martyr of the American Revolution: she died from cholera, contracted while nursing sick soldiers in Charleston.) Whether Elizabeth Jackson ever said any such thing about honor is less important than Andrew Jackson's willingness to attribute so central an aspect of his character to her. Honor was, after all, central not only to his view of gender relations—men must fight to protect ladies' honor—but also to his understanding of public service and political obligations.[34]

Andrew Jackson's willingness to attribute his defining principles to his mother jars with a final role, or lack of one, that widowed mothers were sometimes thought to play in their sons' lives, that of cipher. In certain circles, Andrew Jackson's brilliant future might have been predicted from his posthumous birth. Many years after the Civil War, a Federal Writers' Project interviewer recorded former slave Moses Lyles's comments on just such a natal portent. "My old marster and mistress have two girls, Miss Annie and Miss Lillie, dat was livin' when Marster die," Lyles recalled. "Just a few weeks after he die, here come young Marse John into a troubled land, in de last year of de war, '65. What you think of dat? Niggers 'low dat's what give him da power dat him have. You never hear 'bout dat? Well, they do say, when a male child come after de father's death, dat male child gwine to be a big man in all sorts of ways."[35] Andrew Jackson certainly fit the description of a "big man," but whether because of or despite his father's early death is open to debate. More important for present purposes, Moses Lyles's folk wisdom implies the irrelevance of widowed mothers. His story can be read as saying that posthumous sons succeeded because they were born free from the restraints of a heavy paternal hand.[36] Alternatively, perhaps Lyles meant that the lack of a father's care forced a man to be self-reliant from an early age. Neither version suggests that mothers figured in their sons' careers for good or ill. Yet in slaveholding families, at least, widows played instrumental roles in transferring tangible property and intangible influence to the next generation. How well, how often, and with what consequences for particular men—whether, in other words, political success bore any statistically significant relationship to having a widowed mother—lies beyond the scope of this book. Here, it is enough to note that some widows promoted their sons politically as well as economically and that they could do so because while voting was a male prerogative, pulling political strings was not.

For slaveholding widows, using their connections to promote their own interests or their kinsmen's public careers seemed entirely natural. They and most of their peers saw no more reason to separate friendship and political interests than they did family and economic ones.[37] As a result, cronyism played as prominent a role in politics as it did in the economy. Embedded in this political culture was a set of assumptions about the social order: certain people were suited to lead. For slaveholding southerners, the most basic qualifications were whiteness and maleness, but questions of breeding, bearing, education, refinement, and wealth also played a central role. At times, these aspects of rank and class far outweighed the question of gender, which loomed so large in suffrage and other formal political rights. What this race, gender, and class-saturated understanding of social order implied for slaveholding widows' household mastery, especially in conflicts with white men beyond their own families, is the subject to which we must now turn.

INTERACTIONS AMONG southeastern whites of different socioeconomic positions were rarely either harmoniously collaborative or starkly unequal. Instead, southeastern whites jostled with each other steadily along a number of material and cultural axes, and the outcomes of their disputes were highly contingent on a number of factors beyond the obvious categories of race, class, and gender. As numerous political historians have argued, republican ideology played a particularly important role in shaping how southeastern whites understood themselves and each other. For decades after the Revolution, Americans north and south debated the relationship between economic, social, and political independence. In strict republican terms, financial reliance and personal autonomy were simply incompatible. The difficulty in reconciling them produced both personal anxiety and constant conflict, as individuals, especially white men, sought to assert their own or deny others' claims to true independence. Slavery added fuel to the fire in two ways: it exemplified the degradation of dependency, and it encouraged whites to treat violence as a normal form of communication.

Consequently, disagreements that might otherwise have been minor easily escalated, as white southerners (especially men) sought to repel any hint of slavishness.[38] As a result, while in purely economic terms we might expect a male planter to have some obvious, predictable, and stable superiority over an overseer, the two men had a shared interest in protecting the patriarchal and property relations on which mastery depended. Alternatively, the overseer's vested interest in his own independence prompted some to rebel or even form alliances with others in opposition to their employers.

In this context, slaveholding widows ought to have been at an extreme disadvantage. Where white men learned from childhood to assert themselves by fist and writ, white women learned the milder arts of influence, self-abnegation, and submission. And yet, widows did not automatically quail when they confronted white men who sought to undermine their authority in one way or another. They did, however, need help defending their mastery. Their ability to get that help changed over time in ways that illustrate an important shift in the political meanings of both widowhood and mastery.[39] In the early republic, widowed planters' mastery not only threatened some men's claims to mastery but also seems to have prompted collusion across lines of class against female usurpers. In the antebellum decades, however, similar conflicts revealed the planter class's inclination to uphold elite privilege across lines of gender, contrary to the democratic implications of universal white manhood suffrage. Throughout the period, conflicts between slaveholding widows and white men also reflected the parties' relationships with others in the neighborhood, the presence (or absence) of an audience, and extrinsic factors such as the Southeast's increasing socioeconomic stratification.

During the Revolutionary era, white American women's public visibility and political significance dramatically increased. The post-Revolutionary settlement, by contrast, featured a marked backlash against female independence. While women's education received a distinct boost and the 1790s witnessed an explosion in elite women's political activities, popular magazines attacked the notion of gender equity and lambasted single women for avoiding the womanly destiny of coverture.[40] Reasserting female subordination was intimately linked to the Revolution's implications for racial and class hierarchy. The war years had profoundly challenged the political power of elites (tidewater and lowcountry elites in particular) and the institution of slavery itself. From Virginia to Georgia, male planters sought ways to accommodate some changes, while rolling back others. In formal political terms, that often meant extending suffrage rights and political representation to more white men while tightening up a slave institution that had been seriously challenged by war and economic disruption. In the informal politics of daily life, it could easily mean undermining widowed planters' authority in the name of patriarchal prerogative or even of politically expedient alliances with less wealthy men.[41]

Virginia planter Martha Turberville's struggles to defend her household exemplify the difficulties of widowed planters in the early republic. In 1799, her neighborhood included one James A. Thompson, whose plantation bordered her own. The two had a far from neighborly relationship, however, and at one point, Turberville charged that Thompson had stolen from her. She also maintained that Thompson had "procured or occasioned the murder of her former Overseer," George Baber. In response, Thompson promptly sued her for slander. The fact that he bothered to sue suggests that a widow's words posed a real threat to a man's mastery, but the suit itself also suggests widows' vulnerability. When the suit came to trial, Martha Turberville's new overseer, Henry King, became a key figure in the drama, as a material witness against her. Overseer King testified that Turberville had indeed accused Thompson of stealing from her and murdering overseer Baber. King further claimed that she accused him of being in league with Thompson from the start. Assuming that Martha Turberville truly believed her neighbor guilty of theft and murder, and her own overseer of conspiracy, then she must have felt beleaguered indeed. If her neighbor had killed Baber and installed a replacement to facilitate his thieving ways, her claims to mastery had been thrice undone: first by the theft, second by the murderous attack on one of her dependents, and finally by the legal attack on her personal honor through the slander suit. If, however, the slander accusation was baseless and her overseer was lying about her words in the course of a lawsuit, then her control over her household and its dependents was no less in doubt.[42]

Nearly a decade later, another Virginia planter's effort to control an overseer reinforces this picture of white men's alliance against widowed slaveholders, even in the absence of conspiracy. Early in 1807, overseer John Thompson (no known relation to Turberville's neighbor) found himself in the middle of Susannah Wilcox's ongoing quarrel with her son-in-law. As we have seen, Wilcox and James Hubard had an uneasy relationship at the best of times, levying accusations and counteraccusations of improper and even illegal conduct. In one particularly unsettling incident, Hubard accused Wilcox of trying to suborn his overseer, John Thompson.

Hubard had hired Thompson to overseer a tract of land over which Wilcox herself claimed authority. One day, as Thompson reported to Hubard, Susannah Wilcox insisted that he visit her. At this meeting, she demanded an explanation of his actions. She also ordered him "not to attend" to Hubard's directions, but to "take the Tob[acc]o notes out for her." As soon as Hubard learned of this encounter, he wrote a furious letter to Thompson, demanding to know what had happened and, more particularly, what commitments Wilcox might have extracted from him. In responding, Thompson temporized. He admitted that he had promised to "obey" Wilcox, which must have enraged Hubard. But Thompson hastily added that he told Wilcox he could obey her only if she had "authority" over the property in question. Thompson closed his exculpatory letter by saying that he would be glad to have his responsibilities clarified. This could hardly have satisfied Hubard, who would surely have preferred a promise to defy Susannah Wilcox and her claims at all costs.[43]

John Thompson's description of Susannah Wilcox's behavior is very much in keeping with her subsequent conduct toward her son-in-law, and it nicely captures her forcefulness. When Wilcox told overseer Thompson that she retained "the immediate controul of the Whole Estate" until her dispute with her son-in-law was settled, she was simply too formidable for Thompson to deny her to her face even though he had a clear contractual obligation to Hubard. Thus, he hedged. Yet Thompson did ultimately side with Hubard against Wilcox. Whether or not he consciously chose "loyalty to other men," his expressed concern for his contractual obligation bespeaks the power of men in this society.[44] After all, the law itself reflected, enshrined, and operated within patriarchal principles, and Thompson had reason to predict that Hubard would prevail at law. Viewed in that light, Thompson's willingness to pay Wilcox any mind at all testifies to her considerable authority.[45]

The same year, 1807, saw Martha Turberville facing renewed trouble with her neighbors. Again, the problem concerned theft. As Martha complained to her only son, Gawin, another overseer's death left her "to the murcy of a set of the most abandoned wretches that ever any body lived by in this world." Here, Martha was not complaining that she could not manage her slaves without an overseer. She complacently assumed that "I can have the Crop made myelf with Vincent," one of her male slaves, "who follows my derections as he has done all the winter." The problem was with her neighbors. "You know," she wrote Gawin, "some white body is nessry" to look after "the stock & things of the plantation." Without a white man around, her neighbors found it too easy to "come & steal I say steal the sheep cows & Hogs. . . . & although the negroes see them take them I have no redress as thay are no Evidence." That is, slaves could not testify against "the most abandoned" of white "wretches," but another white person could.[46] Martha herself could testify, of course, but she was not likely to be in a position to witness the thefts; ladies might inspect the fields in the daytime, but they could not spend their nights lurking about to catch thieves in the act.

Martha Turberville's complaint illustrates how useful an overseer could be in defending household mastery. A reliable overseer could be indispensable for a planter with too much property to look after personally, especially in upholding his employer's authority over both slaves and troublesome neighbors. But good overseers were rare, according to planters, and a bad one could be "fatell bad," in one planter's view.[47] Since widowed planters had even less inclination than their male peers to stand around in the fields, they found overseers both particularly useful, if they accepted female authority, and particularly threatening, because they often did not. Martha Turberville clearly had trouble keeping her overseers loyal—and alive—while crusty Susannah Wilcox was probably enough to put any self-respecting man's back up. Their contemporary, Lucy Thornton, unhappily felt herself incapable of restraining her overseer, who beat her slaves "in the most cruel manner."[48]

Fortunately for widows, their authority as employers hinged on more than their gender and their personal forcefulness. Instead, it owed much to the social, economic, and cultural conditions which shaped overseers' options. A pair of antebellum overseers who worked for Martha Jackson in the 1840s suggest how hard material facts of need and opportunity constrained overseers' actions and self-presentations. In the late 1830s, Henry Smith earned a higher salary than his employer could actually afford. As his employer's creditor, Smith was respectful but not especially deferential. When Martha sought to alter his salary, Smith informed her that he could get his old wages—a generous $500 per year—from one of her neighbors. Later, he told her he was retiring from overseeing altogether, which he could afford since he owned not only land but a slave, acquired from Jackson herself in part payment of his past-due wages.[49] Few overseers enjoyed Smith's comparative independence, more typically enduring considerable economic insecurity. While financial worries made some volatile, it made others anxious to please.[50] Such was the case with Smith's hand-picked replacement, Vincent Pierson. Pierson's career underscores Smith's comparative independence. For starters, Pierson received significantly less for managing the same plantation: $275 in 1847 as compared to Smith's $500. Pierson's letters to Martha Jackson also indicate his less advantageous position. Smith's written English resembled many planters', while idiosyncratic spellings riddled Pierson's letters. Their letters also varied in content. While Smith almost never sought Jackson's approval, Pierson asked her how to draw up a check, whether to set the slave women to spinning, and when to sell her cotton.[51] As the plantation continued to struggle, he grew progressively more defensive, recognizing that if Martha was disappointed, whether financially or otherwise, it would be "impossible for me to prosper." He also worried that it was "very paneful to your feelings for me to bee complaining to you so much" about lacking for hands and livestock. Pierson's dependence on his job did not automatically make him, or any other overseer, slavishly deferential, but it forced him to weigh his manly independence against his very real reliance on his wages.[52]

Among overseers as a class, however, both Pierson and Smith represented success stories. After eight years, Pierson left overseeing, having finally saved enough to buy "a little home," but he owned no slaves and had "impaired" health.[53] Smith was significantly more fortunate. Over the course of the early nineteenth century, economic conditions in the Southeast made it more and more difficult for overseers to buy land, let alone slaves. By the 1840s and 1850s, many employees and tenant farmers never managed to buy land of their own or lost what little they had to foreclosure. Charles Bolton suggests that by 1850 landlessness had become a permanent status for a growing number of poor whites in the Southeast. As a result, the landless increasingly depended on slaveholders for employment and land. Moreover, men who needed employment increasingly found they could not depend on annual contracts. In the 1850s, widowed planters joined their male peers in employing white men more often and in hiring them by the day. Some of these day laborers even worked as overseers, which could only have depressed other overseers' wages, security, and independence.[54] During the same period, Gavin Wright observes that any reasonably competent slaveholder could make a profit "from capital gains alone."[55]

Overseers' declining economic position may have made them more useful to widowed planters because men who could not afford to lose their jobs made more reliable agents in defending widows' mastery. Natalie Sumter's diary provides a particularly clear illustration of this role. In January 1841, a brewing quarrel between Sumter and another resident of the district exploded into open conflict. At stake was a piece of land. Sometime before his death, Natalie's husband had bought the land and begun to plant it. At some point after Thomas Sumter died, the seller, a Dr. Yates, had a change of heart; he wanted to renege on the deal and repossess the land.[56] Consequently, he refused to accept the final payment from Natalie Sumter. On the morning of January, Dr. Yates came to see Natalie, swearing that he would "take possession of the land." Yates's visit was an aggressive move; he arrived uninvited, unannounced, and so early in the morning that Sumter was still "in my bed." Charging right into her "chamber," he talked at her for two hours. "At last," Sumter "beg'd" him to retire to the parlor "while I got up."[57]

Given some privacy, Sumter seized the offensive. She sent for her overseer, Mr. Cox, whom she had hired just three weeks before. Sumter dispatched Cox "to go & take possession of the land & make the Negroes work there today." (Occupying the land with her overseer and some of her sixty-plus slaves gave the lie to Yates's claim to possess it.) Sumter's stratagem succeeded. Later that day, Cox reported that "Dr Yates went to the field" as he had threatened. When he arrived, however, he found Cox and the slaves already at work. Frustrated, Yates "told the Negroes he would shoot them." (Sumter's diary does not indicate that the two white men had guns, but their presence may be safely assumed.) Fortunately, Yates's bravado failed him, and he ceded the field, sending Sumter "a receipt for what I owe him." The next morning, she paid off the debt with two notes worth $111. Summing up the day's adventure, Sumter concluded that "the poor man is creasy." As far as the diary is concerned, there the conflict ended.[58]

Invading Sumter's house, claiming her land, and threatening her slaves were all unmistakable attacks on her mastery. Approaching a male planter in this way was a near guarantee of violence, but Yates knew Natalie Sumter would never try to shoot or horsewhip him, as a man might. He may even have expected her to cower in petticoated dismay. He might have also considered that so gross an insult to her would prompt one of her three grown sons to come after him.[59] In the event, neither happened. Sumter prevailed, and she did so not by relying on her sons but by sending her own overseer to defend her rights. In this context, Cox was an employee who could be ordered to stand around in an icy field all day. But Cox was also something more: a white man with the masculinity, the physical presence, and the potential for force that Sumter herself lacked.[60] A very similar understanding of what overseers could do for widowed planters informed William Gilmore Simms's novel *Woodcraft*. An important subplot concerns the widowed Mrs. Eveleigh's reliance on her "attentive and respectful" overseer, Mr. Fordham. In addition to his regular duties, he provides exceptional assistance.[61] Early in the novel—set in South Carolina in the closing days of the Revolution—Mrs. Eveleigh seeks to recover some slaves that the retreating British have stolen. The British Colonel Moncrief stonewalls her, claiming that her slaves are not in his camp. Undaunted, Mrs. Eveleigh sends Fordham to clamber through a British hulk, where he recovers the Eveleigh bondspeople from among other confiscated slaves. Fordham becomes even more indispensable on the return home: when a band of brigands assaults the traveling party, Fordham saves Mrs. Eveleigh, her son, and the slaves. With these heroics under his belt, Fordham can clearly claim "decisive and earnest manliness" despite working for a woman.[62]

As employees dependent upon their wages, overseers made logical extensions of slaveholding widows' authority, but even in a climate of contracting economic opportunity, they remained as much a potential threat as a resource. An extreme example involves Ada Bacot, whose first husband was killed by his overseer in a fight.[63] Even in the absence of violence, widows' reliance on overseers had some risks. When a widow looked to an overseer to do things she would or could not do herself, she put herself at least partially in his power. He might, for instance, arrogate more power than she wished to surrender or commit her to actions she had not intended. As a general pattern for widows' response to trouble, moreover, relying on overseers—or any male agent—suggested that only white men could guarantee widows' mastery. Once Dr. Yates arrived in the disputed field, for example, his quarrel with Natalie Sumter became a confrontation with Mr. Cox, and her victory now hinged on Cox's refusal to back down. In fiction, slaveholding widows' reliance on male agents similarly compensated for and confirmed their own shortcomings as masters. Antebellum novels that featured widowed planters typically made men the guarantors of female authority. In Tucker's *Valley of the Shenandoah*, Colonel Grayson's death all but ruins his family financially, and his widow cannot solve the estate's problems alone. Instead, she depends on her husbands' male friends to protect her interests. One friend spares her an unpleasant interview with a grasping creditor, Mr. Hatchett. Another ensures that she retains a foothold in gentility: a small house and farm, eight slaves, and a carriage and horses. With such staunch allies, Mrs. Grayson can afford to be a paragon of gentle patience, quite similar to Virginia Cary's equally fictional Emilia.[64] When overseers served widows as reliable agents, and male planters served as chivalrous friends, they became instrumental in widows' success. This represented only a minor advance over the starker disputes of the early republic because men continued to decide widows' fate. However, antebellum widows did not always need white men to act on their behalf, nor did their connections assume that they did.

Especially suggestive evidence of male planters' willingness to let widows fight their own battles—in the process closing ranks against lesser whites —comes from a South Carolina widow's dealings with her employee in 1854. When Matthew Singleton died in 1854, he left his substantial properties in his widow Martha's care.[65] One of her duties as Matthew's executor was to finish a capital improvement project he had begun, which involved building a road and rebuilding part of a house. Matthew had hired one Robert Carter to oversee slaves on this project, and after his death, Martha's mother told Carter that Martha was "desirous" for him "to remain and take charge of the place." Almost immediately thereafter, however, Martha brought in someone else to supervise Carter himself. Offended, Carter complained strenuously about this attack on his dignity: "Count de Saisille [Choiseul] has been brought here to do the work that belongs to me, as if I was not competent." Carter's words—"the work that belongs to me"—suggest that he saw his employment almost as a kind of property, perhaps a way of asserting his status as a skilled and independent white man. While Carter admitted his employer's authority to a certain degree, he resented being set up for failure. Having come to supervise Carter's work, de Choiseul left "no orders" for how Carter should proceed and "represented my unfinished work to the ladies as all wrong." "Such an act," Carter remarked, "was very unsatisfactory to me." In Carter' view, this interloper had made Mrs. Singleton "dissatisfied with me," a conclusion he drew from her refusal to let him borrow a horse to go to church. All of these complaints appeared in a letter Carter drafted in the hopes of clarifying the chain of command between Martha Singleton and himself. In closing, he indicated a compromise that would preserve his dignity: he would complete the task "according to Mrs Singletons wishes" but "no person (*Mr Loundes & Dr King excepted*) is to interfere with my work." He also insisted on "the use of a Horse to go to Church."[66]

Instead of addressing this letter to "the Ladies"—Singleton and her mother—directly, Carter sent it to Dr. King, a connection of Singleton's. Without explicitly asking the favor, the letter suggested that King might plead Carter's case to Singleton. Carter "thought it best to explain my circumstances to you so as not to give offence to any"; as Singleton's peer, King could express himself more freely than Carter himself and could presume to advise the recently bereaved widow. As it happened, Carter was sorely disappointed in his hope that Dr. King would take his part against "the Ladies." Instead, King seems to have handed Carter's letter—and Carter himself—over to Singleton. In her reply, Singleton systematically refuted each of his claims. It was "obviously" Carter's "duty" to obey any of her agents. It was equally his "duty" either to explain that he "had not understood" that agent's instructions or to "have apologized for knowingly disobeying them." With regard to the horse, Singleton accused him of lying: "you sent me a message requesting that use of a horse to bring, from Hendersonville, a conveyance which has been *loaned* you. By your letter to Dr King, I find that you had already purchased a Buggy." Worse, he brought the offending carriage onto her place "without either asking or receiving my permission." Furthermore, "you have also, enlarged the gate in the Henderson road, which I consider, to say the least, a very great liberty." Carter's insistence on designating his own supervisors proved the last straw. "I cannot allow you to dictate from which friends I shall or shall not receive advice and assistance," she told him. "As your views & mine of the duties and position of a gardener differ so widely, I shall have no occasion for your services an other year." Singleton flatly denied Carter's claim that he owned his job and must be allowed to perform it as he saw fit, an interpretation that made employment compatible with republican independence.[67]

In this triangular dispute, Dr. King rejected Carter's attempt to recruit him as an ally in an implicit appeal to shared white manhood. Instead, King sided with Martha Singleton, but not by acting on her behalf. His virtual inaction implied that Singleton was fully competent to handle the problem. It also suggested that Carter was Singleton's dependent far more than he was his own man and, thus, not in the same league as King. In the charged atmosphere of the 1850s, a politically astute planter might well hesitate to say this directly to a member of the voting public. This was, after all, a time when throughout the Southeast those who were not already well-off could vote but found it ever harder to buy slaves and land, the bases of republican independence according to most white southerners. As a result, planters had to tread delicately if they wanted to stave off open class-based rebellion from below. In this and similar cases, planter men could obscure any insult to democratic manhood, if they had to, by appealing to chivalry; they were not repressing other white men but simply assisting widows. Instead of having to make a stark choice between property and patriarchy, therefore, antebellum planters had a third option: siding with property and chivalry against the socioeconomic leveling implicit in yeomen's version of mastery.[68]

Among antebellum planters, Dr. King was by no means unusual in refusing both to side with an overseer and to undercut a fellow planter's authority over her (or his) employee. A few years later, a Virginia planter made a similar choice when a pair of overseers threatened to jeopardize his relationship with a fellow planter. Mary Ann Hendrick's decision to sell a plantation to one Charles Alexander in 1857 created the occasion. In the process of moving her property off the plantation and Alexander's onto it, the two planters' overseers, Mr. Wade and Mr. Gill, "had a fuss about" who owned the locks on the corn cribs, smoke houses, and other outbuildings. Hendrick's overseer, Gill, apparently told her that he argued the subject with Wade, Alexander's overseer. Hendrick then approached Alexander herself to sort out the matter. "Surprised & pained," Alexander initially denied knowing anything about "the locks or 'the fuss,'" but later recalled a conversation with his overseer and acknowledged that "shortly after moving my negroes to the place purchased from you and carrying a set of locks with me, Mr Wade told me that there were a plenty of locks on the plantation attached to the houses, I then in a casual way told him that they were mine, but that if you sent for them to send them to you, but if Mr. Gill wanted to carry them off to tell him that they were mine (I did not suppose that you knew anything about what was on the place) This statement is the best that I can give you as it made no impression on my mind —it being of a casual character. I regret the necessity of sending you this note, but am not willing to be misunderstood. I am sure if it were not for the *feeling* existing between our overseers neither you nor I would have ever heard any thing of this matter. I am very respectfully your *friend*."[69] With this letter, Alexander sought to prevent a minor misunderstanding from becoming a more damaging disagreement. He evidently cared little about the locks per se, but he was very concerned that his word and thus his honor had been tainted by his apparent lie (that is, the claim that he knew nothing about "the fuss"). Clarifying the situation was a "necessity," but this did not mean apologizing for an innocent mistake, because in the context of an honor-bound society, there were no innocent mistakes. To defend his honor, Alexander drew careful distinctions about other people's words. Alexander flatly refused to accept an overseer's word, and in that sense, he questioned both Gill's and Mary Ann Hendrick's authority. Yet this refusal reflected disdain not for Hendrick but for Gill; if Hendrick herself claimed the locks, he would respect her word. In short, Alexander redeemed himself by blaming the overseers. Had there not been some "*feeling*" between them, Hendrick and he would never have had to trouble with the locks. Alexander's letter thus aligned himself and Hendrick against the overseers, implying that gentlemen and ladies would not lower themselves to be implicated in lesser men's quarrels.[70]

Antebellum literary sources suggest a similar pattern in which conflicts involving slaveholding widows intersected with questions of social hierarchy. Tucker's *Valley of the Shenandoah* asserts gentry privilege at least as staunchly as female dependence. The Graysons themselves are financially ruined, yet Mrs. Grayson never loses her social standing. In contrast, her social circle refuses to admit the grasping Mr. Hatchett despite his prosperity. Simms's *Woodcraft* contained a similar dynamic. There, the role of Hatchett is filled by the war profiteer, M'Kewn. Like Hatchett, M'Kewn is "emulous of the best social position," and he uses his money "without stint or limit" to "secure it." In the end, however, the planters refuse to grant any social consequence to someone who has gained his money through traitorous opportunism.[71]

In addition to questions of chivalry and rank, a final consideration helped shape the outcome of slaveholding widows' conflicts with white men—the audience. Even in the sparsely settled rural South, few conflicts occurred in complete isolation. An audience of her own peers, for example, typically strengthened a widow's hand in negotiating with an aggressive neighbor or an insubordinate overseer. When Dr. Yates burst into Natalie Sumter's bedchamber on that cold January morning in 1841, he had more of an audience than he could have anticipated. The previous evening, slaves visiting Sumter's plantation had gotten into a fight, "which frightened us & kept us up till one in the morning." The next morning, Natalie and the slaves' owners—her friends, Mrs. Spann and Mr. Nelson—conducted a three-hour "trial" of the alleged culprits, Caesar and Edmund. The two planters were thus present when Yates arrived and likely gave Natalie moral support during his harangue. They proved an important resource in another way, too; when Natalie finally convinced Yates to leave her room so she could finish dressing, she sent Mrs. Spann with him to the parlor. Thus occupied, Yates apparently did not notice that Sumter was stealing a march on him by dispatching her overseer and field hands to the contested land.[72]

Slaves constituted an equally important audience. In Martha Singleton's quarrel with Robert Carter, his initial protest owed a great deal to the fact that Singleton's agent, Count de Choiseul, had rebuked him in front of the very slaves whom Carter was supervising. Refusing to play the slave to the Count's master, Carter quit: "I said in presence of the men that I should not go back to it, he should have the credit and faults of his own work for himself." In her reply to Carter, Martha Singleton focused in on this critical fact. Carter rejected her authority before the one audience that mattered most. "By your own account," she stated, "you said to the negroes engaged in the work that you 'should not return to it &c' thus setting them the example of disrespect to me, and absenting yourself for three weeks from the work it was your duty to execute, whether it accorded with your ideas of taste or not." Lurking in Singleton's words is the implication that Carter himself had acted like a slave whose truancy deprived Singleton of his labor and her right to judge, instruct, and discipline him.[73] The slave audience had a further implication for Singleton's handling of the fracas. Carter based his complaint in outraged manhood. Singleton gave the conflict another valence entirely by refocusing on his public flouting of her authority. In claiming that he set "the example of disrespect," she suggested that he had encouraged her slaves to disobey. As she undoubtedly knew, fomenting slave resistance was a serious offense under southern law, and her peers would have little inclination to take Carter's side— or hire him—if she tarred him with the brush of inciting disobedience.[74]

Martha Singleton may not have been consciously playing to an audience of fellow planters, but other widows clearly used virtual audiences to strengthen their claims. Perhaps the best example concerns Martha Jackson's attempt to cut overseer Henry Smith's salary, which she considered "*enormously* great."[75] She observed to Smith that "your salary has been a large & clear one. We on the contrary, have each year, met with disappointment in our crop." Implying that so skewed an apportionment of risk and gain was unreasonable, she offered to pay Smith five dollars per bale of cotton for the coming year, 1841. At that rate, he would receive his $500 only if she received the hundred-bale crop she considered reasonable.[76] Relying on more than mathematical logic to justify this change, she framed this proposal in terms of her maternal and legal obligations. Martha explained that she was "acting under a great responsibility"; as her husband's executor, she was "bound, to obtain such terms in my transactions, as shall appear proper to others as well as to myself." These others she had in mind were neither her children, nor even her husband's kin, all of whom had an immediate legal interest in her conduct. Instead, she claimed that "those whom my daughters may marry" might reproach her for being "extravagant or imprudent." Martha Jackson was indeed potentially accountable to the men who would eventually marry her daughters (in 1847 and 1852), but it was quite a leap to introduce these still hypothetical husbands into her negotiation with Smith. Imagining those prospective sons-in-law enabled Martha to represent herself as acting under compulsion, much like Martha Richardson, Natalie Sumter, and Lucy Freeman masked their own intentions with the claim that they were merely fulfilling their husbands' last wishes.[77]

William Gilmore Simms took an imagined audience to an extreme in *Woodcraft* in a scene pitting the aristocratic Mrs. Eveleigh against the blackguardly M'Kewn. The scene takes place late in the novel when Mrs. Eveleigh has already helped her friend Captain Porgy recover his slaves from M'Kewn's confederate, Colonel Moncrief, and thwarted M'Kewn's plot to foreclose on a mortgage he holds on Porgy's lands. Aware that Mrs. Eveleigh has opposed his interests, M'Kewn pays her a visit during which he insults her with the "sneering" accusation that Captain Porgy is her "*particular* favorite*," implying that her professed friendship masks an illicit romantic or sexual attachment. Mrs. Eveleigh takes offense, and "breathing equal scorn and nobleness," she offers to teach M'Kewn his manners: "I have been a soldier's wife; and . . . if it needs, for the assertion of my womanly dignity, that I should lift the weapon of the man, I shall feel no womanly fears in doing so. If you have any scruples, sir, in resenting personal indignities as men are apt to do, I have none; and though I have many friends, sir, who would cheerfully do battle in my cause, I would not suffer one of them to incur any peril of life or limb, while I am able to stand and confront the insolent, myself." This offer of violence places Mrs. Eveleigh well beyond the pale of genteel womanhood, but the scene makes her a figure not of ridicule but of heroism: the narrator likens her to Zenobia and Boadicea, two ancient widows who successfully led their people to battle.[78] Like the rest of Simms's fictional oeuvre, this scene is profoundly polemical, and yet it captures something important about white social relations in the antebellum Southeast. When facing insurgent white men, widowed ladies did not always have to wait for gentlemanly rescuers; instead, they could summon up the authority of their class and gender to rescue themselves.

William Gilmore Simms's scene affirmed not only the transcendent importance of wealth in southern social relations, but also the distinctive opportunity that wealthy widowhood afforded to assert social hierarchy. Mrs. Eveleigh arguably makes M'Kewn more powerless (at least in this confrontation) than any man could: she has called him on his ungentlemanly behavior, but because of her sex, he cannot challenge her to a duel, and because of her social status, he cannot simply thrash her either. William Gilmore Simms may not have known it, but there were real-life parallels to Mrs. Eveleigh. Mississippi newspaper editor Harriet N. Prewett, for example, capitalized on her immunity to dueling. When her husband died in 1849, Prewett took over the *Yazoo City Weekly Whig* and ran it until 1859. A violent partisan, Prewett attacked Democratic editors with language that would ordinarily have provoked a duel. As Christopher Olsen observes, "One can imagine the frustration of men obsessed with honor and public insults who knew the 'editress' was safe from their reprisals." Perhaps they felt a little like the fictional M'Kewn, stunned and stymied by their female antagonist. Harriet Prewett was as exceptional in life as Mrs. Eveleigh in fiction, but Simms's creation bears an uncanny resemblance not only to the fiery "editress" but to more conventional widows like Martha Singleton, Martha Jackson, and Natalie Sumter, who summoned up their multiple and intersecting privileges to defend their claims to mastery.[79]

IN CLOSING, it is worth recalling the Revolutionary setting that characterizes *Woodcraft* and several other Simms novels. In the 1850s, fire-eating southerners suggested that the South was the true heir of the American Revolution, a legacy the North had despoiled. The Revolution thus provided a potent backdrop for exploring the South's strengths and dangers, which Simms and other writers addressed more frontally in their nonfiction. To someone like Simms, the Revolution contained models not only for the South's political leaders, but also for its women. His review of Elizabeth Ellet's *Women of the Revolution* makes the point explicitly. While the review was generally favorable, Simms took the opportunity to make three key points. First, he extolled Ellet for her attention to "female virtue and patriotism . . . in the Southern section of the Union." The observation that Ellet had, in fact, gathered two-thirds of her material from the South supported the region's claim to be the true heir of the American struggle for independence. Second, Simms used Ellet's research and local lore to argue that, at moments of "doubt and peril," women could help their country by "overcoming the ordinary weaknesses of the sex." Most critically, while Ellet emphasized the Revolution's popular origins, Simms ascribed it solely to society's highest classes. He argued that women's service to the Revolution, which Ellet had so painstakingly documented, proved that the planter class had led the struggle; only among the higher orders, he averred, could women wield such authority.[80]

In this view, the ruling class comprised "the leading Men and Women,"[81] not just the leading men. And sometimes, the leading women were widowed householders, with the prerogatives of both mastery and ladyhood to summon up and defend. As Simms's writings suggest, in the figure of the slaveholding and especially the planter widow, gender hierarchy both masked and reinforced class privilege. Consequently, even as patriarchal thinking became ever more important in southern political discourse and public institutions, the region's growing socioeconomic inequality and urgent need to defend slavery from northern aggression both enhanced slaveholding widows' authority and gave their male peers new reasons to recognize, endorse, and even celebrate it.

CHAPTER 6

Worried in Body and Vexed in Heart

Slaveholding widows enjoyed far more personal autonomy and influence than did most white women of their era and region, but the power to determine at least some of the twists and turns in their own—and others' lives—came at a price. Losing their husbands broke some women's hearts, ruined others' health, and imposed weighty, usually uncomfortable, responsibilities on all of them. Assuming so many manly obligations had an impact on their sense of themselves, yet slaveholding widows were rarely introspective in their letters, diaries, and other writings. In myriad ways, however, they left indications that they could act masterfully without in fact feeling masterful or embracing their expanded powers. One could hardly hope to find a real-life widow who more closely matched the fictional Mrs. Eveleigh in bravado than Martha Richardson, yet even this self-proclaimed carver of her own fortune found that protecting her interests had its costs. "I have been worried in body and vexed at heart," she wrote; "I had not recovered my voyage, before I had to do much writing and then to undertake the journey to Charleston—there I had to wait four days in anxious agony of mind—It has cost me to lawyers six hundred & fifty dollars besides traveling &c—and shall I forget all this?"[1] Richardson's words reveal both her comparative freedom and the toll that fictive mastery exacted. She could travel as she pleased, and she could spend substantial sums defending her even larger property interests, but that very self-assertion brought emotional and physical strain.

For all that slaveholding widows varied in their age, fortune, location, and connections, several concerns were common to most: self-mastery, uselessness, and dependence. All struggled to control themselves as well as their households, and most found self-mastery at least as elusive as mastery over others. Widows' wills suggest that by life's end they had made some peace with their position as female masters. In keeping with what Suzanne Lebsock has called "personalism," their legacies suggest both a general concern for their kinswomen and an effort to consider particular needs among their heirs. At the same time, their wills reveal the ease with which they used property to express themselves and mold the future.[2] Other points in widowhood, however, involved emotional, psychological, spiritual, and even physical conflict, as women sought to comprehend their situation and govern themselves. Shortly after their husbands' deaths, widows often became "prostrate," an emotional and physical reaction suggesting both protest against and escape from the realities of their new position. This initial near-incapacitation generally yielded to various efforts to cope mentally as well as practically. For many, a key problem beyond loneliness and grief was the struggle to submit to God's will, as their religion demanded. This Christian idiom became the most common means for widows to express their campaign for self-mastery, which for most was a lifelong struggle.

The same circumstances that challenged widows' self-control could also make them feel useless in the world. Like their married peers, slaveholding widows typically judged themselves in terms of whether they were needed, especially by their immediate kin. For all the work they did, widows had their doubts on this subject, especially if they had no children as well as no husband "to lavish any affection upon," as Ada Bacot complained after burying her husband and two daughters.[3] Keeping busy with managerial concerns afforded limited protection against this feeling by occupying their attention. Some widows found even this imperfect refuge beyond their reach, however, as chronic or acute illness made them unable to keep up with either their work or their pleasures. Close kin to uselessness was dependence. Across the life cycle, slaveholding women had a more complex understanding of dependence than either contemporary law or social theory would have suggested; in ending slaveholding women's legal marital dependence, widowhood ironically exposed many of them to new and, to them, more uncomfortable forms of dependence.

Whether they felt overwhelmed, futile, or helpless, slaveholding widows often imagined death as a relief. In this period, most slaveholders believed or at least hoped that death would bring them to heaven where they would rejoin their beloved dead. This escapist vision brought comfort to some but grief to others who felt uncertain that they (or their dead) were worthy of heaven. Another possible escape, remarriage, could prove equally unreliable in practice. Slaveholding widows did not, as a rule, seek new husbands, even if they looked back with longing on what they remembered as happy, protected wifehood. Widowed mothers had to consider whether their children would have a good stepfather, and even childless and laboring widows thought twice about reentering coverture. For some, remarriage fulfilled their fondest hopes, but others discovered they would have been far wiser to have remained single. One such case involved South Carolina's Marion Deveaux, Martha Singleton's sister-in-law and Natalie Sumter's neighbor. Marion's second marriage, to clergyman Augustus Converse, proved a nightmare. Through her friends' intervention, however, she escaped her abusive husband. Her story thus had a happier ending than most, and it provides further proof of the decisive difference that wealth and connections made in slaveholding widows' lives.[4]

IN THE SLAVEHOLDING South, most widowhoods ended in death, not remarriage, and because most widows died from illness or old age, they had time to reflect on their lives, which women suddenly snatched off through violence, accident, or childbirth did not. Most widows did not, however, write letters or diaries to preserve their thoughts in the final months or years of widowhood. Only a very narrow slice of the Old South's white women wrote anything at all for the sake of pleasure, introspection, or immortality. A substantially broader cross section, however, wrote wills in which they left hints about their relationships, their self-images, and their beliefs about the world they were soon to leave. As Suzanne Lebsock has observed about the free women of Petersburg, slaveholding widows' testamentary choices illuminate their special concern for female relations and friends.[5]

In the early nineteenth century, southeastern statutes of distribution provided that an intestate decedent's children would share equally in his or her estate.[6] Writing wills allowed individuals to personalize their bequests, ensuring that a particular child received specified items instead of a mathematical share of the whole. By specifying which bed, dress, or teaspoons descended to which child, widows expressed a particular relationship with both their heirs and their belongings. Domestic articles, for example, suggested the bond created—for better and worse—between mothers and daughters as they performed the wide range of women's domestic chores. Esther Brandon's 1821 will allowed her three unmarried daughters to claim whatever "household furniture" they had made (a category which likely comprised linens rather than what we would today call furniture). The care with which some women described comparatively unvaluable household and personal items, as opposed to more expensive livestock and farm equipment, suggests another way that their self-image remained entwined with female housework and the possibility of sharing it with other women.[7]

Writing a will also allowed parents to give unequal legacies to their children. Thus, fathers typically gave their most valuable properties to sons rather than daughters, and they often distinguished among children of the same sex as well. For their part, slaveholding widows gave most of their personal property to female heirs. This practice reflected the simple fact that they owned items like aprons, linens, and cookware, and since housekeeping was women's work, few saw any reason to give such things to men. Some even bequeathed linens and kitchenware to daughters-in-law rather than sons. By the same token, widows left most of their land and slaves to men. However, widows with land or slaves were significantly more likely to bequeath it to women than men were. In North Carolina's Rowan County, for example, more than half of the landed widows bequeathed some or all of their land to female heirs, usually daughters, but only a quarter of the landed male testators gave land to their daughters. Similarly, 60 percent of the slaveowning widows and under 40 percent of the slaveowning men bequeathed slaves to female heirs. At times, this favoritism simply redressed a previous imbalance in favor of sons. Thus, Mary McNeely gave "more to my daughters and less to my son because he received a larger share of his Fathers Estate."[8] In addition to commenting on past patterns, wills also looked forward. Some widows tried to protect their daughters by shielding their legacies from current or future husbands. In 1821, Catharine Foy reserved her daughter's bequest to her and the heirs of her body. The following year, Catherine Barger stipulated that her son-in-law "shall have no right nor claim" to his wife's legacy. Charleston's Mary Motte similarly restricted her daughters' legacies to their "separate and exclusive use," reinforcing their previous marriage settlements.[9] These legacies could give a wife somewhat greater leverage or independence in her marriage by giving her an income of her own. They also provided a buffer against financial reverses because creditors could not seize a wife's separate property to pay her husband's debts. Finally, a separate estate ensured that a woman would have more than her minimum dower thirds if she outlived her husband. Creating separate estates in this fashion never became commonplace before the Civil War, but mothers more often reserved property to women and their heirs than did fathers.[10]

This preference for female heirs was far from automatic, however. In their wills, widows considered their children's behavior and circumstances, often rewarding their more affectionate offspring. Elizabeth Tomlinson received a more generous legacy than her siblings because she "staid with" and "waited on" her mother. "Infirm & blind" Catharina Garinger favored Lewis Peck over his siblings because he had incurred "great trouble & expence" to care for her. Sarah Elliott's will similarly provided her son Abner with "some remuneration for his care and attention."[11] In considering their children's needs, meanwhile, widows attached particular significance to widowhood itself. Some, like Eliza Flinn and Jane Cocke, often concluded that widowed daughters needed help more than their sons or other daughters did.[12] Elizabeth Leonard left the bulk of her estate to her widowed daughter; she reasoned that widows needed the most financial help, and she further justified her choice by reflecting that her other children had done quite well in previous distributions of the family wealth. As we have seen, Charleston's Eliza Flinn rewrote her will to give her newly widowed daughter a greater share of her estate.[13] In privileging female heirs, protecting their inheritances, and making widowhood a factor in bequests, slaveholding women acknowledged both their emotional investment in other women and the peculiar hazards of widowhood.

A subtler pattern emerges from considering whom widows named as heirs. In addition to giving generously to kinswomen and friends, they tended to have more female than male heirs, and to have more female heirs generally than men did. When slaveholding widows bequeathed property to kin other than their own children, for example, they showed a slight preference for nieces over nephews, granddaughters over grandsons. Childless widows typically left more or most of their property to sisters or mothers as opposed to brothers. Widows with few or no surviving relations made bequests to friends, who were almost invariably other women. The profusion of female heirs—and the comparative generosity of their legacies —suggest that widows found special value in their female networks even though as widows they relied heavily on men for financial, legal, and managerial help.[14] By preferring their female kin and friends, slaveholding widows offered up a quiet counterweight to the more conservative contemporary visions of woman's place.[15] While most widows never remarried, for example, few if any encouraged their daughters to remain single. Instead, widows used their property and legal discretion to offer their daughters some financial protection within marriage. Slaveholding widows' decisions to favor female kin and friends also reflected their own relationships with men. These women knew full well how much they depended on male kin and friends, yet their wills evince no obligation to repay this help and little of the fulsome gratitude that occasionally accompanied requests for manly assistance. Slaveholding widows had two somewhat contradictory reasons to take men's help for granted. On the one hand, receiving help from men reflected the historical conventions of feminine dependence and masculine protection. On the other, it was also an example of the reciprocal assistance that kinsmen and women extended each other, a pattern in which gender hierarchy played a secondary role. Both interpretations rendered men's help ordinary and normative, not something that demanded special recognition.

Widows' wills suggest how far they had traveled from the conservative norm of female self-abnegation in yet a further way. Not only did their wills favor women, widows, and female control over property, their very existence also suggested widows' sense of possession, both of property and of themselves. In writing wills, widows took full advantage of ownership instead of acting as if they had merely borrowed their property, held it on another's sufferance, or had only a custodial interest in it. They behaved, in short, as if they had the moral as well as the legal right to do what they pleased with the property they owned. Their wills also bespoke a sense of entitlement with regard to drawing obvious distinctions among their children, distinctions which the probate process would eventually make public. Their choices did not suggest the arbitrary power of an absolute patriarch, but then again, neither did most men's in the early nineteenth century since more paternalist notions of parental patriarchy had largely supplanted the stricter authority of earlier generations. Wielding their pens—and their property—as tools of self-representation and judgment, testating widows acted with a masterly sense of authority near the close of life.

AS SOURCES OF information about widows' property, relationships, and attitudes, wills are invaluable. For providing a general picture of widowhood, however, they are deeply flawed in that they tend to reflect the mind-set of women who had typically been widowed for long enough to become habituated to its distinctive demands and opportunities. Letters and diaries, especially from earlier in widowhood, provide a much more mixed sense of women's state of mind than the resignation evident in their wills.[16] Particularly important in early widowhood was the struggle for composure; widows labored mightily to keep their emotions in check as befit their secular responsibilities, social propriety, and religious duty. Their repeated failures—bouts of wild grief, despair, lassitude, and rage—were ironically a sign of the importance they attached to the elusive goal of self-mastery.

Slaveholding women's initial reactions to their husbands' deaths often suggested a decisive loss of mental and bodily self-possession. Lucy Thornton and Martha Cocke felt that their losses nearly killed them; Thornton recalled a "fatal shock" and Cocke a "*fatal blow*" which destroyed her "peace of mind." A year after John Wesley Lewis died, Catherine assumed she would soon follow him to the grave. Ada Bacot's diary suggests that she too expected to die; after four years alone, Bacot recalled a time when she never imagined she would live so long. At times, new widows became physically ill. Martha Cocke complained that she could not sleep at night, suffering from "almost constant pain in the brest with a considerable loss of strength and flesh." Fifty years later, Pocahontas Hairston experienced similar symptoms. According to her father, she was "confined to her bed —2/3s of the time" and was "utterly broken down—physically."[17] Widowhood also elicited a language of mental stupefaction. Pocahontas's father described her as "evidently stunned, by the agony she had endured." Caroline Laurens feared for her sanity. The morning after her husband died, she wrote, she "awoke at the dawn of day quite bewildered." She knew she "had met with a great loss, but at first I could not think what it was." When memory returned, "I sighed & mourned aloud . . . I thought I should lose my reason." When Howell Cobb's sister-in-law Mary Athena Lamar lost her husband suddenly, her Cobb connections worried that she had apparently "lost her sense." So unrestrained was Mary Athena's anguish that she frightened her young daughter, Sissa, who was for several days "unwilling to go where her mother was."[18]

These extremes of stunned or hysterical behavior may have provided a refuge from the pressure widows felt to master their feelings. Caroline Laurens's first days of widowhood were unusual, but her "sense of propriety" was not. Her husband died on a ship returning from an unsuccessful European tour that the couple had undertaken to improve his health.[19] During nearly three weeks of travel between John's death and her arrival back home in South Carolina, Caroline's "sense of propriety dictated, that I should command my feelings in so public a situation." She confided to her diary that she would "have been greatly relieved by giving vent to nature & crying aloud," but she felt bound to maintain her composure, and in any case, she had "not a single friend" on board the ship "to weep with." When she finally reached family and comparative privacy, she found "inexpressible" "relief & comfort" in her mother-in-law's arms. Yet immediately after this release, she hastened to regain control. As she recalled, "I did not wish my children to see me before I was able to command my self."[20]

Christian teachings demanded more than the surface appearance of self-control. Most slaveholders believed that "the awful visitations of Death" reflected "the inscrutable providence of God." Because "God knows what is best," it was "impious" and "sinful" to "murmur or repine." Yet for slaveholding widows like Martha Cocke and Catherine Lewis, true submission to divine providence did not come easily.[21] In the months after her husband's death, Martha Cocke recognized that she must "endeavour to submit with patience," but fully twelve years later, she continued to protest "the hardness" of fate. Nonetheless, "I will supress all disposition to murmur," she continued wearily, "knowing it to be unavailing and that it has a tendency to increase rather than lessen the evil of which we complain." Catherine Lewis also sought resignation, but years after her husband died, she admitted, "I cant feel but that I would give ten thousand worlds to have him back." Another three years later, she felt "more resigned," but still fell short of being "perfectly submissive."[22] This language of submission could be taken as a sign of weakness and passivity, but to slaveholding widows, it meant struggle and even strength. Slaveholding widows frequently observed that God demanded resignation, but apparently God did not create that feeling of acceptance. Instead, individuals had to forge it in themselves, and most found it extremely difficult to bring themselves to an appropriate state of mind and heart. As they fought and prayed for resignation, they took comfort from the thought that "what God makes necessary He gives strength to us to perform."[23] As Elizabeth Lee announced to her brother, "you will find me strong in mind and willing to submit." Using very similar language, Caroline Marx admired newly widowed Eliza Ruffin's "strength of mind and resignation."[24]

Widows of the early republic often framed their efforts at submission and self-governance as a contest between reason and emotion. As Martha Cocke put it, in the midst of mourning, reason was "weak" and "flimsy" in comparison to "feeling or nature." Caroline Laurens believed her reason was strained to the breaking point by the effort to stifle her emotions and avoid giving "vent to nature." These bereaved women fought to reduce their passions to the more moderate feelings of resignation. Immoderation, as Benjamin Franklin's writings most famously suggested, imperiled mind, soul, and health. Uncontrolled grief also had the potential to injure widows' secular interests in managing property and serving their families.[25] Widows born in the antebellum generation had a slightly different problem with the balance between reason and emotion. The diffusion of sentimentalism, widespread in print culture, and evangelicalism, the dominant religious mode in the white South, both placed considerable stress on emotional expression, especially for women. However, the ability to rein in their feelings was a practical and social necessity. Shortly before the Civil War, Ada Bacot congratulated herself for keeping her composure during one of many quarrels with her father and her eldest brother. In her diary, she recalled that they berated her steadily for a variety of sins, and "twas by the strongest effort I could scarsely restrain my tears." Refusing to give way, she "got up quietly" and left the room. Yet while she had won a small victory in avoiding public weeping, she lost another one. Once she retired to her room, she hoped "to relieve my wounded heart in tears," but she discovered that "as I had checked them, they will not now flow."[26] The strength needed to master themselves and their situation, in other words, left at least some women feeling unable to release their feelings in tears, a quintessential sign of womanliness in antebellum sentimental culture.

The effort to regulate their emotions may also have prompted some widows to accuse themselves of religious dullness. In addition to lamenting her "*want* of resignation to the will of God," Presbyterian Paulina Legrand complained of her "wicked unbelieving heart—and of coldness & deadness in religion."[27] Occasionally, fellow Presbyterian Dolly Burge "felt that a Friend was near to me one that sticketh closer than a brother!" More often, however, she felt discontented with her own spirituality, fretting that she felt "little enjoyment in religion" and that she made "so little improvement in the Divine life that I am ashamed." Baptist Keziah Brevard similarly complained that her heart had "grown cold in religious duties."[28] Evangelicalism's disdain for worldly things only aggravated the problem by prompting slaveholding widows to blame their religious deadness on their few consolations. After her husband and child died, Dolly Burge lamented that even now she was "glued yet to earth & the things thereof." Widowed mothers brooded that cherishing their children demonstrated their worldliness. Baptist Martha Jackson worried throughout her life that she paid too much attention to secular matters. Three years into her marriage to Henry Jackson, she fretted that she had used sickness as an excuse to abandon her religious writings when the real reason lay elsewhere. "Oh the deceitfulness of the heart," she lamented, "that is ever willing to avail itself of every specious pretext. The true cause was coldness & deadness of soul arising from temporal prosperity. . . . The inestimable gifts of a kind, tender & indulgent Husband, & lovely interesting Infant . . . have led me too much into Egypt." After Henry's death, Martha remained concerned about these profane attachments. Like many widowed mothers, she delighted in her "dear children, for whose sake alone . . . life is desirable." Yet she also feared that her love for Henry, Sarah, and Martha "keeps me at a distance from thee." Thus the very relationships that gave slaveholding widows some joy—and provided their most powerful incentive to manage their property well—could provoke gnawing religious guilt.[29]

Antebellum widows also thought harshly of themselves for the sin of anger. Keziah Brevard's problems with her slaves engendered a near-constant campaign against her own temper. In her diary, she admitted that she "often" felt angry, and she regularly prayed for help in checking "all sinful risings in this breast of mine." Despite her efforts "to conquer every sin I have," she found anger a difficult "master" to resist. Despairing of her "unmanageable" heart, she wrote in July 1860 that "I wish I knew what produced anger in the human body." Had she chosen to recognize it, she could have seen a clear relationship between her fits of temper and her slaves, especially her domestic servants. The day her house slaves served up "a mess of a dinner," for example, she vented her feelings in her diary and, most likely, on her slaves' bodies, noting, "Sometimes my anger rises in spite of all I can do." Over the next few days, Brevard repeatedly gave way to "pettish" outbursts over "trifles." She marveled that "a trifle" often caused anger "to blaze sky high in a twinkling—then if God does not check it changes man or woman into a demon." From childhood on, slaveholding women heard and read that they should be mild and complaisant, restraining their own feelings in the service of others. At the same time, they found "the trials of domestic life," to use Virginia Cary's phrase, ample provocation and excuse for rage. Once widowed, their emotional strain increased in tandem with their responsibilities.[30]

Ill health formed yet another obstacle in widows' quest for self-mastery. Decade after decade, women complained that sore eyes, colds, or more severe afflictions kept them from work and pleasures. In 1792, her children's sickness and her own, "violent & incessant," prevented Penelope Dawson from keeping up with her duties. "Almost worn out," she finally picked up her pen to write a long overdue letter to Hannah Iredell, passing along family news and following up on some neglected business. In the early fall of 1821, Eliza Flinn's eyes became so inflamed "that I could not wear my Glasses to read or write." At seventy-five, Paulina Legrand suffered a more permanent deterioration in her eyes, explaining, "I am not well and one of my Eyes still soar. . . . Excuse this scroll I write in hast & in pain." Natalie Sumter rarely let emotions color her diary, but bouts of sleeplessness and fever led her to complain of being "tired to Death."[31] Ada Bacot found that her health problems aggravated her uneasy relationship with her father. After yet another argument, Ada hoped "to gain by degrees a better command of myself," but her physical state interfered. "My health is miserable," she wrote, and "there are time[s] when" headaches, sleepless nights, and general malaise made her "very nearly crazy."[32] At the extreme, slaveholding widows lost partial or full control over themselves. Shortly before her death in 1858, Elizabeth Lee found herself "a criple for the remainder of life unable to move to the right or left." She could still hold a pencil to write, but she had to be placed in her chair by her granddaughter and nurse. Lucy Thornton spent her last eight or nine years in even worse shape, completely bedridden and "deprived" of her "mental powers."[33]

The state of medical science in the nineteenth century probably aggravated widows' sufferings. Although American doctors generally disavowed the "heroic" extremes practiced by the likes of Benjamin Rush in the 1790s —massive doses of mercury and torrential bleedings—they continued to prescribe blisters, purgatives, emetics, and bloodletting.[34] Seeking to correct Pocahontas Hairston's disordered state, a doctor gave her "external applications . . . on the back of the neck, & spine &c." Patients also drank medicines including toxic ingredients like mercury as well as useful but potentially dangerous opiates. Natalie Sumter's pharmacopeia included calomel (a mercury compound), the purgative jalap, and several emetics, including salts, castor oil, and snakeroot. Perhaps as much because of these medicines as her illness itself, she occasionally reported that she could not "do anything in great pain with a fever & not in my right senses."[35] While the medical equation of balance with health usually complemented the imperatives of self-mastery, at the end of life, every slaveholding widow lost the battle to control herself and her household. The medicines some took to relieve their pain further loosened their grasp.[36] During the last days of her terminal illness, Louisa Alexander was "constantly under the influence of opium." Looking at "her sunken & pain marked face," her son Adam concluded that "her end cannot be far distant" and hoped above all "that she may be kept easy, for that seems to me all that can be done." A few days later, he observed that "she has been so stupified with opiates for the last few days, that it has been impossible to have any communications with her." The prevalence of opium and laudanum in slaveholders' cupboards strongly suggests that many slaveholders spent at least some time in a drugged state.[37]

In its various guises of balance, submission, resignation, and composure, self-mastery left a great deal to be desired; it was both a scant comfort and an unreachable goal. Small wonder, then, that slaveholding widows sometimes lapsed into despair or lassitude. A decade into her widowhood, Martha Cocke still wrestled with low spirits and their adverse impact on her physical well-being. As a kinswoman observed, she needed "some object in taking exercise, more than mere health." She herself knew "the necessity of it," but found it "impossible to rouse herself to exertion, without some added stimulus." Eventually, Martha decided to seek that stimulus in renting and managing a farm, shouldering responsibilities she had previously delegated to male agents. Like Martha Cocke, many slaveholding widows found that while the twinned tasks of self- and household mastery were taxing, even exhausting work, they were nonetheless preferable to other possibilities, such as idleness, uselessness, and dependence.[38]

WHEN ADA BACOT left her father's house in the spring of 1861 to return to her own plantation, she confronted the unhappy difference between her present and her past. She recalled that, when she first went to Arnmore, "twas to be the mistress of the house a loving husband provided." Returning four years after he died, she knew that "I shall be constantly reminded of my former life there, under how different circumstances do I now go there. Memory carrys me back to the happy time, & fills my eyes with tears." While Bacot half-expected the dead to haunt her, she also feared that she would be "lonly." Yet being at Arnmore had some consolations. Ten days after moving, she "began to feel quite settled alredy, & I dont think I am to be so lonly as every one predicts." She added sagely, "If I am twill not be because I've not a plenty of work."[39] Keeping busy in one's own household had a great deal to commend it, especially for a woman like Bacot who could not comfortably live with her closest relations. Householders could also take pride in successful harvests, and those who, like Lucy Freeman, finally made ends meet after years of struggle likely felt a particular satisfaction. Living in comparatively "independent circumstances" did not, however, automatically assuage widows' feelings of uselessness and insignificance although it did keep at bay the ignominy of dependence.[40]

Even the busiest widow sometimes questioned the value of her labors. Executing her husband's estate, supervising a farm in Georgia, raising her daughters, advising her extended family, and absentee-managing a plantation in Alabama kept Martha Jackson occupied but not necessarily cheerful. Particularly depressing were the abysmally low cotton prices, which made her doubt she could ever pay off her debts. After three years, she mused that she might be better off dead; then, she would cease to be a burden to her family and could join her husband in heaven. Jackson's relations scolded her for such gloom, insisting that "your day of usefulness is not passed," and indeed she remained an important resource to her family until shortly before her death in 1853. Her relations' reliance on her, and their ardent affirmation that her "advice and counsel is still needed," lifted her spirits only temporarily, however, and she continued to need such reassurances until she died.[41] At Arnmore, meanwhile, Ada Bacot learned that being "my own mistress" did not abate her feelings of worthlessness. Similarly, Keziah Brevard's diary documents an impressive degree of managerial and hands-on work in and around her household, yet she felt that "if I had been torpid all my life I would have been as useful." Shortly before her fifty-eighth birthday, she again mused, "If I had been a useful woman these many years what a happiness 'twould be to take a retrospect of them —I cannot see what I have done to any one or in any cause to make me feel I have been useful in my generation."[42]

Childlessness exacerbated the insecurities of women like Keziah Brevard and Ada Bacot. Raising children proved as essential to most slaveholding women's sense of self as marrying; without children, many felt incomplete. Being a mother confirmed both a woman's essential femininity and the value of that femaleness. Having borne and buried children was not enough; these women had an advantage over those who had never even been pregnant, but they too lacked the ongoing validation of motherhood. Above and beyond the grief that mothers felt for their dead children, these widows also missed children's affection and the sense of purpose that mothering had provided. Childlessness posed a particular threat to widows because they spent so much of their time enmeshed in masculine responsibilities. Quite simply, motherhood helped anchor slaveholding widows' identities as women. As a wife, Catherine Lewis grumbled about her rowdy sons and resented that motherhood limited her ability to visit far-flung kin. As a widow, she continued to find her sons difficult, especially her eldest, but she also came to treasure them as living memorials of her husband. Drawing on her experience, Lewis later urged her newly widowed sister-in-law to "live in & for your children who are a part & parcel of him whom above all others you loved & clung to." Maternal obligations also had practical import in providing widows with a distinctively feminine means of self-representation. Lewis pronounced herself "willing to do anything to make a support for my family," making a virtue of her need to run a boardinghouse.[43] Simultaneously female masters and self-sacrificing mothers, widows like Catherine Lewis did not so much bridge the customary gender divide in slaveholding society as they walked on both sides of the line. For the childless, meanwhile, mastery alone could not compensate for the lack of both husbands and children. "Sad & alone," Ada Bacot characterized her existence as "cold, tame, & worldly." Keziah Brevard compared herself unfavorably to her sister-in-law, Peggy Brevard, who was "so much happier than I am." Keziah ascribed the difference to Peggy's motherhood, sighing, "She has more to interest her with the world than I have—a good daughter—intelligent & well informed—a Son in law whom she may be proud off & bright Grand Children growing up around her—all these make her live her youth over." Keziah struggled to convince herself that she did not "envy my sister—no—no," but she still felt that Peggy "has been a useful woman while I have been a blank." In Keziah's own estimation, all her success as a widowed planter with more than two hundred slaves could not compensate for her unhappy and childless marriage.[44]

While Keziah Brevard and Ada Bacot found their "independent circumstances" morally and emotionally dull or "blank," other widows who struggled with dependence might gladly have traded places. Like their male peers, slaveholding women saw dependence as a potentially humiliating and degrading status. As Serena Lea remarked to her sister Martha Jackson, "A dependent situation must I know be a dreadful one."[45] These women did not usually consider their own dependence within marriage in this light. In this case, Serena was writing not about herself as a *femme covert* but about her widowed sister-in-law, Emily Rootes. Before Jaquelin Rootes died in the summer of 1840, he and his family were living with the Leas, apparently because of his illness and alcoholism. After his death, Emily and the children continued to live with the Leas since Jaquelin had not left enough property for them to have a household of their own. When

Serena wrote her sister Martha about the horrors of dependence, Emily was debating her options. She could remain where she was, with the Leas. She could also move back to Virginia, where her mother lived; her mother had offered financial assistance if she returned from Alabama. Both of these situations left her uncomfortably dependent, however, and in the end, Emily Rootes chose a third course, remarriage. From her (and Serena Lea's) point of view, this was a step away from, not toward, a shameful sort of dependence. In marriage, it was right and proper for women to rely on their husbands financially. For an otherwise competent adult woman, however, being financially dependent upon someone other than a husband was something else again. Receiving help from relations did not make widows feel humiliated or guilty, but too pronounced a reliance was uncomfortable. As one financially beholden widow concluded, she simply could not remain "entirely dependent on my father for maintenance."[46]

Slaveholding women were not alone in disliking female financial dependence outside of marriage. Entrusted with the interests of his widowed aunt, Judith Archer, and her daughters, Richard T. Archer was certain his mandate included protecting their financial security and autonomy, declaring, "They are in circumstances if they wish it to board in any genteel house in any city or to live in comfort and independence wheresoever they may fix. I should but poorly repay the affection and confidence with which they rely on me if I could consent to let them live in a state of dependence even on a brother. This they never shall be reduced to while I live."[47] Even when the real culprit was bad luck or the volatile business cycle, depending on kin reflected poorly on a widow and on her husband's memory. Raised in a political culture that celebrated republican independence, slaveholding widows easily became uncomfortable with both implications. Similarly, Richard T. Archer apparently felt honor-bound to protect his aunt's propertied independence.

Most slaveholding widows who needed help from others did not, like Emily Rootes, opt for the fuller dependence of coverture, but rather found other means to minimize the stigma of financial dependence on others. Simplest to reconcile with their own and their dead husbands' dignity were episodic and usually reciprocal debts to family and friends. These posed no problem because they were an expression of personal attachments. At times, however, widows received favors, assistance, or money which they could not reciprocate. In these cases, the letters in which they expressed their gratitude can seem self-abasing. Yet the language of thanks itself became a sort of payment, as Ann Wheeler's letters to her benefactor and cousin Ruth Hairston suggest. Ann Wheeler could hardly hope to avoid financial dependence. While she earned some money sewing, and hoped her sons would one day be able to support her, she also leaned heavily on Ruth Hairston's bounty. For at least four years, Ruth paid for the tuition, board, and clothing of Ann's son Charlie. Ruth also sent cash directly to Ann for her other children. Because Ann could not return these favors in money or kind, she repaid them with praise, deference, and information. In her letters, she passed along the rewarding news that Charlie's teacher "has never seen a better boy, or a better scholar." Ann included this information because "I know it is a source of great pleasure to you to know that your kindness has not been thrown away on a worthless boy." She continued, "I hope & pray . . . that he will make you proud to know, that you have made him what he is." With these words, Ann made Ruth Hairston instrumental in her son's future success, but she also used their familial connection to soften charity's otherwise chafing obligations. By offering up this and other family news that Ruth might not otherwise have gotten, Ann made the much richer woman at least somewhat indebted to her, which indirectly offset her own financial debt.[48]

Even more than letters to beneficent family members, widows' correspondence with charitable friends and strangers illustrates their discomfort with dependence. In writing to a benefactor, Mary Campbell wrestled with the fact that she could only return "a small pittance" in exchange for "many and great obligations conferred on me." In signing her letter as "your forever obligated friend & obedient, Humble servant," Campbell encapsulated her dilemma: Charles Mortimer's assistance so far exceeded the ordinary give and take between friends that her obligation to him permanently inflected their relationship. Unlike a debt to a bank or a commercial creditor, her debt to Mortimer could never be discharged with money. Indeed, only an "unmindful, or ungreatfull" person could ever feel completely independent of so great a benefactor. Campbell's language evokes the trope —and trap—of dependence in general and feminine dependence in particular. As it happened, however, Campbell remained largely independent, perhaps thanks to Mortimer's help. At her death, she owned some three dozen slaves and considerable personal property.[49]

Widows' efforts to reconcile their dignity with dependence become even clearer in an unusual series of letters from the 1850s. The letters followed the publication of a short article about Samuel Hairston (Ruth Hairston's son-in-law) which described him as "the richest man in Virginia." At least one version of the widely reprinted article noted his generosity as well as his wealth, and this prompted dozens of people from across the United States to write Hairston, asking him to employ them, buy their land, or give them money. Among the petitioners—all apparently unsuccessful—were three southern widows. First to write was a widowed planter from Louisiana. Mrs. Baillio explained that her husband had owned a large plantation, but like many other planters he died heavily indebted. Unless his property could be sold for "something like an equivalent for its value," she and her children would be left "pennyless." She urged Hairston to "save a helpless family from ruin" by buying her plantation. (The newspaper article had included the improbable claim that he needed to buy a new plantation every year just to accommodate his slaves' natural increase.) To excuse her boldness in thus soliciting an utter stranger, Mrs. Baillio appealed to motherhood, asking, "What will not a mother with eight little children dependent on her, strive to do to better their fortunes?" Yet Mrs. Baillio did not rest her case with that reference to defenseless, pathetic widowhood. Instead, she simultaneously represented herself as a sensible, resourceful planter and framed the purchase of her plantation as a business opportunity for him, not just a charity to her. In making this proposal, Mrs. Baillio knowledgeably discussed price and acreage as well as the deflating impact of the "European War" and lands in Texas on prices in her region, which framed her approach to Hairston as a conversation among planters, not a petition from sub- to superordinate.[50]

The second southern widow to write Hairston was Pamela Crisp of Yanceyville, North Carolina. This nonslaveholder wasted no words trying to represent herself as a peer or obscure that she was asking for charity. Instead, she baldly stated her desperation, writing, "I have been so unfortunate as to loose my husband I am left with 2 children & entirely dependent. I haven a servant nor a home I dont own a particle of property of any sort—I was reading in the paper of your large amount of property, & I though[t] I would write you of my situation begging you to help me in any you think proper." This letter made no pretense that its author could return a favor or repay a debt. Crisp further revealed her humility (although not necessarily humiliation) when she forbore to specify just what type or amount of assistance would be most useful.[51]

The third supplicant, Lucetta Clove, fell somewhere between Crisp and Baillio in her circumstances, and her letter reflects the difficulty of reconciling her petition with her social aspirations. Writing from Culpeper, Virginia, Clove explained that her husband "had not been in business long enough to accumulate much" before he died. As a result, "with no friend to lend me a helping hand," she found herself "behindhand" in paying his debts even though she had made "every exertion and gleaned every point." When she saw the Hairston article, she claimed, "The thought at once flashed into my mind perhaps this good man whom the Lord has so bountifully blest . . . might bestow a mite upon me if I would ask it and make known my need." This inspiration did not, however, immediately lead her to write Hairston because deciding to approach a stranger for aid was "a great struggle I assure you." Only the reflection that "I have no one to protect me now no strong arm to sustain me and keep me from the hardship of unceasing labour" emboldened her to write. Clove's letter omitted none of slaveholding widowhood's most sympathetic associations. With just a few lines, she evoked the widow's proverbial desolation and isolation, her noble resolve to support her family, and God's promise to be "a friend to the widow." Perhaps the most important thread in this widow's tapestry, however, was chivalry, which had the power to convert a poor woman's shameful dependence—and even more shameful solicitation of a stranger—into the seemly appeal of a lady to a gentleman. To work this alchemy, Clove had to demonstrate her right to be considered a lady. Both the physical appearance of her letter and its content spoke in her favor. Her penmanship and diction bespoke a certain refinement while her observation that widowhood had imposed the "hardship of unceasing labour" implied her membership in that small class of women who did not consider hard work an ordinary condition of life. To seal her case, Clove asserted her moral delicacy, requesting, "Should you not choose to notice this letter, please Sir burn it and think no more of it." Clove knew full well that writing this letter to a stranger made her unusually vulnerable to dishonor, and she signaled her own propriety precisely by expressing her worry that Hairston would think ill of her. In contrast, Pamela Crisp could barely aspire to the damsel-in-distress trope that Clove employed, while Mrs. Baillio paired it with a businesslike approach to a peer.[52]

That slaveholding widows with the powers of fictive mastery still worried about being shamefully useless and dependent suggests both the strength and weakness of their position. On the one hand, however discontented and even helpless they felt, they had the social privileges of whiteness and ladyhood, the material compensations of comparative (or absolute) wealth, and enormous power over their own dependents, especially their slaves. On the other hand, slaveholding widows' emotional discontent confirms that they could not make householding and slave management the be-all and end-all of their identities. While those activities confirmed white men's gender identity, they bore a more indirect, even vexed, relationship to white women's. To avoid threatening their femininity, slaveholding widows almost had to cast their masterful activities in terms of service to their husbands' memories or, better, their own children. But even when maternity anchored their feminine identities, slaveholding widows often longed for an escape. Eventually, they all found one of sorts: most in death, and a few in remarriage.

WHILE MANY slaveholding widows looked back on marriage with regret and longing, their papers suggest that most spent more time dreaming about reuniting with their husbands in heaven than about creating a heaven on earth with a new husband. In other words, they looked forward to death, not remarriage. While the slaveholding South had no tradition of acceptable suicide, and widows shuddered "at the imputation of such a crime," death was, after all, a certainty while a happy marriage was anything but, as some of them knew from experience. Not all widows had the opportunity to remarry, but even those with desirable suitors still hesitated in part because they envisioned themselves so completely through the lens of duty to their dead husbands.[53]

Through months, years, and even decades of widowhood, slaveholding women imagined heaven as the place where they would rejoin their husbands and where "parting will be no more."[54] Ignoring gloomy predictions that death "severed" earthly connections, slaveholders hoped that familial and conjugal bonds would prove eternal. Thus, Ann Swann painstakingly transcribed excerpts concerning "Recognition of Friends in a future state of heaven" and "Knowledge of each other in Heaven" into her commonplace book, reflecting her hope of rejoining her husband and children.[55] Tellingly, even women whose married lives had not always been very happy looked forward to reuniting with their husbands. During her marriage, Catherine Lewis complained of her husband's selfishness far more candidly than many wives. Openly "envying men the pleasure they enjoy," she grumbled that her domestic duties meant that she was rarely "out of sight of" her hearth and cradle, while her husband was free to travel as he pleased. Once John Wesley Lewis died, however, Catherine found the travails of a boardinghouse keeper and mother of several orphaned children even more restricting, and the idea of heaven all the more delightful.[56]

For some widows, however, belief in heaven as a place of reunion itself caused pain. Among the evangelical sects, some despaired of having a soul-saving conversion experience. Even those who had been reborn felt themselves spiritually deficient at one point or another, and at those times, thoughts of heaven could grieve rather than console. Mary Athena Lamar "never felt that my sins were forgiven," and she nearly despaired of conversion. Worse, her husband died "unassisted by Divine comfort" (and perhaps had been murdered by his slaves), which made it harder for her to take any solace from her faith. Caroline Laurens excoriated herself for neglecting her husband's spiritual state. Had she discussed religion more often, she believed, "he would have had his mind so calmed . . . he would have resigned himself to God with out a struggle." As it happened, Laurens feared her husband's soul might not "be resting in peace." Natalie Sumter likewise felt uncertain that her "departed husband & child" were in heaven, but as a Catholic, she at least could read masses for their souls and pray that God would be "merciful" to them so that "we may be happy in Eternity."[57]

Although escapist thoughts of heaven could lead widows to dwell overmuch on death, most found the subject less confusing than remarriage, a secular solution to the problems of widowhood. In part, this confusion stemmed from and reflected a broad decline in the frequency of second or third marriages. In the colonial South, widows and widowers alike typically remarried quickly. By the nineteenth century, however, widows' rates of remarriage had declined significantly while widowers continued to remarry regularly. (This southern trend echoed contemporaneous patterns in the North and England.) At first glance, this reluctance to wed again may seem curious, given slaveholding women's dissatisfaction with their widowed state. Yet while most found widowhood no picnic, they had good reason not to rush into remarriage, as the profile of those who remained single suggests. Poor widows, childless women, and mothers who wanted a father for their young children were the most likely to remarry. In contrast, slaveholding women who had passed their childbearing years were especially unlikely to marry, as were the wealthiest women. Rich widows had little need to marry, provided that they could manage their properties themselves or find agents to do so. In addition, they had reason to fear coverture. Even a separate estate only partially mitigated the loss of control over themselves and their property, and many women held their dowers only as long as they remained widowed, a powerful incentive to stay single.[58] Less tangibly, widows' habit of attributing their actions to devotion to their dead husbands likely inhibited some of them from imagining a new one. Widows' uncertainty about remarriage also appeared in their use of biblical teachings. The promise that God would be "a husband to the widow and a father to the fatherless" appeared to give widows some trouble. When Catherine Lewis referenced this text, for example, she ignored the idea that she might have a divine husband. Instead, she wrote only of the "'widows God and Father of the fatherless.'"[59] Others also concentrated on the promise of a heavenly father for their orphaned children and omitted the husband. A condolence letter written to Martha Singleton assured her that God would be a "father" to her as well as her children. Combined with low rates of remarriage, these words may indicate a sense that widows need not and perhaps should not remarry.[60]

Some widows did seek remarriage, however, and for most, no single motive took priority.[61] Instead, practical and emotional factors combined to make an offer irresistible. After Samuel Lewis died in the fall of 1843, his widow Dolly supported herself as a teacher. This career provided some personal satisfaction and enabled Dolly to support herself, yet she still felt lonesome and somewhat purposeless. In February 1848, she fretted that "this keeping house without a man I don't much like." Dolly's feelings about housekeeping probably owed something to the fact that she had outlived three children as well as her husband; living only for herself and her work was simply not enough.[62] Being childless, lonely, and financially struggling did not prevent widows from approaching a new marriage with gravity and hesitation, however. In her diary, Dolly left an unusually explicit record of her concerns and hopes as she considered marrying Thomas Burge in the winter of 1849–50. Late in 1849, Lewis accepted Burge's proposal, but she quickly regretted her decision and poured out her doubts in one of her diary's longer passages: "What have I done? Am I not dreaming? What means it all. Why these heavy forebodings? Oh, my Father Who art in Heaven give me the assurance of a right heart in this matter. Let me feel that I am under thy Heavenly Guidance and direction in this. . . . I have often joked & laughed about marrying & though I have when asked always refused yet I am caught this time. Is my heart truly interested? Do I love him to whom I am about to commit my all of earthly happiness? Can I take upon myself the most solemn of all oaths to Love Honour & Obey one to whom I am so utterly a stranger! . . . Can I add to the happiness and comfort of Him who offers me his name?"[63] Dolly's words speak volumes about the esteem in which she held marital commitments.

Thomas Burge's proposal had much to commend it. He was a major planter, and marrying him would enable Dolly to stop teaching. She would also gain a house of her own to live in, instead of boarding with another couple. Not least important, at thirty-two she could still hope to conceive a child.[64] Yet she believed that if she did not have "a right heart," she could not fulfill her duties as a wife. The commitment to "Love Honour & Obey" was even more "solemn" in this case because Thomas had several children by a previous marriage. Though deeply attracted to motherhood, Dolly worried whether she could "be to *His Darlings* all that his departed one was." In great trouble, she closed her entry with the prayer "that He who calmed the troubled waters may speak peace and quietness to me."[65]

Tormented by doubts, Dolly Lewis broke her engagement, but in the end, she did marry Thomas Burge and quickly thanked her good fortune at finding "a protector & a home." Housekeeping took on an entirely new meaning in a "pleasant home" filled with "a loving companion & beautiful children." A year later, Dolly remembered that she had approached her wedding vows "with trembling & fear," but now, she wrote exultantly, "It has been a year of happiness a year of *heartrest* for after striving & toiling alone for years in this cold hearted world thus to find a heart that truly loves & a home full of every comfort. O How my heart expands with love to him that has thus taken me to himself."[66] Nine years later, she remained satisfied with her choice, taking up her pen to "record the loving kindness of my husband always thoughtful of my happiness." These words were an elegy; Thomas had died a few weeks earlier. Some months later, having returned from taking the midnight train through Georgia, Dolly reflected that "none can tell how much I miss Mr. Burge & how gloomy everything seems without him." Her experience suggests a possible reason other widows avoided remarriage; it created the risk of redoubled loss, which rarely grew easier through repetition.[67]

Remarriage could have other unpleasant if less serious consequences. When Ruth Hairston's first husband died, for example, she was then Ruth Wilson, a thirty-year-old woman with a thirteen-year-old daughter and doting in-laws who competed for her company. A year after his son's death, John Wilson still referred to Ruth as his "dear daughter" and himself as her "affectionate Father." When Ruth remarried, however, the Wilsons' fondness apparently evaporated. Newly wed Ruth Hairston seemed surprised, even annoyed, at the change in her relationship with her former in-laws: "I rote for Col Wilson family to dine with us on sataday but none of them came, I think that I have discharged my duty and if tha are not disposed to be friendly I shall let them alone." The family papers provide no explicit explanation, but the timing suggests that the Wilsons disapproved of either the speed of Ruth's remarriage or her choice of husband.[68] Several decades later, Emily Rootes's remarriage brought no cheers of joy from her in-laws either. Some months after the wedding, Serena Lea remarked that Emily "appears to be very happy with Mr Hagy but I must say I never gave my consent to the match nor am I satisfied with it now he is a good man & when I say that I have said all I think she might have done better." Serena Lea's family pride was apparently hurt by this union, which was rather ironic given that her brother had almost certainly died a dipsomaniac.[69]

An important bone of contention in many remarriages involved widows' property. While that was not likely an issue in Emily Rootes's remarriage, it may well have been in Ruth Wilson's. Much to her cost later in life, she remarried without any legal agreement to protect the property she held in right of her first husband. Nor was there any such arrangement for property that might descend to her daughter, which might explain the Wilsons' ire at Ruth's remarriage. Unlike Ruth Wilson, many widows took care to protect their property through separate estates, but negotiating a prenuptial property agreement was its own hurdle. Eliza Grist, her brother, James Washington, and her second husband, Dr. Reuben Knox, discovered as much in 1840. In this case, the push for a separate estate seems to have come not from Eliza but from James. While he acknowledged that Knox was "worthy," he still thought it "desirable that your property should be settled on yourself." Hard times following the Panic of 1837 surely influenced Washington's thinking. Knox was "now engaged in business," and the region had recently witnessed "such disaster in commercial transaction."[70] At her brother's instigation, Eliza raised the issue with Reuben Knox. Seemingly taken aback, he remarked on her "great anxiety" to preserve "a competence of this worlds goods" for herself and her young son. However carefully Eliza and her brother framed the need for a separate estate, Knox could hardly help but resent the reminder that he could all too easily become ruinously indebted. Yet Eliza insisted, and he agreed. Thus, like many propertied widows, Eliza Grist reentered coverture in a different state than most first-time brides—with a much broader range of managerial experience and with a greater degree of prospective financial security.[71]

As these property arrangements suggest, remarriage did not erase all aspects of widowhood, but it did redistribute the managerial burdens. Widows' new husbands often became the executors or administrators of their predecessors' estates. They could also become their stepchildren's legal guardians.[72] However, even when these new husbands proved themselves worthy through competent management of their wives' and their stepchildren's property, mothers still worried about the emotional consequences of remarriage.[73] Eliza Knox's concerns for her orphaned son bespeak some of the considerations that complicated remarriage and perhaps deterred some women from it altogether. Although Eliza seems to have been quite content with her second husband, she worried that the son of her first marriage would never warm to his new father. She urged her son Franklin Grist to write more frequently to Reuben, and even ask him for favors, "because I think it would please him . . . and appear more like you confided in him as a father." Several years later, observing that her son "has always felt diffidence and hesitency in expressing his mind and feelings," Eliza assured her husband that Franklin was "much attached to you and he desires always to regard your wishes and advice altho he sometimes falls short of it." There is no evidence that Franklin Grist disapproved of his mother's remarriage, and what Reuben Knox thought about his stepson's diffidence is likewise unclear. But Eliza Knox's own role as mediator between her husband and her son suggests some lingering tension. The ripples caused by Eliza's first marriage seem to have been relatively minor, yet even this case reflects the complications of remarriage for widows and their families.[74]

The greatest reason not to remarry, however, was the risk that a new husband would prove abusive. When Sumter District planter Marion Deveaux placed her "earthly happiness" in the care of Reverend Augustus L. Converse, she could not have imagined the troubles that awaited her. A man of no particular fortune or connections, Augustus quickly tried to assert dominion over Marion and her property. Augustus had only a parish living, but Marion had a life interest in her father's True Blue plantation, which in the early 1850s produced more than 150 bales of cotton annually, and at least a third of her husband's estate. This contrast was embarrassing enough, and it could not have helped that Marion quite unusually continued to manage True Blue early in her marriage (with the help of her brother and other advisers). Even more peculiarly, she received business letters and accounts under the name of Deveaux although she quite properly called herself Marion Converse.[75]

Apparently finding Marion's comparative independence insupportable, Augustus took steps to assert his rights over her and her wealth. He be-

lieved, not without reason, that he had a clear claim on the True Blue profits because Marion's father had bequeathed them to her for life, and because a wife's money (as opposed to real property) indubitably became her
husband's upon marriage.[76] Thus, in December 1853, he "ordered *all* the
Cotton now on hand to be handed to the Rail Road for transportation." As
Marion angrily reported to her brother Matthew Singleton, Augustus
planned to "place the proceeds in some Bank, where it shall *only* be subject to his order, until the expenses of the Plantation &c are paid, when the
nett income will be divided *by him*, between us." Worse, Augustus planned
"to sell without any reserve (if he can) all my share in the residuary" of her
father's estate. "*This is not with my consent*," Marion urgently informed
Matthew, "since I do not, of course know what may fall to me that I would
like to retain." In an effort to keep the cotton profits, as well as her share of
her father's estate, Marion tried not only to enlist her brother's help but
also to convince a cousin, Richard Richardson, to act as her trustee.[77] An
extraordinary letter she received around the same time may have stiffened
her resolve. From Charleston, a J. Hamilton wrote to "insist upon your taking such steps as *exhonerate* you from a *false* position & place the pledges
of your first love where by nature & association they should be." Instructing Marion to come to Charleston, Hamilton asked whether she had forgotten "the features and exalted virtues" of her first husband, making explicit what other friends had perhaps been unwilling to say, namely, that
Marion's second marriage had been a woeful mistake.[78]

Matters in the Converse household steadily deteriorated, and in 1854,
a particularly fierce argument had Augustus reaching for his gun and Marion flying to refuge among her slaves. That escape saved Marion for the
moment, but it apparently confirmed Augustus's fear that her disobedience was provoking the slaves to flout his orders as well. He punished them
for sheltering Marion, and later he also beat her severely. At that point,
she sought shelter with her family, and the larger community began to take
notice. In 1855, the Protestant Episcopal Church "degraded" Converse from
his ministry after finding him guilty of an "unprovoked and cruel beating"
against his wife. By 1856, Marion and her lawyers started the arduous
process of securing a legal separation that would remove her, her property,
and her daughters from Augustus's power. To the end, Augustus continued in his "course of unkindness" toward his wife. In February 1857, he
summarily fired Miss Kimmey (a paid companion, teacher, or governess)
because, in Marion's words, "he found her a restraint" in his cruelty, and

"he thought her, too much *my friend*." Later in the same month, a special session of South Carolina's equity court approved a settlement in which Augustus Converse accepted over $24,000 in exchange for granting Marion "separate use" of her remaining property. South Carolina law did not allow divorce, but it did authorize a separation that would end a husband's claim to his wife's person and property. Raising this enormous sum severely strained Marion's resources and permanently indebted her to her son-in-law, John Burchell Moore. That was less important, however, than obtaining a crucial degree of freedom from her disastrous second husband. Afterward, Marion resumed her old name along with the management of True Blue. By all indications, she and her friends acted as if she had never remarried.[79]

Like other widows in trouble, Marion Converse relied on her relations and friends. Although her brother died in 1854, her son-in-law helped her make arrangements to pay off Augustus, and he also became his sister-in-law's guardian, replacing her disgraced former stepfather. (In his will, Moore restricted his wife's legacy so that any subsequent husband could not control it, and he urged her to do the same with any property she might receive from other sources.) From Charleston, Mr. Ingraham and Mr. Petigru advised Marion and John Moore how best to get rid of the "scoundrel" and "villain." Mr. Ingraham instructed Moore to "fix him in *writing*, and do not depend on his word." He and Petigru also offered to help raise nearly half of the sum needed to pay Converse. A female friend (possibly Betty Coles) was delighted to learn that Marion was finally rid of "that grasping bad old man," an outcome she described as passing "from darkness to Light." Urging Marion "to forget all the harshness & unkindness," she reminded Marion of her far-flung friends, of the "affection which has been heaped upon you," and "of Mr Dulles coming all the way from Washington in mid Winter. John Burn coming such a distance &c &c." Such reassurances could not undo the past, of course, but Marion Deveaux was exceptionally fortunate; not only did she escape her husband, but her friends made light of her heavy debt to them. In his 1862 will, for example, her son-in-law left Marion $500 "to be invested in some trinket as a momento of me." More important, he excused her from repaying her $18,825.25 debt to him "except as she may desire." Finally, he gave her a lifetime interest in his property in the admittedly unlikely event he left no issue and she survived her daughter.[80]

Like Marion Converse, untold numbers of slaveholding women faced domestic abuse for years with the sanction if not approval of the law, but unlike her, many had little or no support even from their own relations. Most husbands were never publicly rebuked for cruelty, let alone deemed "revolting" by an equity court judge, as Augustus Converse was. Marrying again allowed women to exchange a burdensome and emotionally barren widowhood for the protective custody of coverture, but the status offered no guarantees and few protections for women, even the wealthy and well connected. On the whole, slaveholding women did not much like being widowed, but those who could afford to stay single had good reason to eschew the matrimonial gamble and focus instead on their hopes of heaven.[81]

AMONG NINETEENTH-CENTURY slaveholders, widowhood encompassed both the duty and the authority to perform customarily masculine work for the benefit of the surviving family, particularly children. In other words, a widow was allowed, even required, to do things well beyond the wife's and deputy husband's purview. Throughout widowhood, but especially in the first several years, slaveholding women had commercial and legal obligations that far exceeded anything that even the most competent deputy planter had to face. Slaveholding women had many roles during their widowhoods, some simultaneous, some sequential. They were householders, executors, and testators. They were also mourners, mothers, and sometimes brides. Finally, they were neighbors, clients, and employers.

While widowhood altered gender roles in socially significant ways, shifts in gender identity were less automatic, more individual, and thus more difficult to track. Widows often held on to the expectation that men would take care of them, an expectation rooted in race and class as well as gender. Nevertheless, at different points, financial necessity, law, family pride, and maternal devotion coerced and inspired widows to tackle their new duties. Slaveholding widows were not simply broken (or even bending) reeds; they were also, as Martha Richardson boasted, carvers of their own fortune although they never acted in a vacuum.[82] But most slaveholding women did not experience widowhood in this way; rather than representing a new opportunity to seek and wield power, it brought an unsought endowment of rights, properties, and responsibilities which they neglected at their peril. Fulfilling a panoply of usually masculine roles, however, endangered neither their self-understanding as privileged ladies, nor the gender order writ large. Slaveholding widows were fundamentally conservative. They endorsed not only the South's racial and class hierarchies but also its fundamental gender inequality. Indeed, they relied upon it. When the nation dissolved into Civil War, however, the old verities became increasingly uncertain. During the war, most slaveholding widows became busier than ever, and some found new purpose in serving their state and nation. But for most, fully occupied hands were no protection against material scarcity, redoubled mourning, crushing anxiety, Union occupation, and, ultimately, defeat.

CHAPTER 7

What Will Become of Us!

During the war, most of the Confederacy's adult white men served in the military,[1] and their absence required white women to fill their shoes as best they could. In itself, this was nothing new; the novelty—and the vastly increased challenge—lay in the ways that war altered the meaning and context of slaveholding women's substitution for men. At the level of ideology, wartime poems, songs, and stories exaggerated gender differences: delicate white womanhood symbolized the cause for which brave men fought and died.[2] In reality, while Confederate women were indeed symbols, they were also actors, but in a vastly different setting than before. During the war, every aspect of householding, ladyhood, and mastery became much more difficult to sustain. Combining women's and men's work, as slaveholding widows had routinely done before the war, became a radically different proposition in the context of mass death, economic devastation, redoubled slave resistance and emancipation, Union invasion, and newly overt class conflict.

Before the presidential election of 1860, slaveholding widows joined with the nation in speculating anxiously about the future. That fall, Keziah Brevard observed that "these are perilous times" for "our *dear dear Country*." She greeted the news of Abraham Lincoln's victory with a shocked "Oh My God!!!," remarking that she "had prayed that God would thwart his election in some way." Keziah's fears centered less around the safety of the federal union than that of slaveholders and slavery itself. In one entry, she fretted that "we know not what moment we may be hacked to death in the most cruel manner by our slaves," egged on, as she imagined, by northern Republicans. Equally gruesome to her were the imagined consequences of emancipation. "No soul on this earth is more willing for justice than I am," she proclaimed, "but the idea of being mixed up with free blacks is *horrid*!!" Her fellow South Carolinian Ada Bacot also deplored Lincoln's election, but she envisioned its consequences for herself rather differently. Far from being consumed by fear, she vowed that if her state did not "take some decided measure this time" in response to northern provocation, "I will never trust to South Carolina again." After secession, she also anticipated that war might give her a new purpose that life at Arnmore could not provide, namely, serving her state by nursing Carolina's wounded soldiers.[3]

Even those widows not haunted by Keziah Brevard's particular nightmares rarely regarded the prospect of war quite as Ada Bacot did; instead, they worried about its economic and personal costs. Eliza Roberts hoped for peace because "times are hard" already. She depended on "kind Friends" for a place to live because she could not afford rent in Charleston. Fellow Charlestonian Eliza Wilkins was "in a great state of excitement" months before the attack on Fort Sumter because her sons, Martin and Berkeley, were "in military exposure." After the fort fell, widowed mothers far beyond Charleston wondered about their sons' safety. That fateful spring, Virginia planter Mary Ann Hendrick had a son studying at the Virginia Military Institute who wrote home with the news that the cadets threatened to destroy the town of Lexington after some Unionists assaulted one of their fellows. Dissuaded from this course, the cadets instead "stooped all accademic duty"—prematurely, in young Henry's case!—to focus on military drills and tactics. In late May, Mary Ann worried about her eldest son, Robert, then in Richmond, telling him, "If the Federal Troops should advance against Richmond dont you stay to be taken prisoner." Robert Hendrick survived that early threat only to die less than a year later, leaving his mother, siblings, and a new bride to mourn him.[4] Over the months and years that followed, the mounting death toll affected nearly every household.

The war's demand for supplies and manpower, the armies' pillaging, and the Federal blockade together made food, clothes, fuel, and shelter progressively more difficult for both civilians and soldiers to acquire. Disruptions to slavery and the household economy came immediately to some places and more slowly to others, but over time, everyone felt the press of want, and fewer and fewer households had any goods or attention to spare for widowed kinswomen. Compounding widows' financial problems was the war's profound disruption of slavery. The military maw consumed most of the white men on whom slaveholding widows relied to help them surveil and punish their slaves. At the same time, new hopes for freedom, and in some places the proximity of Union troops, prompted slaves to down tools, flee toward Federal lines, or even attack their owners. Enemy advances and occupation turned hard times into desolation. Slaveholding widows lost their dignity, slaves, food stuffs, livestock, furniture, clothes, jewelry, and occasionally their houses to Union (or sometimes Confederate) troops. In this context, maintaining any semblance of mastery or ladyhood demanded considerable ingenuity.[5]

None of slaveholding widows' prewar strategies could entirely compensate for the war's disrupting effects, yet widows clung doggedly to practices strained to the breaking point and to beliefs that failed to match reality far more openly than before. Thus, slave resistance, for example, more often confirmed than unseated widows' racism. Widows also attempted to cope with new situations, such as the presence of enemy soldiers, with familiar methods like appealing to chivalrous impulses or acting haughtily. As Union officers recognized, widows' efforts to uphold their vision of rank and propriety were abundantly political when aimed at an occupying army. They were no less so when directed at other southern whites. Although slaveholding widows sometimes exulted when patriotism united whites across lines of class, they more often sought to reassure themselves and others that no matter how poor they became, they were still superior not only to slaves but to some other whites. That attitude helped protect slaveholding widows from some of the war's worst ravages, but it could only have fanned nonslaveholders' already considerable resentment of the rich man's—and woman's—war.

AS TENS OF thousands of men marched off to defend southern independence, Dolly Burge observed that the South was becoming a sea of "homesteads left with only the sad & lonely wife & mother to look after its interests." To Burge's way of thinking, what made these households "so sad" was less the absence of husbands and sons than the difficulty the women left behind faced in meeting "their temporal necessities." Throughout the Confederacy, even "absolutely needful" food and clothing quickly became first expensive and later difficult to obtain at any price.[6] As inflation and scarcity put even basic supplies beyond their reach, some scrimped, others improvised, and still others scrambled for employment. They also continued the antebellum practice of relying on connections and kin for advice, material aid, and other assistance even though widespread poverty and death made both increasingly difficult.

The war had barely begun before consumers began having trouble with inflation and shortages, including currency. In June 1861, widowed schoolteacher Ariela Pinkind complained that instead of making "small change" for large bills and notes, Charleston retailers gave out "tickets," which Pinkind feared they would later refuse to honor. Official revaluating of paper money posed other problems. Anticipating an April 1864 revaluation, Pinkind could not decide whether to try to collect her debts immediately or to wait. "If I get any money now," she reflected, "after the 1st of April, I will have to lose 33 1/3 per cent, so on $300 have to lose $100." Yet she needed cash to buy basic supplies like molasses, now selling at $12.00 per gallon.[7] Slaveholding women noticed shortages and inflation wherever they lived, but both came especially quickly to Virginia. During a trip from Charlottesville to South Carolina in November 1862, Ada Bacot noticed that provisions were "much more abundant & decidedly cheaper" in North Carolina than Virginia.[8] On a similar trip two years later, Phoebe Pember observed that food was still far more plentiful outside Virginia. In and around Richmond, even the richest people were treating the most commonplace goods as "luxuries."[9] In April 1862 Ada Bacot bemoaned a nearly fivefold increase in the price of calico and marveled that shopkeepers "are not ashamed to tell the prices." That autumn, "very poor calico" cost Winchester's Cornelia McDonald $1.25 per yard while salt was $1 per pound.[10] Not all Virginians suffered equally from high prices and scarcity, however. In the southern part of the state, Mary Ann Hendrick's household enjoyed "a great many comforts & luxuries" unavailable in the far northern town of Leesburg where her daughter-in-law, Haddie, lived. Days before Lee's surrender, Henry Clay Hendrick could still afford to pay an astounding $325 for a pair of "fine Boots."[11] The Deep South also suffered economically, notwithstanding Phoebe Pember's and Ada Bacot's impressions of plenty. In December 1861 Dolly Burge observed that "cotton is unsalable," thanks to the Federal blockade. Salt was selling at eighteen or twenty dollars a sack, "& every thing in like proportion." In June 1862 Dolly paid forty to fifty cents per pound for salt. By January 1864 salt sold at $6 per pound, calico at $10 per yard, and a paper of pins for $6. In November of that year, what Dolly considered "ten cents worth of flax thread" now cost fifty times as much.[12]

Over time, certain goods became unavailable even at grossly inflated prices. In mid-1862, Dolly complained that she had "hundreds of dollars in my pocket book & yet I cannot buy a yard of calico." As she and countless others discovered, some goods could be replaced with a little labor and ingenuity; her daughter, Sadai, presently sported a bonnet fashioned from an old dress. Other slaveholders learned to make their own straw hats. After several false starts, Cornelia McDonald contrived to turn a bag of raw wool into yarn and then cloth. Later, she shredded a cotton mattress and unraveled a length of woolen fringe for their fibers, eventually turning both into clothes for her children. Other much-remarked inventions of necessity included ersatz coffee, the salt recycled from smokehouse floors, and soap made from ashes.[13] Despite this sort of ingenuity—fondly remembered after the war—southern civilians and soldiers suffered widespread and serious deprivation as photographs and descriptions of "emaciated" faces and bodies testify. Phoebe Pember recalled that at Chimborazo Hospital in Richmond real "privations" began in the summer of 1864 when some people were reduced to eating rats. By the war's end, Cornelia McDonald's diet—a single meal of coffee and bread daily—left her "so weak" that she "scarcely had strength" for an evening walk.[14]

Who made do and who starved was largely a matter of money, location, and connections. Prewar wealth, distance from battle-torn or early-occupied areas, and friends and relations with supplies to spare or strings to pull made an enormous difference. Rich planters who lived far from the war's several fronts found their productive regimes comparatively undisturbed for much of the war. They grew some of their own food, which they could also sell, and many continued to grow staple crops such as cotton. Dolly Burge complained about inflation and scarcity, but her family never went hungry. Indeed, for most of the war, her plantation continued much as it had done before. In response to the blockade and the army's need for provisions, she switched some fields to corn, but she still grew cotton, which in 1864 she sold for seventy-five cents per pound. In addition, her plantation produced a great deal of meat; her "thithes" to the Confederacy that March included "three hundred pounds of meat 5 pounds of wool [and] five bushels of oats."[15] In southern Virginia, Mary Ann Hendrick likewise continued to produce at a reasonable pace, adjusting her crop mix to reflect the altered market. Instead of tobacco, she sold wheat, oats, wood, corn, and peas. As a result, she had money in the bank throughout the war and could afford nonessential expenses, such as tuition for her sons.[16]

Throughout the Confederacy, however, such success was rare. Far more common were tales of widows who jury-rigged a living, using a combination of old and new strategies. At first, old coping methods largely sufficed. After a Colonel Harrison of Halifax, North Carolina, died in February 1861, his neighbors and relations rallied around his widow, Mary, ensuring that, despite the unsettled times, her widowhood began like many others in her class and section. Her cousin, Elizabeth Wiggins, helped make the Colonel's shroud, and the whole Wiggins family along with "a concourse of friends & neighbors" attended the burial. On subsequent days, Elizabeth Wiggins and her daughters "walked over to see Cousin Mary" and sent her little gifts of oranges and plants while several other women procured Mary's mourning clothes. Elizabeth's husband visited "to examine the Col. papers" and begin the estate settlement process. Several months later, Colonel Harrison's estate was sold, and Mary received her "appropriation" in the usual way for an intestate estate: court-appointed commissioners designated what specific property would constitute her dower share. Thus, while Mary Harrison surely experienced her early widowhood as a singular catastrophe, her despair, reliance on friends and family, and involvement in the set procedures of estate settlement were quite conventional.[17]

Within a matter of months, however, the dependable mechanisms that had long helped southeastern slaveholders endure widowhood would come under unprecedented strain. Even widows from the wealthier families found their resources and influence dwindling, and many sought new means to support themselves. Daughter to a prominent Savannah family, Phoebe Pember badly needed money during the war, and she relied on the salary she earned as matron of Chimborazo Hospital in Richmond. When the Union's victory ended both the war and her income, she found herself suddenly "houseless, homeless, and moneyless" with only "a box full of Confederate money and a silver ten-cent piece." Cornelia McDonald had important connections as well; Confederate ambassador James M. Mason was her friend, for example, and General Robert E. Lee her occasional guest.[18] Unlike Pember, she also had a large family of children to support, and both before and after her husband died in November 1864, she found making ends meet a constant struggle. In May 1862, Union troops devastated her Winchester homestead, leaving her and her children without the means either to farm or to reach shelter in Richmond. The Confederate defeat at Gettysburg, however, forced them and many others to flee to Lexington. With only sixty-five Confederate dollars "in my pocket," Cornelia could hardly imagine how she would pay for housing as well as food and fuel. As she quickly realized, however, her prewar prosperity could be converted into a means of survival. She sold her dresses, then her jewelry, and finally half of a set of china. Having such goods to convert to cash gave Cornelia a decided advantage over many other refugees, but this alone could not sustain her family, and she began to work as a drawing teacher. Even that proved a slender reed of support. By the war's end, when the family lived primarily on the little she earned by teaching, a full two weeks' wages bought only a pound of bacon, a pound of butter, and some candles.[19]

If the war reduced widows like Cornelia McDonald and Phoebe Pember to wage work, it caused more hardship for those who had depended on their wages all along. Before the war even began, widowed teachers regularly faced uncertain employment. At first, the outbreak of hostilities inspired the hope that "all of the Northern teachers will go away." The northerners' retreat, like male teachers' enlistment, did create new opportunities, but the ranks of would-be teachers among the South's white women simultaneously expanded. Cornelia McDonald's recourse to teaching drawing did not necessarily take a job from anyone else, but longtime teachers noted that the "class of applications" for any position was "large." As the correspondence of Isabella Woodruff with her friends and fellow teachers, Lou Dowell and Ariela Pinkind, suggests, widows continued to use whatever connections they had to find employment in a school, or to scrape together at least a few scholars, but the war made it difficult to retain their students and even collect their fees.[20] By June 1861, Lou Dowell's school had already lost half of its pupils. Six months later, she had lost another ten while Ariela Pinkind had lost all but two of her music students. "Everybody is getting stingy and close," Pinkind grumbled; either they pinched pennies by removing children from school or they bargained down "the price of teaching that they want done for very little, next to nothing." By July 1862, Isabella Woodruff considered taking a position that paid her board but no salary. For a childless widow like Isabella, that sort of offer was barely feasible, but for Ariela, mother of two small children, it meant making a very difficult choice. In November 1862 she had to send her children to her family in Charleston because she "could not make the two ends meet by keeping them" with her in Eatonton, Georgia. Three months later, Ariela was still trying to find a way to live with her children and teach. By that time, she had rejoined her children in Charleston but was sewing uniforms for money, which at fifty cents a day was barely a living. As she glumly remarked, "At present I am worth the big sum of $3.00 after all my hard work of last year."[21]

Being promised a salary was, in any case, no guarantee of payment, a problem for many creditors in this period. In late 1862 Lou Dowell complained that one woman "refuses to pay me" for teaching her two children. Also in 1862 Isabella Woodruff debated accepting a new position, reflecting that she had a "great deal of money owing me, in this neighborhood & find some difficulty in collecting it." A year and a half later, she had to borrow $50 simply to reach a job in Orangeburg, South Carolina. Several months later, a daughter of the family with whom she had been boarding wrote to dun her for $80 (a somewhat unusual undertaking for a young single woman, which itself bespeaks the war's disruptions). Outraged—and quite unable to pay—Isabella reminded her former hosts of their agreement that what she owed in board would "stand as an offset to my tuition bills." Even after being "beat down in my price," she had still expected to earn at least $300, "but altogether I received $116.00 for 9 months," and two of "your young relations . . . never paid a dime." Small wonder, then, that at the end of that year (1864), Isabella wailed that she had tasted no meat for three weeks and was living on "corn bread, homony, molasses, & water." She might have considered herself lucky, however, because she only had to cope with her fellow Confederates. By contrast, Union officials in Winchester, Virginia, closed down the school of widowed Mrs. Eichelberger because one of her teachers had written an ill-considered note about a Union general's "doings" in the area.[22]

Boardinghouse keepers like Catherine Lewis faced related problems. Like teachers, they often met increased competition as more families sought boarders for the sake of additional income. Early in the war, for example, Mary Ann Hendrick began taking in boarders during the school session as did Cornelia McDonald's stepdaughter Mary. Location made a great difference in these ventures. In Richmond, housing quickly grew so short that anyone with a room to rent could command exorbitant prices, or so Judith McGuire thought when she tried to find lodging there.[23] Similarly, upcountry families often took in people fleeing the Union-occupied coastline. (Whether they charged exorbitantly was perhaps a matter of perspective, but some refugees certainly felt exploited in their misfortune.) But someone like Catherine Lewis, whose business had depended on her location in a university town, faced a potentially catastrophic loss of boarders. While the University of North Carolina remained open throughout the war, so many male students and faculty went to war that many other institutions closed down, substantially affecting local economies.[24]

For widows who could not farm, teach, or take in boarders, there were also new jobs created by the war itself. After losing her husband's land to a crooked sheriff, North Carolina's Candace Lee went to Raleigh to "get sewing for the soldiers from the Commissary Department." Ariela Pinkind began sewing for soldiers when she could not make enough money teaching music.[25] Judith McGuire believed that the poor were actually "better off than usual" because of these government jobs. She and her daughters "tried in vain" to get government work, and she supposed "it is right, for there are so many widows and orphans who have a much higher claim to any thing that Government can do for them."[26] Yet war widows were not all equal in the government's eyes; well-connected women had access to more and better government resources. Cornelia McDonald received a much needed $100 from a secret fund for military widows and orphans because a General Pendleton had recommended her as well as his own daughter-in-law as worthy candidates.[27] Former Savannah belle Lou Berrien ended up working for the government in Richmond after her husband, Colonel Bartow, died at First Manassas. Quite likely, her husband's ties to the Davis administration and her own friendship with Varina Davis and Mary Chesnut explain why hers was a comparatively lucrative post. "Cutting bonds—Confederate bonds—for five hundred Confederate dollars a year" compared quite well to the fifty cents per day Ariela Pinkind earned sewing uniforms.[28] Savannah's Phoebe Pember also acquired her position as matron of Chimborazo Hospital through a connection, her friend Mary Randolph, wife of Secretary of War George Randolph.[29]

Widows also relied on another important prewar strategy: drawing from the well of familial generosity. After her husband's death at First Manassas, Lou Bartow received an "urgent" invitation from her brother-in-law "to come and live in his home." Cornelia McDonald's diary and memoir contain numerous examples of the help she received from friends as well as family. During her flight from Winchester, her brother-in-law loaned her money to pay her way from Lynchburg to Lexington. After her husband died, her kin offered to provide homes for her children. Cornelia declined this offer, but she depended on her kinswomen and friends to convert her remaining luxuries into cash. Her cousin Lizzie Tyler arranged for "the disposal of the finery," including a "brocade shot with gold that my husband had brought me from Paris." A Mrs. Powell found a buyer for "a set of onyx and pearls set in Etruscan gold." Friends also helped her cobble together food, fuel, and clothing. "Kind Mrs. Moore" made a set of clothes for her son, Harry, using fabric that Mr. Powell donated. Colonel Gilham sent her a quarter of beef even though he himself had just been burned out of his house. These inestimable acts of compassion could not, however, keep pace with the steady rise in the number of widows and orphans who needed their friends' and relatives' help. As Cornelia herself recognized, even the most generous "could not give always," and all the altruism in the world could not overcome the Confederacy's shortage of everything but death.[30]

INEXTRICABLY LINKED with widows' financial woes was the problem of sustaining slavery, both economically and socially. Well before the Emancipation Proclamation, even before secession itself, slavery's uncertain political future threatened both the perception and reality of slaveholders' control. The war tended to increase widows' sensitivity to signs of discontent and rebellion among slaves and simultaneously destabilized the slave regime itself. In removing so many white men from the home front, the war substantially decreased all slaveholders' ability to discipline and exploit their slaves, and the wartime economy made it increasingly difficult even to feed and clothe them. Together, these trends gave slaves more opportunity and more reason to disobey, malinger, steal, talk or strike back, and run away. Compounding slaves' own actions, Union soldiers destroyed farms and encouraged or forced slaves to leave their homes. In this context, the surprise is not that many slaveholding widows became both more fearful and more contemptuous of African Americans, free or slave, but rather that any of them continued to view themselves and their slaves through mastery's fractured lens.

Even before the war broke out, some slaveholding widows observed a heightened level of slave defiance. In January 1861 Ada Bacot grumbled that some slaves "were found away from home with out a pass." Later that year, she was "much worried" by some slaves' "misbehavior." In April, Keziah Brevard's fears of being "hacked to death" by slaves coincided with witnessing a slave child's refusal to call white children "master." If slave children were now rebels, what could slaveholders expect from their parents?[31] Worries about slave disloyalty—or worse—became especially acute in areas where Union armies operated.[32] Candace Lee, for example, worried that "even faithful Aunt Pallas," who had refused freedom under her husband's will, would "turn traitor" when the Yankees came.[33] Throughout the Confederacy, slaveholders watched in sick dismay as slaves turned the old racial order on its head. In occupied Winchester, Virginia, Cornelia McDonald raved that "negroes can assemble in any numbers, and if they choose can jostle and crowd ladies off the pavement into the gutter as may suit their convenience." Under Brigadier General Milroy's rule, Cornelia believed, slaves "are the only people who have any rights or liberty, and of the latter they have an undue share." To protest this change, she took the grave risk of sending Milroy an anonymous "valentine," satirizing his evident preference for slave women over white ladies.[34] Ada Bacot had a similar reaction while working as a nurse in Charlottesville where she made the unsettling discovery that Virginia slaves talked back when rebuked. "The little yellow boy William," for example, argued with her order to call another widow's young son "Master." Falsely confident that her own slaves would never behave thusly, she noted that "Virginia negroes" were far less "servile" and made housekeeping "any thing but pleasant." In fact, Ada's personal maid Savary also began to give "trouble," enough so that Ada was tempted to sell her.[35] In Charleston the following year, Ariela Pinkind crabbed that she "had to cook" for herself because the slave she had hired refused to come to work. Another hiree's complaint that Pinkind's home was "*too confining*" also forced her to look for new help. Truculence, malingering, and even self-appointed holidays were not necessarily signs of slavery's imminent collapse. Before the war, many planters found it necessary to ignore "misbehavior" or grant holidays that slaves would have taken anyway. Yet Pinkind's comment that Liddy's owner "could not make her come" bespeaks slaves' widespread refusal to work at antebellum paces.[36]

Even more dreadful to anxious widows was the prospect that slaves might harm them physically, a fear that exploded from dormancy even before the war began. Keziah Brevard believed that "we are in the very midst of enemies" and lay awake at night "thinking of our danger." At least once she suspected her slaves were trying to poison her, and she could scarcely believe that houses "without a white gentleman at home" would long remain "safe" from slave attack.[37] Less alarmist than Brevard, Ada Bacot initially felt safe staying alone at Arnmore, describing herself as unafraid that "any thing would harm me." By the fall of 1861, however, unexpected events began to frighten her, and she panicked when an unfamiliar man appeared on her porch late one night. While she soon realized he was in fact her overseer, she wondered whether she could have defended herself, thinking, "Some times I think I could then again I fear not, I fear I am nothing more than a weak woman at last." When she learned that another widowed planter, Mrs. Witherspoon, had apparently been "smothered in her bed," she realized no one could be sure that "we are safe." Still disposed to trust her house slaves, whom she believed "very fond of me," she thought "twould take very little" for the others to "put me out of the way."[38] Fears of slave violence were far from groundless, but many more slaves had both opportunity and provocation to put their owners out of the way than ever did so. As before the war, black women and poor white women remained much more vulnerable to sexual and other assault than slaveholding women.[39] In some families, moreover, slaveholders continued to view at least their own favored slaves as protectors, not enemies. In Albemarle County, Virginia, for example, a Mr. George and his sons depended on their "houseman," William, "to protect Mistress Nancy and her two daughters" when they went off to war.[40]

As William's role in the George household suggests, the same military mobilization that left some widows feeling unprotected in a sea of slaves often increased widows' dependence upon particular slaves, especially those men whom they considered reliable advisers and potential leaders among their fellows. White men's mobilization meant that few widows could rely on a brother, son, or cousin to help them decide when and what to plant, and even before the war brought new financial hardship, few could afford an overseer. (Overseers became even more costly when planters had to pay $500 to exempt a man from conscription.) In this context, many Confederate women continued to prefer a slave's aid to no help at all. Some preferred slave men's help even when white men were available. Georgia widow Peggy Sybert "turned off" her overseer and put a slave "in his place to manage things and look after the work." Similarly vexed by overseers who did nothing but "act biggity," Mary Brice told her absent husband that "what she couldn't see to when he was away, she'd pick out one of de slaves to see after."[41]

While white men's mobilization increased slaveholding widows' reliance on male slaves for advice, the war's economic hardships made the largely female domestic slave force even more important to widows' self-representation as ladies. Cornelia McDonald remembered that she nearly starved during the war, yet she rarely did without domestic help. During the Union occupation of Winchester, Margaret cared for the baby and Aunt Winnie cooked and did laundry. McDonald also hired a third domestic, Lethea. Another nurse, Catherine, ran away early in the war, but was returned to her, "starved" and "forlorn." Cornelia McDonald's descriptions of life in Lexington suggest a bizarre combination of privilege and hardship. To many of her peers, the definitive sign of her remaining status would have been the simple fact that she did not do her own cooking; she "got a negro woman near to bake our bread, and if we had meat, to cook it for me." On the other hand, she only had "a small skillet and a tea kettle for cooking utensils," and the family soon discovered "that it took more money than we could command to buy comfortable food and provide fuel." After her husband's death, she continued to hire a servant to cook "our poor dinner," but because she could not "afford her light and fuel to sit by," the slave left every evening to visit her friends. In Charlottesville, Ada Bacot relied not only on her personal servant Savary but also on Matilda and Annie, who kept up the house where she and the other South Carolinians boarded. Laundry and childcare were the sticking point for Ariela Pinkind. In complaining about her low income, she noted that "I make barely enough to pay for my washing and Eliza's wages." Pinkind's insistence that other women do these tasks reflected her priorities at two levels: she needed to save her time for teaching, and her chance of attracting music students depended in part on her ability to maintain the appearance of a refined gentlewoman.[42]

During the war, slaveholding widows found themselves forced to accommodate many changes within the slave regime, but few jettisoned either their racism or their illusions of mastery. Rather than converting widows to abolition, slaves' heightened rudeness and open disobedience more often convinced widows that blacks must remain enslaved and that a biracial free society was lunacy. Isabella Woodruff believed that slaves gossiped about their owners because they were not morally equipped to appreciate the value of a lady's or gentleman's reputation. Keziah Brevard confided to her diary that the very idea of free blacks revolted her; "half barbarians," they were no more "prepared for freedom" than "the beasts of the field." Ada Bacot expressed less revulsion than Brevard, but she too maintained strict ideas about racial difference. While working in a Charlottesville hospital, Ada strongly objected to having a slave's bed set up on her ward; she had "no idea of having my ward turned into a negro house." Bacot did not particularly care where the slaves actually slept, but to her way of thinking, having their beds placed somewhere where she might see them violated an important barrier.[43]

Slaveholding widows sought to resist the war's corrosive effects on slavery in a variety of ways. Some simply lived in denial, clinging to the hope that the Confederacy would prevail and slavery would survive. Early on, of course, many believed the war would be quick and glorious. In this spirit, Ada Bacot offered to help refugees from the South Carolina lowcountry to "find places for their negroes" on the assumption that they would eventually be returned to work on coastal plantations.[44] Such efforts to protect slave property became more quixotic as the war dragged on. In September 1864, for example, Dolly Burge played host to a "camp" of forty refugee slaves who belonged to a Marietta slaveholder who had fled the battles around Atlanta. By this time, Union advances had already disrupted work on Burge's own plantation. In early August, for example, she noted that "servants & all scarcely know what to be about," and "work of all kind is laid aside."[45] Notwithstanding these clear reminders that slavery's future was being decided on the battlefield, many slaveholders continued to cast their relations with their slaves in the familiar light of beneficent mastery. As if nothing had changed, in August 1861 Elizabeth Wiggins noted that "today is the negroes holliday dinner."[46] The following Christmas in Charlottesville, Ada Bacot's slaves "burst into the room crying Christmas gift." Following the successful harvest of some 300 bushels of wheat in the summer of 1864, Dolly Burge gave "a supper" to her slaves, which they "enjoyed hugely." Dolly's other diary entries mingled concerns about inflation and news from the front with utterly mundane entries about getting wheat and corn ground, hiring out slaves, "breaking up for peas," and "cutting wheat."[47]

Whatever prosperity and discipline individual widows like Dolly Burge managed to sustain generally vanished with the arrival of hostile forces. While many civilians had little or no contact with Union troops during the war, others had to scamper out of their way, or learn to cope with an invading force. In 1864, regular Union raids from New Bern, North Carolina, kept Ann Swann "on the wing" with "half our things packed" for a speedy departure beyond their reach. Civilians in much of northern Virginia faced occupation much earlier in the war. In mid-1862 Haddie Hendrick, Mary Ann Hendrick's widowed daughter-in-law, reported that the Federals in her area were cutthroats and fiends.[48] Around the same time, advancing troops turned Cornelia McDonald's green fields into mud, splintered her fences, shattered her windows, and made off with her supplies. Three years later, her house was "so ruined as to be uninhabitable." Nor could she contemplate resuming farming even if she could have hired laborers, for "nothing could be cultivated as there was not a fence on the place, and we could by no possibility replace them."[49] Slaveholding widows in central Georgia and South Carolina faced equal or greater devastation from Sherman's army in 1864 and 1865. Rumors of Sherman's advance frightened Candace Lee much as British activities had alarmed Jean Blair during the Revolution because she had heard "horrible stories . . . of what might happen to her daughters" at the hands of "the enemy." While Lee's children escaped personal insult, their household fell pray to straggling soldiers, who "searched our house thoroughly" and took whatever they pleased. Union torches destroyed two of Keziah Brevard's houses.[50]

Dolly Burge's diary provides a particularly detailed account of what such attentions meant to a widowed planter. In late July 1864 rumors of Union looting nearby prompted Dolly Burge to make slaves bury her china and silver, hide her clothes in their cabins, and drive the livestock into the swamp. Although she escaped serious losses then and in August, in late November her luck ran out. Returning from a trip to Social Circle, Dolly heard that "the Yankees were coming!" Two days later, she saw "large fires like burning buildings" and began again to disperse her possessions. Her overseer and a slave took her mules into the swamp while several other slaves assisted her in hiding smoked meats in a fodder stack. Dolly herself camouflaged a $200 barrel of salt as a leaching tub in a slave's garden, and she instructed her hands to hide their own things as well. The following day, the Yankees came. "Like Demons they rush in," she wrote. "My yards are full. To my smoke house my Dairy Pantry kitchen & cellar like famished wolves they come breaking locks & whatever is in their way. The thousand pounds of meat in my smoke house is gone in a twinkling my flour my meal my lard butter eggs pickles of various kinds both in vinegar & brine. Wine jars & jugs are all gone. My eighteen fat turkeys my hens chickens & fowls. My young pigs are shot down in my yard & hunted as if they were rebels themselves."[51] Burge's present-tense description captures the whirlwind nature of the soldiers' movements. By her calculation, their visit left her "poorer by thirty thousand dollars than I was yesterday morning." She also claimed to be "a much stronger rebel."[52]

Burge's continued commitment to the Confederate cause, and to the cause of slavery more generally, becomes clear in the way she used the rhetoric of benevolence to describe the loss of her slaves. She wrote, for example, that the soldiers had marched her slaves off "at the point of the bayonet," and "one (Newton) jumped into bed in his cabin & declared himself sick another crawled under the floor a lame boy he was but they pulled him out & placed him on a horse & drove him off. . . . Jack came crying to me the big tears coursing down his cheeks saying they were making him go. I said stay in my room but a man followed in cursing him & threatening to shoot him if he did not go. Poor Jack had to yeild." This scene proved her inability to protect her slaves against outsiders as a master should, but it also suggested something more, that the soldiers had abducted her slaves, which in turn implied that her slaves had wills of their own and, crucially, did *not* want to leave her but instead had to be coerced into abandoning her plantation. An earlier experience with Union soldiers likely helped Dolly Burge interpret her slaves' departure in this way. In August of that year, a group of twenty-six Yankees demanded breakfast, robbed her over-seer, "seared" a house, and took "three of my best mules." "None of my servants went with them," however, for which Dolly felt "very thankful."[53]

What Dolly Burge did not acknowledge was that slaves had reasons of their own to remain where they were. Staying put, even to the point of re-sisting Union soldiers, might make the best sense, depending on the sol-diers' behavior, the slaves' history with their owner, and their own invest-ment in the farm or plantation. In Dolly Burge's case, the first group of Yankee soldiers her slaves encountered had pretended to be stragglers from Confederate Joseph Wheeler's cavalry, a lie which might well have made the slaves suspicious. On both occasions, soldiers' destructiveness likely did not endear them to slaves either. Soldiers stole everything of value that they found in and around the slaves' cabins, insisting that the cloth-ing and other goods they found could only have belonged to the whites. They also treated the slaves themselves roughly; Dolly complained that "my women could not step outside the door without an insult."[54] Given this taste of their supposed liberators, the Burge slaves perhaps reflected that Dolly had treated them comparatively well. While they surely knew that only their labor enabled her to keep feeding and clothing them, per-haps they appreciated the special dinners, the "candy pulling," and the chance for "enjoying themselves right merrily dancing & frolicking" with which she rewarded their labors. Dolly also allowed them to earn money and acquire property. Finally, the land itself probably had meaning for them: not only had they buried their dead there, but they also had plots which Dolly let them farm for their own benefit. They may even have imagined that if they remained, they would gain title when the North won, which in late 1864 seemed increasingly likely. At this point, they could not have predicted that Reconstruction would disabuse so many of their hopes.[55]

For their part, slaveholding widows like Dolly Burge regarded their slaves' reluctance to depart as testimony to their own mastery. In mourning her lost slaves, Dolly crafted an elegy for antebellum master–slave relations: "My poor boys my poor boys, what unknown trials are before you. How you have clung to your mistress & assisted her in every way you knew how. You have never known want of any kind. Never have I corrected them. A word was sufficient it was only to tell them what I wanted & they obeyed!"[56] Even on plantations where planters' and slaves' interests most thoroughly articulated, this idyll of uncontested authority and uncoerced obedience bore little relationship to the facts.[57] Dolly Burge's words here assuredly say more about her own emotional state in the aftermath of the Sherman tornado than about what really happened on her plantation before his visit. And yet, before we conclude that Sherman's men eviscerated Dolly Burge's pretense of mastery, leaving her only the illusory comforts of false memory, we would do well to consider how she described her slaves in the weeks and months that followed. Christmas found her still employing the language of benevolent care. About her missing "boys," she wrote, "How I miss them." On December 24 and 25, she recorded her truncated Christmas preparations. She had "no cakes, pies, or confectionary" and "nothing to put in even in Sadais stocking," nor could she live up to her obligation to provide "gifts for my servants." Come Christmas morning, Sadai "could not believe" that she had no presents, and she retreated to bed, "sobbing." Afterward, "the little negroes all came in [saying] 'Christmas gift mistress Christmas gift mistress,'" whereupon Dolly herself "pulled the cover over my face" and cried as well.[58]

The holiday season exposed Dolly's inability to provide the treats and gifts for her slaves that they (and she) expected, but the failure did not prompt her to abandon the ideal of generosity, nor to imagine washing her hands of slaves once and for all. Dolly was, in fact, unprepared for emancipation, which she learned about on May 17, 1865; "I hear to day that our negroes are all freed by the US government. This is more than I anticipated yet I trust it will be a gradual thing." It was not, and for the next two weeks, Dolly heard a series of "conflicting rumors" about what the order meant. Ultimately, she told her slaves "they were free to do as they liked," but she remained confused about her needs and obligations. On the one hand, she wondered, "What can I do without them?" On the other, she asked, "What provision shall I make for them," believing it was still "my duty to make some provision for them." Ultimately, like many of her peers, she hired back those who agreed to "go on with their work & obey as usual," an arrangement which in many former slaveholders' minds should be slavery in all but name. On Christmas Day 1865, a recognition of fundamental change vied with Dolly's longing for continuity. This year, Sadai had gifts in her stocking, some of which she shared with "eight little ne-groes sitting around her gazing upon the treasures." The freedpeople also received their own gifts, an index that Dolly's household economy had sig-nificantly recovered from the previous year's devastation. After describing this scene—which could equally well have been penned in any number of years before 1861—Dolly wrote, "'Tis the last Christmas we shall prob-ably be together Freedmen!" Yet even now, she clung to the idea that for-mer slaveholders had custodial obligations to their former slaves. The next month, she marveled that some of her peers could "allow them to wander about & perish," words that reflect the entrenched assumption that many if not most African Americans could not provide for themselves.[59] Like thousands of her peers, Dolly Burge had lost her slaves and, with them, much of her fortune, but her beliefs about the reciprocal obligations of whites and blacks—care and obedience, respectively—remained intact through the Confederacy's collapse, surrender, and reincorporation into a (nominally) free nation.

FURTHER EVIDENCE of slaveholding widows' dogged resistance to change comes from the ways they continued using chivalry and gentility to shape their negotiations with other whites, both the Union invaders and their fellow Confederates. Slaveholding widows reacted in various ways to their experiences of Union invasion and occupation, but many if not most be-lieved that their behavior in the enemy's presence revealed both patriotism and propriety (or their absence). Some women privileged the former, ex-pressing their politics through open acts of contempt. In occupied New Or-leans, these reached such heights that General Benjamin Butler famously warned that any woman who acted disrespectfully could in turn be treated as a prostitute.[60] A safer approach involved treating the enemy with scrupu-lous reserve.[61] That was Cornelia McDonald's course through most of her time in occupied Winchester, both maintaining a posture of "loftiness" and "scorn" and taking pains to act "as if they were not there." If she was "obliged to pass very near them" on the streets or even in her own house, she "did so without being, or seeming to be aware of their presence." Even a friendly adjutant, who "often brought some delicacies for the children" and spent hours "with my little Hunter in his arms," received the cold shoul-der. She never invited him into her parlor and would speak to him only in the hallway. From Richmond, Phoebe Pember reported a similar reserve.

While there was no "stepping aside with affectation," there was also "no assimilation between the invaders and invaded." Richmond's women "simply totally ignored their presence."[62]

For all this hauteur, slaveholding widows often needed to interact with the enemy, to request a guard against looters, for example, or petition for the return of confiscated property. In those cases, they used familiar strategies, playing up their maternity, their feminine dependence, and their right to be treated as ladies. In Winchester, repeated demands that Cornelia McDonald surrender her house for use as a Union hospital or headquarters forced her to negotiate with those she usually snubbed. After a year of occupation, one such demand finally broke her "power of resistance, and all my self command." She "burst into tears," as did her children, who cried "violently without knowing why." Embarrassed by this scene, Major Butterworth suggested that she speak with his superior, General Milroy. When Milroy pleaded that he had to follow orders, she argued with him. Refusing to let him deny his agency in this way (as widows themselves often did), she claimed instead that he alone could determine her fate. That permitted her the complementary position of supplicant, petitioning for the privilege of "a shelter for my sick children." Milroy granted her plea, and whatever his reasons, his decision confirmed for McDonald the rhetorical utility of dependent widowhood.[63]

If bereaved and desperate motherhood went hand in glove with petitioning, the supposed prerogatives of the fairer sex suggested ways of being "less at a disadvantage." When Cornelia McDonald returned home from town one day early in the war, she found a group of Federal officers on her front steps. Before speaking a word, she "walked deliberately up the steps until I reached the top one" in order to be "on a level with them." Another Winchester widow, Mary Lee, informed a captain that "we demanded the courtesy that every lady has the right to expect from every gentleman."[64] Dolly Burge judged Union officers and soldiers in light of this expectation. As the bluecoats approached her house in 1864, she walked "to the gate to claim protection & a guard." After her first guard abandoned his post, a Vermont colonel ordered two other men to stand guard, but Dolly took little comfort from them because "they were Dutch & I could not understand one word they said." None of these men amounted to much in Dolly's eyes, but she assessed another man, "Mr. Webber from Illinois & a Captain," quite differently. He promised to protect her house from the torch, telling her that he knew her brother Orrington, who lived in Chicago. Reflexively assuming the prerogative of judging others' gentility, Dolly wrote, "He felt for me & I give him & several others the character of gentlemen."[65]

Positioned as she was on her plantation (however despoiled), Dolly Burge could safely assume that the Union's men would recognize her standing as a planter and a lady. Beyond the residences that anchored their social status, however, slaveholding widows took pains to demonstrate their claim to ladyhood through dress. After the occupation of Richmond following General Lee's surrender, Phoebe Pember was determined not to abandon the Confederate patients who remained at Chimborazo Hospital. Among other things, this meant contriving to find food and other supplies for their use. To this end, she visited the Federal Headquarters where she applied for the right to use her ambulance and gather food for her patients. Beforehand, she dressed for battle. As she described it, her "full-dress toilette" evinced both the need to improvise and a ramrod determination to look the lady: she wore boots, a black and white homespun dress, "white cuffs and collar of bleached homespun, and a hat plaited of the rye straw picked from the field back of us, dyed black with walnut juice, a shoe-string for ribbon to encircle it; and knitted worsted gloves." However ersatz, her hat, cuffs, collar, and gloves apparently communicated to the Union officials she met because they granted her request. On another occasion, Pember simply "put aside" the bayonets of Union soldiers blocking her path and proceeded to help herself to supplies remaining in the hospital commissary.[66]

Phoebe Pember's expectation that she could continue doing her job even under Union occupation suggests that she imagined her work not as a political act which the enemy might rightfully oppose, but rather as an apolitical mission of mercy. That assumption was explicit in Cornelia McDonald's response to the demand that she take a loyalty oath before being allowed "to buy necessaries for my family." She claimed that "it could not be a matter of importance what women thought or wished on the subject."[67] Her antagonist in this encounter, General Milroy, knew better, however. So did her neighbor, Mary Lee, who described McDonald as "one of the talking heroines."[68] Union officials were not entirely consistent on this point, however. While Union commanders knew that women were some of the worst "rebels," they also tended to treat women's resistance differently from men's. Cornelia McDonald was never punished for her "'audacity,'" for example, but her young son, Harry, was once arrested on suspicion of having hit a Federal officer with a snowball, and he was also beaten up for proclaiming his Confederate loyalties. Not all women benefited from this gendered privilege, however; wealthy and well-connected women stood the best chance of escaping violence. During the war, untold numbers of southern women endured rape, other violence, and sometimes even murder, but most of these unfortunates were either slaves or poor white women—precisely those who had been most vulnerable to assault before the war—or Unionists.[69]

CONFEDERATE LADIES' insistence on the privileges of gender and class applied not only to Union officers but also to their fellow white southerners. Difficult as it was to play the lady with the enemy, slaveholding widows found it even more challenging to sustain the mystique of privilege over other southerners when all faced the prospect of being burned out of their houses, forced to flee advancing columns, or reduced to supping on hominy and water. But few if any were willing to relinquish their own self-assessment as ladies, and they continued to measure gentility in much the same ways as before the war, attaching particular significance to dress, work, and behavior. In part because the war made the first two signs of ladyhood harder to sustain, behavior became all the more important. New anxieties about their own status, however, rarely made the cohort more sympathetic to the less fortunate.

During the war, slaveholding widows sometimes expressed surprise at what they found themselves wearing and doing. Maintaining fashionable dress proved a constant struggle, even for widows whose mourning dictated a fairly plain wardrobe. Susie Richmond remarked that even the most stylish women of Charleston and Savannah were "obliged to get any thing they can get for to wear" because few stores had "any goods." While in Charlottesville, Ada Bacot had to settle for a bonnet she did not like, for example, because she could not find a better one. (South Carolina patriot to the core, she observed that "it will do for this place.") Late in 1862, Ada also found herself riding in a wagon she "could never had made up my mind to ride through our village in." But Charlottesville at war was not Darlington District at peace, and she consoled herself with the thought that "every body here" did "the same."[70] In November 1864 Dolly Burge marveled at the changes war had brought to her (above and beyond the damage to her plantation). After accompanying her slave on an errand by mule-wagon, she wrote, "Never did I think I would have to go to mill. Such are the changes of life"—or rather of war.[71] Mary Green, Cornelia McDonald's stepdaughter, found herself in an even more embarrassing predicament during her flight from Winchester. Her hasty packing left her in an "un-becoming plight"; traveling by stagecoach in a "calico morning dress" while carrying a "white bundle" of "forgotten articles" tied up in an old sheet, she looked far too rustic to be considered a lady. As a result, during her journey, "she missed the attention she had a right to expect," except on the few occasions when she happened to meet "some one who knew her or her family" from better times.[72]

Slaveholding widows were determined to keep up a semblance of gentility precisely because of these status-blurring predicaments. Candace Lee intended that her children be "as well dressed as our neighbors" even if they had to use homespun and recycled trimmings in lieu of new goods.[73] Cornelia McDonald found it "plenty of work" simply keeping her growing children's "knees and elbows covered," but to her it was no less important that they look good as well. She spent considerable energy, for example, turning some old curtain fringe into a "very pretty plaid for Nelly's frocks." She paid equal attention to her eldest son when he resolved to join the army. By this point—March 1864—the McDonalds were nearly penniless, but Cornelia still believed it a "great consideration" to outfit him properly. She exchanged a "remaining piece of finery" for some gray cloth to make his uniform because "coarse and rough as it was, it was worn by the best of the land." Cornelia also knew that "a white collar was indispensable, as it was then and must always be the distinguishing badge of a gentleman."[74]

Widows were particularly intent on maintaining social distinctions when they were engaged in unusual activities, such as hospital nursing. Throughout the war, although some celebrated the uplifting influence of a tender lady nurse, many Confederate men and women remained concerned that "such a life would be injurious to the delicacy and refinement of a lady." Working in a hospital indeed proved challenging for women like Phoebe Pember and Ada Bacot, who were accustomed to "all the comforts of luxurious life."[75] After a period of adjustment, Ada Bacot valued her nursing enough that she was inclined to accept an 1863 offer to become a hospital matron. In this case, she believed her gentility would stand her in good stead; slaves had "a higher respect" for her and her Charleston comrade Marie Lesesne than for humbler whites, and "therefore we can manage them more easily." Yet Bacot ultimately refused the position, convinced by her friends' arguments that "I had never been accustomed to labour" and could not do the work "except at the expence of comfort, pleasure, & health."[76] If she could not do it, she and her peers thought they knew who could, namely, "the common class of respectable servants," who had a life-long familiarity with manual housework. Pember, for one, described the women she hired to assist her at Chimborazo as "inefficent and unedu-cated women, hardly above the laboring classes." While they lacked the manners and, she thought, morals of "the better class of people," they like slaves were supposedly "more amenable to authority." As it happened, Pember found her female assistants a real trial. One turned out to be an al-coholic and had to be fired. Another assumed a delicacy that prevented her from doing any work. Pember found her patients' female relations equally appalling, sneering that they considered it "a patriotic duty not to be afraid or ashamed under *any* circumstances." She also passed judgment on their letters, "queer mixtures of ignorance, bad grammar, worse spelling, and simple feeling." These "irresistibly ludicrous" letters would, she thought, be excellent sources of "public amusement," were it not for the "love that filled them chastened and purified them."[77]

Hospitals further tested elite women by putting them in close and often intimate proximity to strange men. Ada Bacot and Phoebe Pember often found ordinary soldiers either disgusting or comical in every way, from their speech to their physical appearance, favorite foods, and utter igno-rance of genteel manners. "Expression was not a gift among the common soliders," Pember opined. (Educated nurses often wrote letters for the il-literate and wounded.)[78] Both women felt more comfortable tending to men who were "generaly polite & genteel looking" because these men were ap-proximately their social equals and less likely to shock them with uncouth words or behavior.[79]

Coarse patients were not nurses' only problem. Equally troubling were the male members of the hospital staff, who did not always treat ladies with the consideration they believed their due. Phoebe Pember had particular problems in this regard: her authority over patients and male ward work-ers placed her in competition with male surgeons, who vied with her for control over the patients' diet and the hospital's rations. Pember handled these conflicts much as antebellum widows dealt with troublesome neigh-bors or overseers: relying on lower-status men she could command and on high-status men who supported her. Following a quarrel in Pember's "of-fice" over whiskey rations, an angry surgeon astonished her when he "kicked back the door" to her "private room" to resume the fight. She in-structed him to leave, and when he refused, she "called to the sentry to order up a sergeant and file of the guard." As "the ring of their muskets outside sounded," she told the surgeon he had five minutes to leave or be "taken to the guard-house." The offending surgeon spluttered that "he would make me know my position," but he soon decided that "discretion was the better part of valor, and left." While she made no formal complaint, the man was removed from the hospital shortly thereafter, "no doubt to that Botany Bay—'the front.'" Shortly thereafter, the whiskey battle resumed. When she disputed another surgeon's attempt to alter the standard ration for a patient, he reacted angrily, challenging her to document her disbursement of whiskey for the previous fifteen months. When an exchange of letters failed to satisfy him, he forwarded the letters to the surgeon-in-chief. He refused to act, in essence endorsing Pember's conduct. Next, the surgeon sent an official complaint to the military governor of the department of Henrico, who "read it all with some amazement" and returned it, "again without response." At that point, some "waggish" surgeons decided to have some fun with their colleague. They urged him to take his complaint to Secretary of War Reynolds, which he did, presumably unaware that Pember was the Secretary's personal friend. The "unlucky documents" became a great joke "at one of the charming breakfasts which his wife was in the habit of giving," at which Pember was a regular and welcome guest. After that, the surgeon "kept out of my way."[80]

Pember's determination not to back down owed a great deal to her conviction that the surgeons were "not all gentlemen, although their profession should have made them aspirants to the character." This particular man, moreover, was merely a "contract surgeon" (the lowest medical rank), and before the war, he had been "a bar-keeper in a Georgia tavern." Pember herself was "accustomed to be treated with extreme deference and courtesy by the highest officials connected with the government." For such a woman, being challenged by a barman was "appalling." Nor was she alone in finding his presumption ridiculous; Pember's prominence and the surgeon's low status surely explain why his fellow surgeons set up him for embarrassment, instead of closing ranks with him to discipline a woman who challenged masculine authority. Pember's encounter with these two doctors echoes countless prewar occasions when slaveholding widows' connections with prominent men or employment of overseers enabled them to stand up to (and over) white men who disputed their authority. Moreover, rather like Dr. King had done in Robert Carter's dispute with Martha Singleton, the surgeon-in-chief, the military governor, and the secretary of war not only did not side with the disgruntled man, but also chose inaction. In refusing to dignify the complaint, they let Pember's authority stand on its own. This scene thus encapsulates the distinctive position of the elite slaveholding widow. More than almost any other white southern women, she possessed her status in her own right, rather than coming under the umbrella of any (living) man. Small wonder, then, that slaveholding widows sedulously insisted on drawing stark distinctions not only among women, but among men as well: their version of mastery depended on policing the boundaries of rank in both genders.[81]

FOR ALL THE AUTHORITY that widowed ladyhood endowed, slaveholding women were not invulnerable. Not only did they suffer along with other white women and all civilians, they also faced distinctive hazards as widows. Within and beyond hospitals, slaveholding widows relied heavily on behavioral signs of respectability as they found it increasingly difficult to maintain other markers of ladyhood, such as elegant clothes and well-fed, leisured bodies. Concerns about keeping a dignified distance from men outside their immediate families had constrained slaveholding widows' sociable activities even before the war, especially for those young enough to consider remarriage and to seem sexually desirable. During the war, these issues became all the more fraught. For starters, the rising death toll engendered considerable competition among women for the attentions, and especially the wedding vows, of the remaining hale men. Single women sometimes complained that it was unfair for a widow to seek a new husband when they had never had the chance to marry. Equally important, war bred far more contact among strangers than was common before the war, especially among strangers who could not easily infer each others' social position. Refugeeing and poverty in particular eroded the supposedly reliable signs encoded in location, connections, dress, and demeanor. In this context, even the staunch patriot Ada Bacot dared not cheer aloud for a Confederate regiment that was passing through Charlottesville because it would have been undecorous.[82]

Working as nurses and matrons exposed slaveholding women to piles of amputated legs and the embarrassment of working in wards with men clad only in hospital gowns. It also entailed the risk that a lonely soldier might regard their kindness as something more. Ada Bacot worried that one of the soldiers she attended was "inclined to over rate my little attentions." She felt very embarrassed when another invalid, a young lieutenant who was the relative of friends and not her patient, asked her to wash his face and comb his hair. She "hesitated a good while," but when she realized that "he couldent realy use his hands," she consented to perform "Mrs. Coats' duty." Bacot had been visiting with Lieutenant Harllee as an acquaintance, not a nurse, and she found the blurring of sociability with the businesslike intimacies of nursing quite uncomfortable.[83] When Harllee wrote her a personal letter thanking her for her nursing, she struggled to write a reply that accurately reflected her sentiments, namely, "a very kindly feeling . . . but nothing more." She showed her response to fellow widow Marie Lesesne, who pronounced it "just the thing." Maintaining propriety was a matter not just of self-respect but of honor and even employment. Another widow who worked with Marie Lesesne and Ada Bacot in Charlottesville was fired, following questions about her conduct. Bacot remarked, "I thought if a woman did not behave as a woman ought she could not expect consideration from any one." Her friend Dr. McIntosh agreed, saying that "she had not acted in any way to command the respect or attention of a gentleman." On another occasion, Ada and Marie jointly "scolded" a young nurse for failing to recognize that soldiers "might not put the right construction upon her motives." The outspoken and fiercely intelligent Louisa McCord took this risk extremely seriously in the hospital she managed. According to her friend, Mary Chesnut, she blamed the nurses as much as the soldiers. "Mrs. McCord says a nurse, who is also a beauty, had better leave her beauty with her cloak and hat at the door," Chesnut noted. When a "lovely lady nurse" repeated a story about a soldier asking for a kiss, McCord's "fury was 'at the woman's telling it.'" McCord feared, "very properly," that such tales would bring "disrepute" upon her hospital, as "she knew there were women who would boast of an insult if it ministered to their vanity."[84]

It was not only in hospitals that widows worried about seeming either too lighthearted or too interested in men. Mary Chesnut sneered in her diary about another young widow, who quickly transferred her affections from her dead husband to a new love. Even more shocking was a woman she saw canoodling on the train with a man. When others not unreasonably assumed this man was her husband, the woman "drew herself up proudly" and explained that she was a widow and the man her cousin, and that "I loved my dear husband too well to marry again." (This story mirrors countless ancient tales of faithless widows consoling themselves with new lovers.)[85] Another anecdote in Chesnut's diary suggests a proper lady's response to such a scandalous sight. When a Mrs. Preston found herself on a train with some "'strictly unfortunate females,'" she neither "made a fuss" nor "fidgeted." Instead, she reacted with "quiet self-possession," calmly ignoring "all that she did not care to see." Traveling sometimes made slaveholding women themselves the subjects of unsettling comment. While Cornelia McDonald was traveling by boat to meet her husband (who died before she arrived), she was "annoyed" to hear two young girls speculate that she was "a widow, been married twice." Worrying that this meant she looked inappropriately "festive," she sought out a mirror and was "reassured" to see only "a thin, anxious face and black garments." Any number of twice-widowed women would have disputed the association between remarriage and undue levity, but McDonald recognized that, fairly or not, her contemporaries sometimes looked askance at widows for remarrying and for socializing too gaily.[86]

Young South Carolina teacher Isabella Woodruff agonized over these issues throughout the war. She had cause because she depended on her reputation even more than most widows since no slaveholders would hire a woman of questionable virtue to teach their young daughters. Complicating the situation significantly was the fact that she actually had several suitors.[87] As her friend Ariela Pinkind reminded her, "You know *widows* and especially *young widows* are so liable to be *censured* for the least things, without the slightest cause. . . . I am afraid if you do not take him people will set you down as a flirt and coquette."[88] At least two abortive courtships produced no obvious damage to Isabella Woodruff's reputation, but she had new cause for concern in the spring of 1864 when she was accused of standing between a husband and wife.[89] At the time, Isabella had been corresponding with a C. H. A. Woodin, a recent acquaintance whom she knew to be married. Concerned that their epistolary friendship loaned itself to a scandalous interpretation, she urged him to get his wife's approval. Apparently he failed, for in June 1864, Mollie Woodin herself wrote Isabella: "I seat myself to drop you a note in regard to the correspondence betwixt yourself and my husband (C H A Woodin) you wished to know in one of your epistles to him if I was knowing to the correspondence; he has shown me several of your letters and I do object for the correspondence to be continued any longer betwixt you two and the acquaintance of yours being of short duration and another thing to be considd he being a married man and you a single lady, I don't think that you ought to be corresponding therefore I wish it to be discontinued so you have got my opinion of the matter." What Isabella thought about this letter is unclear, but she hastened to put the "'green eyed monster'" to rest. She assured Mrs. Woodin that "the correspondence you speak of is *purely literary* & was carried on with your concent. Your husband I firmly believe *loves you devotedly*. I like to hear a man speak affectionately of his wife & sister & *that* was why I was willing to write to him." Attempting to seal her case, she added a confidential piece of information, that while she was "a 'single Lady,'" her heart was "occupied" and "to all intents & purposes" she was as good as married.[90]

The object of Woodruff's affections at this point was Charles Holst, whose wife Jeannette had died in January 1864. Woodruff had corresponded with Holst since 1859 with his wife's apparent approbation. Disdaining those couples who lived like "cats & dogs," Jeannette Holst assured Isabella that "my husbands friends are my friends." Whatever the nature of the friendship during Jeannette's life, Charles and Isabella married a year and a half after her death. Their courtship proved a stormy one, in part because economic hardship kept them apart and delayed their wedding, and in part because Charles failed to appreciate Isabella's vulnerability. (He was, if anything, more sensitive to her independence as a self-supporting widow.) In the spring of 1865, for example, Charles let it be known that he had invited Isabella to stay at his house while simultaneously pleading that he could not yet marry her for want of money. Incensed, she told him to "cultivate self control! It is not pleasant to me to be talked about, even though no harm be said!" She admitted that she ought "to listen & be guided in a great measure by you," but she reminded him that she had obligations to others. "There are others, also interested, & whose voice must be listened to, though they speak from the silent land," she told him. "Father said daughter, never place yourself or allow yourself to be placed for an instant in any questionable position! My husband on his death bed said, I leave you & my name to God & yourself. Were that name to become tarnished through my residence with or love for yourself, you could never do any thing that would sweeten the bitter thought!"[91] Like many a widow before the war, Isabella Woodruff referenced her dead husband (and father) to justify criticizing Holst and to insist that she was honor-bound to behave as she did. Unlike the many slaveholding men who appreciated this argument, Holst apparently did not get the message. Isabella again had to chide him for writing about her to others, "contrary to my express desires." This time, she herself was too angry for prudence; since he did not care "whether my name becomes a town talk," she suggested that he "extend your enquiries in any direction you please." Perhaps he might consult with "the Governor of this State, Georgia, or Florida" to investigate her character. Behind the anger in this letter lay its date—the day that she and Charles ought to have married—and the continued vulnerability of her liminal position between widowhood and coverture.[92]

Isabella Woodruff knew what Charles Holst apparently did not fully appreciate, namely, that women's reputations, and especially those of young widows, were more vulnerable than men's when it came to courtship, emotional intimacy, and marriage. As Meta Grimball observed of two women she met in Charleston, being "much talked about" made any woman "not desirable" as a friend. In her correspondence, Isabella protected both herself and her suitors by refusing to name them, which made it difficult for her to understand how Charles Holst could publicize their affection in his own letters to third parties. Being talked about was not the only risk; worse still was the prospect that she might be seen, as some widows were, as the initiator in the relationship, as a daring widow who had ensnared a man's affections away from his wife.[93]

Explicit testimony about the supposedly predatory widow is hard to come by in the antebellum or the wartime South, thanks to the slaveholders' typical prudery about sexual matters. Outside the South, however, the husband-hunting widow was a staple in British comic theater in the late eighteenth and early nineteenth centuries, for example, and appeared throughout early modern European sacred and profane literatures.[94] Fragmentary evidence of the trope's persistence in the Confederacy can be deduced from the comments of slaveholders and former slaves. Decades after emancipation, Savilla Burrell of Winnsboro, South Carolina, asserted that her owner's second wife had "captivated" him, explaining, "You know widows is like dat anyhow, 'cause day done had 'sperience wid mens and wraps dem round their little finger. . . . Young gals have a poor chance against a young widow like Miss Mary Ann." Eliza Hasty, also of Winnsboro, had a similar opinion, describing one of her former owner's children: "Her is a widow, just lak I is a widow. De only difference is, I's black and her is white. Her can see well enough to run after and ketch another man, but I's bland and can't see a man, much less chase after him." Whether African Americans imbibed this attitude from whites or developed it independently, the image of sexually experienced and aggressive widows suggests that widows ran a real risk that their behavior would be interpreted unfavorably.[95] Sexually forward widows became all the more ominous during the Civil War in what was perhaps a displaced anxiety about the chastity of the region's many wives left alone on the homefront. Promiscuous widowhood also took on new meaning at this time because southern whites already dreaded that slave emancipation would drag the region into a slough of sexual depravity, a fear aggravated by the suspicion that white widows might initiate interracial liaisons. At least as important, if not more so, was the sense that unchaste or merely flirtatious widows cast doubt on the very purpose and value of men's battlefield sacrifices: if they would be dishonored after death, why should they lay down their lives?[96]

MORE WAS AT STAKE in slaveholding widows' concern with propriety and disparagement of ordinary men and women than a prissy attachment to morality and cleanliness. As before the war, widows' elitism had implications beyond sociability, beyond even their investment in ladyhood as a source of protection. These became especially explicit in their reactions to the Confederacy's battlefield losses and ultimate defeat. Phoebe Pember described the Virginia soldiers as "the very best class of men in the field." A "hardier race" than the Gulf State's men, the Virginians also possessed "more civilized tastes." This preference for Virginia soldiers, like Ada Bacot's prejudice in favor of South Carolinians, suggests the Confederacy's inability to create a truly national patriotism.[97] But it also reflected a persistent faith in the reality, and the *political* impact, of class as well as state distinctions.

Summing up the year 1861 in her diary, Dolly Burge lamented "the horrors of war" and "the privations the hardships to which our soldiers are exposed." Despite this universal concern for southern men in arms, she also remarked that "some of the best blood of the country has been spilled." In her and other widows' minds, ordinary people's sufferings might elicit compassion, but it was the "best" men's deaths that they imagined would determine the nation's fate. As the war drew to its bloody close, Cornelia McDonald's comments about the high levels of desertion from Lee's army reflects this distinction. She pitied the men who deserted because their families were starving, yet she nonetheless "felt a scorn" for "deserters" because she believed that desertion reflected a weak character as well as a strong attachment to family. To her mind, the Confederacy became despotic at the end, but only to the humbler sort. The poor "knew that they would be as well off under one government as another," and thus to them "it was oppression to be forced into the army." In contrast, "to those whose education and habits of life made them enthusiastic, or whose pride acted as an incentive for them to endure and suffer, as was the case with the higher classes, it wore no such aspect." McDonald believed—and she was not alone in this—that "if the brave, the well born and the chivalrous could have done all the fighting, there would have been no shrinking, no desertion." And, she presumably assumed, no defeat, no surrender, and no end to slavery.[98]

In some ways, slaveholding widows' dependence on slave labor reached its apogee at precisely the moment of the institution's greatest weakness. Less able than ever to rely on other whites for financial and other assistance, widows' ability to house, feed, and clothe themselves rested squarely on their slaves' increasingly dubious willingness to labor for them. Relatedly, because ladyhood was arguably more important than ever, so too was slave women's labor. Little changed in this regard with emancipation. While many slaveholding women proclaimed that they were thankful to shed their obligations to slaves, few if any imagined that this meant doing without black women's domestic labor. For Cornelia McDonald, for instance, the prospect of having to dismiss her one remaining servant encapsulated her desolation. In the "dreary days" after the war ended, she was "so weak from hunger that I could scarcely go up and down stairs." By August 1865, she "had lost the feeling that God cared for us. . . . [T]he whole dreadful situation was shown to my doubting heart; the empty pantry, for even the beans and bread were exhausted, and I should have to send the servant away." For days, she longed for death.[99]

Although less despairing, her contemporary Ann Swann was no more enthusiastic about housekeeping without domestic servants. During the summer and early fall of 1865, Ann lived with various relatives. She apparently enjoyed her peripatetic existence, and she also relished the signs of familial affection. "When I think that your Fathers Relations have made so much of me," she wrote to her daughters, "it is the more gratifying." Such tangible and intangible support had long been critical to widows, but as the remainder of the letter reveals, more was at stake here. Ann did not want to return to her own house in Wilmington because she doubted that she "could fill any of the Servants places." Without slaves to do "so much of the drudgery," Ann had little interest in householding.[100] Age played some role in her reluctance; at 69, she had good reason to shun heavy housework. Equally important, however, slaveholding women's self-image had long had everything to do with their ability to avoid most of the heavy and unpleasant kinds of domestic work, or at least to choose what they would and would not do. The war compelled many a slaveholding woman to wash her own clothes, cook her own food, and clean her own room, but they rarely considered that this work truly lay in their proper sphere. As one slaveholding woman described in the waning days of the war, "'Newport has taken the cooking, and we are all ladies again.'"[101] One slaveholding man, Thomas Dabney, famously thought it more appropriate to do the washing himself than to have his daughter do it. (General Sherman had promised to bring southern women to the washtubs, rightly understanding that this image implied the Confederacy's utter defeat.)[102]

For the Confederacy's slaveholding widows, and perhaps especially for women widowed before the war, the loss of slave labor cut particularly deep. Slave management typically caused widows their greatest problems, yet it was precisely access to slave labor that preserved these widows' status as ladies, which in turn secured their respect and authority in the eyes of friends, family, and subordinates. Doing the managerial work of elite men posed comparatively little threat to slaveholding women's gender identity and social standing as long as they retained their freedom from most forms of women's manual labor. Even those widows who had to labor for their own support as boardinghouse keepers or teachers preserved their standing—as long as they had slaves to demarcate them as ladies. Before the war, Catherine Lewis depended on slaves Martha and Alana to "do all my washing and ironing" for her Chapel Hill boardinghouse. After the war's end, Lewis noted that all her kinswomen looked "ten years older than they did three weeks ago." This rapid aging had many causes, among which was the fact that "the negroes are all turned loose to ramble about & do what they please"; working as domestic servants did not much please most newly freed black women.[103] When women like Martha, Alana, and Savary obtained their freedom, women like Catherine Lewis and Ada Bacot had to struggle in new ways to define themselves as ladies. This was a struggle of truly historic proportions: southerners had measured the elevated status of elite white women through the gap between their work and that of enslaved women since the late seventeenth century. Looking at the postwar period, some of the clearest evidence of former slaveholders' reluctance to let the old order die can be found in their refusal to let freedwomen retire from laboring in white peoples' homes.

The Civil War compromised slaveholding widows' ability to act as masters while retaining the status of respectable ladies by threatening the material and ideological bases of slaveholding society. Antebellum strategies began to fail not simply because many more women suddenly became widows, but also because the war removed the white men—kinsmen, neighbors, and overseers—who complemented white widows' authority. And yet, even with their families mowed down or scattered, and their livelihood in shambles, Confederate women continued to benefit from the familiar languages of widows' determination, maternal sacrifice, familial mutualism, and, above all, racial and class superiority.

Epilogue

Slaveholding widows' fictive mastery existed because they participated in the slave system of social and economic domination and because slaveholding men time and again refused to carry their belief in female subordination to its logical conclusion. Enforced across the board and without exception, white women's subordination cost them too much. The same was true of slavery itself, which goes a long way to explaining why mastery was always fictive. When generalizing about the sexes, male slaveholders rarely articulated their faith in or reliance on women, but they expressed both in their actions. This dependence on white women by no means guaranteed companionate let alone happy marriages, families, and households. Doing men's work did not make women men's equals: women generally had little choice in the matter, and the relationship was profoundly unreciprocal because men avoided women's work at all costs.[1] Like gender ideology, mastery was coherent and forceful, and it structured behaviors throughout the Old South, but there was no one-to-one correlation between the ideology and the practice. Even as an idea, mastery hinged on the contradictory fictions that subordinates willingly consented and that masters could dominate others' hearts and minds. Yet despite their imperfect mastery, slaveholders held the fate of millions in their hands.

Collectively, widows helped ensure the orderly transfer of property, authority, and, ultimately, power between generations of these slaveholders. They had all the more influence because their gender drew a veil over the way that slavery produced systemic inequality among whites. Just as slave-holding men could use white racism to gloss over socioeconomic differences between themselves and the nonslaveholding majority, slaveholding widows deployed gender ideals in similar ways. Whether they represented themselves as imperious ladies or dependent ones, they tacitly—and largely unconsciously—replaced the material axis of wealth with the ideological one of gender. Gender in turn shaded into morality. Slaveholding women claimed the right to assistance on the basis of their delicacy, a quality which suggested innate virtue but in practical terms depended on being white and at least moderately well off. Even as widows drew attention to gender difference, they also assumed that they enjoyed most of slaveholding men's privileges. Those they lacked—chiefly political rights—they did not generally want. Slaveholding widows also modified gender expectations by carrying out both men's and women's work. Still, gender difference mattered in everything they did, especially when they performed men's work. Slaveholding widows laid no groundwork for egalitarian feminism; their crossing of gender lines constituted no self-conscious challenge to sexual inequality, no alternative to patriarchy. However, by doing work normatively assigned to both genders, they confounded the contemporary presumption that women and men were fundamentally different sorts of beings, intellectually, morally, and physically.

THE CIVIL WAR and its aftermath complicated slaveholding widows' ideas about gender roles and interactions. On the one hand, their sufferings made many long to be rescued and protected, a longing whose frustration, Drew Faust argues, prompted many women to withdraw their support from the Confederacy. On the other, most recognized the difference between their desires and their options, and when it came down to it, they refused to be dependent if they could avoid it. Or, as they would have put it, they refused to be burdensome to their friends and relations. A description of Lou Bartow in Mary Chesnut's diary recalls slaveholding women's discomfort with financial dependence on men other than their own husbands. Chesnut observed that Bartow's brother-in-law, Judge Carroll, urged her to live with him after her husband died. However, Bartow knew that supporting her as well as his "large family" would be difficult, and she "will not be an added burden to him." Apparently Carroll made a sincere effort to change her mind, but "in spite of all he can say, she will not forego her resolution." "She will," Chesnut said, "be independent."[2]

Some widows mourned their dependence as a sign of how far they had fallen from their prewar glory. Such was Cornelia McDonald's lament in the months immediately following General Lee's surrender. "How often I wished then," she wrote, "that of all the land their father had owned, I had only a few acres on which I could live with my children and try to make a living." Cornelia's fantasy did not extend so far that she longed not to work at all. If they had still had land, she presumed, "None of us would have shrunk from labour." What "almost broke" her heart, however, was the fact that her two elder sons had to "work as hired labourers for other people!" Other former slaveholders were laboring in fields too, of course, but as Cornelia knew, working for hire "was so different" from working one's own land, for "that would have been independence." For the first time, Cornelia could not easily distinguish her family from humble day laborers and tenant farmers of "the lowest level," whom she was accustomed to consider almost a different species. Rescue of a sort came her way not long thereafter, however. Thanks to General Pendleton, she received $100 in recognition of her husband's public service; her stepson gave her some money he had collected from his father's debtors; and a friend loaned her $300. Cornelia herself resumed her teaching, and she was "able in various ways to take care of my family till they were fitted to be of use."[3]

Other widows were equally determined not to become dependent, however much they relied on their kin and friends for help. In August 1865 Ann Swann resolved that she would not be a burden to her widowed daughter, stating, "I look forward to taking in work. . . . Sallie must work also. We cannot be dependent on Ann that cant tell what she will do herself for her little ones." This ethic of self-reliance occasionally formed a basis to criticize men who were not living up to their responsibilities. Whereas Cornelia McDonald took comfort from her sons' and stepsons' willingness to do their part, Ann Swann rebuked one of her sons for failing to do his. Ann's son had been occupying his mother's house rent-free for several years (another instance of widowed mothers' desire to help all their children, not only daughters and widows). But now, Ann desperately needed to rent her house out, so she wrote to inform her son that he would have to move out and look for tenants for her. Perhaps anticipating some resistance, she reminded him that she could have rented the house for the previous three years of his occupancy, "but I could not bring myself to say so to you, as I knew you had not wherewith to pay, your oft repeated sickness keeping you back in your business." Times had changed, however, and if his widowed mother and sister could earn their own support, so could he.

"Do as we all are going to do," she wrote. "Turn over a newe Leaf, begin to *work*, & *save*, as we have never done before. . . . my dear Son if you will only give up your habits of indulgence, and follow *duty*, . . . your future is still open to you to support your family." Ann Swann recognized that in hard times, men might not be able to support their womenfolk, but they at least had to try.[4]

Not all Confederate women echoed Ann Swann's efforts to shame their sons and husbands into action, but the contrast between female energy and male passivity was often marked and remarked upon. To some eyes, the listlessness of men like young Mr. Swann may also have compared unfavorably with the entrepreneurial energy of freedmen and women. From the scantiest of material foundations, southern blacks did their utmost to live, as the saying went, under their own vine and fig tree. They reconstructed their families whenever possible, built churches, schools, and mutual assistance societies, and entered formal politics. One such man, Byrl Anderson of Virginia, became both a farmer on his own account and an adviser to his white widowed neighbor, Mrs. Goode. "When Mrs. Goode came to these parts," he recalled, "she got me as her personal adviser for her farm. I used to tell her what things to plant in certain kinds of land and she always had success with her crops." Their relationship resembled antebellum patterns except that Anderson showed Goode the kind of attention that she expected but failed to receive from white men. Or at least that seems to be the message in her claim that Anderson knew "'more about how to treat a white lady than any white man in Virginia.'"[5]

These unfavorable comparisons between white and black men, and between white men and women, could only have aggravated gender and racial tensions in the postwar period. They may even have contributed to the construction of the rape complex in which black men were always and everywhere dangerous beasts, white women vulnerable innocents, and white men their indispensable defenders. After the war, freedpeople in general, and the Freedman's Bureau, black voters, and the Republican Party in particular constituted both a provocation and a threat to southern whites. Cornelia McDonald was not alone in fuming that "the negroes were at all times encouraged to be impudent and aggressive" while "every day" federal agents crafted "some new and oppressive prohibition or arbitrary command."[6] Over the coming years, hard-line southern Democrats fanned the flames of racism to white-heat and helped doom Reconstruction. Newspapers shrieked that all black men were murderers, rapists, and thieves just waiting to strike at hapless whites.[7] Once Reconstruction ended, black men's "uncontrollable hypersexuality" was nearly an article of faith among southern whites.[8] Their dread of the "black superpenis," to use Eugene Genovese's startling term,[9] made it possible to interpret the simple fact of a white woman's "being alone in the house with an African-American man" as an attack on her honor and on white dominion in general. This in turn justified lynching on the premise that only a very short and slippery slope separated a black man's minor familiarity from out-and-out rape. (In reality, specific accusations of sexual aggression were absent from most lynchings.)[10]

Against this grim backdrop, what do we make of Byrl Anderson and Mrs. Goode? Does his knowing "how to treat a white lady" simply reflect a black man's need to preserve the most scrupulous propriety in order to avoid a lynch mob's attentions? Had Mrs. Goode in fact "got" Anderson as a sexual partner as well as an adviser, as myths about sexually voracious widows would suggest? Whatever their relationship, Anderson was terribly vulnerable. Not only was he helping out a white woman who lived alone, he also had his own farm and had even been a union organizer.[11] And yet, while more research is needed on postwar relationships between freedmen and white widows in particular, we ought not read Anderson's relationship with Goode solely through the long shadow of lynch law. For starters, Anderson took pains to represent himself as an assertive, confident man who refused to play the slave to anyone's master. Equally important, Mrs. Goode represents something rather different than the flower of southern womanhood as defined by white vigilantes. For a widow like Mrs. Goode, being treated like a lady did not mean being confined to the narrowest of pedestals. She was, after all, running her own farm household, an enterprise in which she relied not on white men's physical protection but on a black man's practical assistance.

Byrl Anderson's relationship with Mrs. Goode thus raises questions about continuity and change, fluidity and rigidity, as the South endured the upheavals of Civil War, Reconstruction, and Redemption. In one sense, their interaction suggests the dramatic differences for African Americans between the pre- and postwar Souths, for better and for worse. Born a slave, Anderson was now a free man. He was a farmer, perhaps on his own land, perhaps as a tenant, but not, apparently, as a sharecropper. Moreover, he apparently took pride in not being Goode's employee; he "wasn't on no salary," but rather helped her out in a neighborly way.[12] Of course, he had to be scrupulously careful to treat her like a lady because, now that he was no one's property, no white person had a vested financial interest in protecting him from the ultimate penalty should he one day stand accused of insulting or attacking her. She thus retained considerable latent power over him, even as she relied on his aid. In another sense, Byrl Anderson's work for Mrs. Goode simply perpetuated an antebellum pattern of elite women's reliance on enslaved men to help them manage farms and plantations. She even gave him presents and money every Christmas, much as her predecessors had done for favored slaves. This continuity points up the underappreciated flexibility of white women's gender roles before and after the war. It also highlights their persistent inability to hand over all responsibilities to the white men who were supposedly their providers and protectors. Finally, it suggests how the gaps between the ideal and the real in race and gender prescriptions continued to create odd opportunities for interactions across the color line.

NOTES

Abbreviations Used in Notes

AFP   Archer Family Papers, VHS
AHFP   Alexander-Hillhouse Family Papers, SHC
ASFP   Arnold and Screven Family Papers, SHC
BFP   Burwell Family Papers, SHC
CFP   Cocke Family Papers, VHS
Duke   Special Collections Library, Duke University, Durham, N.C.
DWPP   Douglas Watson Porter Papers, SHC
EWGKP   Elizabeth Washington Grist Knox Papers, SHC
GFP   Grimball Family Papers, SHC
HFP   Hubard Family Papers, SHC
IARWP   Isabella Ann Roberts Woodruff Papers, Duke
JBGD   John Berkeley Grimball Diary, SHC
JFSP   John Francis Speight Family Papers, SHC
JPFP   Jackson and Prince Family Papers, SHC
JSP   John Steele Papers, SHC
NARA   National Archives and Records Administration
NCDAH   North Carolina Department of Archives and History, Raleigh
NDSD   Natalie DeLage Sumter Diary, SHC
PP   Peckatone Papers, VHS
RMDP   Robert Marion Deveaux Papers, Duke
SCL   South Caroliniana Library, University of South Carolina, Columbia
SHC   Southern Historical Collection, Wilson Library, University of
           North Carolina, Chapel Hill
VHS   Virginia Historical Society, Richmond, Va.
WGP   William Gilliland Papers, Duke
WHFP   Wilson and Hairston Family Papers, SHC
WHP   William Huntington Papers, VHS

Introduction

1. Allgor, *Parlor Politics*, 19–20; Fields, *"Worthy Partner,"* xix–xxvii.
2. Hagler, "Ideal Woman."

3. McCurry, *Masters of Small Worlds*, 6, 87, 177; Young, *Domesticating Slavery*, 86–89, 110–17.

4. Cary, *Letters on Female Character*, 48 (see also vi, 21, 193, 195); Adams, *Elements of Moral Philosophy*, 115, 145; *American Gleaner*, August 1, 1807; *Christian Index*, March 8, 1844; Chandler, *Address on Female Education*, 4, 10–23.

5. Catherine Lewis to Emma Lewis, March 20, 1839, JFSP; Wyatt-Brown, *Southern Honor*, 224; Clinton, *Plantation Mistress*, 31, 74, 191; Bynum, *Unruly Women*, 88–110.

6. McCurry, *Masters of Small Worlds*, 6, 85, 92.

7. On the early nineteenth-century expansion of suffrage and representation in the United States, see Keyssar, *Right to Vote*, part 1.

8. Boyd, *Papers of Thomas Jefferson*, 5:696.

9. Eliza Chapman to Mary Ferrand, July 8, [1840], Robert Cochran to Mary Steele, October 9, 1836, JSP; James Powell Cocke to Caroline Cocke, January 9, 1812, Charles Cocke to Jane Segar Cocke, February 19, 1812, Extract from Family Bible, Genealogical Notes, CFP; Whitcher, *Widow Spriggins*, 144, 155; Southworth, *Widow's Son*, 96–103, 119; *Fifth Annual Report*, 6; *Christian Index*, February 21, 1845, see also February 9, March 15, and March 29, 1844; Eliza Schley to Henry Jackson, April 22, 1837, Sarah Cobb to Martha Jackson, n.d., JPFP; Lucy Freeman to Thomas Nelson, February 7, 1836, Jessie Vaughan Papers; *Rules of the Society*; *Southern Cultivator*, December 6, 1843; *South Carolina Weekly Museum*, June 3, 1797; *Virginia Literary Magazine*, December 9, 1829; *Southern Rose*, October 26, 1833; Kerber, "Republican Mother," 187–205; Kierner, *Beyond the Household*, 182–84. For the recognition that some wives might welcome widowhood, see Sarah Screven to Martha Richardson, August 8, 1819, ASFP; Serena Lea to Martha Jackson, July 25, 1840, JPFP; Mary Ferrand to Ann Ferrand, March 30, 1836, JSP.

10. Haywood, *Manual of the Laws*, 237–40; Moore and Biggs, *Revised Code of North Carolina*, chapter 18; Salmon, *Women and the Law of Property*, 5, 141–43. Cf. Wilson, *Life after Death*, chapter 2.

11. In the formerly French and Spanish controlled Southwest, Roman and Catholic influences allowed somewhat more recognition of African-American and mixed-race wives and widows. I have chosen not to study slaveholding widows of color because they were so few in number, especially outside of cities like Charleston and New Orleans, and because I am interested in the implications of widowhood for racially as well as economically privileged women in a patriarchal, slaveholding society. Clinton and Gillespie, *Devil's Lane*, pt. 4; Cott, *Public Vows*, 32–35.

12. As Victoria Bynum argues, where poor white and free black mothers were concerned, southern courts doubted both their economic and their moral ability to raise good children. Bynum, *Unruly Women*, 100.

13. Some wealthy widows lived off investment income, such as stock dividends, without having any responsibility for managing capital. Widows of men in partnerships or corporations—increasingly common in the North—rarely had the option of becoming managers because these enterprises did not descend lineally

like a family business. For an exception to this general rule, consider Deborah Powers of Lansingburgh, New York. When her husband died circa 1830, she took over the management of his oil-cloth making factory. Appleby, *Recollections of the Early Republic*, 2–3, 21–24. That widows could become planters but not lawyers, doctors, or merchants suggests one way in which professionalization and the spread of industrial capitalism created new levels of gender segregation in the economic lives of elite women. Davidoff and Hall, *Family Fortunes*; Smith, *Ladies of the Leisure Class*.

14. Fields, *Worthy Partner*, 371.

15. Martha Cocke to Caroline Cocke, April 9, [1812], July 17, 1812, CFP; Clinton, *Plantation Mistress*, 170.

16. Martha Cocke to Caroline Cocke, n.d., and M. Cocke to Caroline Cocke, n.d., CFP; Bellows, *Benevolence among Slaveholders*, 44. Cf. Catherine Kenan Price to Elizabeth Blanks, [November 1844], Elizabeth J. (Holmes) Blanks Papers.

17. Fox-Genovese, *Within the Plantation Household*, 204–7; Wyatt-Brown, *Southern Honor*, 240, 242; McCurry, *Masters of Small Worlds*, 17, 121; Weiner, *Mistresses and Slaves*, 35–37, 56–59; Faust, *Mothers of Invention*, 12, 32, 55.

18. Ada W. Bacot Diary, February 11, 1861, Ada W. Bacot Papers.

19. Catherine Edmonston quoted in Fox-Genovese, *Within the Plantation Household*, 110. For an insightful analysis of how kin and especially sibling relationships crosscut patriarchal marriages, see Glover, *All Our Relations*. Cf. Clinton, *Plantation Mistress*, 36–51; Fox-Genovese, *Within the Plantation Household*, 101–45.

20. Partial exceptions to this rule can be found among widows who worked as government printers or who received monopoly rights to a ferry. Spruill, *Women's Life and Work*, 263–67, 302–4; King, "'What Providence Has Brought Them to Be,'" 154, 160.

21. Wyatt-Brown, *Southern Honor*, 172; Stowe, *Intimacy and Power*, 5–49; Freeman, *Affairs of Honor*.

22. Berlin, *Confederate Nurse*, 27.

23. M. Cocke to Caroline Cocke, n.d., CFP; Fields, *Worthy Partner*, 328–30.

24. Ada W. Bacot Diary, esp. September 23, 1860, April 25, 1861, Ada W. Bacot Papers.

25. Catherine Lewis to Emma Speight, May 20, 1848, April 4 and July 8, 1853, and March 27, 1855, JFSP.

26. Records of the School of Law, July 1988; Lucy Freeman to Jesse Vaughan and wife, and to Thomas Henry Vaughan and wife, November 30, 1835, Jessie Vaughan Papers. On brother-sister relations, see Glover, *All Our Relations*, 60–62, 70–71, 76–78.

27. For subregional differences within the South, see, for example, Joyner, *Down by the Riverside*; Morgan, *Slave Counterpoint*; Rivers, *Slavery in Florida*; Olwell, *Masters, Slaves, and Subjects*; Dusinberre, *Them Dark Days*; Freehling, *Road to Disunion*; Moore, *Emergence of the Cotton Kingdom*; Malone, *Sweet Chariot*; Young, "Ideology and Death"; Schwalm, *Hard Fight for We*.

28. Bynum, *Unruly Women*, 26, 32.

29. Before the Civil War, fully one-third of Petersburg, Virginia, households were female-headed. Female householders were also quite common in Orange County, North Carolina, perhaps because Durham, Chapel Hill, and the Orange Factory Cotton Mill offered employment opportunities. In contrast, Stephanie McCurry reports that 16 percent of the free household heads in 1850 in St. Peter's Parish, Beaufort District, South Carolina, were women, and 12 percent were black. (If half of the black householders were female, then 10 percent of the total householders were white women.) McCurry, *Masters of Small Worlds*, 52 n. 31; Lebsock, *Free Women*, xv–xvi, 116, 176–77, 194, 240; Bynum, *Unruly Women*, 32, table 1.5; Oakes, *Ruling Race*, 50; Pease and Pease, *Ladies, Women, and Wenches*, 10–11, 39–40; Manuscript Federal Population Census for 1790 and 1850, Rowan County, North Carolina.

30. By contrast, in 1790, in Claremont and Clarendon Counties, Camden District, South Carolina, the average slaveholding was over 10, and the median 6. Manuscript Federal Population Census, 1790, for Rowan County, North Carolina, and Camden District, South Carolina. Census data for female householders is an imperfect substitute for the (unavailable) number of widows; however, it provides a useful measure of women's risk of householding, and since most women did not become householders without being widows, it allows some tentative deductions about the frequency and visibility of widowed householding.

31. Lebsock, *Free Women*, xv–xvi, 116, 176–77, 194, 240; Oakes, *Ruling Race*, 50; Pease and Pease, *Ladies, Women, and Wenches*, 10–11, 39–40; Federal Population Census for 1790 and 1850, Rowan County, North Carolina. On female and male mortality and life expectancies in dangerous, disease-ridden Mississippi, see Morris, *Becoming Southern*, 194.

32. Hamilton, *Plea for the Liberal Education of Woman*, 5.

33. In 1800, even the wealthiest planter women were often indifferent writers and worse spellers. By 1860, standards for feminine handwriting and prose style had increased dramatically, as had the overall curricula in girls' schools. Farnham, *Education of the Southern Belle*.

34. See, for example, Pease and Pease, *Ladies, Women, and Wenches*; Lebsock, *Free Women*, 147, 157; Scott, *Southern Lady*, 14–16, 35–36.

35. Anne Isabelle Iredell to Maria Skinner, July 10, 1812, Skinner Family Papers; Ada W. Bacot Diary, March 8, 1861, Ada W. Bacot Papers.

36. Harris, *Plain Folk and Gentry*, 1–2; Fox-Genovese, *Within the Plantation Household*, 43.

37. Fox-Genovese and Genovese, *Fruits of Merchant Capital*, chapter 9; Genovese, *Roll, Jordan, Roll*.

38. Harris, *Plain Folk and Gentry*, 6–7; Bolton, *Poor Whites of the Antebellum South*.

39. Ford, *Origins of Southern Radicalism*, 68–69, 103–4, 108–12.

40. Fox-Genovese, *Within the Plantation Household*, 41, 43; McCurry, *Masters of Small Worlds*, 16–19, 85, 92, 127; Ford, *Origins of Southern Radicalism*, 372–73. For gender and class politics elsewhere in the new United States, see Branson, *These Fiery Frenchified Dames*; Ginzberg, *Women and the Work of Benevolence*.

41. McCurry, *Masters of Small Worlds*, 16–19, 85, 92, 106.

42. The literature on slave mastery in theory and practice is enormous: see, for example, Morris, *Southern Slavery and the Law*; Bardaglio, *Reconstructing the Household*; Franklin and Schweninger, *Runaway Slaves*; Harris, *Plain Folk and Gentry*; Young, *Domesticating Slavery*. On mastery and self-control, see Faust, *James Henry Hammond*, 181–84, 283, 376; Brown, *Good Wives*, 324–28; Isaac, *Transformation of Virginia*, 39–40, 132, 339, 344–49; Stowe, *Intimacy and Power*, 22, 26; McTyeire, Sturges, and Holmes, *Duties of Masters to Servants*.

43. Berlin, *Confederate Nurse*, 27; Faust, *James Henry Hammond*.

44. McCurry, *Masters of Small Worlds*, 121 and 92–129 passim.

45. On the power of myth and ideology, see Fields, "Ideology and Race," 144, 150, 161; Fields, "Slavery, Race, and Ideology," 110–11.

46. For a useful perspective on how slaves' and owners' interests could "articulate," see Morris, "Articulation of Two Worlds," 982–1007.

47. Faust, *Mothers of Invention*, 70, 251, see also 10, 56, 78; Faust, "Altars of Sacrifice," 1215.

Chapter 1

1. Cary, *Letters on Female Character*, 188; Adams, *Elements of Moral Philosophy*, 147.

2. Charles Cocke to Jane Cocke, February 19, 1812, CFP; Isaiah 36:6.

3. Chapter 2 picks up another aspect of southern legal culture that centrally concerned slaveholding widows: the laws of slavery and the institutions that enforced them.

4. Bennett and Froide, *Singlewomen in the European Past*; Mate, *Daughters, Wives, and Widows*; Mirrer, *Upon My Husband's Death*, 3; Cavallo and Warner, *Widowhood*; Barron and Sutton, *Medieval London Widows*; Carr and Walsh, "Planter's Wife," 555, 569; Salmon, *Women and the Law of Property*, 143 and 141–84 passim; Gundersen and Gampel, "Married Women's Legal Status," 114–34; Haywood, *Manual of the Laws*, 224–26, 237–41; Reeve, *Law of Baron and Femme*, chapter 3; Cushing, *First Laws of Georgia*, 313, 414; *Acts of the General Assembly of the State of Georgia, 1838*, 201; *Acts of the General Assembly of the State of Georgia, 1839*, 145, 148–49; *Acts of the State of Georgia, 1849 and 1850*, 152–54; Iredell, *Treatise on the Law of Executors*, 5–117; Moore and Biggs, *Revised Code of North Carolina*, chapters 38, 43, 64, 118–19.

5. Barron and Sutton, *Medieval London Widows*, introduction; Cushing, *First Laws of Georgia*, 313; Cushing, *First Laws of North Carolina*, 1:488–92; Gundersen and Gampel, "Married Women's Legal Status," 119; Moore and Biggs, *Revised Code of North Carolina*, 604–5, chapter 64; Haywood, *Manual of the Laws of North Carolina*, 240–41; Hawks, *Digested Index*, 417; Reeve, *Law of Baron and Femme*, 36–37; Salmon, *Women and the Law of Property*, 141, 226–27. After 1791, widows of intestates in South Carolina could take their dower in fee simple, which removed any protection against their husbands' creditors. Salmon, *Women and the Law of Property*, 171.

6. Lebsock, *Free Women*, xix, 130, 138–41; Morris, *Southern Slavery and the Law*, 71; Meyers, *Common Whores*, 129–30.

7. Carr and Walsh, "Planter's Wife," 542, 545–47, 550; Salmon, *Women and the Law*, 171–72.

8. Carr and Walsh, "Planter's Wife," 556; Snyder, "'Rich Widows,'" 143; Meyers, *Common Whores*, chapter 6.

9. Snyder, "'Rich Widows,'" 174.

10. Carr and Walsh, "Planter's Wife," 556–57; Carr, "Inheritance in the Colonial Chesapeake," 171, 179, 196; Snyder, "'Rich Widows,'" 9, 143, 182–84; Spruill, *Women's Life and Work*, 349; Smith, "Inheritance and the Social History of Early American Women," 64; Norton, "The Evolution of White Women's Experience," 603; Speth, "More Than Her 'Thirds,'" 23; Brown, *Good Wives*, pt. 3; Lebsock, *Free Women*, 38; Crowley, "Importance of Kinship," 560; Erickson, "Property and Widowhood in England," 156–57.

11. Hannah Corbin Correspondence, PP; Fields, *Worthy Partner*, xx.

12. Franklin, *Autobiography*, 108; King, "'What Providence Has Brought Them to Be,'" 152, 155–56, and 147–66 passim.

13. Franklin, *Autobiography*, 108; King, "'What Providence Has Brought Them to Be.'"

14. On the limited validity of wives' contracts, see Salmon, *Women and the Law of Property*, 43–44, 53; Norton, *Founding Mothers and Fathers*, 84–85; Reeve, *Law of Baron and Femme*, 79–80, chapter 8.

15. Ulrich, *Good Wives*, 40, see also 36–50; Anzilotti, *In the Affairs of the World*, 164–75.

16. Franklin, *Autobiography*, 108; King, "'What Providence Has Brought Them to Be,'" 155–56; Bushman, *Refinement of America*.

17. Mary Campbell to Lord Dunmore, n.d., Spotswood Family Papers. On well-connected men's ability to engross land and political power, see, for example, Kars, *Breaking Loose Together*, chapter 2.

18. Ballagh, *Letters of Richard Henry Lee*, 1:394 n. 24; William Flood to Hannah Corbin, February 16, 1775, PP. The subscription raised £81, but the project was never completed, and Richard Henry Lee eventually returned the money.

19. Higginbotham, *Papers of James Iredell*, 1:282–86.

20. Elizabeth Steele to Ephraim Steele, May 16, 1778, JSP.

21. Elizabeth Steele to Ephraim Steele, October 25, 1780, Ephraim Steele Papers.

22. Olwell, *Masters, Slaves, and Subjects*, 245.

23. Higginbotham, *Papers of James Iredell*, 2:84, 225, 239.

24. Ibid., 239, 244, 249–51, 257.

25. Ibid., 245; Kierner, *Beyond the Household*, 89.

26. Kierner, *Beyond the Household*, 89.

27. Elizabeth Steele to Ephraim Steele, [March] 19, 1781, JSP.

28. Olwell, *Masters, Slaves, and Subjects*, 266; Kierner, *Beyond the Household*, 88–89, 99.

29. Kierner, *Beyond the Household*, 42–43.

30. Boyd, *Papers of Thomas Jefferson*, 5:704–5.

31. Olwell, *Masters, Slaves, and Subjects*, 225.

32. Norton, *Liberty's Daughters*, 212; Olwell, *Masters, Slaves, and Subjects*, 262–64; Pinckney, *Letterbook of Eliza Lucas Pinckney*, xxxiii–xxiv; Gillespie, *Free Labor*, 3–5.

33. Higginbotham, *Papers of James Iredell*, 2:246, 266; Boyd, *Papers of Thomas Jefferson*, 5:688; Kierner, *Southern Women in Revolution*, 32.

34. Kierner, *Southern Women in Revolution*, xix, xxi.

35. Ibid., 7, 42–43, 48, 57.

36. Ibid., 31, 60, 88.

37. Ibid., 38.

38. Ballagh, *Letters of Richard Henry Lee*, 1:392–94.

39. Boyd, *Papers of Thomas Jefferson*, 4:692, 5:689.

40. Byrd represented herself as a good citizen and wronged innocent, but her position was far more complicated; Turberville's men had invaded her house because she had allegedly misused a flag of truce for her own purposes, namely recovering stolen property from the British—after the governor had explicitly banned the practice—and perhaps also engaged in illegal commerce with the enemy. Boyd, *Papers of Thomas Jefferson*, 5:689–91, 703.

41. Isenberg, *Sex and Citizenship*.

42. Kierner, *Beyond the Household*, 111. For the Revolution's impact on American women generally, consult Norton, *Liberty's Daughters*; Kerber, *Women of the Republic*.

43. Clinton, *Plantation Mistress*, 29–30.

44. Lebsock, *Free Women*, 192.

45. Kierner, *Beyond the Household*, 203.

46. Susan Davis Nye Hutchison Diary; JSP; JPFP; Lebsock, *Free Women*, 147–49; Hufton, "Women without Men," 135–36.

47. Susan Davis Nye Hutchison Diary, October 19 and December 30, 1826, January 19, 1828, August 8, 1829, January 9, 1830, and June 29, 1833. For Adam Hutchison's exclusion from communion and suspension from his congregation, see entry on August 8, 1831.

48. Susan Davis Nye Hutchison Diary, October 4, 1833. For Susan Hutchison's partial knowledge of her husband's finances, see October 21, November 20, and December 14, 1826, February 10, February 23, April 14, and August 1, 1827, January 9, January 19, and October 16, 1828; for Adam Hutchison's use of a substitute, see January 31 and February 1, 1833. For a former slave's memory of his mistress acting as head during her husband's illness, see Perdue, Barden, Phillips, and Virginia Writers' Project, *Weevils in the Wheat*, 55.

49. Martha Cocke to Caroline Cocke, November 19, 1810, CFP; Lebsock, *Free Women*, chapter 6; Anzilotti, *In the Affairs of the World*, 164–65.

50. James Oakes makes this point in passing in Oakes, *Ruling Race*, 50. For plantation mistresses' work, see, for example, Weiner, *Mistresses and Slaves*, chapter 2.

51. Paulina Pollard to Paulina Legrand, August 18, 1840, Henry Carrington

Papers; Weiner, *Mistresses and Slaves*, 10, 35–37; Perdue, Barden, Phillips, and Virginia Writers' Project, *Weevils in the Wheat*, 55; Henry Jackson to Martha Jackson, November 26 and 29, 1836, JPFP; Peter Wilson Hairston to Samuel Hairston, May 3, 1852, also letters from Samuel Nowlin to Ruth Hairston, 1840s and 1850s, WHFP. Mary Beth Norton coined the term "fictive widows" to describe wives who acted as if their husbands were irrelevant, and who were thus strikingly unlike the actual widows in my study. Norton, *Founding Mothers and Fathers*, 403, see also 140.

52. John Steele was away from home for two months in 1790, three in 1791, three in 1792, two in 1793, five in 1796, two in 1797, four months in 1800, all of 1801, and most of 1802. In this period, he served two terms in Congress and was Comptroller of the Treasury under George Washington. JSP.

53. John Steele to Mary Steele, October 14, 1791, January 1 and February 15, 1793, September 1, September 15, and December 15, 1796, January 12, 1797, January 19, 1802; Mr. Haywood to John Steele, January 6, 1808; John Steele to David Anderson, October 30, 1808; Bills of Sale, dated March 26 and May 18, 1812, JSP.

54. John Steele to Mary Steele, December 15, 1796, JSP. On the evolution of written instruments and the litigated economy in Connecticut, see Mann, *Neighbors and Strangers*; Dayton, *Women before the Bar*. Mary Beth Norton suggests that married women knew something about men's "standards of interaction," but she implies that this knowledge made little difference in acclimating widows to the formal economy. Norton, *Founding Mothers and Fathers*, 161, see also 155–61; Fox-Genovese, *Within the Plantation Household*, 205.

55. John Steele to Mary Steele, March 1, 1792, September 1, 1796, see also March 3, March 25, and November 25, 1792, October 6, 1796, February 3, 1797, JSP.

56. John Steele to Mary Steele, December 22, 1796, JSP.

57. John Steele to Mary Steele, July 3, October 6, and December 22, 1796, January 19 and June 26, 1802, JSP.

58. Crowley, "Importance of Kinship," 565; Main, *Tobacco Cultivation*, chapter 5; Anzilotti, *In the Affairs of the World*, 137–44; Meyers, *Common Whores*, 129–30.

59. Wills of James Blair, 1800, Book D; William Nesbit, 1799, Book C; Joseph G. Gillespie Sr., 1840, Book I; John Eller, 1820, Book H, NCDAH. Pease and Pease, *Ladies, Women, and Wenches*, 105–6. This section is based primarily on data from Rowan County, North Carolina; Charleston, South Carolina; and Petersburg, Virginia. Unless otherwise noted, wills quoted in the text are from Rowan County.

60. In contrast, in Bucks County, Pennsylvania, two-thirds of the husbands who wrote wills in the 1790s assigned their widows less than dower. Lebsock, *Free Women*, 45; Speth, "More Than Her 'Thirds'"; Carr, "Inheritance in the Colonial Chesapeake," 161, 182; Carole Shammas, "Early American Women." Gwen Gampel and Joan Gundersen suggest that husbands treated their widows somewhat better in Virginia than in New York, but compare David Narrett's interpretation

of the Dutch influence on New York. Gundersen and Gampel, "Married Women's Legal Status"; Narrett, "Men's Wills." For wealth as a variable in bequests to widows, see Lebsock, *Free Women*, 36, 44; Boswell, *Her Act and Deed*, 40, table 1, 71, table 3, 100, table 4.

61. Main, *Tobacco Colony*, 82; Speth, "More Than Her 'Thirds,'" 15–19; King, *Abstracts, Fairfax County*; King, *Abstracts, Loudon County*; King, *Abstracts, Frederick County*; Chappelear and Hatch, *Abstracts of Louisa County*; Headly, *Wills of Richmond County*; Hudson, *Census for Lincoln County*; Carr and Walsh, "Planter's Wife," 46; Ditz, *Property and Kinship*, chapter 8; Main, *Tobacco Colony*, chapter 5.

62. Wills of Christian Zimmerman, 1790, Book D, Frederick Weehon, 1800, Book E, see also William Ford, 1841, Book I, NCDAH; Speth, "More Than Her 'Thirds,'" 19, 29; Lebsock, *Free Women*, 26–27, 46, 76; Todd, "The Remarrying Widow"; Carr and Walsh, "Planter's Wife," 556, 560. Inheritance law and restricted tenures constrained those who wanted to buy and sell land freely, but widows rarely speculated in land even when they had the option. Lebsock, *Free Women*, 24, 42–44, 126–28; Salmon, *Women and the Law of Property*, 7, 169, 227 n. 4.

63. Between 1790 and 1860 in Rowan County, North Carolina, 88 percent of testators sampled had children, and the fathers averaged five children apiece. In Lincoln County, Georgia, over the same period, a remarkably similar 87 percent had children, with a slightly lower average of four children per family. In several longer-settled counties in Virginia, the vast majority of husbands who wrote wills also had children. A significant percentage of testators—20 percent, sometimes 30—in the surveyed counties mentioned grandchildren in their wills, which suggests that the testators themselves were at least in their forties, if not substantially older. Headly, *Wills of Richmond County*; Hudson, *Census for Lincoln County*; Speth, "More Than Her 'Thirds,'" 15–21; Wills of John Morrison, 1790, Book C, William Cupplus, 1800, Book E, John Mowra, 1819, Book H, James Womack, 1820, Book H, Henry Fraley, 1830, Book H, Thomas C. Gillespie, 1848, Book K, Eli Gaither, 1809, Book G, Rowan County, NCDAH; Carr and Walsh, "Planter's Wife," 46; Lebsock, *Free Women*, 38, 45.

64. Ditz, *Property and Kinship*, 32–36.

65. Wills of Edmund Palmer, 1810, Book H; William Pack, 1800, Book F; Stephen Weavel, 1820, Book H; Thomas Wilkerson, 1792, Book C; John Mowra, 1819, Book H; Thomas Anderson, 1820, Book H, NCDAH.

66. Wills of William Anderson, 1839, Book I, John Irvin, 1809, Book G, George Cauble, 1850, Book K, Hugh Horah, 1820, Book H, Rowan County, NCDAH; Will of Willis Alston (copy), January 21, 1835, Archibald Davis Alston Papers; Hudson, *To Have and to Hold*.

67. Wills of David Fraley, 1849, Book K, and James Graham, 1840, Book I, Rowan County, NCDAH.

68. Wills of Abel Armstrong, 1799, Book C; George Bost, 1848, Book K; Matthias Garner, 1831, Book H; Richard Gillespie, 1830, Book H; Philip Yost, 1848, Book K; John Bodenhamer, 1820, Book H; Matthias Phifer, 1849, Book K, Rowan County, NCDAH.

69. Headly, *Wills of Richmond County*; Hudson, *Census for Lincoln County*; Boatwright, *Status of Women*, 99. For colonial patterns in the choice of executor, see Carr and Walsh, "Planter's Wife"; Speth, "More Than Her 'Thirds.'" On the duties of an executor, see also Lebsock, *Free Women*, 36–40.

70. According to the 1810 census, John Steele owned 74 slaves, which made him second only to John Kelly, with 96. Manuscript Federal Population Census, 1810, Rowan County, North Carolina.

71. In 1814, John Steele owned 115 slaves, 860 acres on Grants Creek valued at three dollars per acre, a 788 acre plantation on the Yadkin river, 351 acres in Flat Swamp, 414 acres of "much worn" land, and several houses and lots in Salisbury, the county seat. If these were the lands he owned at his death, then in terms of acreage if not value, Mary Steele received slightly more than one-third of the realty, not counting the Salisbury lots. List of John Steele's Taxable Property, April 10, 1814, JSP; Will of John Steele, Book G, Rowan County, NCDAH.

72. Will of John Steele, Book G, Rowan County, NCDAH.

73. John Steele to Mary Steele, June 26, 1802, JSP. See also Lee, *The American Revolution*, 59.

74. Carter, *Diary of Dolly Lunt Burge*, xxxii, 75–76, see also 55, 58–91, 124, 144.

75. Adams, *Elements of Moral Philosophy*, 164–65; Cary, *Letters on Female Character*, 87; Hamilton, *Plea for the Liberal Education of Women*, 27; *Southern Cultivator*, August 2, 1843; Pease and Pease, *Family of Women*, 34.

76. Lebsock, *Free Women*, 121–22; Young, *Domesticating Slavery*, 233–34.

Chapter 2

1. Carter, *Diary of Dolly Lunt Burge*, 95–97.

2. Martha Richardson to James Proctor Screven, April 16, 1817, ASFP.

3. The debate over slaveholders' capitalist or paternalist (or feudal), promarket or antimarket orientation has raged for years. See, for example, Genovese, *Roll, Jordan, Roll*, *World the Slaveholders Made*, and *Slaveholders' Dilemma*; Ford, *Origins of Southern Radicalism*; Oakes, *Ruling Race*; Curtin, *Rise and Fall of the Plantation Complex*. Jeffrey Robert Young has recently argued that the two sides merge when we appreciate how deeply market culture shaped the South and, in particular, helped produce paternalistic proslavery in the antebellum South. Young, *Domesticating Slavery*, 3–15.

4. Perdue, Barden, Phillips, and Virginia Writers' Project, *Weevils in the Wheat*, 317–18; Wood, *Gender, Race, and Rank*, 34–36.

5. Joseph Jackson to Martha Jackson, September 22, 1840; Henry Rootes Jackson to Sarah Jackson, n.d. (probably 1842), January 7 and June 10, 1842; Joseph Jackson to Martha Jackson, May 6, 1842, JPFP. I am using "yeoman" to indicate widows who did not have enough to make their own work primarily managerial. In that sense, my yeoman widows are comparable to yeoman farmers, although even widows rarely performed field labor.

6. This and the next example concern women from the Southeast who mi-

grated west either before or during widowhood. They are included here in part because rich caches of letters by widows who farmed with only a handful of slaves are rare and also because their experience of migration was a common one in the early nineteenth century.

7. Lucy Freeman to Jessie Vaughan, December 26, 1837, Jessie Vaughan Papers; McCurry, *Masters of Small Worlds*, 48, 62, 78–85.

8. Felix Gilbert to Sarah Hillhouse, various dates, AHFP; Zaccheus Collins to Elizabeth Lee, May 16, 1800, Richard Bland Lee Papers; Glover, *All Our Relations*, 13; Stowe, *Intimacy and Power*, 165, 171–74, 187–90; Pease and Pease, *Family of Women*, 32–34.

9. Lucy Freeman to Jessie Vaughan, June 20, 1839, Jessie Vaughan Papers; Freehling, *Prelude to Civil War*, appendix A, table 1.

10. Lucy Freeman to Jessie Vaughan, December 26, 1837, June 20, 1839, Jessie Vaughan Papers.

11. Caroline Burke to William Gilliland, February 3, 1843, March 10, 1844, July 15, 1848, February 8, 1854, Rebecca Younge to William Gilliland, January 10, 1848, John Prior Burke to William Gilliland, March 10, 1844, July 29 and November 28, 1850, October 1853, WGP; Pease and Pease, *Family of Women*, 32. The predominance of women and children among Caroline Burke's and Lucy Freeman's slaves is typical both of yeomen slaveholders in general and widows in particular. McCurry, *Masters of Small Worlds*, 48–49.

12. Caroline Burke to William Gilliland, March 2, 1854, WGP.

13. Ibid.

14. Domestic slaves were usually girls too young for full-time field work. Unless they were highly skilled, domestics hired at low rates. Weiner, *Mistresses and Slaves*, chapter 1.

15. Catherine Lewis to Emma Speight, October 16, 1845, November 24, 1847, JFSP.

16. Susan Davis Nye Hutchison Diary, [March] 25, July 25, and November 6, 1840, see also May 14 and November 19, 1838, March 19, 1840. Hutchison also had white help; at Christmas in 1840, she mentioned a "young orphan girl Margaret" (December 25, 1840).

17. Shammas, "Black Women's Work," 5–28; Lebsock, *Free Women*, 127–29; McCurry, *Masters of Small Worlds*, chapter 2; Brown, *Good Wives*, chapter 4; Harris, *Plain Folk and Gentry*, 65–66, 75; Johnson, *Soul by Soul Life*, 88–92, 101–2.

18. Weiner, *Mistresses and Slaves*, 23–71; Kierner, *Beyond the Household*, 139–79; Fox-Genovese, *Within the Plantation Household*, 196–97; Scott, *Southern Lady*, 3–21.

19. Tucker, *Valley of the Shenandoah*, 1:201; Cary, *Letters on Female Character*, 28–29, 30–33, 79.

20. NDSD, July 12, July 22, August 11, October 4, December 19, December 24, and December 26, 1840; John B. Moore to Rev. J. V. Welch, September 16, 1858, RMDP; Rawick, *American Slave*, 12(2):108–9; "Daily Expenditures for 1842," Plantation Accounts, 1841–42, JPFP.

21. Rawick, *American Slave*, 2(1):190, 12(2):132, 12(1):320; Joseph Jackson to Sarah Jackson, January 1, 1847, Joseph Jackson to Martha Jackson, January 12, 1847, Vincent Pierson to Martha Jackson, January 21, 1844, Martha Jackson to Sarah Jackson, December 27, 1852, Henry Jackson to Martha Jackson, November 29, 1836, February 11, 1844, July 12, 1845, September 7, 1844, and Plantation Day Book, November 5, 1851, JPFP; JBGD, December 25, 1832; NDSD, December 24, 1840; Perdue, Barden, Phillips, and Virginia Writers' Project, *Weevils in the Wheat*, 98, 195; Brown, *Good Wives*, 372; Faust, *James Henry Hammond*, 99–104.

22. Perdue, Barden, Phillips, and Virginia Writers' Project, *Weevils in the Wheat*, 40; Vincent Pierson to Martha Jackson, June 7, 1845, JPFP; Ada W. Bacot Diary, September 8, 1862, Ada W. Bacot Papers. Being sold in order to be united with family is reminiscent of the strange experience some fugitive slaves faced in the North: being sold to someone who would free them. See, for example, Jacobs, *Incidents in the Life of a Slave Girl*, 301. The intersection of marriage and sale on the Abbott plantation also confirms Walter Johnson's analysis of the centrality of the market in shaping slavery. Johnson, *Soul by Soul*, 17–18, 111–12.

23. Carter, *Diary of Dolly Lunt Burge*, 99; Plantation Day Book, November 5, 1851, JPFP; Morgan, *Slave Counterpoint*, 358–65; Schwalm, *Hard Fight for We*, 14, 25, 60–63.

24. Plantation Day Book, September 8 to November 5, 1851, JPFP. On picking rates, see Blassingame, *Slave Community*, 182. On incentives to slave workers, see Scarborough, *Overseer*, 180. On 1851 cotton prices, see Freehling, *Prelude to Civil War*, appendix A, table 1.

25. NDSD, July 4, 1840; Agnes Hairston to Ruth Hairston, February 28, 1844, WHFP; Sterling Adams to Ruth Hairston, June 9, 1854, WHFP; JBGD, August 17, 1834; Rawick, *American Slave*, 12(1):206, 14:105.

26. NDSD, July 4, 1840; Genovese, *Roll, Jordan, Roll*, 545; Faust, *James Henry Hammond*, 99–104. *Roll, Jordan, Roll* has many critics, but it is still a core text on paternalism. For more recent works, see Young, *Domesticating Slavery*; Christopher Morris, "The Articulation of Two Worlds"; Joyner, *Shared Traditions*; Brown, *Good Wives*. For scholars who argue against the paternalist interpretation, see, for example, Oakes, *Ruling Race*; Malone, *Sweet Chariot*; Tadman, *Speculators and Slaves*. On evangelicalism and slavery, see Mathews, *Religion in the Old South*; Heyrman, *Southern Cross*; Isaac, *Transformation of Virginia*, 300–301, 310.

27. Young, *Domesticating Slavery*, 8–11.

28. See, for example, NDSD, July 4, July 10–15, July 18, August 6, September 6, October 16, November 15, November 16, November 28, and December 28, 1840, and February 5, February 23, June 11, and July 8, 1841.

29. For Tucker's fictional Mrs. Grayson as Lady Bountiful, see Tucker, *Valley of the Shenandoah*, 2:318. For widows' purchases of provisions and other plantation expenses, see Account of Paulina Legrand with Isaac Read and Co., September 1, 1819, Henry Carrington Papers; Bill of N. M. Martin Brothers and Co., July 29, 1857, W. Robert Leckie Papers; Bill of David and Ro. Maitland, February 4, 1794, CFP; Adams and Frost to Marion Deveaux, March 3, 1855, and In-

graham and Webb to John Berkeley Moore for Marion Deveaux, September 25, 1855, RMDP; Henry Smith to Martha Jackson, June 22, 1840, Joint expenses at plantation for 1849 and 1850, Vincent Pierson to Martha Jackson, April 9, 1844, and March 29, 1845, JPFP; Mary Pursley in account with Martha Turberville, December 3, 1794, PP; Account Book, 1838–42, Jacob Rhett Motte Papers; Bill of G. M. Thompson and Co., January 9, 1855, RMDP; Account of Lucy Burwell with Alexander Boyd, February 9, 1822, BFP; Rawick, *American Slave*, 15(2):148, 3(3):195, 12(1):320, 12(2):120. On slaveholders' production of food crops, see Wright, *Political Economy of the Cotton South*, 55–74; McCurry, *Masters of Small Worlds*, 67, table 2.9; Faust, *James Henry Hammond*, 118.

30. Perdue, Barden, Phillips, and Virginia Writers' Project, *Weevils in the Wheat*, 42; Codicil to the Will of Mary Motte, May 17, 1837, Jacob Rhett Motte Papers. For slaves' efforts to ingratiate themselves, perhaps with an eye to avoiding sale, see, for example, Martha Jackson to Sarah Jackson, December 27, 1852; Henry Jackson to Martha Jackson, November 29, 1836; Vincent Pierson to Martha Jackson, February 11, May 28, and September 7, 1844, July 12 and 26, 1845, JPFP. See also Margaret Steele to Mary Steele, September 7, 1818, JSP; Faust, *James Henry Hammond*, 99–104; Morgan, *Slave Counterpoint*, 348; Genovese, *Roll, Jordan, Roll*, 609–12; Wyatt-Brown, "Mask of Obedience," 1228–53.

31. Marriage Settlement between Martha J. R. Jackson and Hezekiah Erwin, JPFP; Wills of Tristim Skinner, 1853 and 1857, Skinner Family Papers; Malone, *Sweet Chariot*, 88–89, 211–16, 269; Morris, *Southern Slavery and the Law*, 99–101.

32. Joseph Jackson to Martha Jackson, September 22, 1840; Henry Rootes Jackson to Sarah Jackson, n.d. (probably 1842), January 7 and June 10, 1842; Joseph Jackson to Martha Jackson, May 6, 1842, JPFP.

33. Marie-Louisa-Beatrix-Stephanie-Natalie DeLage de Volude, known as Natalie, married Thomas Sumter Jr. in 1802 when she was just twenty and he in his early thirties. He died in June 1840 and she in August of the following year. Records in the Sumter-DeLage Family Papers indicate that the royalist DeLage family fled during the French Revolution, at which point young Natalie came to the United States, where she met Thomas Sumter.

34. NDSD, July 1–4, July 10–15, July 18, July 25, August 6, September 6, October 16, November 15, November 16, November 28, December 12, and December 28, 1840, February 5, February 23, June 11, and July 8, 1841; Rawick, *American Slave*, 12(2):108, 15(2):67; Pease and Pease, *Family of Women*, 34. McCoy perhaps intended to disparage Cotton by comparing her to an overseer, but it is worth noting the implication that in McCoy's experience, at least, male planters might be inattentive.

35. Linnaeus Bolling to William Acres, November 31, 1805, HFP.

36. Paulina Legrand to William Huntington, September 19, 1839, WHP.

37. NDSD, July 6, 1840, February 23, 1841. On deaths and damage caused by lightning, see, for example, Sarah Jackson to Henry Rootes Jackson, September 12, 1834, and Sarah Cobb to Martha Jackson, August 25, 1846, JPFP; Martha Richardson to James Proctor Screven, June 15, 1821, ASFP; Agnes Hairston to George Hairston, September 27, 1838, WHFP.

38. Vincent Pierson to Martha Jackson, January 21, June 19, August 6, and December 24, 1844, JPFP. On slave "theft," see, for example, Rawick, *American Slave*, 2(2):317; Tinling, "Cawsons, Virginia," 281–91; Genovese, *Roll, Jordan, Roll*, 599–607; Franklin and Schweninger, *Runaway Slaves*, 7, 28, 79–83, 89–93. I am indebted to Seth Cotlar for bringing the Cawsons source to my attention.

39. James Wills to Susannah Wilcox, December 28, [1787], HFP.

40. Will of Mary Chastain Archer, May 28, 1841, Richard T. Archer to Capt. James Hobson, June 16, 1835, AFP; Archibald Alston to Sarah Alston, June 24, 1853, Will of Sarah Alston, 1858, Archibald Davis Alston Papers.

41. NDSD, August 18, 1840; Abraham Van Buren to Marion Deveaux, January 20, 1856, Account of Ingraham and Webb, March 24, 1857, RMDP; Perdue, Barden, Phillips, and Virginia Writers' Project, *Weevils in the Wheat*, 37, 42; Rawick, *American Slave*, 15(2):129, 14(1):77–78, 308, 3(4):148, 12(2):107–8; Hughes, "Slaves for Hire," 260–86. On plantation life cycles and their impact on slaves, see Malone, *Sweet Chariot*, chapter 2; Morris, *Southern Slavery and the Law*, chapter 4.

42. Martha Richardson to James Proctor Screven, April 16, 1817, ASFP. For an exception, see accounts of slave hire, 1819–1820, William Patterson Smith Papers.

43. JBGD; HFP; WHFP; Henry Smith to Henry Jackson, March 10 and May 3, 1840, Henry Smith to Martha Jackson, August 23, 1840, Martha Jackson to [James Addison Cobb], n.d., Martha Jackson to Sarah Jackson, October 26, 1848, JPFP; Freehling, *Prelude to Civil War*, appendix A, table 1.

44. Vincent Pierson to Martha Jackson, December 24, 1844, JPFP. Pierson's letters contain one reference to illness and injuries in 1843, twelve in 1844, nine in 1845, nine in 1846, six in 1847, none in 1848, and three in 1849. See also miscellaneous accounts for 1847 and 1851 in Personal Account book of Martha Jackson and Henry Jackson, 1819–20.

45. Henry Smith to Martha Jackson, July 11, 1840; Martha Jackson to Henry Smith, October 26, 1840; overseer's contract, 1847; and Estate Appraisal, 1847, JPFP.

46. James Wills to Susannah Wilcox, December 22, 1789, Nathan Wells to Susan Hubard, December 16, 1814, HFP; Caroline Burke to William Gilliland, March 10, 1844, WGP; Account Book, 1847–1855, March 21, 1853, Mary G. Franklin Papers.

47. Martha Cocke to Caroline Cocke, November 14, 1813, CFP.

48. Plantation Account Book, 1850, "Division of Crop for 1852," Plantation Day Book, Martha Jackson, 1851, JPFP. On slaveholders' response to slaves' mortality and morbidity, see, for example, Young, "Ideology and Death"; Ann Patton Malone, *Sweet Chariot*, 315 n. 6.

49. Dr. Neeson's Account, paid December 20, 1847, James Lamkin Papers; Fett, *Working Cures*, 119, 148, 152, 189.

50. Henry Smith to Martha Jackson, June 22, July 11, and September 5, 1840, JPFP. On July 11, Smith reported that Patty had a "Rheumatic affection" which he and his wife were attending, but this letter likely preceded Jackson's response to the June 22 letter. For owners' conflicts with slaves over slave health care, see Fett, *Working Cures*.

51. For slaveholding women's ideas of domesticity, see Weiner, *Mistresses and Slaves*, chapter 3; Kierner, *Beyond the Household*, chapter 5.

52. NDSD, July 25, August 7, August 17, August 27, September 15, October 6, October 8, November 11, and December 6, 1840, January 23 and February 4, 1841; Moore, *Plantation Mistress*, 41, 75–76, 83, 95.

53. Keziah Goodwyn Hopkins Brevard Diary, March 28, 1861.

54. NDSD, September 7, September 12–13, October 16, November 19, and December 6, 1840, February 4, 1841; Elizabeth Lee to Anna Washington, September 25, [1832 or 1835], Richard Bland Lee Papers. Elizabeth Lee was Richard Bland Lee's widow. Lee had built Sully plantation on land inherited from his father in northern Virginia. Lee served in the Virginia legislature and the U.S. House of Representatives, and he briefly held a judgeship before dying in the spring of 1827.

55. Martha Richardson to James Proctor Screven, December 19, 1818; Addendum by Delia Bryan in Georgia Bryan to Mrs. Forman, November 17, 1821; Sarah Screven to Delia Bryan, November 13, 1822, ASFP.

56. Cary, *Letters on Female Character*, 173; Martha Richardson to James Proctor Screven, February 25, 1821, ASFP.

57. Faust, *Mothers of Invention*, 63, see also 54, 56, 62–65; Faust, "Trying to Do a Man's Business," 197–214. Faust argues that James Henry Hammond concluded that violence signified a loss of control. Faust, *James Henry Hammond*, 72–73, 89–91, 99–104. Marli Weiner suggests that slaveholding women's fear of slaves curbed their violence. Weiner, *Mistresses and Slaves*, 87.

58. Perdue, Barden, Phillips, and Virginia Writers' Project, *Weevils in the Wheat*, 16, 194–95, 284, 309–10; Rawick, *American Slave*, 15:170, 193, 199, 300–301, 2(1):11; Wood, *Gender, Race, and Rank*, 42.

59. Catherine Lewis to Emma Lewis, August 9, 1838, JFSP; Perdue, Barden, Phillips, and Virginia Writers' Project, *Weevils in the Wheat*, 16, 63, 173, 285, 309; Rawick, *American Slave*, 15:45, 300–301; Wyatt-Brown, *Southern Honor*, 142. For a different interpretation of maternal violence, see Faust, "Trying to Do a Man's Business."

60. Catherine Lewis to Emma Lewis, August 9, 1838, JFSP.

61. Vincent Pierson to Martha Jackson, May 28, 1844, JPFP. Born in 1828, Hester had her first child in 1847 and her second in 1851. When Henry Jackson's estate was divided among his four heirs in 1847, Hester was assigned to Martha Jackson's elder daughter.

62. Rawick, *American Slave*, 3(4):158, 12(2):108, 15(2):6; Perdue, Barden, Phillips, and Virginia Writers' Project, *Weevils in the Wheat*, 102; Account Book, 1838–42, Jacob Rhett Motte Papers; Plantation Account Book—Estate of Adam Alexander, AHFP; Samuel Hairston to sheriff, February 7, 1820, W. Beavers to Mrs. R. Wilson [Ruth Hairston], February 26, 1816, WHFP; JBGD, May 6, 1840; Sarah Cobb to Sarah Jackson, May 6, 1847, JPFP; Mary Steele to Mary Ferrand, October 18, 1835, JSP; Payment for jailing and boarding a slave, June 10, 1818, William Patterson Smith Papers; William Akers's receipt, August 14, 1815, HFP.

63. Philip Ludwell Lee to Hannah Corbin, December 22, n.d., PP.

64. Perdue, Barden, Phillips, and Virginia Writers' Project, *Weevils in the Wheat*, 16, 190, 273–75; Rawick, *American Slave*, 2(2):290, 15:67, 169–70, 193, 300, 2(1):157, 12(2):108, 130, 92–93; Margaret Steele to Mary Steele, September 7, 1818, JSP; Keziah Goodwyn Hopkins Brevard Diary, September 18, 1860; Catherine Lewis to Emma Speight, August 9, 1838, JFSP; Tinling, "Cawsons, Virginia."

65. Lucy Thornton to [Mrs. Rootes], November 25, 1799, JPFP; Faust, *James Henry Hammond*, 100; Brown, *Good Wives*, 327, 350–61.

66. Keziah Goodwyn Hopkins Brevard Diary, September 18, 1860.

67. Ibid.

68. Holding slaves for life debarred some widows from this form of punishment, but the possibility of hiring out enabled them too to hold the prospect of separation from kin over a slave's head.

69. JBGD, September 9, 1849. Johnson argues that white women did not go to the slave pens in New Orleans, for example, to buy and sell slaves, but white women did deal directly with slave traders, buyers, and sellers in other locations. Johnson, *Soul by Soul*, 100, 92–102 passim, 164, 172–88; Rawick, *American Slave*, 12(2):131. On transportation, see also Egerton, *He Shall Go Out Free*, appendix.

70. Peter Wilson Hairston to Ruth Hairston, January 4, 1856, "Peremptory Sale of Negroes!," WHFP; Wiencek, *Hairstons*, 94, 96–97, 114–15.

71. Hodes, *White Women, Black Men*; Hodes, "Wartime Dialogues," 235, 230–42; Painter, *Soul Murder and Slavery*; Woodward and Muhlenfield, *The Private Mary Chesnut*, 42–43; Sommerville, "Rape, Race, and Castration"; Hall, "'The Mind That Burns,'" 328–49; Schwarz, *Twice Condemned*, 92–114; Faust, *Mothers of Invention*, 56–62; Weiner, *Mistresses and Slaves*, 135–37, 166–70; Rothman, *Notorious in the Neighborhood*. Evidence of interracial sex in the Old South overwhelmingly involves heterosexual pairings, but we cannot altogether rule out the possibility of homosexual sex. On nineteenth-century white women's friendships and sexuality, see Smith-Rosenberg, "Female World of Love and Ritual," 53–77.

72. While early eighteenth-century planters tended to regard all white women as naturally lustful, by the mid-nineteenth century, white southern men usually believed that elite white women were free from improper sexual desire. See Chapter 7, below, and Bynum, *Unruly Women*, 88–95, 101–2, 107, 109–10; Brown, *Good Wives*, 328–34; Sommerville, "Rape, Race, and Castration"; Fischer, "'False, Feigned, and Scandalous Words'"; Gilmore, *Gender and Jim Crow*, 72.

73. Bynum, *Unruly Women*, 88–93.

74. On quasi-caste differences between domestics and field hands, see, for example, Gomez, *Exchanging Our Country Marks*, 219–43; Schwalm, *Hard Fight for We*, 31, 34–37.

75. NDSD, September 1, 1840.

76. NDSD, August 7, August 17, October 6, October 8, and November 11, 1840, January 23, 1841; JBGD, September 9, 1849; Scott, *Domination and the Arts of Resistance*, 133, 187–201.

77. Elizabeth Lee to Anna Washington, September 25, [1833], Richard Bland

Lee Papers; Parker, *Stealing a Little Freedom*, 741; NDSD, July 4, August 3, August 10, August 21, September 15, November 11, and November 30, 1840, January 4, 1841; Franklin and Schweninger, *Runaway Slaves*, 22, 24, 617–19.

78. Meaders, *Advertisements for Runaway Slaves*; Wood, *Gender, Race, and Rank*, 54–55.

79. Schwarz, *Twice Condemned*, 92–114, 160–62, 164, 209–14, 282–83, 291–93, 297; Berlin, *Confederate Nurse*, 49; Moore, *Plantation Mistress*, 54, see also 31, 86; Egerton, *Gabriel's Rebellion*, 38, 78; Faust, *Mothers of Invention*, 56–62; Weiner, *Mistresses and Slaves*, 87, 135–37, 166–70; Sarah Cobb to Martha Jackson, May 22 and June 19, 1848, JPFP, Breen, "'Storm of Terror.'" Faust notes that some Confederate women preferred a black man's protection to no male help at all (*Mothers of Invention*, 62).

80. Receipt of payment to William Bolling, January 24, 1830, Francis Gildart Ruffin Papers; Rawick, *American Slave*, 15:6; Perdue, Barden, Phillips, and Virginia Writers' Project, *Weevils in the Wheat*, 102; Certification by Vincent Redman, January 26, 1798, Martha Corbin Turberville to Daniel Mealey, July [16], 1804, PP; W. Beavers to Mrs. R. Wilson, February 26, 1816, Samuel Hairston to sheriff, February 7, 1820, WHFP; JBGD, May 6, 1840; Sarah Cobb to Sarah Jackson, May 6, 1847, JPFP; Mary Steele to Mary Ferrand, October 18, 1835, JSP; Receipt of payment from Thomas Smith to Hugh B. Gwyn for jailing and boarding a slave, June 10, 1818, William Patterson Smith Papers; Receipt of payment from William Akers for Susan Hubard, August 14, 1815, HFP; Account Book, 1838–42, Jacob Rhett Motte Papers; Plantation Account Book—Estate of Adam Alexander, AHFP; Meaders, *Advertisements for Runaway Slaves*.

81. Cushing, *First Laws of South Carolina*, 1:205; Cushing, *First Laws of Georgia*, 1:119. Sometimes the community or the state interfered with a slaveowner's actions, as when they regulated the treatment of slaves or took the punishment of rebels out of their owners' hands. For slavery as a legal institution, see Morris, *Southern Slavery and the Law*, esp. chapter 8; Cushing, *First Laws of South Carolina*, 1:205–7; Cushing, *First Laws of North Carolina*, 1:85–95, 152, 371; Cushing, *First Laws of Georgia*, 1:119, 458; *Acts of the General Assembly of the State of Georgia, 1841*, 135.

82. Brown, *Good Wives*, 290. The eighteenth-century court decisions concerning slaves were by no means universally hostile to female slaveholders: for example, of ninety-four victims of theft by slaves who brought charges in Virginia between 1770 and 1774, nine were women "who successfully brought charges against another owner's slaves in the same courts men used to protect themselves." Schwarz, *Twice Condemned*, 121.

83. It is important, however, not to overstate white men's assumption that women's slaves were especially unruly. Of the two hundred slaves tried for conspiracy and insurrection in Virginia between 1785 and 1831, for example, only 10 percent were owned by women, a figure in line with female slaveholders' representation in the general population. Among the Virginia slaves convicted on these serious charges, those owned by women were no more likely to be executed. Similarly, female owners appeared among the slaveholders whose slaves were accused of conspiring

with Denmark Vesey in 1822 in proportion to their numbers in the Charleston area. *Trial Record of Denmark Vesey*; Schwarz, *Twice Condemned*, appendix. For nineteenth-century southern women's encounters with the law with reference to class and paternalism, see Bardaglio, *Reconstructing the Household*, pt. 1; Bynum, *Unruly Women*, chapter 4; Wyatt-Brown, *Southern Honor*, 261.

84. Perdue, Barden, Phillips, and Virginia Writers' Project, *Weevils in the Wheat*, 317–18.

85. NDSD, July 1, 1840; Will of John Steele, Book G, Rowan County, NCDAH.

86. NDSD, June 16, 1841; Ada W. Bacot Diary, February 11, 1861, Ada W. Bacot Papers.

87. Lucy Freeman to Jessie Vaughan, June 20, 1839, Jessie Vaughan Papers; Carter, *Diary of Dolly Lunt Burge*, 108, 110; Johnson, *Soul by Soul*, 102. The once-heated debate over how much work slaveholding wives did revolved in part around this verbal appropriation. Few if any historians, however, have doubted the gulf between words and reality in the case of male slaveholders. See, for example, Clinton, *Plantation Mistress*, 25–27; Weiner, *Mistresses and Slaves*, chapter 2.

88. Martha Jackson correspondence, 1840–53, JPFP; John Prior and Caroline Burke correspondence, 1848–54, WGP; 1829 and 1830 Tax Receipts for Eliza R. Ruffin, Hanover County, Virginia, Francis Gildart Ruffin Papers; Tucker, *Valley of the Shenandoah*, 2:154, 213–15, 240.

89. See note 9 above and Moore, *Plantation Mistress*, 10; Pease and Pease, *Family of Women*, 32–33, 163.

90. Faust, *James Henry Hammond*, 99, see also 89–90; "Prayer for a Woman who has lost her Husband," AFP; Fox-Genovese, "Family and Female Identity," 16, 19; Stowe, *Intimacy and Power*, 22; Brown, *Good Wives*, 290, 365.

91. Faust, *James Henry Hammond*, 99, see also 89–90.

Chapter 3

1. Lebsock, *Free Women*, 35; Wyatt-Brown, *Southern Honor*; Lewis, *Pursuit of Happiness*, 169–230; Brown, *Good Wives*, 339–42, see also 284, 324, and pt. 3 generally; Stowe, *Intimacy and Power*, 88–96, 130, 142–53; Fox-Genovese, *Within the Plantation Household*, 203; Young, *Domesticating Slavery*, 148–58, 180–82, 214–18, 234.

2. *Christian Index*, December 8, 1835; Fitzhugh, *Cannibals All!*, 201, 206, 217–18; Crowley, "Importance of Kinship," 560–62. For maternal rights, see Bardaglio, *Reconstructing the Household*, chapter 3.

3. Adams, *Elements of Moral Philosophy*, 390; Kulikoff, *Tobacco and Slaves*, 259–60; Censer, *North Carolina Planters*; Glover, *All Our Relations*; Lebsock, *Free Women*, 22, 32–35.

4. The differences between wives and widows in this regard was more a matter of degree than kind: both wives and widows depended on their extended kin and helped them in return, but widows generally did more of both.

5. Richard T. Archer to Mary Archer, May 17, 1823, AFP; Higginbotham, *Papers of James Iredell*, 1:99; Adams, *Moral Philosophy*, 246; Morris, *Southern Slav-*

ery and the Law, 7–8, 448–49 n. 41; Bardaglio, *Reconstructing the Household*, 24–34, 241–42 n. 70; Karlsen, *Devil in the Shape of a Woman*, 80–116.

6. Daniel [Grinnon] to Martha Jackson, May 28, 1829, Martha Jackson to Daniel [Grinnon], June 19, 1829, Sarah Cobb to Martha Jackson, March 4, 1853, JPFP; Caroline Burke to William Gilliland, February 3, 1843, WGP; Caroline Adams to William Blanks, August 28, 1844, Caroline Adams to Elizabeth Blanks, October 29, 1844, Elizabeth J. (Holmes) Blanks Papers; Harriet Brown to Marion Deveaux, Sr., May 12, [1860?], RMDP; JBGD, July 27, 1844; Sarah Screven to Martha Richardson, August 8, 1819, ASFP; Josiah C. Skinner to Maria Skinner, September 14, 1819, Skinner Family Papers; M. E. Lewis to Emma Lewis, February 4, [1839], Catherine Lewis to Emma Speight, October 16, 1845, October 7, [1846], and July 3, 1860, JFSP; Lucy Freeman to Jessie Vaughan, February 28, 1836, June 20, 1839, and May 26, 1844, Jessie Vaughan Papers; Bethenia [Ewing] to [Agnes Hairston], September 10, 1831, Green Pryor to Ruth Hairston, October 15, 1831, Agnes Hairston to Peter and George Hairston, October 2, 1843, Ann Wheeler to Ruth Hairston, March 6, 1859, WHFP; Isabella Woodruff to Charles Holst, March 16, 1865, IARWP. On mourning visits among eighteenth-century Virginia gentry women, see Brown, *Good Wives*, 303.

7. Receipts for Charlie Wheeler's tuition and board, June 10 and 15, 1857, January 23 and July 10, 1858; Ann Wheeler to Ruth Hairston, August 7, 1857, March 6, 1859, January 24, 1861, WHFP.

8. Catherine Lewis to Emma Speight, May 20, 1848, see also October 16, 1845, JFSP.

9. Peter Hairston to Ruth Hairston, May 29, 1814, February 9, 1815, August 5, 1821, WHFP; JBGD, October 12, 1832, September 15, 1833, October 14, 1839, April 10, 1843.

10. Copartnership Agreement between John Wilkes and Martin L. Wilkins (1823), Will of Martin L. Wilkins, July 2, 1838 [copy], John Berkley Grimball to Gouverneur M. Wilkins, January 2, August 14, and December 12, 1844, GFP; JBGD, February 5 and July 8, 1838, May 16 and 19, 1843, February 24 and October 7, 1844, February 1, 1849, January 22, 1850.

11. Bills and Accounts from Alexander Boyd, 1818–1822, BFP; Account of Pauline Legand with Archibald Vaughan, 1835–36, Archibald Vaughan Papers; John Wilson to Isabella Glenn, November 26, 1808, Glenn Family Papers; letters of Caroline and John Prior Burke to William Gilliland, WGP; Williams Rutherford to Sarah Jackson, December 26, 1846, JPFP; Perkins, "The Consumer Frontier," 505–6.

12. Henry Cook to Annabella Porter, November [10], 1824, DWPP.

13. Williams Rutherford to Sarah Jackson, December 26, 1846, Lucy Thornton to Martha and Mary Rootes, February 16, 1807, Mary Ann Cobb to Martha Jackson, January 1838, Serena Lea to Martha Jackson, October 5, 1843, JPFP; NDSD, July 16, October 18, and December 24, 1840, January 14 and July 21, 1841; Delia Bryan to Sarah Screven, October 21, 1822, ASFP; M. Hubard to Susan Hubard, n.d. and December 25, 1812, HFP; Fanny Binda to Marion Deveaux, n.d., RMDP; Adam Alexander to Sarah Alexander, December 12, 1827,

AHFP; Eliza Wilkins to John Berkeley Grimball, June 20, 1839, GFP; Robert Cochran to Mary Steele, January 20, 1836, JSP; Catherine Lewis to Emma Speight, October 16, 1845, November 24, 1847, JFSP; William Cabell to Paulina Legrand, May 24, 1822, Henry Carrington Papers; Mrs. G. Tucker to Ruth Wilson, July 12, 1811, E. H. Rowland to Ruth Hairston, June 14, 1840, Fanny Hairston to Ruth Hairston, January 24, 1860, Peter Wilson Hairston to Ruth Hairston, March 20, 1857, WHFP; Gillespie, *Free Labor*, 14–16, 74, 75. On agency, see Chapter 4 below, and Kierner, "Hospitality, Sociability, and Gender," 449; O'Connor, "'I Hear the Little Basket.'"

14. John Prior Burke to William Gilliland, November 28, 1850, WGP.

15. For Eliza Wilkins, see JBGD; Louisa Alexander to Sarah Alexander, November 28, 1834, AHFP; Sarah Screven to James Proctor Screven, February 3, 1819, ASFP.

16. John Prior Burke to William Gilliland, April 6, 1848, November 8 and December 2, 1849, WGP; Chappell and Richter, "Wealth and Houses," 8.

17. Sarah Hillhouse to Sarah Alexander, July 5, 1832, AHFP.

18. Will of Stephen Cocke, November 7, 1794, and correspondence of Jane Cocke and James Powell Cocke, CFP.

19. Martha Cocke to Caroline Cocke, n.d., November 18, 1812, December 20, 1814, CFP; Lucy Thornton to Mrs. Rootes, November 25, 1799, Sarah Cobb to Sarah Jackson, May 18, 1845, Serena Lea to Martha Jackson, December 10, 1845, Martha Jackson's Answers to Interrogatories, June 16, 1846, JPFP; Deposition of Nancy Foscue, n.d., Foscue Family Papers; Will Alexander to John Steele, November 8, 1806, JSP.

20. Richard T. Archer to Capt. James Hobson, June 16, 1835, AFP; Stephen Cocke Archer to James Powell Cocke, August 19, 1831, "List of Debts to be secured by the General Deed," n.d., Will of Stephen Cocke, November 11, 1794, Agreement between Anne B. Cocke and Peter Field Archer, et al., January 23, 1806, Richard T. Archer to James Powell Cocke, December 12, 1835, CFP.

21. JBGD, February 8, 1837; Codicil to the Will of Eliza Flinn, October 7, 1843, GFP; Receipts for tuition and board of Charles Wheeler, June 10 and 15, 1857, January 23 and July 10, 1858, Ann Wheeler to Ruth S. Hairston, March 6, 1859, August 7, 1857, WHFP; Joseph Dulles to Ann Lovell, April 25, 1835, Ann (Heatly) Reid Lovell Papers; Lebsock, *Free Women*, 142–45.

22. Martha Richardson to James Proctor Screven, March 2, 1817, June 15 and December 20, 1821, Trust Agreement, January 7, 1829, ASFP.

23. Catherine Lewis to Emma Lewis, December 11, 1838, August 1, 1840, JFSP. As surrogate parents for orphaned grandchildren, widows also wielded substantial influence; see Sarah Alexander to Adam Alexander, December 14, 1826, AHFP, and letters between Margaret and Ann Ferrand and Mary Steele, JSP; Fox-Genovese, *Within the Plantation Household*, 107–12; Clinton, *Plantation Mistress*, 25.

24. Martha Richardson to James Proctor Screven, April 21, 1833, ASFP.

25. Will Alexander to John Steele, November 8, 1806, JSP; Deposition of Ann (Nancy) Foscue, n.d., Foscue Family Papers.

26. Serena Lea to Martha Jackson, December 10, 1845, November 20, 1852;

Martha Jackson's Answers to Interrogatories, June 16, 1846; Emily Hagy to Martha Jackson, April 22, 1846, JPFP.

27. Mary Spotswood Campbell to John Spotswood, January 10, 1791; Will of John Spotswood, 1756, Spotswood Family Papers.

28. Linnaeus Bolling to Susannah Wilcox, February 10, 1810, HFP.

29. James Powell Cocke to Caroline Cocke, September 15 and November 11, 1814, Charles Cocke to Jane Cocke, April 8, 1813, June 16, 1816, and May 26, 1840, Martha Cocke to Caroline Cocke, November 18, 1812, CFP; JBGD, August 17, 1836; Adams, *Elements of Moral Philosophy*, 376; Stowe, *Intimacy and Power*, 130, 144–46; Brown, *Good Wives*, 340–42. Cf. Lewis, *Pursuit of Happiness*, 24, 27, 36. On letter-writing and emotions, see Halttunen, *Confidence Men and Painted Women*, 88–96, 118–19; Stowe, *Intimacy and Power*, 142–53.

30. JBGD, August 17, 1836, February 21, 1834, see also April 8, August 27, and May 4, 1834, May 28, 1836, November 30, 1837, January 18, 1838, February 23, May 28, and December 25, 1839, October 30 and November 7, 1840, January 1, 1841, December 21, 1843, March 17, July 27, and January 23, 1844; Louisa Alexander to Adam Alexander, March [9], 1837, AHFP; Stowe, *Intimacy and Power*, 154 and 122–63 passim.

31. Lucy Freeman to Jessie, Martha, Thomas Henry, and Mrs. Vaughan, November 30, 1835; Lucy Freeman to Thomas Nelson, February 7, 1836; Lucy Freeman to Jessie and Mrs. Vaughan, February 28, 1836, Jessie Vaughan Papers. On migration's relationship to familial bonds, compare Censer, "Southwestern Migration," 407–26; Baptist, "Migration of Planters," 527–54; Cashin, *Family Venture*.

32. Brown, *Good Wives*, 321; Catherine Lewis to Emma Speight, November 24, 1847, see also November 25, 1845, March 27, 1855, JFSP; Catherine Lewis to Kenelm H. Lewis, October 16, 1858, Catherine Lewis to William Figures Lewis, June 18, 1842, Lewis Family Papers; Lewis, *Pursuit of Happiness*, 24, 36, 172–73; Kierner, *Beyond the Household*, 169–70; Lebsock, *Free Women*, 17–18, 48–53.

33. On the desirability of preserving familial privacy by settling disputes privately instead of at law, see, for example, C. A. Brown to George Rives, September 8, 1858, George S. Rives Papers.

34. Equity initially developed in England as a complement to common law, in which the principle of fairness carried more weight than common-law precedent. See Reeve, *Law of Baron and Femme*; Salmon, *Women and the Law of Property*, 7–10, 18, 38–40, 105, 115–18; Basch, "Equity vs. Equality," 297–318; Morris, *Southern Slavery and the Law*, 7, 448 n. 41; Basch, "Invisible Women," 346–66. Widows were not always better off in equity than at law, however; Ruth Hairston had a "legal right" in her husband's Tennessee lands, for example, but not an "equitable one." Peter Wilson Hairston to Ruth Hairston, June 15, 1852, WHFP.

35. Copy of the will of Gawin Corbin, October 9, [1760], PP. Corbin named a kinsman, his wife, and three of her brothers as his executors, but only his wife and one of her brothers chose to qualify.

36. This George Turberville was a relation of the Major George Turberville whose invasion of Westover so affronted Mary Willing Byrd in 1781.

37. Gawin Corbin's will did not specify that Martha's property be reserved to

her sole and separate use, or use any similar language that could give her a separate estate after marriage. Consequently, any realty she received from her father became her husband's for his lifetime, and any personalty became his outright. Copy of the will of Gawin Corbin, October 9, [1760]; George Turberville to James Mercer, October 2, 1774; [George Turberville] to [Richard Henry Lee], February 26, 1783, PP.

38. James Thruston Hubard to [unknown], September 9, [1810]; James Thruston Hubard to Susannah Wilcox, n.d., HFP.

39. James Thruston Hubard to Susannah Wilcox, [1806], HFP.

40. James Hubard died intestate and his wife declined the administration of his extremely indebted estate. James Thruston Hubard to Susan Hubard, n.d., HFP. On the post-Revolutionary backlash, see Kierner, *Beyond the Household*, 111–18, 137. On men's reaction to separate estates, see, for example, Lebsock, *Free Women*, 58–67.

41. George Turberville to James Mercer, October 2, 1774, PP; John Thompson to James Thruston Hubard, May 2, 1807, James Thruston Hubard to Susan Hubard, December 3, 1806, James Thruston Hubard to John Miller, July 11, 1809, Linnaeus Bolling to Susannah Wilcox, November 2 and 6, 1810, Linnaeus Bolling to James Thruston Hubard, November 4, 1810, HFP.

42. In contrast, political disputes among men often involved vicious insults, which in turn produced brawls and duels. See, for example, Olsen, *Political Culture and Secession*, 49–53, 172–75; Greenberg, *Honor and Slavery*; Freeman, *Affairs of Honor*.

43. Martha Richardson to James Proctor Screven, April 16, 1817, ASFP.

44. Martha Richardson to James Proctor Screven, November 29, 1819, ASFP; Bynum, *Unruly Women*, 67–68; Salmon, *Women and the Law of Property*, 114–15.

45. For the Hairston clan's tangled history, see Wiencek, *Hairstons*.

46. Peter Wilson Hairston to Ruth Hairston, May 29, 1852, January 26, 1853, James M. Whittle to Ruth Hairston, May 24, 1852, WHFP; Wiencek, *Hairstons*, 112–25.

47. Peter Wilson Hairston to Ruth Hairston, June 8, 1852; James T. Harrison to Ruth Hairston, October 9, 1852; James Whittle to Ruth Hairston, January 14, 1853; Peter Wilson Hairston to Ruth Hairston, August 9, 1853, WHFP. For the legal status of bastards and slaves with regard to inheritance, see, for example, *Acts of the State of Georgia, 1849 and 1850*, 172; Hawks, *Digested Index*, 129; Haywood, *Manual of the Laws*, 226; Moore and Biggs, *Revised Code of North Carolina*, chapter 28.

48. James T. Harrison to Ruth Hairston, October 9, 1852; John Gilmer to Ruth Hairston, July 11, 1855, WHFP.

49. James M. Whittle to George Hairston, September 4, 1845; John Gilmer to Ruth Hairston, July 11, 1855; 1861 Agreement, WHFP.

50. Peter Wilson Hairston to Ruth Hairston, June 12 and December 13, 1852, January 16 and January 26, 1853; Peter Wilson Hairston to Samuel P. Wilson, January 24, 1853; Transcripts from Probate Court, April Session, 1852, Lowndes County, Mississippi, WHFP.

51. Peter Wilson Hairston to Ruth Hairston, January 26, 1853; Peter Wilson Hairston to Samuel P. Wilson, January 24, 1853, WHFP.

52. Peter Wilson Hairston to Ruth Hairston, June 12, 1852; James Whittle to Ruth Hairston, July 25, 1854, WHFP.

53. Peter Wilson Hairston to Ruth Hairston, April 15, May 8, and June 12, 1852, January 16, 1853, Peter Wilson Hairston to Samuel P. Wilson, January 24, 1853, Receipt of payment by Peter Wilson Hairston, August 4, 1853, WHFP; Peter Wilson Hairston to George Hairston, April 4, 1853, Hairston Family Papers.

54. Affinal relations were not always as close as blood kin, but they too could provide considerable support. Jean Blair, Marion Deveaux, Martha Jackson, Penelope Lowther, Martha Cocke, Martha Richardson, Catherine Lewis, and Natalie Sumter all had very positive relationships with brothers-in-law, sons-in-law, or more distant connections by marriage. Wood, "Fictive Mastery," 259–60.

55. As Suzanne Lebsock has suggested, the low rates of remarriage among financially comfortable widows, especially those with children, confirm that they preferred to retain control over their finances, households, and persons whenever possible. See Chapter 6 below and Lebsock, *Free Women*, 26–27.

56. Wyatt-Brown, *Southern Honor*, 234–36, esp. 235; *Southern Cultivator*, August 2, 1843; Cary, *Letters on Female Character*, 21; Tucker, *Valley of the Shenandoah*, 2:179; Blennerhasset, *Widow of the Rock*; Carey, *Fragment*; Southworth, *Widow's Son*; Sawyer, *Merchant's Widow*.

Chapter 4

1. Ditz, "Shipwrecked," 51–81. For Pennsylvania women managing property and businesses, see Wilson, *Life after Death*, chapter 4.

2. Julia Cherry Spruill's invaluable study of colonial southern women includes a dazzling array of women's economic and specifically commercial activities. Scholars of later generations have found less evidence of white women's economic activity, especially among slaveholding women. Suzanne Lebsock is a key exception. Spruill, *Women's Life and Work*, esp. chapters 12–13; Lebsock, *Free Women*, chapter 6; Kierner, *Beyond the Household*, 2, 172–74; Wyatt-Brown, *Southern Honor*, 240–42; Snyder, "'Rich Widows,'" 198, 202–3; Anzilotti, *In the Affairs of the World*, esp. chapters 4–6.

3. See, for example, McCurry, *Masters of Small Worlds*, 97; Isaac, *Transformation of Virginia*, 57; but cf. Olsen, *Political Culture and Secession*, 104–5; Varon, *We Mean to Be Counted*, 71–136.

4. Lewis Utzman's receipt, August 15, 1815, JSP; Receipt of payment from R. Williams, May 4, 1825, BFP; John Day's receipt, November 25, 1857, W. Robert Leckie Papers. Widows also paid for special monuments for their husbands. See, for example, James A. Washington to Eliza Grist, October 7, 1839, Elizabeth Washington Grist Knox Papers; Memorandum, n.d., Ann (Heatly) Reid Lovell Papers; Jesse Pearson to Mary Steele, [fragment, ca. April 1816], JSP.

5. Hamilton, Lemoine, and Pannill (later Robert Hamilton and Co.) to Lucy Burwell, October 7, 1822, April 10, 1823, and October 8, 1825, BFP; Reynolds

and Bros.'s receipt, December 6 and November 17, 1855, WHFP. For mid-nineteenth-century mourning customs, primarily in the northern United States, see Halttunen, *Confidence Men and Painted Women*, 124–52.

6. Hugh Campbell to Mary Steele, August 27 and September 26, 1815; Mary Steele to Walker and Atkinson, September 27, 1815, JSP.

7. Estate sale of Nicholas Click, December 12, 1832, Click Family Papers; John E. Foscue Estate Sale, July 1849, Simon Foscue Sr. Estate Sale, November 1814, Foscue Family Papers; Lucy Freeman to Thomas Nelson, February 7, 1836, Lucy Freeman to Jesse Vaughan and Wife, February 28, 1836, Jessie Vaughan Papers; Tucker, *Valley of the Shenandoah*, 2:202, 203–4, and 201–15 passim; NDSD, July 3, 1840; Cushing, *First Laws of Georgia*, 1:414; Cushing, *First Laws of South Carolina*, 1:201, 2:491–95; Haywood, *Manual of the Laws*, 5, 6, 8; Cushing, *First Laws of North Carolina*, 1:28–29; Moore and Biggs, *Revised Code of North Carolina*, 282–83, 318; *Acts of the State of Georgia, 1849 and 1850*, 37–39, 92–98; *Acts of the State of Georgia, 1855–'56*, 144. According to the 1850 Federal Population Census, Caroline Foscue possessed $3,333 of real estate and 48 slaves.

8. Johnson, *Soul by Soul*, 12–14, figure 20 (preceding p. 117); Morris, *Southern Slavery and the Law*, chapter 5.

9. Accounts of Susannah Wilcox with Walke, Lackland and Co., September 22, 1798, with John Hendrick, February 11, 1799, and with Rives, Higginbotham and Co., November 9, 1802, HFP; Hamilton, Lemoine, and Pannill (later Robert Hamilton and Co.) to Lucy Burwell, October 7, 1822, April 10, 1823, October 8, 1825, BFP; Account of Paulina Legrand with Archibald Vaughan, 1835–36, Account Book of Archibald Vaughan, Archibald Vaughan Papers; Reynolds and Bros.'s receipt, November 17 and December 6, 1855, WHFP; Bill of Pearson and Murphy, May 27, 1816, JSP; John M. Wright's receipt, August 12, 1857, W. Robert Leckie Papers; Ford, "Self-Sufficiency, Cotton, and Economic Development," 261–67; Wright, *Political Economy of the Cotton South*, 164–76; Gillespie, *Free Labor*, 14–18, 96–98, 119.

10. Accounts and receipts, folder 7, BFP; letters and receipts, folders 2 and 3, DWPP; Reynolds and Bros.'s receipts, December 6 and November 17, 1855, Millner Tinsley's receipts, March 9, 1855, and January 19, 1856, John W. Holt's receipt, October 30, 1857, J. A. Hampton's receipt, June 4, 1859, and correspondence of Samuel Nowlin, Reynolds and Bros., Winfree and Watkins, and Sandy River Mill, 1841–59, WHFP; McCurry, *Masters of Small Worlds*, 96–99; Chappell and Richter, "Wealth and Houses."

11. NDSD, August 5, September 15, September 29, October 2, October 7, October 9–10, November 19, and November 30, 1840, January 26, 1841.

12. Absalom Taylor's receipt, September 21, 1775, Alexander Long's receipt, July 10, 1819, John Steele's Taxable Property, 1814, JSP; James B. Cain's receipt, January 1, 1824, Runa Lockwood's receipt, December 18, 1824, DWPP; [Als] Blankinship's receipt, March 1, 1825, BFP; Payment—Elizabeth Alston, January 14, 1841, Archibald Davis Alston Papers; Millner Tinsley's receipts, March 9, 1855, and January 19, 1856, John W. Holt's receipt, October 30, 1857, J. A. Hampton's receipt, June 4, 1859, WHFP. Cf. Boydston, *Home and Work*; Gillespie, *Free*

Labor, 91, 96–104. For the use of slave artisans, see Hannah Corbin to George Turberville, n.d., asking to borrow Lancaster Dick to repair her house, PP.

13. NDSD; correspondence, 1841–1859, WHFP; Archibald Vaughan accounts, 1835–36, Archibald Vaughan Papers; John M. Wright's receipt, August 12, 1857, W. Robert Leckie Papers; John R. Lark's bill, March 29, 1821, Richard Bullock's bill, May 19, 1821, and Account of Alexander Boyd, February 9, 1822, BFP; Miscellaneous Receipts, 1824, DWPP; Dr. Neeson's Account, paid December 20, 1847, James Lamkin Papers.

14. Note, however, that poor households could not afford to buy foodstuffs or fuel in bulk and thus regularly made small purchases (often at higher prices). Boydston, *Home and Work*, 132; Stansell, *City of Women*, 49–50.

15. Henry Cook and A. G. Boyd were sons-in-law, and Alexander Boyd a brother-in-law. Heard and Cook to Annabella Porter, November [10], 1824, DWPP; genealogical notes, BFP; summons, December 23, 1857, W. Robert Leckie Papers.

16. Mary Steele to Walker and Atkinson, September 27, 1815, JSP.

17. Slaveholders both used the U.S. mail and entrusted letters to slaves or fellow whites—friends, neighbors, or relations. For slave couriers, see Richard Eppes to [Jane Cocke], November 14, 1795, CFP; Ruth Wilson to Peter Wilson, May 2, 1802, Sterling Adams to Ruth Hairston, July 25, 1863, WHFP; Hamilton, Lemoine, and Pannill to Lucy Burwell, December 11, [1821], October 7, 1822, Robert Hamilton and Co. to Lucy Burwell, October 8, 1825, BFP; Peter Wilson Hairston to George Hairston, August 1, 1852, George Hairston Papers; Gundersen, "Kith and Kin."

18. Hugh Campbell to Mary Steele, August 27 and September 26, 1815, Mary Steele to Walker and Atkinson, September 27, 1815, Mary Steele to Ann Nessfield, October 16, 1805, JSP; Hamilton, Lemoine and Pannill to Lucy Burwell, December 3 and 11, 1821, Robert Hamilton and Co. to Lucy Burwell, October 8, 1825, James Lowry and Co. to Lucy Burwell, January 1, 1824, BFP.

19. JBGD, August 22, 1834, February 8, 1837, February 5 and July 8, 1838, May 16 and 19, 1843, October 7, 1844; John Lankford's receipts, June 11, 1818, and March 18, 1819, Seth Stubblefield's receipt, January 1, 1819, William Patterson Smith Papers; receipts by hand of William Porter, June 16 and March 2, 1824, DWPP; William H. Battle to Lucy Battle, February 10, 1857, Battle Family Papers.

20. Fields, *Worthy Partner*, 398; James Powell Cocke to Caroline Cocke, December 14, 1811, James Powell Cocke in account with William Powlett, January 2, 1828, CFP; William H. Cabell to Paulina Legrand, April 6, 1840, see also June 22, 1820, June 26, 1821, May 24, 1822, Henry Carrington Papers; Mary Steele to Walker and Atkinson, July 10, 1816, Jesse Pearson to Mary Steele, n.d., Mary Steele to Jesse Pearson, n.d., Robert Cochran to Mary Steele, January 10, 1818, April 6, 1816, JSP; Joseph Dulles to Anne Lovell, November 28, 1833, Ann (Heatly) Read Lovell Papers; John Miller to Edm[un]d W. Rootes, January 9, 1810, Linnaeus Bolling to Susannah Wilcox, November 9, 1809, Bill against Susannah Wilcox, July 31, 1806, HFP; Receipts of payment from Caroline Foscue, Foscue Family Papers; Sarah Ann Tazewell to Mary Claiborne, December 19, 1853, Jones Family Papers; Receipt of payment from Martha Turberville, January

29, 1833, PP; Eliza Blackwell's receipt, June 14, 1827, BFP; Mary G. Franklin in account with Marcus Franklin, 1847, Account Book 1847–55, Mary G. Franklin Papers.

21. Fields, *Worthy Partner*, 5–6, 8–9, 13, 25–28, 35–36, 41–44, 48, 57; Account of Mrs. Hannah Corbin and Richard L. Hall with William Molleson, March 1, 1773, PP; T. R. O'Neale's receipt, November 7, 1854, RMDP; David and Ro. Maitland accounts with estate of Stephen Cocke, 1794–96, CFP.

22. Robert Cochran to Mary Steele, December 30, 1816, January 10, 1818, July 7, 1819, JSP; Powers of Attorney, May 21 and December 4, 1852, Peter Wilson Hairston Papers; Contract between Ruth Hairston and John M. Withers, February 4, 1853, WHFP; Linnaeus Bolling to Susannah Wilcox, November 9, 1809, HFP; Account of John Kirkpatrick, December 20, 1825, January 28, 1826, Agreement, December 14, 1826, Agreement, April 7, 1827, Singleton Family Papers, SHC.

23. Penelope Dawson to Helen Iredell, December 8, 1792, Skinner Family Papers; M. Hubard to Susan Hubard, December 25, 1812, January 14 and November 6, 1813, HFP; William Cabell to Paulina Legrand, May 24, 1822, Henry Carrington Papers; Polly Townes to Jane Cocke, February 9, 1823, CFP; O'Connor, "'I Hear the Little Basket'"; Fryer, "Red Birds and Turtles."

24. For examples of printed stationary, see Frederick D. Peters (Petersburg) to [Robert Hairston], January 22, 1823, James Blair (Columbus, Miss.) to Ruth Hairston, August 11, 1855, WHFP; Binford, Brooks, and Gay (Richmond) to [Jane Cocke], November 30, 1835, CFP; N. M. Martin Brothers and Co. (Richmond) to Mary Ann Hendrick, May 12, 1857, W. Robert Leckie Papers; William Bullock Jackson for Anderson and Co. (Savannah) to Sarah Jackson, June 12, 1852, JPFP; Emmet and Cuthbert (New Bern) to Caroline Foscue, December 1, 1855, Foscue Family Papers. Some if not most of the letterhead was printed in the North, but it seems unlikely that merchants who went to the trouble to buy customized letterhead would have accepted designs that bore no relationship to actual or desired patterns in southern commerce.

25. Power of Attorney (Walter Lindsay), July 5, 1777, Power of Attorney (Mary Steele), December 28, 1817, JSP; Account of Zaccheus Collins, n.d., Richard Bland Lee Papers.

26. Sarah Cobb to Martha Jackson, February 12, 1846, JPFP; Agreement, April 16, 1857, Haddie Grey to Mary Ann Hendrick, March 30, 1867, W. Robert Leckie Papers.

27. Randolph, *Virginia Housewife*, xii; *Southern Cultivator*, April 5, 1843; *South Carolina Weekly Museum*, January 1, 1797; *Southern Agriculturalist*, April 1830; James A. Washington to Eliza Washington, August 22, 1822, EWGKP; Richard T. Archer to Mary Archer, May 17, 1823, AFP; Sarah Cobb to Henry Rootes Jackson, June 5, 1834, JPFP; Martin Wilkins to John Berkeley Grimball, January 11, 1850, GFP; Richard Singleton to [unknown], June 6, 1850, RMDP.

28. For domesticity's influence on southern culture, see Kierner, *Beyond the Household*; Weiner, *Mistresses and Slaves*. Cf. Fox-Genovese, *Within the Plantation Household*, 61–68, 78–81.

29. J. C. Dobbin to Elizabeth Blanks, September 13, 1844, Elizabeth J. (Holmes) Blanks Papers; Sale of Douglas Watson Porter's personalty, December 12, 1826, DWPP; Sale of Roger J. Williams's perishable estate, December 21, 1830, BFP; Sale of Thos. Goodson's estate, October 28, 1840, James Dove Papers; Sale of Henry Norman's estate, December 5 and 6, 1831, Henry Norman Papers; George Hairston for Ruth Hairston to [unknown], July 8, 1852, WHFP; Harriet H. Branham Diary, February 11, 1863.

30. Tucker, *Valley of the Shenandoah*, 1:202, 215, and 201–15 passim.

31. Charles Crenshaw's will (1790), Sarah Crenshaw's will (1803, 1808, 1818), Charles Crenshaw's will (1808, 1818 [canceled], 1820), Crenshaw Family Papers; Copy of the will of Gawin Corbin, [unknown] to [a Corbin executor], February 26, 1783, PP.

32. Thomas Smith to William P. Smith, February 6 and March 30, 1822, William Patterson Smith Papers; C. A. Brown to George Rives, September 8, 1858, George S. Rives Papers; John Steele to Thomas Jefferson, July 1, 1802, Will of John Steele, 1815, copy, JSP; Richard B. Lee to Zaccheus Collins, 1813 (fragment), Richard Bland Lee Papers.

33. Peter Wilson Hairston to [George] Hairston, January 3, 1853, WHFP; George Weir to Susannah Wilcox, August 19, 1797, John Barret and Company to Susannah Wilcox, July 21, 1789, John Miller to Archibald Austin, August 29, 1810, Linnaeus Bolling to Susannah Wilcox, September 1, 1804, November 9, 1809, Thomas L. to Susannah Wilcox, July 25, 1810, James Bullock to Susan Hubard, September 1814, Richard Theweate to Susan Hubard, December 11, 1816, HFP; Martha Turberville to Joseph James Monroe, August 6, 1802, James Dishman to Gawin Corbin Turberville, May 28, 1806, PP; NDSD, September 1840; William H. Cabell to Paulina Legrand, January 1, [182?], see also June 6, 1819, Henry Carrington Papers; Carter, *Diary of Dolly Lunt Burge*, 103.

34. George H. Wethers to Mary Steele, January 7, 1823, Joseph Hampton to Mary Steele, n.d., JSP; Carter, *Diary of Dolly Lunt Burge*, 98, 103.

35. Cary, *Letters on Female Character*, 45; *Acts of the State of Georgia, 1839*, 144; Nancy White to Mrs. Thomas Cowan and Mrs. Michael Brown, December 30, 1835, quoted in Susan Davis Nye Hutchison Diary; Gilman, *Poetry of Travelling*, 337; King, "'What Providence Has Brought Them to Be'"; Spruill, *Women's Life and Work*, chapters 12–14; Lebsock, *Free Women*, chapter 6; David Jaffee, "Peddlers of Progress," 511–35. Cf. Pease and Pease, *Family of Women*, 31.

36. Ann Green Swann Diary, August 19, 1855, Swann Family Papers; Heath, "North American Railroads," 40–53; Weiman, "Economic Emancipation," 71–93.

37. Cohen, "Safety and Danger"; Cohen, "Women at Large," 44–51; Lewis, *Ladies and Gentlemen*; Brown, *Good Wives*, 272–76, 281–82; Clinton, *Plantation Mistress*, 9, 90, 109; Kerber, "Separate Spheres," 9–39. On travel hazards in a later era, see Welke, *Recasting American Liberty*, chapter 2.

38. Simms, *Eutaw*; Simms, *Woodcraft*; Ball, *Fifty Years in Chains*, 150–52, 154, 166, 178–79. Cf. Daniels and Kennedy, *Over the Threshold*; Bardaglio, *Reconstructing the Household*, 3–4, 33–34, 74; Bynum, *Unruly Women*, 74–75, tables 3.3, 3.4.

39. On chaperones for young single women, see, for example, John Steele to Margaret Steele, March 12, 1807, JSP; Martha Jackson to Daniel [Grinnon], June 19, 1829, JPFP.

40. Carter, *Diary of Dolly Lunt Burge*, 35, 98–99, 101, 103, 109, 177, 180; NDSD, September 10–16, October 12, and November 16, 1840, January 11, March 20, and April 1, 1841.

41. See note 34 above.

42. Martha Richardson to James Proctor Screven, November 29, 1819, ASFP; JBGD, February 23, 1859; McCord, *Louisa S. McCord*, 342; NDSD, September 23, 1840, April 1, 1841; Martha Jackson to Joseph Jackson, August 10, 1849, JPFP; Carter, *Diary of Dolly Lunt Burge*, xxxii, 100, 104–5.

43. Martha Jackson to Joseph Jackson, August 10, 1819, JPFP; Carter, *Diary of Dolly Lunt Burge*, 100. On early nineteenth-century etiquette, see, for example, *Laws of Etiquette*, 66; Leslie, *Behavior Book*; Parkes, *Domestic Duties*.

44. Carter, *Diary of Dolly Lunt Burge*, 100; McCord, *Louisa S. McCord*, 284.

45. McCord, *Louisa S. McCord*, 284.

46. Will of Alexander Spotswood, 1756, Spotswood Family Papers; Tax Receipt, November 27, 1794, Will of Gawin Corbin Turberville, 1806, PP; Order on Wheeler and [illegible], n.d., HFP; Margaret Steele to Mary Steele, January 15, 1815, Bill from George Gibby, June 26, 1818, Tax Receipt, May 5, 1818, JSP; Tax Receipts, January 3, 1814, January 14, 1815, AHFP; Will of Dr. George Haig, January 4, 1790, Jacob Rhett Motte Papers; Will of Willis Alston, January 21, 1835, Archibald Davis Alston Papers.

47. Fields, *Worthy Partner*, xxi; Allison and Co.'s receipt, February 1, 1819, JSP; Catherine Lewis to Emma Lewis, June 20, 1839, JFSP; N. [Leffties]'s receipt, December 15, 1812, HFP; Sarah Mangum's receipt, August 7, 1830, Francis Gildart Ruffin Papers; E. Cuthbert's receipt, May 30, 1854, Foscue Family Papers; Duke and Parrish's receipt, September 1, 1855, Alice B. Payne George Papers; Samuel Peniston's bill, April 2, 1814, Reynolds and Bros.'s receipt, December 6, 1855, WHFP; Henry Woodworth's bill, November 29, 1823, BFP; Birchetts and Puryear's bill, February 5, 1805, CFP; Receipt of Duke and Parrish, September 1, 1855, Alice B. Payne George Papers. For British and American mourning customs and traditions, see Halttunen, *Confidence Men and Painted Women*, 136–43; Faust, *Mothers of Invention*, 188–91; Faust, *James Henry Hammond*, 116; Cunnington and Lucas, *Costume for Births, Marriages, and Death*, 148–51, 244–69.

48. Mary Meade to Jane Cocke, n.d., Charles Cocke to Jane Cocke, n.d., David and R. Maitland's bill, December 17, 1794, CFP; Mary Steele to Thomas Cowan, July 17, 1816, Wilkinson and Horah's receipt, October 19, 1820, JSP; Hamilton, Lemoine, and Pannill to Lucy Burwell, October 7, 1822, BFP; M. Hubard to Susan Hubard, n.d., HFP; Fields, *Worthy Partner*, xxi.

49. Catherine Lewis to Emma Speight, June 1, 1846, JFSP.

50. On wives' confinement to their homes, see Catherine Lewis to Emma Speight, September 27, 1838, April 4, 1839, March 6, 1841, JFSP. Wives, chil-

dren, and slaves did, of course, leave the household without permission, but they could not do so with impunity. The slave patrol regularly molested slaves whether they had passes or not, for example, and husbands could accuse their wives of breaking their marital vows if they traveled without permission or strayed from home for too long. See, for example, Charles Holst to Isabella Holst, June 9, 1869, IARWP; Franklin and Schweninger, *Runaway Slaves*, 149–81; Bynum, *Unruly Women*, 75, table 3.4.

51. Catherine Lewis to Emma Speight, March 27, 1855, JFSP; Farnham, *Education of the Southern Belle*.

52. Many who moved west found their prospects only marginally improved, in part because the rich, who also migrated in large numbers, carried their wealth and connections with them. Moving west did have one advantage for poor southern whites: looser requirements for suffrage. The western states lifted property qualifications earlier and more thoroughly than most of the southeastern states. Keyssar, *Right to Vote*; Bolton, *Poor Whites*, 52–53, 114–17, 134–37, 165.

53. Susannah Wilcox to Edward and Samuel Jones, April 16, 1810; Edward and Samuel Jones to Susannah Wilcox, n.d. (written on her letter of April 16, 1810, to the Joneses), HFP.

54. For this evolution in Connecticut, consult Mann, *Neighbors and Strangers*; Dayton, *Women before the Bar*.

55. James Brandon to Rowan County surveyor, November 3, 1778, JSP.

56. Bond of John Powell Cocke, September 26, 1813, CFP; Bond of John Berkeley Grimball and Eliza Flinn, March 8, 1828, GFP; Sarah Cobb to Martha Jackson, January 11, 1852 (bears a stamp), Indenture of Martha Jackson and Sarah Jackson, January 11, 1850 (uses printed indenture form), JPFP; Bond of Spotswood Burwell and William A. Burwell (uses a printed form intended for slave hires), January 3, 1827, BFP; Tax Receipt, September 1, 1859 (uses a printed form), Foscue Family Papers; Fields, *Slavery and Freedom*.

57. Mary Steele to Walker and Atkinson, April 13, 1816, Robert Cochran to Mary Steele, September 13, 1816, Mary Steele's checks drawn on Bank of North Carolina, 1816–17, JSP; Martha Richardson to James Proctor Screven, December 19, 1819, Sarah Screven to James Proctor Screven, October 4, 1819, ASFP; Charles Cocke to Jane Cocke, June 6, 1816, CFP; J. H. Drew to Eliza Ruffin, October 30, 1829, Mr. Claiborne to Eliza Ruffin, October 20, 1830, Francis Gildart Ruffin Papers; James A. Washington to Eliza Grist, October 7, 1839, EWGKP; Henry Rootes Jackson to Sarah Jackson, July 29, 1842, Vincent Pierson to Henry Rootes Jackson, January 13, 1844, Joseph Jackson to Martha Jackson, September 9, 1846, JPFP; Winfree and Watkins to George Hairston, September 3, 1855, WHFP; William H. Battle to Lucy P. Battle, January 10, 1857, Battle Family Papers; Keziah Goodwyn Hopkins Diary, September 27, 1860; Baptist, *Creating an Old South*, 112–19; Baptist, "Migration of Planters," 544–45.

58. Hugh Campbell to Mary Steele, August 27 and September 26, 1815, JSP; James Duffel to Peter Hairston, November 13, 1815, "Richmond Letter Sheet Prices Current," March 1, 1860, WHFP.

59. J. and J. D. Kirkpatrick's account, November 1, 1859, with penciled notation by Peter Bacot, Peter Samuel Bacot Papers; Harris and Wilson to Alice George, August 5, 1858, Alice B. Payne George Papers.

60. Chesnut, *Diary from Dixie*, 255.

Chapter 5

1. While more research is necessary, my evidence suggests that widowhood made little difference in many slaveholding women's charitable and religious activities. While their expanded personal and financial freedom spurred some to deeper commitments, others encountered significant obstacles in the shape of new demands on their time, attention, and purse. On charitable activities in the South, see Bellows, *Benevolence among Slaveholders*; Pease and Pease, *Web of Progress*, 144–52, 191–92; Varon, *We Mean to Be Counted*, chapter 1; Lebsock, *Free Women*, 142, 240; Wood, *Gender, Race, and Rank*, chapter 3.

2. McCurry, *Masters of Small Worlds*, 129; Ford, *Origins of Southern Radicalism*, 372–73.

3. Martha Richardson to James Proctor Screven, March 3, 1817, September 16, 1820, ASFP.

4. Caroline Marx to Eliza Ruffin, November 26, 1829, Francis Gildart Ruffin Papers.

5. Louisa Frederika Schmidt Alexander to Louisa Alexander, August 3, 1843, AHFP. Notes penciled on Alexander's letter indicate that her son was a Whig and her son-in-law a Democrat.

6. Elizabeth Oldham to Peter Hairston, March 19, 1817, WHFP.

7. Serena Lea to Sarah Jackson, December 13, 1844, JPFP; Green Pryor to Ruth Hairston, May 6, 1848, WHFP; Catherine Lewis to Emma Speight, August 1 and September 8, 1840, JFSP.

8. Ryan, *Women in Public*; Allgor, *Parlor Politics*; Branson, *These Fiery Frenchified Dames*; Jacob, *Capital Elites*; Wood, "'One Woman So Dangerous,'" 237–75; Isenberg, *Sex and Citizenship*; Varon, *We Mean to Be Counted*.

9. Fields, *Worthy Partner*, 342, 351–52, and 325–401 passim; Malone, *Jefferson and His Time*, 6:443.

10. American Colonization Society to Dolley Madison, July 6, 1836, Franklin Literary Society to Dolley Madison, August 8, 1836, Mr. Scantland and E. M. Haines (Independent Highlanders) to Dolley Madison, July 15, 1836, Democratic Young Men's Convention to Dolley Madison, July 8, 1836, Citizens of Petersburg to Dolley Madison, July 12, 1836, Louisa County Court to Dolley Madison, July 11, 1836, Fluvanna Court House to Dolley Madison, August 22, 1836, Dolley Payne Todd Madison Papers; Citizens of the Town of Madison to Dolley Madison, July 1836 (copy), Dolley Madison Project.

11. Fields, *Worthy Partner*, 328, 332, 342, 351–52, 363, 397.

12. Ibid., xxix–xxxii, 373–74, 378.

13. Eliza Schley to Sarah Jackson, June 24, 1840; Demosthenian Society to Martha Jackson, April 27, 1840, JPFP.

14. Fields, *Worthy Partner*, 331–32, 334, 340–41, 348, 365, 374, 384, 390; Newman, *Parades and the Politics of the Street*; Waldstreicher, *In the Midst of Perpetual Fetes*, 138–39, 160.

15. Malone, *Jefferson and His Time*, 6:444.

16. Fields, *Worthy Partner*, xxvii.

17. Ibid., 400–401. (Sources differ on Sargent's political fate.)

18. This paragraph is based on material drawn from Varon, *We Mean to Be Counted*, 88–93.

19. I owe a real debt to Chris Olsen for his willingness to share research from his unpublished book manuscript, "Politics as Ritual: A Cultural History of Voting and Running for Office in Antebellum America."

20. "James Jackson," in Wilson and Fiske, *Appleton's Cyclopaedia of American Biography* [electronic edition].

21. Finding Aid, JPFP; Powell and Fish, *Dictionary of North Carolina Biography*, 3:2–3, 1:112–18.

22. Mary Campbell to Lord Dunmore, n.d., Spotswood Family Papers; Fields, *Worthy Partner*, xxix–xxxii, 373–74, 378; Caleb McNulty to Dolley Madison, January 1, 1844 (copy), Dolley Madison Project.

23. Brant, *James Madison*, 523–24.

24. Martha Jackson to Mr. Camak, October 29, 1840, July 29 and August 4, 1841, JPFP.

25. Kierner, *Beyond the Household*, 125; Bellows, *Benevolence among Slaveholders*, 17.

26. James Powell Cocke to Caroline Cocke, December 18, 1810, December 4, 1811, Martha Cocke to Caroline Cocke, October 6 and December 21, 1813, CFP.

27. Fields, *Worthy Partner*, 392–93.

28. Howell Cobb to Martha Jackson, June 23, 1847, Martha Jackson to Sarah Cobb, March 19, 1847, Sarah Cobb to Martha Jackson, December [1], 1846, see also Serena Lea to Sarah Jackson, December 13, 1844, Joseph Jackson to Henry Rootes Jackson, October 21, 1844, JPFP; Green Pryor to Ruth Hairston, May 6, 1848, Peter Wilson Hairston to Ruth Hairston, November 10, 1857, WHFP; Catherine Lewis to Emma Speight, August 1 and September 8, 1840, JFSP. For young, single women's politics, see Margaret Steele to John Steele, December 8, 1811, William Ferrand to Mary Ferrand, August 14, 1839, JSP.

29. Charles Cocke to Jane Cocke, April 6, 1822, CFP; Sarah Cobb to Martha Jackson, November 15, 1843, JPFP.

30. Col. J. H. Watson to Henry R. Jackson, October 9, 1841; George R. Gilman to Henry R. Jackson, October 13, 1841; Wilson Lumpkin to Henry R. Jackson, October 13, 1841; Martha Jackson to Charles Jenkins, October 10, 1841; Martha Jackson to Mr. Bullock, October 19, 1841; Charles Jenkins to Martha Jackson, October 15, 1841; see also Martha Jackson to Henry Jackson, n.d. [ca. 1830], JPFP.

31. Mary Washington had the right to work her slaves on one portion of her husband's land and to employ them on a different plot while quarters were built for her. Instead, she simply occupied Ferry Farm, George's portion, even after he came of age. Freeman, *George Washington*, 1:74, 190, 193, 232, 2:17–18, 40, 84,

107, 199, 246, 387, 390. Dalzell and Dalzell, *George Washington's Mount Vernon*, 191, 198.

32. Malone, *Jefferson the Virginian*, 1:12, 31–32, 37, 116, 216; Ellis, *American Sphinx*, 27.

33. Hammond, *Secret and Sacred*, 15, 64, 91, 102, 295; Bleser, *Hammonds of Redcliffe*, 146 n. 1; Faust, *James Henry Hammond*, 39–45, 58–63, 311, 375.

34. Remini, *Life of Andrew Jackson*, 5, 8–9; Kerber, "Republican Mother"; Norton, *Liberty's Daughters*, 248–50; Randolph, *Virginia Housewife*, xii; *Southern Rose*, January 19, 1831, October 26, 1833, October 6, 1843.

35. Rawick, *American Slave*, 3(3):139–40.

36. This interpretation would mesh nicely with Joan Cashin's interpretation of young men's choices to migrate away from stifling families in the Southeast, although Jane Censer and Edward Baptist have cogently disputed Cashin's conclusions about migration and family. Cashin, *Family Venture*; Baptist, "Creating an Old South"; Censer, "Southwestern Migration."

37. For a case in which personal and political loyalties clashed in spectacular fashion, see Wood, "'One Woman So Dangerous.'"

38. On slaveholding women's attitudes toward dependence, see Chapter 6 below.

39. The argument is made here through suggestive moments in planters' papers, but court records would likely reward further research in this area.

40. Branson, *These Fiery Frenchified Dames*, 97, 125–42, 148; Kierner, *Beyond the Household*, 115.

41. On the war and its aftermath, see, for example, Olwell, *Masters, Slaves, and Subjects*, 221–83; Young, *Domesticating Slavery*, 57–122; Kulikoff, *Tobacco and Slaves*, 300–313, 416–20; Frey, *Water from the Rock*, 78–148.

42. A third possibility, that Martha Turberville had manufactured the accusations against Thompson and King, is not readily supported by the evidence. Deposition of Henry King, 1798, in the suit of James A. Thompson v. Martha Turberville, Westmoreland County Court, PP. On discord between overseers and planters generally, see Scarborough, *Overseer*, chapter 5. On slander suits, mostly involving sexual slurs, see Fischer, "Sexual Slander and Racial Ideology"; Bynum, *Unruly Women*, 41–44, 98. On trespass and related affronts to mastery, see McCurry, *Masters of Small Worlds*, chapter 1; Wyatt-Brown, *Southern Honor*, 379–80.

43. John Thompson to James Thruston Hubard, May 2, 1807, HFP.

44. Ibid.; Olsen, *Political Culture and Secession*, 104.

45. For a similar case, see George Turberville to James Mercer, October 2, 1774, PP.

46. Martha Turberville to Gawin Corbin Turberville, May 9, 1807, PP.

47. John Wilson to Isabella Glenn, September 12, 1808, Glenn Family Papers. Planters (and slaves) usually held overseers in "social disesteem." Scarborough, *Overseer*, 43.

48. See notes 43 and 45 above, and Lucy Thornton to Mrs. Rootes, November

15, 1799, JPFP; Archibald Ritchie to Eliza Ruffin, February 8, 1830, Francis Gildart Ruffin Papers; Scarborough, *Overseer*, 6–7, 43.

49. Henry Smith to Martha Jackson, July 25, 1840; Henry Rootes Jackson to Martha Jackson, November 3, 1840; Henry Smith to Henry Jackson, March 15, April 3, and May 3, 1840, JPFP.

50. Scarborough, *Overseer*, 5–6, 13, 29, 43, 47, 49.

51. Henry Smith to Henry Jackson, February 15, March 10, and March 15, 1840; Vincent Pierson to Martha Jackson, January 13, January 21, February 11, March 9, April 9, and September 7, 1844, JPFP.

52. Vincent Pierson to Martha Jackson, April 20, 1845, JPFP, Scarborough, *Overseer*, 6, 9–10, 41–43; Joyner, *Down by the Riverside*, 68.

53. Vincent Pierson to Martha Jackson, January 21, May 4, 1844, February 4, April 20, and August 9, 1845, June 8 and August 24, 1846, JPFP.

54. Isaac Read and Co.'s account, September 1, 1816, WHP; Robert Wood's account, September 2, 1816, JSP; William Morris's bill, June 26, 1815, William [Hunt]'s receipt, August 20, 1815, W. Cole's account, December 9, 1815, Edward Atkinson's receipt, October 25, 1856, John A. Hampton's receipt, May 2, 1857, WHFP; Account Book, 1847–55, references to John Fowler, 1852–53, and to Mr. Clark, 1853, Mary G. Franklin Papers; William H. Rudd's bill, July 20, 1857, Lewis G. Meacham's receipt, April 29, 1863, W. Robert Leckie Papers; Bolton, *Poor Whites*, 12–16; Lebsock, *Free Women*, 126–27; Gillespie, *Free Labor*, 110, 114–15, 123.

55. Wright, *Political Economy of the Cotton South*, 141; Morris, *Southern Slavery and the Law*, 132; Ford, *Origins of Southern Radicalism*, 335–37; Harris, *Plain Folk and Gentry*, 72–93. Wright argues that high slave prices in the 1850s made slaveholders feel more confident about and committed to slavery, while James Oakes suggests the opposite. Wright, *Political Economy of the Cotton South*, 145–48; Oakes, *Ruling Race*, 229–30.

56. According to the manuscript census returns for 1840, there were three householders named Yates in Sumter District. Two owned no slaves, but Robert E. Yates's household included twenty slaves and one educated white man, so he was probably the Dr. Yates of Sumter's diary. 1840 Manuscript Federal Population Schedules, Sumter District South Carolina.

57. NDSD, January 21, 1841.

58. NDSD, January 20 and 21, 1841.

59. Stephanie McCurry uses a similar incident—a case of trespass and personal violence between a South Carolina yeoman and planter—to suggest how ordinary whites as well as planter grandees had access to mastery. She argues that "although the rigorously observed boundaries of lowcountry households and the prerogatives of proprietors did not reflect, in the first instance at least, the particular needs of yeoman farmers, the claim of yeomen as property holders and heads of households to those legal and customary principles could not be denied." McCurry, *Masters of Small Worlds*, 17.

60. NDSD, January 19–21, 1841; McCurry, *Masters of Small Worlds*, 17, 206–7.

61. Simms, *Woodcraft*, 52–53; Tucker, *Valley of the Shenandoah*, 2:40, 44; Fox-Genovese, *Within the Plantation Household*, 203.

62. Simms, *Woodcraft*, 52–55, 373–74.

63. Berlin, *Confederate Nurse*, 4; Scarborough, *Overseer*, 45.

64. Tucker, *Valley of the Shenandoah*, 1:40, 214, 2:159, 292.

65. J. Dyson to Martha Singleton, [May 6, 1856], Singleton Family Papers, SCL.

66. Robert Carter to Dr. King, September 20, 1854, Singleton Family Papers, SCL. Mr. Lowndes was almost certainly related to Martha Singleton through her mother, and Dr. King was probably a friend and perhaps a kinsman as well.

67. Martha Singleton to Robert Carter, September 27, 1854, Singleton Family Papers, SCL. Calling Carter a gardener may even have been an insult if he preferred to consider himself a mechanic, craftsman, or artisan. Gillespie, *Free Labor*, 104–7.

68. In contrast, see how George Fitzhugh's arguments about the natural incapacity of women, children, and slaves for self-rule took the conventional wisdom to an extreme and left little room for the day-to-day realities of female authority over people and property. Fitzhugh, *Cannibals All!*, 201, 214, 217–18, 220, 232.

69. Charles Alexander to Mary Ann Hendrick, February 23, 1857, W. Robert Leckie Papers.

70. This interpretation owes much to Kenneth Greenberg's analysis of lies, but in applying his conclusions to a controversy between a male and a female planter, it challenges the usual restriction of such matters to white men. Greenberg, *Honor and Slavery*, chapter 1; Wyatt-Brown, *Southern Honor*, 227, 233–35.

71. Tucker, *Valley of the Shenandoah*, 1:41–44, 157, 159–60, 2:154, 178, 202, 209, 292; Simms, *Woodcraft*, 409.

72. NDSD, January 20 and 21, 1841, see also January 3, 15, and 16, 1841.

73. Robert Carter to Dr. King, September 20, 1854; Martha Singleton to Robert Carter, September 27, 1854, Singleton Family Papers, SCL.

74. Freehling, *Road to Disunion*, 98–101, 110–13; Harris, *Plain Folk and Gentry*, 64–65.

75. Martha Jackson to John A. Cobb, n.d., JPFP.

76. Martha Jackson to Henry Smith, October 26, 1840; Martha Jackson to Joseph Jackson, August 10, 1849; Joseph Jackson to Martha Jackson, September 22, 1840, JPFP. For overseers' wages, see Genovese, *Political Economy of Slavery*, 276; Scarborough, *Overseer*, 27–31.

77. Martha Jackson to Henry Smith, October 26, 1840, JPFP.

78. Simms, *Woodcraft*, 411, and 408–12 passim, see also 372; Pease and Pease, *Family of Women*, 31.

79. Olsen, *Political Culture and Secession*, 178.

80. Simms, "Review of *Women of the Revolution*," 334–35, 324–25, 342, 345. Cf. *Ladies' Repository*, 265–69. See also 1833 Reminiscences, Swann Family Papers; Emma Edwards Holmes, "Life Sketches of the Revolution," "Reminiscences," and "Tales of a Grandmother," Wilmot Stuart Holmes Papers; Wirt, *Sketches of Patrick Henry*, 84, 140; Kennedy, *Horse-Shoe Robinson*, 55–60, 411–

16, 463–72; *Virginia Literary Magazine*, March 3, 1830; Wyatt-Brown, *Southern Honor*, 234–35. Consider also the depiction of Mrs. Motte in biographies of General Francis Marion: Simms, *Life of Francis Marion*, 235–38; Horry and Weems, *Life of General Francis Marion*, 220–21; *Life of General Marion*, 186.

81. Charles Holst to Isabella Woodruff, June 26, 1858, IARWP.

Chapter 6

1. Martha Richardson to James Procter Screven, November 29, 1819, ASFP; Simms, *Woodcraft*, 411–12.

2. Lebsock, *Free Women*, xix, chapter 5.

3. Berlin, *Confederate Nurse*, 32.

4. On womanly sacrifice, especially for family, see Faust, *Mothers of Invention*, 17, 23; Fox-Genovese, *Within the Plantation Household*, 192; Lebsock, *Free Women*, 165.

5. A few wives and some single women also wrote wills, but most female testators were widowed. Unlike the women of Petersburg and Charleston, rural slaveholding women appear not to have made many special bequests to slaves or to have freed them. Lebsock, *Free Women*, 130, 133, and 130–45 passim; Weiner, *Mistresses and Slaves*, 151–52, 274 n. 61; Salmon, *Women and the Law of Property*, 112–14; Wood, *Gender, Race, and Rank*, 36–37. Like the parallel section in Chapter 1, the following discussion is based on qualitative data from throughout the Southeast and from quantitative analysis of wills from Rowan County, North Carolina. Also as in Chapter 1, unless otherwise specified, wills quoted or paraphrased in the text come from Rowan County. Wood, "Fictive Mastery," chapter 2. See also Lebsock, *Free Women*, 130–37; Ditz, *Property and Kinship*, 26–27; Anzilotti, "In the Affairs of the World," 115–32.

6. Salmon, *Women and the Law of Property*, xvi.

7. Wills of Esther Brandon, 1816, Book H; Elizabeth Stuart, 1792, Book D; Agnes Irwin, 1803, Book C, Rowan County, NCDAH.

8. Will of Mary McNeely, n.d. (1855 session), Book K, Rowan County, NCDAH. Lebsock finds that men in Petersburg usually gave equal shares to their children. Lebsock, *Free Women*, chapter 5, esp. 130.

9. Wills of Catharine Foy, 1821, Will Book H, Catherine Barger, 1822, Book H, Rowan County, NCDAH; Second Codicil to Mary Motte's Will, December 31, 1842, Jacob Rhett Motte Papers.

10. Will of Mary Motte, Jacob Rhett Motte Papers; Deposition of Martha Jackson, June 16, 1846, Indentures, June 27, 1847, June 15, 1852, JPFP; Will of [unknown] Gibbons, Book D, Chatham County, Georgia, Georgia Department of Archives and History; Wills of Jane Trotter, Elizabeth Torrence, Susan Beard, Catherine Weant, Elizabeth Fitzgareth, Mary Locke, Mary Anderson, Books E, H, I, and K, Rowan County, North Carolina, NCDAH; Lebsock, *Free Women*, xix, 76, 78; Salmon, *Women and the Law of Property*, 83, 115–16; Censer, *North Carolina Planters*, 65–68, 70–71, 74–76, 79; Stowe, *Intimacy and Power*, chapter 2, esp. 50–51, 63–64.

11. Wills of Mary Mahan, 1829, Book H; Catherine Garinger, 1797, Book G; Sarah Elliott, 1852, Book K; Mary McNeely, n.d. (1855 probate session), Book K; Susannah Moore, 1798, Book E, NCDAH.

12. Codicil to the Will of Eliza Flinn, October 7, 1843, GFP; Stephen Cocke Archer to James Powell Cocke, August 19, 1831; Richard T. Archer to James Powell Cocke, n.d., CFP; Richard T. Archer to Capt. James Hobson, June 16, 1835, AFP.

13. Wills of Elizabeth Leonard, 1803, Book G, Eleanor Faust, 1837, Book I, Fanny Winders, 1843, Book I, NCDAH; Codicil to the Will of Eliza Flinn, October 7, 1843, GFP.

14. Wood, "Fictive Mastery," chapter 2.

15. Lebsock, *Free Women*, xix, chapter 5; Smith-Rosenberg, "Female World of Love and Ritual."

16. Carter, *Diary of Dolly Lunt Burge*, 50; Harriet Singleton to Martha Singleton, May 6, 1853, Singleton Family Papers, SCL; Higginbotham, *Papers of James Iredell*, 1:98.

17. Lucy Thornton to Mrs. Rootes, November 25, 1799, Lucy Battaille Thornton Papers; Martha Cocke to Caroline Cocke, April 9, [1812], and July 17, 1812, CFP; Catherine Lewis to Lucy Battle, April 20, 1843, Battle Family Papers; Ada W. Bacot Diary, January 1, 1861, Ada W. Bacot Papers; Benjamin W. S. Cabell to George Hairston, February 27, 1857, John Tyler Hairston Papers.

18. Benjamin W. S. Cabell to George Hairston, February 27, 1857, John Tyler Hairston Papers; Caroline Olivia Laurens Diary, October 19 and 20, 1827; Sarah Cobb to Martha and Sarah Jackson, June 19, 1848, JPFP; Martha Cocke to Caroline Cocke, April 9, [1812], July 17, 1812, CFP.

19. Caroline Olivia Laurens Diary, June 1, 1826, June 7, 1827.

20. Caroline Olivia Laurens Diary, October 19 and November 9, 1827; Elizabeth Lee to Cornelia Lee, June 21, [n.y.], John Bland Lee Papers. On self-control in American culture, see, for example, Hemphill, *Bowing to Necessities*; Halttunen, *Confidence Men and Painted Women*.

21. Charles Cocke to Jane Cocke, April 13, 1812, November 4, 1819, CFP; John McPherson Berrien to Elizabeth Lee, November 1, 1852, James Bland Lee Papers; Eliza Kennedy to Sarah Jackson, March 4, 1849, JPFP; "Prayer for the Woman who has lost her husband," AFP; Catherine Lewis to Emma Speight, October 7, 1846, JFSP.

22. Martha Cocke to Caroline Cocke, July 17 and November 18, 1812, December 21, 1824, CFP; Catherine Lewis to Emma Speight, October 16, 1845, May 20, 1848, see also October 27, 1846, JFSP; Sarah Screven to James Proctor Screven, March 18, 1820, ASFP; Eliza Schley to Sarah Jackson, June 24, 1840, JPFP. For references to grace, see, for example, Serena Lea to Martha Jackson, October 5, 1843, Sarah Cobb to Martha Jackson, n.d. [ca. 1840], JPFP; Ann Swann to [her children], 1864, Swann Family Papers; James Augustus Washington to Elizabeth Grist, May 18, 1836, EWGKP; Harriet Brown to Marion Deveaux, May 12, [1860], RMDP; Caroline Burke to William Gilliland, March 2, [1854], WGP; Caroline Olivia Laurens Diary, September 14 and October 18–20, 1827; Agnes

Hairston to Peter and George Hairston, October 2, 1843, WHFP. For the meager compensations of religion, see Lewis, *Pursuit of Happiness*, 95–105.

23. Carter, *Diary of Dolly Lunt Burge*, 18.

24. Elizabeth Lee to Zaccheus Collins, March 27, 1827, Richard Bland Lee Papers; Caroline Marx to Eliza Ruffin, November 26, 1829, Francis Gildart Ruffin Papers; Keziah Goodwyn Hopkins Brevard Diary, November 18, 1860; Catherine Lewis to Emma Speight, October 27, 1846, JFSP; Ann Swann to [her children], 1864, Ann Swann to [her son], August 27, 1865, Swann Family Papers; Serena Lea to Martha Jackson, October 5, 1843, JPFP; L. Carter [Flirrol] to Mrs. Mattie R. Singleton, September 11, 1854, Singleton Family Papers, SCL; Caroline Burke to William Gilliland, March 2, 1854, WGP; Weiner, *Mistresses and Slaves*, 65; Hentz, *Planter's Northern Bride*, 257, 274.

25. Martha Cocke to Caroline Cocke, July 17, 1812, CFP; Caroline Olivia Laurens Diary, October 19, 1827; "Susie" to Martha Singleton, October 14, 1854, Singleton Family Papers, SCL.

26. Ada W. Bacot Diary, March 17, 1861, Ada W. Bacot Papers.

27. Rev. Robert Anderson to Paulina Legrand, May 16, 1815, Henry Carrington Papers.

28. Carter, *Diary of Dolly Lunt Burge*, xii, xxviii, 4, 17, 27, 41, 46–47; Keziah Goodwyn Hopkins Brevard Diary, September 15, 1860, see also Moore, *Plantation Mistress*, 32; Heyrman, *Southern Cross*, 128.

29. Carter, *Diary of Dolly Lunt Burge*, 41; Martha Jackson's religious writings, February 22, 1821, April 13, 1846, Sarah Cobb to Sarah Jackson, February 26, 1846, Joseph Jackson to Martha Jackson, September 20, 1848, JPFP; Lewis, *Pursuit of Happiness*, 70–105.

30. Moore, *Plantation Mistress*, 21, 30, 43, 49, 66, 97, 105–7; Cary, *Letters on Female Character*, 20; Wyatt-Brown, *Southern Honor*, 145, 158, 227.

31. Penelope Dawson to Hannah Iredell, December 8, 1792, Skinner Family Papers; Eliza Flinn to John Berkeley Grimball, September 27, 1821, John Berkeley Grimball Papers, SCL; Paulina Legrand to William Huntington, April 29, 1838, WHP; NDSD, August 1, September 18–19, and October 7, 1840, January 24–28, 1841.

32. Ada W. Bacot Diary, April 25, 1861, Ada W. Bacot Papers.

33. Elizabeth Lee to Fanny Reading, February 1858, Richard Bland Lee Papers; Obituary of Lucy Thornton, by Martha Jackson, Lucy Battaille Thornton Papers; Benjamin W. S. Cabell to George Hairston, February 27, 1857, John Tyler Hairston Papers; Martha Cocke to Caroline Cocke, April 9, [1812], and July 17, 1812, CFP. For the relationship between mastery and medicine, see Faust, *James Henry Hammond*, 376–78; Fett, *Working Cures*, 50, 52.

34. Slaveholders administered these treatments to slaves as well as themselves: Lucy Thornton to Martha Rootes, n.d., and Sarah Cobb to Martha Jackson, n.d., JPFP; Mary Cocke to Jane Cocke within James Cocke to Jane Cocke, October 2, 1799, Birchetts and Puryear, November 9, 1802, CFP; Eliza McNamara to John and Mary Steele, January 12, 1815, JSP; Deane and Page's bill, July 11, 1816, HFP; Sarah Screven to James Screven, October 4, 1819, ASFP; Goodman and

Co.'s account, January 9–August 13, 1821, Singleton Family Papers, SHC; James and Nathaniel Daniel's bill, January 1, 1822, BFP; Ezekiel S. Tally's receipt, July 3, 1829, Francis Gildart Ruffin Papers; Elizabeth Lee to Anna Washington, September 25, [1835], James Bland Lee Papers; NDSD, September 18–19 and November 25, 1840, Dr. Neeson's Account, James Lamkin Papers; Keziah Goodwyn Hopkins Brevard Diary, October 1, 1860.

35. NDSD, May 1–3, 1841; Benjamin Cabell to George Hairston, February 27, 1857, John Tyler Hairston Papers; Rosenberg, *Explaining Epidemics*, 63–70.

36. Drew Faust has suggested that James Henry Hammond took this concern with internal and external control to a particular extreme; including his own bowels in the list of things he must dominate, he took regular, toxic doses of "mercury-based laxatives" and frequently used enemas. Faust, *James Henry Hammond*, 377.

37. Adam Alexander to Sarah Alexander, September 28–October 4, 1846, AHFP; Elizabeth Lee to Fanny Reading, February 1858, Elizabeth Lee to Anna Washington, September 25, 183[3], Richard Bland Lee Papers; Martha Jackson, "Lucy Thornton's obituary," Lucy Battaille Thornton Papers; Benjamin W. S. Cabell to George Hairston, February 27, 1857, John Tyler Hairston Papers; Martha Cocke to Caroline Cocke, April 9, [1812], and July 17, 1812, CFP. Opium and laudanum formed a regular part of the planter's pharmacopeia for their own use and for slaves'. Henry Woodworth's account, November 20, 1835, BFP; R. Barrus and Son's account, March 10, 1854, March 21, 1856, Foscue Family Papers; J. P. Morriss's receipt, July 16, 1815, HFP; Susan Davis Nye Hutchison Diary, May 10, 1827; "Sundries Sent Mrs J Singleton by Boat February 20 1822," Singleton Family Papers, SHC; Pearson and Murphy's bill, May 27, 1816, JSP; NDSD, February 14, 1841; Sarah Alexander to Adam Alexander, January 18, 1824, AHFP; David and R. Maitland's bill, December 17, 1794; William Flood to Hannah Corbin, January 3, 1780, PP; B. [Dural]'s receipt, March 11, 1829, Francis Gildart Ruffin Papers; J. C. James's account, July 1858, WHFP; Rosenberg, *Explaining Epidemics*, 15, 63, 147.

38. M. Cocke to Caroline Cocke, n.d., CFP; Pease and Pease, *Family of Women*, 187.

39. Ada W. Bacot Diary, May 1 and 10, 1861, Ada W. Bacot Papers.

40. Mary Ann Cobb to Martha Jackson, March 7, 1844, JPFP.

41. Ibid.; Serena Lea to Martha Jackson, November 20, 1852, JPFP.

42. Ada W. Bacot Diary, May 1, 1861, Ada W. Bacot Papers; Moore, *Plantation Mistress*, 71, 96.

43. Catherine Lewis to Emma Speight, October 31, 1860, November 25, 1845, JFSP; Mrs. [A. X.] Baillio to Samuel Hairston, June 6, 1854, Lucetta Clove to Samuel Hairston, December 12, 1859, WHFP.

44. Ada W. Bacot Diary, May 1 and November 11, 1861, Ada W. Bacot Papers; Moore, *Plantation Mistress*, 55.

45. See notes 40 and 44 above, and Serena Lea to Martha Jackson, April 25, 1842, JPFP.

46. Serena Lea to Martha Jackson, July 25, 1840, April 25, 1842, January 5,

1846, Serena Lea to Sarah Jackson, December 13, 1844, JPFP; J. Sanderson to [Simon Foscue], October 22, 1827, Foscue Family Papers.

47. Richard T. Archer to James Powell Cocke, December 12, 1835, CFP; Richard T. Archer to Capt. James Hobson, June 16, 1835, AFP.

48. Receipts for Charlie Wheeler's tuition and board, June 10 and 15, 1857, January 23 and July 10, 1858; Ann Wheeler to Ruth Hairston, August 7, 1857, March 6, 1859, January 24, 1861, WHFP.

49. Mary Campbell to Charles Mortimer, n.d., and Inventory of Mary (Dandridge) Spotswood Campbell Estate, n.d. [sometime after March 1791], Spotswood Family Papers.

50. Mary W. Crook to Samuel Hairston, June 5, 1854; Mrs. A. [X.] Baillio to Samuel Hairston, June 6, 1854, WHFP.

51. Pamela Crisp to Samuel Hairston, July 25, 1854, WHFP.

52. Lucetta Clove to Samuel Hairston, December 2, 1859, WHFP.

53. Martha Cocke to Caroline Cocke, July 17, 1812, CFP.

54. Lucy Freeman to Jessie Vaughan, February 28, 1836, see also June 20, 1839, Jessie Vaughan Papers; Ann Wheeler to Ruth Hairston, March 3, 1859, see also Rev. J. D. Kilpatrick to Ruth Wilson, April 24, 1814, WHFP; Josiah C. Skinner to Maria Skinner, September 14, 1819, Skinner Family Papers; Henry Carrington to Paulina Legrand, September 15, 1822, Henry Carrington Papers; Catherine Lewis to Emma Speight, November 27, 1844, October 16, 1845, November 24, 1847, JFSP; Charles Cocke to Jane Cocke, February 19, 1812, CFP; *Christian Index*, February 23, 1845, November 2, 1848.

55. Ann (Green) Swann commonplace book, October 18, 1835, 1840, 1841, Swann Family Papers; Green Pryor to Ruth Hairston, January 28 and September 18, 1810, October 15, 1831, April 9, 1838, December, 29, 1840, and May 6, 1848, Ann Wheeler to Ruth Hairston, August 7, 1857, WHFP; Lucy Freeman to Jessie Vaughan, June 20, 1839, Jesse Vaughan Papers; *Christian Index*, December 8, 1835.

56. Catherine Lewis to Emma Speight, March 20 and April 4, 1839, August 1, 1840, October 27, 1846, JFSP; Eliza Schley to Henry Jackson, July 8, 1835, Mary A. Hutchinson to Martha Jackson, October 18, 1837, Sarah Cobb to Martha Jackson, March 4, 1853, JPFP.

57. Mary Athena Lamar to Sarah Jackson, February 1 and August 28, 1849, JPFP; Caroline Olivia Laurens Diary, September 14, 1827; NDSD, December 31, 1840, see also September 17, October 17, November 16, December 15, and December 17, 1840, January 15, May 15, and July 17, 1841.

58. In Petersburg, Virginia, between 1784 and 1860, about half of those widowed at or under thirty remarried. Less than one-third of widows in their thirties and only 9 percent of those over forty remarried. Of widows under forty, only 29 percent of the richest quartile remarried. Researching three eighteenth-century Virginia counties, Linda Speth found that 9 percent of testators' widows "are known to have contracted a second marriage." Lebsock, *Free Women*, 26–27; Speth, "More Than Her 'Thirds,'" 27. Based on her study of 750 planter genealogies,

Catherine Clinton suggests that only 7.5 percent of plantation mistresses had two or more marriages. Clinton, *Plantation Mistress*, 78, appendix A, table 1. Her text states that "7 percent of widowed plantation mistresses" remarried, but her table shows that 7.5 percent of *all* women surveyed married more than once. Marli Weiner finds that some widows remarried for the sake of having a husband to care for their slaves. Weiner, *Mistresses and Slaves*, 94–95. While none of the widows studied here admitted to marrying for this reason, some contemporaries believed this to be a common pattern. See Bayard, *Travels of a Frenchman*, 45–46. On remarriage in Europe, see Kuiper, "Noble Widows," 156; Hufton, "Women without Men," 124; Dupaquier, *Marriage and Remarriage*. Widows' remarriage aroused controversy in the early Christian church (see, for example, 1 Tim. 5:5, 5:11–14), but in the nineteenth-century South, the question had little theological significance. Buitelaar, "Widows' World," 12–13; Bremmer, "Pauper or Patronness," 33–40, 45–49; van der Toorn, "Public Image of the Widow," 27.

59. *Christian Index*, November 16, 1844; Rev. J. D. Kilpatrick to Ruth Wilson, April 24, 1814, WHFP; Catherine Lewis to Emma Speight, November 27, 1844, October 16, 1845, November 24, 1847, JFSP; Psalms 68:5–6, 146:9; Sir. 4:10; Deut. 24:17–18; 2 Kings 4:1–7; 1 Kings 17:8–24; Luke 21:1–4.

60. L. Carter Flirrol to Martha Singleton, September 11, 1854, Singleton Family Papers, SCL; Abram M. Allen to Eliza Ellison, October 30, 1864, Henry Alderson Ellison Papers; Delia Bryan to Sarah Screven, August 14, 1822, ASFP; Moore, *Plantation Mistress*, 30; Ann Wheeler to Ruth Hairston, August 7, 1857, WHFP.

61. Wood, "Fictive Mastery," 163–74.

62. Carter, *Diary of Dolly Lunt Burge*, 8.

63. Ibid., 46–47.

64. Ibid., xxix–xxx.

65. Ibid., 46–47.

66. Ibid., 52, 59. Punctuation altered for clarity.

67. Ibid., 95–96, 100.

68. John Wilson to Ruth Wilson, February 23, 1815; Ruth Hairston to Peter Hairston, March 3, 1816; Nancy R. Wilson to Ruth Wilson, February 27, 1814, WHFP.

69. Serena Lea to Sarah Jackson, December 13, 1844; Serena Lea to Martha Jackson, July 25, 1840, JPFP.

70. James Washington to Elizabeth Grist, February 25, April 21, and December 8, 1834, May 18, September 1, and October 17, 1836, April 24, 1840, EWGKP. For a summary of the Bank War, see Watson, *Liberty and Power*, chapter 5, 206–10.

71. Dr. Reuben Knox to Elizabeth Grist, July 19, 1840, EWGKP.

72. Elizabeth Knox to Franklin Grist, n.d., Elizabeth Knox to Reuben Knox, May 23, 1850, EWGKP; Reeve, *Law of Baron and Femme*, chapter 5.

73. For a contrary example, see below and J. Hamilton to Marion Converse, November 22, 1853, Singleton-Deveaux Family Papers, SCL.

74. Eliza Knox to Franklin Grist, n.d.; Eliza Knox to Reuben Knox, May 23, 1850, EWGKP.

75. Carter, *Diary of Dolly Lunt Burge*, 47; Catherine Lewis to Emma Speight, April 4, 1853, JFSP; Edwards, *Scarlett Doesn't Live Here Anymore*, 15–16, 23–31.

76. Will of Richard Singleton, July 22, 1848 (copy), Singleton Family Papers, SCL.

77. Marion Converse to Matthew Singleton, December 25, 1853, see also December 21, 1853, Singleton Family Papers, SCL.

78. J. Hamilton to Marion Converse, November 22, 1853, Singleton-Deveaux Family Papers, SCL.

79. J. Hamilton to Marion Converse, November 22, 1853, Marion Converse to Marion Deveaux Jr., [February 1857], Excerpt from Settlement of Converse v. Converse, Extra Equity Court, State of South Carolina, February 20, 1857, Singleton-Deveaux Family Papers, SCL; Marion Converse to Matthew Singleton, December 21, 1853, Singleton Family Papers, SCL; Bishop Thomas F. Davis to Rev. Augustus L. Converse, August 15, 1815, Mr. Ingraham to John Moore, January 21, 1857, Sales of Stock on Account of John B. Moore, February 25, 1857, Ingraham and Webb account with "Mrs. Deveaux," March 24, 1857, Will of John Burchell Moore, May 2, 1862 (later invalidated by himself), Memo, December 18, 1854, RMDP; undated extract from the *Columbia Times*, Singleton Family Papers, SHC; Edwards, *Scarlett Doesn't Live Here Anymore*, 15–16, 23–31.

80. [Betty Coles] to Marion Deveaux, January 11, 1858, Singleton-Deveaux Family Papers, SCL; Sales of Stock on Account of John B. Moore, February 25, 1857, Mr. Ingraham to John Burchell Moore, January 21, 1857, Will of John Burchell Moore, May 2, 1862 (later invalidated by Moore himself), Memo, December 18, 1854, RMDP.

81. Edwards, *Scarlett Doesn't Live Here Anymore*, 24.

82. Martha Richardson to James P. Screven, April 16, 1817, ASFP.

Chapter 7

1. Faust, *Mothers of Invention*, 5–6, 30; McPherson, *Battle Cry of Freedom*, 306–7.

2. Pember, *Southern Woman's Story*, 36; Faust, *Mothers of Invention*, 21; Fahs, *Imagined Civil War*, 65, 68, 120–23; Whites, *Civil War as a Crisis in Gender*, 11–12, 34–35; Bynum, *Unruly Women*, 125.

3. Moore, *Plantation Mistress*, 30, 39, 40, 43, 49, 51, 56, 72, 92–93, 95, 110; Berlin, *Confederate Nurse*, 18–19, 25, 27, 33.

4. Eliza Roberts to Isabella Woodruff, November 20, 1860, IARWP; Margaret Ann (Meta) Morris Grimball Diary, January 12, 1861, Henry Clay Hendrick to Mary Ann Hendrick, April 16, 1861, Mary Ann Hendrick to [Robert or Henry Clay Hendrick], May 31, 1861, W. Robert Leckie Papers; Moore, *Plantation Mistress*, 72; Carter, *Diary of Dolly Lunt Burge*, 113.

5. Whites, *Civil War as a Crisis in Gender*, 64–131; Faust, *Mothers of Invention*, 30–79, 234–47; Faust, *Riddle of Death*; Weiner, *Mistresses and Slaves*, 157–84;

Edwards, *Scarlett Doesn't Live Here Anymore*, 65–84; Rable, *Civil Wars*, 154–201.

6. Carter, *Diary of Dolly Lunt Burge*, 128.

7. Ariela Pinkind to Isabella Woodruff, June 30, 1861, February 28 and March 7, 1864, Georgie V. to Isabella Woodruff, March 20, 1864, IARWP; Harriet H. Branham Diary, March 16, 1863; N. Talley to Mary Ann Hendrick, August 16, 1861, W. Robert Leckie Papers; Escott, *After Secession*, 147–48; Thomas, *Confederate Nation*, 284. For prewar discounting, see, for example, James [Rawlings] to Eliza Ruffin, September 22, 1831, W. H. Roane to Eliza Ruffin, November 1, 1831, Francis Gildart Ruffin Papers; John A. Cobb to Martha Jackson, November [29], 1837, Martha Jackson to Mrs. Thomas, July 6, 1841, JPFP; James Washington to Eliza Grist, April 24, 1840, EWGKP; E. F. Campbell to Mary Jones, February 17, 1841, George Noble Jones Papers; Peter Wilson Hairston to Ruth Hairston, December 21, 1855, WHFP. For wartime currency, see N. Talley to Mary Ann Hendrick, August 22, 1861, W. Robert Leckie Papers; Ariela Pinkind to Isabella Woodruff, June 30, 1861, IARWP; Chesnut, *Diary from Dixie*, 290; Pember, *Southern Woman's Story*, 1.

8. Berlin, *Confederate Nurse*, 162.

9. Pember, *Southern Woman's Story*, 73.

10. Berlin, *Confederate Nurse*, 109; McDonald, *Woman's Civil War*, 95. Cornelia (Peake) McDonald was widowed late in 1864. Her diary, heavily revised after the war, primarily covers the period before her husband's death. She was born in 1822 in Virginia but spent time in Mississippi before moving to Missouri, where she met her future husband Angus, a lawyer. The couple returned to Virginia and were living in Winchester when the war broke out. They had several young children (all under 17), and Angus also had adult children from a prior marriage. Angus McDonald quickly received a colonel's commission in the Confederate army and raised a cavalry regiment, and he later commanded the post at Romney. McDonald, *Woman's Civil War*, 5–7, 12, 254–56, 265–66.

11. Haddie G. Hendrick to Mary Ann Hendrick, August [17], 1864; Receipt of payment from Henry Clay Hendrick, April 7, 1865, W. Robert Leckie Papers.

12. Carter, *Diary of Dolly Lunt Burge*, 122, 128, 142, 157, 158; "Sue" to Isabella Woodruff, August 17, 1861, IARWP; Berlin, *Confederate Nurse*, 109, 111.

13. Carter, *Diary of Dolly Lunt Burge*, 122, 125–26, 128, 156; McDonald, *Woman's Civil War*, 204–12; Ariela Pinkind to Isabella Woodruff, August 4, 1862, May 17, 1863, Susie A. Richmond to Isabella Woodruff, November 28, 1861, IARWP; Lucy Johnston Ambler Diary, July 15, 1863; Pember, *Southern Woman's Story*, 86; Lee, *Forget-Me-Nots*, 156–57; McGuire, *Diary of a Southern Refugee*, 173.

14. Pember, *Southern Woman's Story*, 45–47; McDonald, *Woman's Civil War*, 150, 215, 229–30, 232.

15. Carter, *Diary of Dolly Lunt Burge*, 129, 136, 144–45; Berlin, *Confederate Nurse*, 148.

16. Martin Tannahill and Co. to Mary Ann Hendrick, April 11, 1862, Receipt for payment of tuition, February 19, 1863, miscellaneous receipts, 1864, W. Robert Leckie Papers; Carter, *Diary of Dolly Lunt Burge*, 143; JBGD, October 31, 1861.

17. Elizabeth Slade Wiggins Diary, May 11 and July 1, 1861, February–July 1861 passim.

18. Pember, *Southern Woman's Story*, xiv, 2, 23, 42–43, 57, 88; McDonald, *Woman's Civil War*, 27, 51, 216, 243.

19. McDonald, *Woman's Civil War*, 43–44, 114, 176, 178, 180, 222, 229; Lee, *Forget-Me-Nots*, 149, 156–57.

20. Julia L. Main to Isabella Woodruff, May 20, 1861, Isabella Woodruff to Selina Bingley, October 29, 1863 (copy), IARWP; McDonald, *Woman's Civil War*, 221–22.

21. [Unknown] to Isabella Woodruff, October 27, 1860; Ariela Pinkind to Isabella Woodruff, April 1, June 30, and December 8, 1861, June 27, August 4, August 13, and November 30, 1862, March 1, 1863, but see also May 17, 1863; Julia L. Main to Isabella Woodruff, May 20, 1861; [U. A. Delettre] to Isabella Woodruff, March 2, 1861; A. Girard to Isabella Woodruff, July 23, 1862; Isabella Woodruff to [Unknown], July 27, 1862; Isabella Woodruff to Selina Bingley, October 29, 1863; William B. Henry to Isabella Woodruff, December 25, 1863; Isabella Woodruff to Mrs. Mildred W. Gray, January 10, 1864; Isabella Woodruff to Charles Holst, December 18, 1864, IARWP.

22. Lou Dowell to Isabella Woodruff, October 12, 1862, Isabella Woodruff to [unknown], July 27, 1862, Isabella Woodruff to Mildred W. Gray, January 10, 1864, Mildred W. Gray to Isabella Woodruff, January 18, 1864, Alice Earle to Isabella Woodruff, November 8, 186[4], Isabella Woodruff to Dr. Earle, November 14, 1864, Isabella Woodruff to Charles Holst, November 27, 1864, March 27, 1865, IARWP; McDonald, *Woman's Civil War*, 138.

23. Mary Ann Hendrick to [Henry C. Hendrick], July 14, [1861], W. Robert Leckie Papers; McGuire, *Diary of a Southern Refugee*, 88–92, 172.

24. McDonald, *Woman's Civil War*, 76.

25. Lee, *Forget-Me-Nots*, 149; Ariela Pinkind to Isabella Woodruff, March 1, 1863, IARWP.

26. McGuire, *Diary of a Southern Refugee*, 174, 198, 204, 206.

27. When Cornelia McDonald's husband was being held prisoner at Fortress Monroe, his extended family appealed "constantly . . . to those in power for his exchange." Cornelia recalled that "we wrote to President Davis who was his friend," and to Secretary of War Seddon. Angus's daughter Anne also wrote to a Union general, commandant at Fortress Monroe, "who had been his classmate and friend at West Point." Anne's letter "elicited a favourable response, and an order for his release on parole was sent immediately." Angus McDonald died shortly after his release, before Cornelia could reach him. McDonald, *Woman's Civil War*, 203, 208–9, 212, 245.

28. Chesnut, *Diary from Dixie*, 166; Ariela Pinkind to Isabella Woodruff, March 1, 1863, IARWP.

29. Pember, *Southern Woman's Story*, ix, 12–13.

30. Chesnut, *Diary from Dixie*, 166; McDonald, *Woman's Civil War*, 172, 181, 218, 221.

31. Berlin, *Confederate Nurse*, 27, 33; Moore, *Plantation Mistress*, 92–93, 95, 110.

32. Perhaps the best known case of slavery disrupted occurred on the Carolina Sea Islands where many slaves lived in virtual freedom, farming for themselves after their owners fled. See, for example, Rose, *Rehearsal for Reconstruction*; Schwalm, *Hard Fight for We*, 97–104.

33. Lee, *Forget-Me-Nots*, 159.

34. McDonald, *Woman's Civil War*, 122–23.

35. Berlin, *Confederate Nurse*, 68, 92, 144–45, 158.

36. Ariela Pinkind to Isabella Woodruff, July 5 and December 27, 1863, IARWP. Note the similarity to Jean Blair's conflict with her slave Sarah during the American Revolution, mentioned above.

37. Moore, *Plantation Mistress*, 53–54, 60, 62, 83, 86, 110, 118; Overseer exemption, Singleton Family Papers, SCL; Rable, *Civil Wars*, 85.

38. Ada W. Bacot Diary, February 9, 1861, Ada W. Bacot Papers; Berlin, *Confederate Nurse*, 49, 51.

39. Bynum, *Unruly Women*, 117–19; Weiner, *Mistresses and Slaves*, 135–37, 166–70; Faust, "Trying to Do a Man's Business"; Faust, *Mothers of Invention*, 56–62; Moore, *Plantation Mistress*, 54, 31, 86; Egerton, *Gabriel's Rebellion*, 38, 78; Sommerville, "Rape, Race, and Castration."

40. Perdue, Barden, Phillips, and Virginia Writers' Project, *Weevils in the Wheat*, 167. On white women as fearful of or victimized by slave men, see Bardaglio, "Rape and the Law," 752; Rawick, *American Slave*, 12(1):74; Faust, *Mothers of Invention*, 62; Jordan, *White over Black*, 154; Wyatt-Brown, *Southern Honor*, 50; Breen, "'Storm of Terror.'"

41. Rawick, *American Slave*, 12(1):74, 3(3):169; Faust, *Mothers of Invention*, 62.

42. McDonald, *Woman's Civil War*, 45, 61, 64–65, 101, 140, 154–55, 164, 178, 180, 182, 222, 229–30; Berlin, *Confederate Nurse*, 68, 82, 110; Ariela Pinkind to Isabella Woodruff, December 8, 1861, July 5, 1863, IARWP; Lee, *Forget-Me-Nots*, 149, 156–57; Elizabeth Slade Wiggins Diary, May 11 and July 1, 1861.

43. Isabella Woodruff to Charles Holst, February 11, 1865, IARWP; Moore, *Plantation Mistress*, 39, 42, 44, 49, 58, 65; Berlin, *Confederate Nurse*, 176.

44. Berlin, *Confederate Nurse*, 58; Durrill, *War of Another Kind*, 122; Weiner, *Mistresses and Slaves*, 158, 164; Schwalm, *Hard Fight for We*, 108–15.

45. Carter, *Diary of Dolly Lunt Burge*, 150–51, 154, 156–65; Lee, *Forget-Me-Nots*, 159.

46. Elizabeth Slade Wiggins Diary, August 8, 1861.

47. Berlin, *Confederate Nurse*, 171; Carter, *Diary of Dolly Lunt Burge*, 141, 143, 145–47.

48. Ann Swann to [her children], 1865, Swann Family Papers; Henry Clay Hendrick to Mary Ann Hendrick, April 19, 1861, Mary Ann Hendrick to [Robert or Clay Hendrick], May 31, 1861, Robert Hendrick to Mary Ann Hendrick, February 15, 1862, Martin Tannahill and Co. to Mary Ann Hendrick, April 11 and May 23, 1862, Haddie Hendrick to Mary Ann Hendrick, August 27 186[2], W. Robert Leckie Papers; Lucy Johnston Ambler Diary, July 21–August 9, 1863; McPherson, *Battle Cry of Freedom*, 372–73.

49. McDonald, *Woman's Civil War*, 43–44.

50. Lee, *Forget-Me-Nots*, 161–65; Moore, *Plantation Mistress*, 116; Chesnut, *Diary from Dixie*, 386.

51. Carter, *Diary of Dolly Lunt Burge*, 157–60.

52. Ibid., 163.

53. Ibid., 150–51, 154, 158–62.

54. Ibid., 150, 162.

55. Ibid., 150–51, 154, 158–62; McPherson, *Battle Cry of Freedom*, 809–10; Lee, *Forget-Me-Nots*, 159; Weiner, *Mistresses and Slaves*, 177–80.

56. Carter, *Diary of Dolly Lunt Burge*, 160–61.

57. Morris, "Articulation of Two Worlds."

58. Carter, *Diary of Dolly Lunt Burge*, 166.

59. Ibid., 173–77.

60. McPherson, *Battle Cry of Freedom*, 551–52; Ryan, *Women in Public*, 142–46.

61. Berlin, *Confederate Nurse*, 90, 126.

62. McDonald, *Woman's Civil War*, 24–26, 28, 30, 32, 34, 40–43, 46, 104, 119, 126; Pember, *Southern Woman's Story*, 82–83.

63. McDonald, *Woman's Civil War*, 121, 152–53.

64. Ibid., 26; Mary Lee, as quoted in Faust, *Mothers of Invention*, 198.

65. Carter, *Diary of Dolly Lunt Burge*, 159, 161–62.

66. Pember, *Southern Woman's Story*, 86–88; McDonald, *Woman's Civil War*, 32.

67. McDonald, *Woman's Civil War*, 28, 126, 161.

68. Mary Lee, as quoted in Faust, *Mothers of Invention*, 200. In contrast, while working as a nurse, Ada Bacot celebrated her ability "to be able even this slight way to be of some use to my country." Berlin, *Confederate Nurse*, 82.

69. Faust, *Mothers of Invention*, 200, and 196–219 passim; McDonald, *Woman's Civil War*, 132, but cf. 136. For wartime violence against white southern women, see Edwards, *Scarlett Doesn't Live Here Anymore*, 98; Bynum, *Unruly Women*, 143–44, 148; Fellman, "Women and Guerilla Warfare," 147–65.

70. Susie Richmond to Isabella Woodruff, November 28, 1861, IARWP; Berlin, *Confederate Nurse*, 65, 152.

71. Carter, *Diary of Dolly Lunt Burge*, 165.

72. McDonald, *Woman's Civil War*, 167.

73. Lee, *Forget-Me-Nots*, 156–57.

74. McDonald, *Woman's Civil War*, 221, 222, 228.

75. Pember, *Southern Woman's Story*, 2; Berlin, *Confederate Nurse*, 76–77.

76. Berlin, *Confederate Nurse*, 165, 169, 177–79.

77. Pember, *Southern Woman's Story*, 1, 18–22, 27, 51, 53.

78. Ibid., 14–15; Berlin, *Confederate Nurse*, 113.

79. Berlin, *Confederate Nurse*, 76.

80. Pember, *Southern Woman's Story*, 37–43.

81. Ibid., 12–13, 40–42.

82. Berlin, *Confederate Nurse*, 90, 126. On prewar sociability, see Wood, "Fictive Mastery," 167–71; Lewis, *Ladies and Gentlemen*.

83. Berlin, *Confederate Nurse*, 70, 140; Pember, *Southern Woman's Story*, 12–16.

84. Berlin, *Confederate Nurse*, 69–70, 78–79, 96, 140; Chesnut, *Diary from Dixie*, 166, 203–4; Pember, *Southern Woman's Story*, 13–16.

85. Chesnut, *Diary from Dixie*, 217; Faust, *Mothers of Invention*, 149–50. Studies of widowhood in many different cultures suggest that widows are often considered sexually experienced, aggressive, and even dangerous. Unlike early modern Europe, the Old South did not tend to regard its white women as sexually voracious—that stereotype was largely assigned to enslaved black women. Sommerville, "Rape, Race, and Castration," 74–89; Hodes, *White Women, Black Men*; Pease and Pease, *Ladies, Women, and Wenches*, chapter 7; Tracy, *In the Master's Eye*, 126–37. For northern and European ideas about female sexuality, see, for example, Brown, *Good Wives*, 28–32, 94–98; Stansell, *City of Women*, 20–30; Stone, *Family, Sex, and Marriage*, 281; Hufton, "Women without Men," 145; Whitman, *Price of Freedom*, 21, 33.

86. Chesnut, *Diary from Dixie*, 374–75; McDonald, *Woman's Civil War*, 215.

87. Eliza Roberts to Isabella Woodruff, November 20, 1860, IARWP.

88. Ariela Pinkind to Isabella Woodruff, November 6 and December 8, 1861, June 27 and August 4, 1862, IARWP.

89. Isabella Woodruff to Ariela Pinkind, November 1 and December 6, 1862; Lou Dowell to Isabella Woodruff, January 17, 1863; "Anna" to [Isabella Woodruff], March 22, 1863, IARWP.

90. C. H. A. Woodin to Isabella Woodruff, April 6, 1864; Mollie Woodin to Isabella Woodruff, June 15, 1864; Isabella Woodruff to Mrs. Woodin, June 23, 1864 [copy], IARWP.

91. Jeanette Holst to Isabella Woodruff, August 17 and September 17, 1859; Isabella Woodruff to Charles Holst, August 18, September 6, October 30, November 13, November 27, and December 18, 1864, February 11, 1865; Charles Holst to Isabella Woodruff, November 4 and December 6, 1864, IARWP.

92. Isabella Woodruff to Charles Holst, April 6 and 22, 1865; Charles Holst to Isabella Woodruff, April 22 and May 21, 1865, IARWP.

93. Margaret Ann (Meta) Morris Grimball Diary, March 29, 1861.

94. In Tom Taylor's 1854 play, *Sir Roger de Coverley*, for example, a male character impugns Lady Bellasis's constancy: "Methinks her heart's like a common alehouse, Sir Roger; every one who knocks has a right to lodging and entertainment." Taylor, *Sir Roger de Coverley*, 50; Arden, "Grief, Widowhood, and Women's Sexuality"; Vasvari, "Why Is Doña Endrina a Widow?"; Warner, "Widows, Widowers, and the Problem"; Coyne, *Widow Hunt*; Garrick, *Irish Widow*; Jodrell, *A Widow and No Widow*; Atkinson, *Match for a Widow*; Whitcher, *Widow Spriggins*.

95. Rawick, *American Slave*, 2(1):149, 2(2):253.

96. Chesnut, *Diary from Dixie*, 212, 255.

97. Pember, *Southern Woman's Story*, 27–28. On Confederate nationalism, see Escott, *After Secession*; Faust, *Creation of Confederate Nationalism*.

98. Carter, *Diary of Dolly Lunt Burge*, 165; McDonald, *Woman's Civil War*, 224–25, 232.

99. McDonald, *Woman's Civil War*, 239, 241–42.

100. Ann Swann to [her daughters], September 15, 1865, Swann Family Papers.

101. Charlotte Ravenel, as quoted in Weiner, *Mistresses and Slaves*, 193.

102. Weiner, *Mistresses and Slaves*, 198.

103. Catherine Lewis to Emma Speight, October 16, 1845, November 24, 1847, May 6, 1865, JFSP.

Epilogue

1. For an exception, see Weiner, *Mistresses and Slaves*, 198.

2. Chesnut, *Diary from Dixie*, 166.

3. McDonald, *Woman's Civil War*, 238, 245.

4. Ann Swann to [Willie, John, Fred, or Samuel] Swann, August 27, 1865, Swann Family Papers.

5. Perdue, Barden, Phillips, and Virginia Writers' Project, *Weevils in the Wheat*, 13, and 9–13 passim.

6. McDonald, *Woman's Civil War*, 237.

7. Edwards, *Gendered Strife and Confusion*, 245.

8. Ibid., 11.

9. Genovese, *Roll, Jordan, Roll*, 461–62.

10. Edwards, *Gendered Strife and Confusion*, 244, 250; Gilmore, *Gender and Jim Crow*.

11. Anderson was probably not in imminent danger in speaking so freely because his interlocutor (a Federal Writers' Project interviewer) was black. All but nine of the WPA interviews collected from former slaves in Virginia were conducted by black interviewers. Along with certain characteristics of the sample interviewed, this is generally believed to have made the Virginia testimonies more reliable and representative than those collected elsewhere in the South. Perdue, Barden, Phillips, and Virginia Writers' Project, *Weevils in the Wheat*, xli–xlii.

12. Ibid., 13.

BIBLIOGRAPHY

Manuscripts

Atlanta, Georgia
Georgia Department of Archives and History
  Will Books, Chatham County (microfilm)

Chapel Hill, North Carolina
Southern Historical Collection, University of North Carolina Library
  Alexander-Hillhouse Family Papers
  Archibald Davis Alston Papers
  Arnold and Screven Family Papers
  Mrs. Eleanor J. Baker Papers
  Battle Family Papers
  Brownrigg Family Papers
  Burwell Family Papers
  Click Family Papers
  Crenshaw Family Papers
  Henry Alderson Ellison Papers
  Foscue Family Papers
  Glenn Family Papers
  Grimball Family Papers
  John Berkeley Grimball Diary
  Margaret Ann (Meta) Morris Grimball Diary
  George Hairston Papers
  John Tyler Hairston Papers
  Peter Wilson Hairston Papers
  William Johnston Hall Papers
  Wilmot Stuart Holmes Papers
  Hubard Family Papers
  Susan Davis Nye Hutchison Diary
  Jackson and Prince Family Papers
  Roger Kelsall Papers
  Elizabeth (Washington) Knox Papers
  James Lamkin Papers

Caroline Olivia Laurens Diary
Lewis Family Papers
Alfred Osborn Pope Nicholson Papers
Douglas Watson Porter Papers
Francis Gildart Ruffin Papers
Singleton Family Papers
Skinner Family Papers
John Francis Speight Papers
Ephraim Steele Papers
John Steele Papers
Swann Family Papers
Wilson and Hairston Family Papers
University Archives and Records Service
Records of the School of Law

Columbia, South Carolina
South Caroliniana Library, Manuscript Division, University of South Carolina
Ada W. Bacot Papers
Peter Samuel Bacot Papers
Keziah Goodwyn Hopkins Brevard Diary
John Berkeley Grimball Papers
Singleton Family Papers
Singleton-Deveaux Family Papers
John Stapleton Papers
Sumter-DeLage Family Papers
Natalie DeLage Sumter Diary

Durham, North Carolina
Special Collections Library, Manuscript Department, William R. Perkins
    Library, Duke University
Lucy Johnston Ambler Diary
Anonymous Ledger, 1835–1841
Elizabeth J. (Holmes) Blanks Papers
Harriet H. Branham Diary
Robert Marion Deveaux Papers
James Dove Papers
Mary G. Franklin Papers
William Gilliland Papers
Mary E. Baxter Gresham Commonplace Book
Henry Rootes Jackson Papers
James Jackson Papers
George Noble Jones Papers
W. Robert Leckie Papers
Ann (Heatly) Reid Lovell Papers
James Marshall Papers

Jacob Rhett Motte Papers
Henry Norman Papers
George S. Rives Papers
William Patterson Smith Papers
John Steele Papers
Jessie Vaughan Papers
Elizabeth Slade Wiggins Diary
Isabella Ann Roberts Woodruff Papers

Raleigh, North Carolina
North Carolina Department of Archives and History
  Susan Davis Nye Hutchison Papers
  Iredell Family Papers
  John Steele Papers
  Will Books, Rowan County (microfilm)

Philadelphia, Pennsylvania
National Archives and Records Administration
  Federal Population Schedules, 1790–1860

Richmond, Virginia
Virginia Historical Society
  Archer Family Papers
  Claiborne Barksdale Papers
  Ann Powell Burwell Commonplace Book
  Carrington Family Papers
  Henry Carrington Papers
  Cobb Family Bible Records
  Cocke Family Papers
  Fontaine Family Papers
  Alice B. Payne George Papers
  Hairston Family Papers
  William Huntington Papers
  Jones Family Papers
  Richard Bland Lee Papers
  Dolley Payne Todd Madison Papers
  Peckatone Papers
  Spotswood Family Papers
  Lucy Battaille Thornton Papers
  Archibald Vaughan Papers

Williamsburg, Virginia
Manuscripts Divisions, Earl Gregg Swem Library, College of William and
    Mary
  Jerdone Family Papers

Serials

American Gleaner
Christian Index, for the Baptist Convention of the State of Georgia
Ladies' Repository: A Monthly Periodical, Devoted to Literature, Arts, and
  Religion
Southern Agriculturalist
South Carolina Weekly Museum
Southern Cultivator
Southern Rose
Virginia Literary Magazine

Published Primary and Secondary Sources

Acts of the General Assembly of the State of Georgia, Passed in Milledgeville, at a
  Bi-Ennial Session in November, December, January, February, and March,
  1855–'56. Compiled by John W. Duncan. Milledgeville: Boughton, Nisbert &
  Barnes, 1856.
Acts of the General Assembly of the State of Georgia, Passed in Milledgeville at an
  Annual Session in November and December, 1838. Milledgeville: P. L. Robin-
  son, 1839.
Acts of the General Assembly of the State of Georgia, Passed in Milledgeville at an
  Annual Session in November and December, 1839. Milledgeville: Grive &
  Orme, 1840.
Acts of the General Assembly of the State of Georgia, Passed in Milledgeville at an
  Annual Session in November and December, 1841. Milledgeville: Grieve &
  Orme, 1842.
Acts of the State of Georgia, 1849 and 1850. Milledgeville: Richard M. Orme,
  1850.
Adams, Jasper. *Elements of Moral Philosophy.* Charleston: Folsom, Wells and
  Thurston, 1837.
Allgor, Catherine. *Parlor Politics: In Which the Ladies of Washington Help Build a*
  City and a Government. Charlottesville: University Press of Virginia, 2000.
Anzilotti, Cara. *In the Affairs of the World: Women, Patriarchy, and Power in*
  Colonial South Carolina. Westport, Conn.: Greenwood Press, 2002.
Appleby, Joyce. *Recollections of the Early Republic.* Boston: Northeastern Uni-
  versity Press, 1997.
Arden, Heather. "Grief, Widowhood, and Women's Sexuality in Medieval
  French Literature." In *Upon My Husband's Death: Widowhood in the Litera-*
  ture and Histories of Medieval Europe, edited by Louise Mirrer, 305–19. Ann
  Arbor: University of Michigan Press, 1992.
Atkinson, Joseph. *A Match for a Widow; or, the Frolics of Fancy. A Comic Opera,*
  in Three Acts. Dublin: P. Byrne, 1788.
Ball, Charles. *Fifty Years in Chains; or, The Life of an American Slave.* New
  York: H. Dayton, 1859.

Ballagh, James Curtis, ed. *The Letters of Richard Henry Lee*. 2 vols. New York: Macmillan, 1911.

Baptist, Edward E. *Creating an Old South: Middle Florida's Plantation Frontier before the Civil War*. Chapel Hill: University of North Carolina Press, 2002.

———. "The Migration of Planters to Antebellum Florida: Kinship and Power." *Journal of Southern History* 62 (August 1996): 527–54.

Bardaglio, Peter W. "Rape and the Law in the Old South: 'Calculated to Excite Indignation in Every Heart.'" *Journal of Southern History* 60 (November 1994): 749–72.

———. *Reconstructing the Household: Families, Sex, and the Law in the Nineteenth-Century South*. Chapel Hill: University of North Carolina Press, 1995.

Barron, Caroline M., and Anne F. Sutton, eds. *Medieval London Widows, 1300–1500*. London: Hambledon Press, 1994.

Barton, Keith C. "'Good Cooks and Washers': Slave Hiring, Domestic Labor, and the Market in Bourbon County, Kentucky." *Journal of American History* 82 (September 1997): 436–60.

Basch, Norma. "Equity vs. Equality: Emerging Concepts of Women's Political Status in the Age of Jackson." *Journal of the Early Republic* 3 (Fall 1983): 297–318.

———. "Invisible Women: The Legal Fiction of Marital Unity in Nineteenth-Century America." *Feminist Studies* 5 (Summer 1979): 346–66.

Bayard, Ferdinand Marie. *Travels of a Frenchman in Maryland and Virginia; with a Description of Philadelphia and Baltimore, in 1791*. Ann Arbor: Edwards Brothers, 1950.

Bellows, Barbara L. *Benevolence among Slaveholders: Assisting the Poor in Charleston, 1670–1860*. Baton Rouge: Louisiana State University Press, 1993.

Bennett, Judith M., and Amy M. Froide, eds. *Singlewomen in the European Past, 1250–1800*. Philadelphia: University of Pennsylvania Press, 1999.

Berlin, Jean V., ed. *A Confederate Nurse: The Diary of Ada W. Bacot, 1860–1863*. Columbia: University of South Carolina Press, 1994.

Blassingame, John W. *The Slave Community: Plantation Life in the Antebellum South*. New York: Oxford University Press, 1972.

Blennerhasset, Mrs. Margaret (Agnew). *The Widow of the Rock and Other Poems*. Montreal: E. V. Sparhawk, 1824.

Bleser, Carol, ed. *The Hammonds of Redcliffe*. New York: Oxford University Press, 1981.

Boatwright, Eleanor Miot. *Status of Women in Georgia, 1783–1860*. Brooklyn, N.Y.: Carlson Publishing, 1994.

Bolton, Charles C. *Poor Whites of the Antebellum South: Tenants and Laborers in Central North Carolina and Northeast Mississippi*. Durham: Duke University Press, 1994.

Boswell, Angela. *Her Act and Deed: Women's Lives in a Rural Southern County, 1837–1873*. College Station: Texas A & M University Press, 2001.

Boyd, Julian P., ed. *The Papers of Thomas Jefferson*. 30 vols. Princeton: Princeton University Press, 1950.

Boydston, Jeanne. *Home and Work: Housework, Wages, and the Ideology of Labor in the Early Republic*. New York: Oxford University Press, 1990.

Branson, Susan. *These Fiery Frenchified Dames: Women and Political Culture in Early National Philadelphia*. Philadelphia: University of Pennsylvania Press, 2001.

Brant, Irving. *James Madison: Commander in Chief, 1812–1836*. Indianapolis: Bobbs-Merrill, 1961.

Bremmer, Jan N. "Pauper or Patronness: The Widow in the Early Christian Church." In *Between Poverty and the Pyre: Moments in the History of Widowhood*, edited by Jan N. Bremmer and Lourens van den Bosch, 31–57. London and New York: Routledge, 1995.

Brown, Kathleen M. *Good Wives, Nasty Wenches, and Anxious Patriarchs: Gender, Race, and Power in Colonial Virginia*. Chapel Hill: Published for the Institute of Early American History and Culture by the University of North Carolina Press, 1996.

Bryant, Keith L., Jr. "The Role and Status of the Female Yeomanry in the Antebellum South: A Literary View." *Southern Quarterly* 18 (Winter 1979/80): 73–88.

Buitelaar, Marjo. "Widows' Worlds: Representations and Realities." In *Between Poverty and the Pyre: Moments in the History of Widowhood*, edited by Jan N. Bremmer and Lourens van den Bosch, 1–18. London and New York: Routledge, 1995.

Bushman, Richard L. *The Refinement of America: Persons, Houses, Cities*. New York: Alfred A. Knopf, 1992.

Bynum, Victoria E. *Unruly Women: The Politics of Social and Sexual Control in the Old South*. Chapel Hill: University of North Carolina Press, 1992.

Carey, Mathew. *Fragment. Addressed to the Sons and Daughters of Humanity, by a Citizen of the World*. Philadelphia: Lang and Ustick, 1796.

Carr, Lois Green. "Inheritance in the Colonial Chesapeake." In *Women in the Age of the American Revolution*, edited by Ronald Hoffman and Peter J. Albert. Charlottesville: Published for the United States Capital Historical Society by the University Press of Virginia, 1989.

Carr, Lois G., and Lorena Walsh. "The Planter's Wife: The Experience of White Women in Seventeenth-Century Maryland." *William and Mary Quarterly* 34 (October 1977): 542–71.

Carter, Christine Jacobsen, ed. *The Diary of Dolly Lunt Burge, 1848–1879*. Athens: University of Georgia Press, 1997.

Cary, Virginia. *Letters on Female Character, Addressed to a Young Lady, on the Death of Her Mother*. Richmond: A. Works, 1828.

Cashin, Joan E. *A Family Venture: Men and Women on the Southern Frontier*. New York: Oxford University Press, 1991.

Cavallo, Sandra, and Lyndan Warner. *Widowhood in Medieval and Early Modern Europe*. New York: Longman, 1999.

Censer, Jane Turner. *North Carolina Planters and Their Children, 1800–1860*. Baton Rouge: Louisiana State University Press, 1984.

———. "Southwestern Migration among North Carolina Planter Families: 'The Disposition to Emigrate.'" *Journal of Southern History* 57 (August 1991): 407–26.

Chandler, Daniel. *An Address on Female Education, Delivered before the Demosthenian and Phi Kappa Societies, on the Day after Commencement, in the University of Georgia.* Washington, Ga.: William A. Mercer, 1835.

Chappelear, Nancy, and Kate Binford Hatch. *Abstracts of Louisa County, Virginia, Will Books, 1743–1801.* Berryville: Virginia Book Company, 1964.

Chappell, Edward A., and Julie Richter. "Wealth and Houses in Post-Revolutionary Virginia." In *Exploring Everyday Landscapes: Perspectives in Vernacular Architecture,* edited by Annemarie Adams and Sally McMurry, 3–22. Knoxville: University of Tennessee, 1997.

Chesnut, Mary Boykin. *A Diary from Dixie, as Written by Mary Boykin Chesnut, Wife of James Chesnut, Jr., United States Senator from South Carolina, 1859–1861, and Afterward an Aide to Jefferson Davis and a Brigadier-General in the Confederate Army.* New York: D. Appleton and Company, 1905.

Clinton, Catherine. *The Plantation Mistress: Woman's World in the Old South.* New York: Pantheon Books, 1982.

Clinton, Catherine, and Michele Gillespie, eds. *The Devil's Lane: Sex and Race in the Early South.* New York: Oxford University Press, 1998.

Cohen, Patricia Cline. "Safety and Danger: Women on American Public Transport, 1750–1850." In *Gendered Domains: Rethinking Public and Private in Women's History,* edited by Dorothy O. Helly and Susan M. Reverby, 109–22. Ithaca, N.Y.: Cornell University Press, 1992.

———. "Women at Large: Travel in Antebellum America." *History Today* 44 (December 1994): 44–51.

Cott, Nancy F. *Public Vows: A History of Marriage and the Nation.* Cambridge: Harvard University Press, 2000.

Coyne, Stirling J. *A Widow Hunt.* New York: H. L. Hinton, n.d.

Crowley, John. "The Importance of Kinship: Testamentary Evidence from South Carolina." *Journal of Interdisciplinary History* 16 (Spring 1986): 559–77.

Cunnington, Phillis, and Catherine Lucas. *Costume for Births, Marriages, and Death.* New York: Barnes and Noble Books, 1972.

Curtin, Philip. *The Rise and Fall of the Plantation Complex.* 2d ed. New York: Cambridge University Press, 1998.

Cushing, John, ed. *The First Laws of the State of Georgia.* 2 vols. Wilmington, Del.: Michael Glazier, 1981.

———. *The First Laws of the State of North Carolina.* 2 vols. Wilmington, Del.: Michael Glazier, 1984.

———. *The First Laws of the State of South Carolina.* 2 vols. Wilmington, Del.: Michael Glazier, 1981.

Dalzell, Robert F., Jr., and Lee Baldwin Dalzell. *George Washington's Mount Vernon: At Home in Revolutionary America.* New York: Oxford University Press, 1998.

Daniels, Christine, and Michael V. Kennedy, eds. *Over the Threshold: Intimate Violence in Early America*. New York and London: Routledge, 1999.

Davidoff, Leonore, and Catherine Hall. *Family Fortunes: Men and Women of the English Middle Class, 1780–1850*. Chicago: University of Chicago Press, 1987.

Dayton, Cornelia Hughes. *Women before the Bar: Gender, Law, and Society in Connecticut, 1639–1789*. Chapel Hill: University of North Carolina Press, 1995.

Ditz, Toby L. *Property and Kinship: Inheritance in Early Connecticut, 1750–1820*. Princeton: Princeton University Press, 1986.

———. "Shipwrecked; or Masculinity Imperilled: Mercantile Representations of Failure and the Gendered Self in Eighteenth-Century Philadelphia." *Journal of American History* 81 (June 1994): 51–81.

Dupaquier, Jacques, ed. *Marriage and Remarriage in the Populations of the Past*. London: Academic Press, 1981.

Durrill, Wayne. *War of Another Kind: A Southern Community in the Great Rebellion*. New York: Oxford University Press, 1990.

Dusinberre, William. *Them Dark Days: Slavery in the American Rice Swamps*. New York: Oxford University Press, 1996.

Edwards, Laura F. *Gendered Strife and Confusion: The Political Culture of Reconstruction*. Urbana: University of Illinois Press, 1997.

———. *Scarlett Doesn't Live Here Anymore: Southern Women in the Civil War Era*. Urbana: University of Illinois Press, 2000.

Egerton, Douglas R. *Gabriel's Rebellion: The Virginia Slave Conspiracies of 1800 and 1802*. Chapel Hill: University of North Carolina Press, 1993.

———. *He Shall Go Out Free: The Lives of Denmark Vesey*. Madison, Wis.: Madison House, 1999.

Ellis, Joseph J. *American Sphinx: The Character of Thomas Jefferson*. New York: Alfred A. Knopf, 1997.

Erickson, Amy Louise. "Property and Widowhood in England, 1660–1840." In *Widowhood in Medieval and Early Modern Europe*, edited by Sandra Cavallo and Lyndan Warner, 145–63. London: Pearson Education, 1999.

Escott, Paul D. *After Secession: Jefferson Davis and the Failure of Confederate Nationalism*. Baton Rouge: Louisiana State University Press, 1978.

Fahs, Alice. *The Imagined Civil War: Popular Literature of the North and South, 1861–1865*. Chapel Hill: University of North Carolina Press, 2001.

Farnham, Christie. *The Education of the Southern Belle: Higher Education and Student Socialization in the Antebellum South*. New York: New York University Press, 1994.

Faust, Drew Gilpin. "Altars of Sacrifice: Confederate Women and the Narratives of War." *Journal of American History* 76 (March 1990): 1200–1228.

———. *The Creation of Confederate Nationalism*. Baton Rouge: Louisiana State University Press, 1988.

———. *James Henry Hammond and the Old South: A Design for Mastery*. Baton Rouge: Louisiana State University Press, 1982.

————. *Mothers of Invention: Women of the Slaveholding South in the American Civil War*. Chapel Hill: University of North Carolina Press, 1996.

————. *A Riddle of Death: Mortality and Meaning in the American Civil War*. [Gettysburg, Pa.]: Gettysburg College, 1995.

————. "Trying to Do a Man's Business: Gender, Violence, and Slave Management in Civil War Texas." *Gender History* 4 (Summer 1992): 197–214.

Fellman, Michael. "Women and Guerilla Warfare." In *Divided Houses*, edited by Catherine Clinton and Nina Silber, 147–65. New York: Oxford University Press, 1992.

Fett, Sharla M. *Working Cures. Healing, Health, and Power on Southern Plantations*. Chapel Hill: University of North Carolina Press, 2002.

Fields, Barbara Jeanne. "Ideology and Race in American History." In *Region, Race, and Reconstruction: Essays in Honor of C. Vann Woodward*, edited by J. Morgan Kousser and James M. McPherson, 143–77. New York: Oxford University Press, 1982.

————. *Slavery and Freedom on the Middle Ground: Maryland during the Nineteenth Century*. New Haven: Yale University Press, 1985.

————. "Slavery, Race, and Ideology in the United States of America." *New Left Review* 181 (May/June 1990): 95–118.

Fields, Joseph E., comp. *"Worthy Partner": The Papers of Martha Washington*. Westport, Conn.: Greenwood Press, 1994.

Fifth Annual Report of the Association for the Relief of Jewish Widows and Orphans of New Orleans. New Orleans: Lathrop and Co., 1860.

Fischer, Kirsten. "'False, Feigned, and Scandalous Words': Sexual Slander and Racial Ideology among Whites in Colonial North Carolina." In *The Devil's Lane: Sex and Race in the Early South*, edited by Catherine Clinton and Michele Gillespie, 139–53. New York: Oxford University Press, 1998.

Fitzhugh, George. *Cannibals All!; or, Slaves without Masters*. Edited by C. Vann Woodward. Cambridge: Belknap Press of Harvard University Press, 1960.

Ford, Lacy K., Jr. *Origins of Southern Radicalism: The South Carolina Upcountry, 1800–1860*. New York: Oxford University Press, 1988.

————. "Self-Sufficiency, Cotton, and Economic Development in the South Carolina Upcountry, 1800–1860." *Journal of Economic History* 45 (June 1985): 261–67.

Fox-Genovese, Elizabeth. "Family and Female Identity in the Antebellum South: Sarah Gayle and Her Family." In *In Joy and in Sorrow: Women, Family, and Marriage in the Victorian South*, edited by Carol Bleser, 15–31. New York: Oxford University Press, 1991.

————. *Within the Plantation Household: Black and White Women of the Old South*. Chapel Hill: University of North Carolina Press, 1988.

Fox-Genovese, Elizabeth, and Eugene D. Genovese. *Fruits of Merchant Capital: Slavery and Bourgeois Property in the Rise and Expansion of Capitalism*. New York: Oxford University Press, 1983.

Franklin, Benjamin. *The Autobiography of Benjamin Franklin*. New York: Penguin Books, 1986.

Franklin, John Hope, and Loren Schweninger. *Runaway Slaves: Rebels on the Plantation*. New York: Oxford University Press, 1999.

Freehling, William W. *Prelude to Civil War: The Nullification Controversy in South Carolina, 1816–1836*. New York: Harper and Row, 1966.

———. *The Road to Disunion*. New York: Oxford University Press, 1990.

Freeman, Douglas Southall. *George Washington: A Biography*. 7 vols. Clifton, N.J.: Augustus M. Kelley, 1975.

Freeman, Joanne B. *Affairs of Honor: National Politics in the New Republic*. New Haven: Yale University Press, 2002.

Frey, Sylvia R. *Water from the Rock: Black Resistance in a Revolutionary Age*. Princeton: Princeton University Press, 1991.

Garrick, David. *The Irish Widow, in Two Acts, as It Is Performed, with Universal Applause, at the Theatres in London and Dublin*. Corke: Exshaw, Saunders, 1773.

Genovese, Eugene D. *The Political Economy of Slavery: Studies in the Economy and Society of the Slave South*. Middletown, Conn.: Wesleyan University Press, 1989.

———. *Roll, Jordan, Roll: The World the Slaves Made*. New York: Pantheon Books, 1974.

———. *The Slaveholders' Dilemma: Freedom and Progress in Southern Conservative Thought, 1820–1860*. Columbia: University of South Carolina Press, 1992.

———. *The World the Slaveholders Made: Two Essays in Interpretation*. New York: Pantheon Books, 1969.

Gillespie, Michele. *Free Labor in an Unfree World: White Artisans in Slaveholding Georgia, 1789–1860*. Athens: University of Georgia Press, 2000.

Gilman, Caroline. *The Poetry of Travelling*. New York: S. Colman, 1838.

Gilmore, Glenda Elizabeth. *Gender and Jim Crow: The Politics of White Supremacy in North Carolina, 1896–1920*. Chapel Hill: University of North Carolina Press, 1996.

Ginzberg, Lori. *Women and the Work of Benevolence: Morality, Politics, and Class in the Nineteenth-Century United States*. New Haven: Yale University Press, 1990.

Glover, Lorri. *All Our Relations: Blood Ties and Emotional Bonds among the Early South Carolina Gentry*. Baltimore: Johns Hopkins University Press, 2000.

Gomez, Michael A. *Exchanging Our Country Marks: The Transformation of African Identities in the Colonial and Antebellum South*. Chapel Hill: University of North Carolina Press, 1998.

Greenberg, Kenneth S. *Honor and Slavery: Lies, Duels, Noses, Masks, Dressing as a Woman, Gifts, Strangers, Humanitarianism, Death, Slave Rebellions, the Proslavery Argument, Baseball, Hunting, and Gambling in the Old South*. Princeton: Princeton University Press, 1996.

Gundersen, Joan R. "Kith and Kin: Women's Networks in Colonial Virginia." In *The Devil's Lane: Sex and Race in the Early South*, edited by Catherine

Clinton and Michele Gillespie, 90–108. New York: Oxford University Press, 1998.

Gundersen, Joan R., and Gwen Gampel. "Married Women's Legal Status in Eighteenth-Century New York and Virginia." *William and Mary Quarterly* 39 (January 1982): 114–34.

Hagler, D. Harland. "The Ideal Woman in the Antebellum South: Lady or Farmwife?" *Journal of Southern History* 46 (August 1980): 405–18.

Hall, Jacquelyn Dowd. "'The Mind That Burns in Each Body': Women, Rape, and Racial Violence." In *Powers of Desire*, edited by Ann Snitow, Christine Stansell, and Sharon Thompson, 328–49. New York: Monthly Review Press, 1983.

Halttunen, Karen. *Confidence Men and Painted Women: A Study of Middle-Class Culture in America, 1830–1870*. New Haven: Yale University Press, 1982.

Hamilton, Rev. W. T., D.D. *A Plea for the Liberal Education of Woman: An Address Delivered at the Annual Examination of the Female Seminary*. New York, 1845.

Hammond, James Henry. *Secret and Sacred: The Diaries of James Henry Hammond, a Southern Slaveholder*. Edited by Carol Bleser. New York: Oxford University Press, 1988.

Harris, J. William. *Plain Folk and Gentry in a Slave Society: White Liberty and Black Slavery in Augusta's Hinterlands*. Middletown, Conn.: Wesleyan University Press, 1985.

Hawks, Francis Lister. *A Digested Index of the Reported Cases Adjudged in the Courts of North Carolina from the Year 1778 to 1826*. Raleigh: Bell and Lawrence, 1826.

Haywood, John. *A Manual of the Laws of North Carolina, Arranged under Distinct Heads in Alphabetical Order*. Raleigh, 1801.

Headly, Robert K., Jr. *Wills of Richmond County, Virginia, 1699–1800*. Baltimore: Genealogical Publishing Co., 1983.

Heath, Milton S. "North American Railroads: Public Railroad Construction and the Development of Private Enterprise in the South before 1861." *Journal of Economic History* 10 (1950): 40–53.

Hemphill, C. Dallett. *Bowing to Necessities: A History of Manners in America, 1620–1860*. New York: Oxford University Press, 1999.

Hentz, Caroline Lee. *The Planter's Northern Bride*. Philadelphia: T. B. Peterson, 1854.

Heyrman, Christine Leigh. *Southern Cross: The Beginnings of the Bible Belt*. New York: Alfred A. Knopf, 1997.

Higginbotham, Don, ed. *The Papers of James Iredell*. 2 vols. Raleigh: Division of Archives and History, Department of Cultural Resources, 1976.

Hodes, Martha. "Wartime Dialogues on Illicit Sex: White Women and Black Men." In *Divided Houses*, edited by Catherine Clinton and Nina Silber, 230–42. New York: Oxford University Press, 1992.

———. *White Women, Black Men: Illicit Sex in the Nineteenth-Century South*. New Haven: Yale University Press, 1997.

Horry, Brig. Gen. P., and Mason Locke Weems. *The Life of General Francis Marion, a Celebrated Partisan Officer in the Revolutionary War, against the British and Tories in South Carolina and Georgia*. Philadelphia: Joseph Allen, 1831.

Hudson, Frank Parker. *An 1800 Census for Lincoln County, Georgia*. Atlanta: R. K. Taylor Jr. Foundation, 1977.

Hudson, Larry E. *To Have and to Hold: Slave Work and Family Life in Antebellum South Carolina*. Athens: University of Georgia Press, 1997.

Hufton, Olwen. "Women without Men: Widows and Spinsters in Britain and France in the Eighteenth Century." In *Between Poverty and the Pyre: Moments in the History of Widowhood*, edited by Jan N. Bremmer and Lourens van den Bosch, 122–51. London and New York: Routledge, 1995.

Hughes, Sarah S. "Slaves for Hire: The Allocation of Black Labor in Elizabeth City County, Virginia, 1782 to 1810." *William and Mary Quarterly* 35 (April 1978): 260–86.

Iredell, James. *A Treatise on the Law of Executors and Administrators in North Carolina*. Raleigh: North Carolina Institution for the Deaf and Dumb and the Blind, 1851.

Isaac, Rhys. *The Transformation of Virginia, 1740–1790*. New York: W. W. Norton, 1982.

Isenberg, Nancy. *Sex and Citizenship in Antebellum America*. Chapel Hill: University of North Carolina Press, 1998.

Jacob, Kathryn Allamong. *Capital Elites: High Society in Washington, D.C., after the Civil War*. Washington: Smithsonian Institution Press, 1995.

Jacobs, Harriet A. *Incidents in the Life of a Slave Girl*. Edited by L. Maria Child. Boston: Published for the author, 1861.

Jaffee, David. "Peddlers of Progress and the Transformation of the Rural North, 1760–1860." *Journal of American History* 78 (September 1991): 511–35.

Jodrell, Paul. *A Widow and No Widow*. London: N. Conant, 1780.

Johnson, Walter. *Soul by Soul: Life Inside the Antebellum Slave Market*. Cambridge: Harvard University Press, 1999.

Jordan, Winthrop. *White over Black: American Attitudes toward the Negro, 1550–1812*. New York: W. W. Norton, 1968; reprint 1977.

Joyner, Charles W. *Down by the Riverside: A South Carolina Slave Community*. Urbana: University of Illinois Press, 1984.

———. *Shared Traditions: Southern History and Folk Culture*. Urbana: University of Illinois Press, 1999.

Kars, Marjoleine. *Breaking Loose Together: The Regulator Rebellion in Pre-Revolutionary North Carolina*. Chapel Hill: University of North Carolina Press, 2002.

Kennedy, John Pendleton. *Horse-Shoe Robinson*. N.p.: American Book Company, 1837.

Kerber, Linda K. "The Republican Mother: Women and the Enlightenment— An American Perspective." *American Quarterly* 28 (Summer 1976): 187–205.

———. "Separate Spheres, Female Worlds, Woman's Place: The Rhetoric of Women's History." *Journal of American History* 75 (June 1988): 9–39.

———. *Women of the Republic: Intellect and Ideology in Revolutionary America.* Chapel Hill: University of North Carolina Press, 1980.

Keyssar, Alexander. *The Right to Vote: The Contested History of Democracy in the United States.* New York: Basic Books, 2002.

Kierner, Cynthia A. *Beyond the Household: Women's Place in the Early South, 1700–1835.* Ithaca, N.Y.: Cornell University Press, 1998.

———. *Southern Women in Revolution, 1776–1800: Personal and Political Narratives.* Columbia: University of South Carolina Press, 1998.

King, J. Estelle Stewart. *Abstracts of Wills and Inventories, Fairfax County, Virginia, 1742–1801.* Berryville: Virginia Book Company, 1978.

———. *Abstracts of Wills, Inventories, and Administration Accounts of Loudon County, Virginia, 1757–1800.* N.p., 1940.

———. *Abstracts of Wills, Inventories, and Administration Accounts of Frederick County, Virginia.* N.p., 1973.

King, Martha J. "'What Providence Has Brought Them to Be': Widows, Work, and Print Culture in Colonial Charleston." In *Women and Freedom in Early America*, edited by Larry D. Eldridge, 147–66. New York: New York University Press, 1997.

Kuiper, Yme. "Noble Widows between Fortune and Family." In *Between Poverty and the Pyre: Moments in the History of Widowhood*, edited by Jan N. Bremmer and Lourens van den Bosch, 152–70. London and New York: Routledge, 1995.

Kulikoff, Allan. *Tobacco and Slaves: The Development of Southern Cultures in the Chesapeake, 1680–1800.* Chapel Hill: University of North Carolina Press, 1986.

The Laws of Etiquette; or, Short Rules and Reflections for Conduct in Society. Philadelphia, 1836.

Lebsock, Suzanne. *The Free Women of Petersburg: Status and Culture in a Southern Town, 1784–1860.* New York: W. W. Norton, 1984.

Lee, Jean B. *The American Revolution in Charles County.* New York: W. W. Norton, 1994.

Lee, Laura Elizabeth [Mrs. Jesse Mercer Battle]. *Forget-Me-Nots of the Civil War: A Romance, Containing Reminiscences and Original Letters of Two Confederate Soldiers.* St. Louis: A. R. Fleming Printing Company, 1909.

Leslie, Eliza. *The Behavior Book: A Manual for Ladies (Philadelphia 1854); Etiquette at Washington; Together with the Customs Adopted by Polite Society in the Other Cities of the United States.* Baltimore, 1850.

Lewis, Charlene M. Boyer. *Ladies and Gentlemen on Display: Planter Society at the Virginia Springs, 1790–1860.* Charlottesville: University Press of Virginia, 2001.

Lewis, Jan. *The Pursuit of Happiness: Family and Values in Jefferson's Virginia.* Cambridge: Cambridge University Press, 1983.

Life of General Marion, Embracing Anecdotes Illustrative of His Character, with Illustrations. Philadelphia: Lindsay and Blakiston, 1847.

McCord, Louisa Susanna Cheves. *Louisa S. McCord: Poems, Drama, Biography, Letters*. Edited by Richard Cecil Lounsbury. Charlottesville: University Press of Virginia, 1996.

McCurry, Stephanie. *Masters of Small Worlds: Yeoman Households, Gender Relations, and the Political Culture of the Antebellum South Carolina Low Country*. New York: Oxford University Press, 1995.

McDonald, Cornelia. *A Woman's Civil War: A Diary with Reminiscences of the War from March 1862*. Edited by Minrose C. Gwin. Madison: University of Wisconsin Press, 1992.

McGuire, Judith W. *Diary of a Southern Refugee during the War, by a Lady of Virginia*. Lincoln: University of Nebraska Press, 1995.

McPherson, James M. *Battle Cry of Freedom: The Civil War Era*. New York: Ballantine Books, 1988.

McTyeire, Holland N., C. F. Sturges, and A. T. Holmes. *Duties of Masters to Servants: Three Premium Essays*. Charleston, S.C.: Southern Baptist Publication Company, 1851.

Main, Gloria L. *Tobacco Colony: Life in Early Maryland, 1650–1720*. Princeton: Princeton University Press, 1982.

Malone, Ann Patton. *Sweet Chariot: Slave Family and Household Structure in Nineteenth-Century Louisiana*. Chapel Hill: University of North Carolina Press, 1992.

Malone, Dumas. *Jefferson and His Time*. 6 vols. Boston: Little, Brown, 1948–81.
———. *Jefferson the Virginian*. Boston: Little, Brown, 1948.

Mann, Bruce H. *Neighbors and Strangers: Law and Community in Early Connecticut*. Chapel Hill: University of North Carolina Press, 1987.

Mate, Mavis E. *Daughters, Wives, and Widows after the Black Death: Women in Sussex, 1350–1535*. Woodbridge, England: Boydell Press, 1998.

Mathews, Donald G. *Religion in the Old South*. Chicago: University of Chicago Press, 1977.

Meaders, Daniel. *Advertisements for Runaway Slaves in Virginia, 1801–1820*. New York: Garland Publishing, 1997.

Meyers, Debra. *Common Whores, Vertuous Women, and Loveing Wives: Free Will Christian Women in Colonial Maryland*. Bloomington: Indiana University Press, 2003.

Mirrer, Louise, ed. *Upon My Husband's Death: Widowhood in the Literature and Histories of Medieval Europe*. Ann Arbor: University of Michigan Press, 1992.

Moore, Bartholomew F., and Asa Biggs. *Revised Code of North Carolina*. Boston: Little, Brown, 1855.

Moore, John Hammond, ed. *A Plantation Mistress on the Eve of the Civil War: The Diary of Keziah Goodwyn Hopkins Brevard, 1860–1861*. Columbia: University of South Carolina Press, 1993.

Moore, John Hebron. *The Emergence of the Cotton Kingdom in the Old Southwest: Mississippi, 1770–1860*. Baton Rouge: Louisiana State University Press, 1988.

Morgan, Philip D. *Slave Counterpoint: Black Culture in the Eighteenth-Century Chesapeake and Lowcountry*. Chapel Hill: Published for the Omohundro Institute of Early American History and Culture, Williamsburg, Virginia, by the University of North Carolina Press, 1998.

Morris, Christopher. "The Articulation of Two Worlds: The Master-Slave Relationship Reconsidered." *Journal of American History* 85 (December 1998): 982–1007.

———. *Becoming Southern: The Evolution of a Way of Life, Warren County and Vicksburg, Mississippi, 1770–1860.* New York: Oxford University Press, 1995.

Morris, Thomas D. *Southern Slavery and the Law, 1619–1860.* Chapel Hill: University of North Carolina Press, 1996.

Narrett, David. "Men's Wills and Women's Property Rights in Colonial New York." In *Women in the Age of the American Revolution*, edited by Ronald Hoffman and Peter J. Albert, 91–153. Charlottesville: Published for the United States Capital Historical Society by the University Press of Virginia, 1989.

Newman, Simon P. *Parades and the Politics of the Street: Festive Culture in the Early American Republic.* Philadelphia: University of Pennsylvania Press, 2000.

Norton, Mary Beth. "The Evolution of White Women's Experience in Early America." *American Historical Review* 89 (June 1984): 593–619.

———. *Founding Mothers and Fathers: Gendered Power and the Forming of American Society.* New York: Alfred A. Knopf, 1996.

———. *Liberty's Daughters: The Revolutionary Experience of American Women, 1750–1800.* Boston: Little, Brown, 1980.

Oakes, James. *The Ruling Race: A History of American Slaveholders.* New York: Alfred A. Knopf, 1982.

Olsen, Christopher J. *Political Culture and Secession in Mississippi: Masculinity, Honor, and the Antiparty Tradition, 1830–1860.* New York: Oxford University Press, 2000.

Olwell, Robert. *Masters, Slaves, and Subjects: The Culture of Power in the South Carolina Low Country, 1740–1790.* Ithaca, N.Y.: Cornell University Press, 1998.

Painter, Nell Irvin. *Soul Murder and Slavery.* Waco, Tex.: Markham Press Fund, 1995.

Parker, Freddie L., ed. *Stealing a Little Freedom: Advertisements for Slave Runaways in North Carolina, 1791–1840.* New York: Garland Publishing, 1994.

Parkes, Mrs. William. *Domestic Duties; or Instructions to Young Married Ladies.* N.p., 1829.

Pease, Jane H., and William Henry Pease. *A Family of Women: The Carolina Petigrus in Peace and War.* Chapel Hill: University of North Carolina Press, 1999.

———. *Ladies, Women, and Wenches: Choice and Constraint in Antebellum Charleston and Boston.* Chapel Hill: University of North Carolina Press, 1990.

Pease, William Henry, and Jane H. Pease. *The Web of Progress: Private Values and Public Styles in Boston and Charleston, 1828–1843.* Athens: University of Georgia Press, 1991.

Pember, Phoebe Yates. *A Southern Woman's Story*. Edited by George C. Rable. Columbia: University of South Carolina Press, 2002.

Perdue, Charles L., Thomas E. Barden, Robert K. Phillips, and Virginia Writers' Project, eds. *Weevils in the Wheat: Interviews with Virginia Ex-Slaves.* Charlottesville: University Press of Virginia, 1976.

Perkins, Elizabeth A. "The Consumer Frontier: Household Consumption in Early Kentucky." *Journal of American History* 78 (September 1991): 486–511.

Pinckney, Elise, ed. *The Letterbook of Eliza Lucas Pinckney, 1739–1762.* Columbia: University of South Carolina Press, 1972.

Powell, William, and Peter Graham Fish. *Dictionary of North Carolina Biography.* 6 vols. Chapel Hill: University of North Carolina Press, 1979–96.

Prior, Mary, ed. *Women in English Society, 1500–1800.* London: Methuen, 1985.

Rable, George C. *Civil Wars: Women and the Crisis of Southern Nationalism.* Urbana: University of Illinois Press, 1989.

Randolph, Mary. *Virginia Housewife or, Methodical Cook: A Facsimile of an Authentic Early American Cookbook.* New York: Dover Publications, 1993.

Rawick, George P., ed. *The American Slave: A Composite Autobiography.* 19 vols. Westport, Conn.: Greenwood Press, 1972.

Reeve, Tapping. *The Law of Baron and Femme: Of Parent and Children; of Guardian and Ward; of Master and Servant; and of the Powers of Courts of Chancery.* New Haven: Oliver Steele, 1816.

Remini, Robert V. *The Life of Andrew Jackson.* Condensed edition. New York: Harper and Row, 1988.

Rivers, Larry E. *Slavery in Florida: Territorial Days to Emancipation.* Gainesville: University Press of Florida, 2000.

Rose, Willie Lee. *Rehearsal for Reconstruction: The Port Royal Experiment.* Athens: University of Georgia Press, 1993.

Rosenberg, Charles E. *Explaining Epidemics and Other Studies in the History of Medicine.* Cambridge: Cambridge University Press, 1992.

Rothman, Joshua D. *Notorious in the Neighborhood: Sex and Families across the Color Line in Virginia, 1787–1861.* Chapel Hill: University of North Carolina Press, 2003.

Rules of the Society for the Relief of the Widows and Orphans of the Clergy of the Protestant Episcopal Church in the State of South Carolina. Charleston, 1808.

Ryan, Mary P. *Women in Public: Between Banners and Ballots, 1825–1880.* Baltimore: Johns Hopkins University Press, 1990.

Salmon, Marylynn. *Women and the Law of Property in Early America.* Chapel Hill: University of North Carolina Press, 1986.

Sawyer, Caroline M. *The Merchant's Widow.* New York: Hallock and Lyon, 1849.

Scarborough, William K. *The Overseer: Plantation Management in the Old South.* Baton Rouge: Louisiana State University Press, 1966.

Schwalm, Leslie A. *A Hard Fight for We: Women's Transition from Slavery to Freedom in South Carolina.* Urbana: University of Illinois Press, 1997.

Schwarz, Philip J. *Twice Condemned: Slaves and the Criminal Laws of Virginia, 1705–1865.* Baton Rouge: Louisiana State University Press, 1998.

Scott, Anne Firor. *The Southern Lady: From Pedestal to Politics, 1830–1930.* Chicago: University of Chicago Press, 1970.

Scott, James C. *Domination and the Arts of Resistance: Hidden Transcripts.* New Haven: Yale University Press, 1990.

Shammas, Carole. "Black Women's Work and the Evolution of Plantation Society in Virginia." *Labor History* 26 (Winter 1985): 5–28.

———. "Early American Women and Control over Capital." In *Women in the Age of the American Revolution,* edited by Ronald Hoffman and Peter J. Albert, 134–54. Charlottesville: Published for the United States Capital Historical Society by the University Press of Virginia, 1989.

Simms, William Gilmore. *Eutaw, a Sequel to the Forayers, or The Raid of the Dog-Days.* New York: Redfield, 1856.

———. *The Life of Francis Marion.* New York: Derby and Jackson, 1857.

———[?]. "Review of Mrs. E. F. Ellet, *Women of the Revolution.*" *Southern Quarterly Review* 1 (July 1850): 314–54.

———. *Woodcraft, or, Hawks about the Dovecote.* Edited by Charles S. Watson. New Haven: New College and University Press, 1983.

Smith, Bonnie. *Ladies of the Leisure Class: The Bourgeoises of Northern France in the Nineteenth Century.* Princeton: Princeton University Press, 1981.

Smith, Daniel Scott. "Inheritance and the Social History of Early American Women." In *Women in the Age of the American Revolution,* edited by Ronald Hoffman and Peter J. Albert, 45–66. Charlottesville: Published for the United States Capital Historical Society by the University of Virginia Press, 1989.

Smith-Rosenberg, Carroll. "The Female World of Love and Ritual: Relations between Women in Nineteenth-Century America." Chap. 2 in *Disorderly Conduct: Visions of Gender in Victorian America.* New York: Oxford University Press, 1985.

Sommerville, Diane Miller. "Rape, Race, and Castration in Slave Law in the Colonial and Early South." In *The Devil's Lane: Sex and Race in the Early South,* edited by Catherine Clinton and Michele Gillespie. New York: Oxford University Press, 1998.

Southworth, Emma Dorothy Eliza Nevitte. *The Widow's Son.* Philadelphia: Peterson, 1867.

Speth, Linda. "More Than Her 'Thirds': Wives and Widows in Colonial Virginia." In *Women, Family, and Community in Colonial America,* edited by Linda Speth and Alison Duncan Hirsh. New York: Institute for Research in History and Haworth Press, 1983.

Spruill, Julia Cherry. *Women's Life and Work in the Southern Colonies.* New York: W. W. Norton, 1972.

Stansell, Christine. *City of Women: Sex and Class in New York, 1789–1860.* Urbana: University of Illinois Press, 1987.

Stone, Lawrence. *Family, Sex, and Marriage in England, 1500–1800.* New York: Harper and Row, 1977.

Stowe, Steven M. *Intimacy and Power in the Old South: Ritual in the Lives of the Planters.* Baltimore: Johns Hopkins University Press, 1987.

Tadman, Michael. *Speculators and Slaves: Masters, Traders, and Slaves in the Old South.* Madison: University of Wisconsin Press, 1989.

Taylor, Tom. *Sir Roger de Coverley; or, The Widow and Her Wooers.* London: Hailes Lacy, 1854.

Thomas, Emory M. *The Confederate Nation, 1861–1865.* New York: Harper and Row, 1979.

Tinling, Marion. "Cawsons, Virginia, in 1795–1796." Notes and Documents. *William and Mary Quarterly* 3 (April 1946): 281–91.

Todd, Barbara J. "The Remarrying Widow: A Stereotype Reconsidered." In *Women in English Society, 1500–1800,* edited by Mary Prior, 54–92. London and New York: Methuen, 1985.

Tracy, Susan Jean. *In the Master's Eye: Representations of Women, Blacks, and Poor Whites in Antebellum Southern Literature.* Amherst: University of Massachusetts Press, 1995.

Trial Record of Denmark Vesey. Boston: Beacon Press, 1970.

Tucker, George. *Valley of the Shenandoah; or, Memoirs of the Graysons.* 2 vols. New York: C. Wiley, 1824.

Ulrich, Laurel. *Good Wives: Image and Reality in the Lives of Women in Northern New England, 1650–1750.* New York: Oxford University Press, 1983.

van der Toorn, Karel. "The Public Image of the Widow in Ancient Israel." In *Between Poverty and the Pyre: Moments in the History of Widowhood,* edited by Jan N. Bremmer and Lourens van den Bosch, 19–30. London and New York: Routledge, 1995.

Varon, Elizabeth R. *We Mean to Be Counted: White Women and Politics in Antebellum Virginia.* Chapel Hill: University of North Carolina Press, 1998.

Vasvari, Louise O. "Why Is Doña Endrina a Widow? Traditional Culture and Textuality in the *Libro de Buen Amor.*" In *Upon My Husband's Death,* edited by Louise Mirrer, 259–87. Ann Arbor: University of Michigan Press, 1992.

Waldstreicher, David. *In the Midst of Perpetual Fetes: The Making of American Nationalism, 1776–1820.* Chapel Hill: University of North Carolina Press, 1997.

Warner, Lyndan. "Widows, Widowers, and the Problem of 'Second Marriages' in Sixteenth-Century France." In *Widowhood in Medieval and Early Modern Europe,* edited by Sandra Cavallo and Lyndan Warner, 84–107. New York: Longman, 1999.

Watson, Harry L. *Liberty and Power: The Politics of Jacksonian America.* New York: Noonday Press, 1990.

Weiman, David F. "The Economic Emancipation of the Non-Slaveholding Class: Upcountry Farmers in the Georgia Cotton Economy." *Journal of Economic History* 45 (March 1985): 71–93.

Weiner, Marli Frances. *Mistresses and Slaves: Plantation Women in South Carolina, 1830–80.* Urbana: University of Illinois Press, 1997.

Welke, Barbara Young. *Recasting American Liberty: Gender, Race, Law, and the Railroad Revolution*. New York: Cambridge University Press, 2001.

Whitcher, Frances Mary. *Widow Spriggins, Mary Elmer, and Other Sketches*. New York: George W. Carleton and Co., 1867.

Whites, LeeAnn. *The Civil War as a Crisis in Gender: Augusta, Georgia, 1860–1890*. Athens: University of Georgia Press, 1995.

Whitman, T. Stephen. *The Price of Freedom: Slavery and Manumission in Baltimore and Early National Maryland*. Lexington: University Press of Kentucky, 1997.

Wiencek, Henry. *The Hairstons: An American Family in Black and White*. New York: St. Martin's Press, 1999.

Wilson, James Grant, and John Fiske, eds. *Appleton's Cyclopaedia of American Biography*. 6 vols. New York: D. Appleton and Company, 1887–89.

Wilson, Lisa. *Life after Death: Widows in Pennsylvania, 1750–1850*. Philadelphia: Temple University Press, 1992.

Wirt, William. *Sketches of the Life and Character of Patrick Henry*. Philadelphia: James Webster, 1817.

Wood, Betty. *Gender, Race, and Rank in a Revolutionary Age: The Georgia Lowcountry, 1750–1820*. Athens: University of Georgia Press, 2000.

Wood, Kirsten E. "'One Woman So Dangerous to Public Morals': Gender and Power in the Eaton Affair." *Journal of the Early Republic* 17 (Summer 1997): 237–75.

Woodward, C. Vann, and Elisabeth Muhlenfield, eds. *The Private Mary Chesnut: The Unpublished Civil War Diaries*. New York: Oxford University Press, 1984.

Wright, Gavin. *The Political Economy of the Cotton South: Households, Markets, and Wealth in the Nineteenth Century*. New York: W. W. Norton, 1978.

Wyatt-Brown, Bertram. "The Mask of Obedience: Male Slave Psychology in the Old South." *American Historical Review* 93 (December 1988): 1228–53.

———. *Southern Honor: Ethics and Behavior in the Old South*. New York: Oxford University Press, 1982.

Young, Jeffrey Robert. *Domesticating Slavery: The Master Class in Georgia and South Carolina, 1670–1837*. Chapel Hill: University of North Carolina Press, 1999.

———. "Ideology and Death on a Savannah River Rice Plantation, 1833–1867: Paternalism amidst 'A Good Supply of Disease and Pain.'" *Journal of Southern History* 59 (November 1993): 673–707.

Unpublished Sources

Anzilotti, Cara. "'In the Affairs of the World': Women and Plantation Ownership in the Eighteenth-Century South Carolina Low Country." Ph.D. diss., University of California, Santa Barbara, 1994.

Baptist, Edward E. "Creating an Old South: The Plantation Frontier in Jackson and Leon Counties, Florida." Ph.D. diss., University of Pennsylvania, 1997.

Breen, Patrick H. "'A Storm of Terror': Femininity in the Wake of Nat Turner's Slave Revolt." Citadel Conference on the South. Charleston, S.C., 2000.

Fryer, Darcy R. "Red Birds and Turtles: Robert Pringle and the Culture of Gift-Giving in Colonial Charleston." Citadel Conference on the South. Charleston, S.C., 2000.

The Dolley Madison Project. Virginia Center for Digital History. ⟨http://www.vcdh.virginia.edu/madison/index.html⟩.

O'Connor, Ellen Hartigan. "'I Hear the Little Basket Has Reached Its Destination': Provisioning and Exchange in Eighteenth-Century Charlestonian Families." Citadel Conference on the South. Charleston, S.C., 2000.

Olsen, Christopher, "Politics as Ritual: A Cultural History of Voting and Running for Office in Antebellum America." Unpublished paper.

Snyder, Terri Lynne. "'Rich Widows Are the Best Commodity This Country Affords': Gender Relations and the Rehabilitation of Patriarchy in Virginia, 1660–1700." Ph.D. diss., University of Iowa, 1992.

Wood, Kirsten E. "Fictive Mastery: Slaveholding Widows in the American South, 1790–1860." Ph.D. diss., University of Pennsylvania, 1998.

INDEX

Abbott, Sarah Ann, 45
Adams, Abigail, 106
Adams, Jasper, 15
Adams, John, 106
Agents: and commercial transactions, 84, 87, 88–89, 91, 92, 93, 99, 101; slaveholding widows as, 89–90
Agricultural production, 42, 45, 46, 85, 90
Alexander, Adam, 142
Alexander, Charles, 125–26
Alexander, Louisa, 51, 65, 104–5, 141–42
Alston, Sarah, 31, 45
Alston, Willis, 31
American Colonization Society, 106
American Freedmen's Inquiry Commission, 54
Ames, Fisher, 107
Anderson, Byrl, 196, 197–98, 245 (n. 11)
Anderson, Margaret, 31
Archer, Judith, 145
Archer, Mary, 45, 88
Archer, Polly, 111
Archer, Richard T., 145
Armstrong, Abel, 31
Armstrong, Mary, 31
Austin, Archibald, 92
Authority: and political privilege, 6; and slaveholding widows as household heads, 7; and slave management, 7, 55; and ladyhood, 9, 183; and kinship networks, 13, 70–71, 75–76; and property rights, 13; access to managerial, 17, 19; and wills, 19, 29, 31–32; as executors, 25; familial, 31–32; assumption of, 58; and property disputes, 74, 75; and husband's agency, 77; and white men's political alliances, 117–18, 124, 125; and overseers, 119–27; and audience, 126–28; and class boundaries, 128–29, 130, 182–83; and widows' wills, 136; white men's complement to, 191

Baber, George, 117
Bacot, Ada: as mistress, 6; and slave management, 7; and slave resistance, 12, 58, 168, 169–70; and kinship networks, 101; and overseers, 122; and self-mastery, 132, 137, 139; and illness, 141; and household mastery, 142, 143; and childlessness, 144; and Civil War, 160, 162, 168, 169–70, 171, 172, 179, 180, 181, 183–84, 188; and domestic slaves, 171, 190
Bacot, Peter S., 101
Baillio, Mrs., 147, 148
Banking, 100, 162
Barbour, James, 108, 109
Barbour, Lucy, 108, 109
Barger, Catherine, 134
Bartow, Lou, 167, 194
Battle, Joel, 68
Battle, Polly, 68

Battle, William Horn, 8, 68, 88, 110

Benevolent ideals, 35–36, 41, 43, 48, 51, 59, 173–74, 175

Berry, Fannie, 42

Blacks: and political rights, 3; free black widows, 4, 200 (n. 12); slave women, 33, 94, 169, 174, 179; white women's fears of, 168, 169–70; freedom for, 171; free black women, 190, 196; as freedmen, 196–97. *See also* Domestic slaves; Slave management; Slave relations; Slave resistance; Slavery

Blair, Jean, 20, 21, 22–23, 173, 242 (n. 36)

Bleser, Carol, 113

Boardinghouses: and subordinate role, 7; and deputy husbands, 25; as remunerative work, 36, 39, 97; and kinship networks, 63; and public realm, 93; and commercial transactions, 102; and household mastery, 144; restrictions of, 149; and Civil War, 166; and domestic slaves, 190

Bolling, Linnaeus, 71

Bolton, Charles, 99, 120

Bost, George, 31

Boudinot, Elias, 106

Boyd, A. G., 87

Boyd, Alexander, 87

Brandon, Esther, 134

Brevard, Keziah: and slave management, 49, 52, 53, 59, 140; and property management, 59; and self-mastery, 139, 140, 143, 144; and Civil War, 159–60, 173; and slave resistance, 168, 169; and freedom for blacks, 171

Brevard, Peggy, 144

Brice, Mary, 170

British troops, 21–23

Brown, C. A., 92

Brown, Kathleen, 72

Bryan, Delia, 49

Bullock, James, 92

Burge, Dolly: and property management, 33; and slave management, 35, 42, 58; and travel, 92, 95–96; and religious enjoyment, 139; and remarriage, 151–52; and Civil War, 161, 162–63, 172, 173, 174–76, 177–78, 179, 188

Burge, Sadai, 163, 175–76

Burge, Thomas, 32–33, 35, 151–52

Burke, Caroline, 38–39, 40, 59, 65

Burke, John, 39, 65

Burrell, Savilla, 187

Burwell, Lucy, 64, 84, 85, 87

Butler, Benjamin, 176

Butler, Gabriela, 95

Bynum, Victoria, 8

Byrd, Mary, 22, 23, 24, 205 (n. 40)

Cabell, Joseph, 99

Cabell, William H., 88, 89

Camden, Lord, 20

Camden subscription, 20

Campbell, Alexander, 71

Campbell, Hugh, 87–88

Campbell, John, 71

Campbell, Mary, 19, 70–71, 72, 82, 96–97, 110, 146

Cannon, Sylvia, 42

Carolina Sea Islands, 242 (n. 32)

Carter, Robert, 123–24, 126–27, 182

Cary, Virginia, 2, 15, 41, 49–50, 93, 122, 140

Chancery courts, 62, 74, 75

Charitable institutions, 4

Charity ideals, 35, 228 (n. 1)

Chesnut, Mary, 167, 184–85, 194

Childlessness, 135, 143–44, 150

Children: and widows' legal rights, 4–5; and ladyhood, 10; and personal property, 16; and wills, 29–31, 33, 133, 135, 136, 207 (n. 63); and support of mother, 31; and yeoman farmer widows, 37–38, 39; and education, 38, 39, 59, 63, 64, 66, 67, 146, 164, 165; fatherless children as orphans, 61; and co-residence, 65; and duties to parents, 70–71; and widows' remarriage, 133, 150, 154; and widows' Christian duty, 139–40; and dependency of slaveholding widows, 147; and gender identity, 149; and authority, 157; and Civil War, 164, 167, 168, 177

Chivalry, 124, 126, 148, 161, 176

Christian duty, 41, 52, 132, 138, 139, 151

Civic affairs, 25

Civil War: and domestic slaves, 14, 170–71, 189–90; and slave resistance, 57, 161, 168–69; and gender identity, 158; and ladyhood, 159, 161, 170, 171, 177, 178, 179, 180, 189–90; death toll of, 160, 162, 168, 183; and economic losses, 160–61, 162, 166–67, 168, 170; and class boundaries, 161, 178–83, 188–89, 191, 195; and availability of goods, 162, 163–64; and wage work, 165–67

Clark, Margaret, 51

Class boundaries: and whites, 10–11, 115, 161, 179, 193–94; and white women, 11, 183; and ladyhood, 12, 130, 188; slaveholding widows' assertion of, 14; and corporal punishment, 53; and commercial transactions, 83, 100–101, 102; and clothing, 98, 102, 178, 179–80, 183; and literacy, 98–99; and political involvement, 103, 115, 116, 124; and mastery, 104, 116; and planters, 124, 125; and authority, 128–29, 130, 182–83; and Revolutionary War, 129–30; and widows' remarriage, 150; and class conflict, 159; and Civil War, 161, 178–83, 188–89, 191, 195

Clay, Henry, 108, 109

Clay Association, 109

Clothing: and bereavement, 84, 98, 164, 179; of planter widows, 97–98; and class boundaries, 98, 102, 178, 179–80, 183

Clove, Lucetta, 147–48

Cobb, Howell, 109–10, 111, 137

Cobb, John Addison, 112

Cobb, Sarah, 63, 111

Cobb, Thomas R. R., 110

Cochran, Robert, 89, 90

Cocke, Caroline Lewis, 66, 67

Cocke, Charles, 15, 34, 71, 112

Cocke, James Powell, 66, 67, 71, 88, 100, 111

Cocke, Jane, 45, 66, 67, 72, 89, 112, 135

Cocke, Martha, 5, 7, 47, 67, 100, 137, 138, 142

Code of honor, 6, 83

Cohen, Patricia Cline, 93

Coles, Betty, 156

Collins, Zaccheus, 90

Colonial South, 2, 16, 17, 150

Commercial networks, 18, 19, 100–101

Commercial transactions: and public and private space, 14, 83, 84, 89, 90, 92, 101; and deputy husbands, 26; and slaveholding wives, 33, 84; and consumer and producer roles, 83, 84, 101; and household mastery, 83, 84; and kinship networks, 83, 87, 99, 101; and white women, 83–84, 221 (n. 2); and correspondence, 84, 87, 89, 92, 93, 98, 101, 223 (n. 17); and domestic privacy, 84, 90, 91, 92, 93; and goods not produced domestically, 84; and agricultural production, 85, 90; and multiple retailers, 85–86; and neighbors, 86; and travel, 93, 94, 95, 96–97, 98, 131; and women's unequal terms, 98–99; and written instruments, 99–100; and printed forms, 100; and political involvement, 105; responsibilities of, 157; and Civil War, 162, 163–64

Overseers: slaveholding widows' hiring of, 7; and ladyhood, 10; slaveholding wives' hiring of, 27; and slave management, 44, 45, 46; and corporal punishment, 48, 50–51, 52, 53; and property disputes, 76; and kinship networks, 81; independence of, 116; and authority, 117–27; and Civil War, 170

Panic of 1819, 44
Panic of 1837, 44, 45–46, 69, 153
Paternalism, 11, 42, 43, 62, 74, 208 (n. 3)
Patriarchy: patriarchal roots of masters, 6, 9, 104, 116; democratic application of, 11; and sexual coercion, 54; and conjugal or nuclear family, 61–62; and kinship networks, 70, 82; and subordinate roles, 102, 103; and white men's political alliances, 117, 118; and political discourse, 130
Pember, Phoebe, 162, 163, 164, 167, 176–77, 178, 180, 181–83
Perfect control myth, 12, 13
Personal property, 16, 29, 32, 79
Petigru, James L., 64
Petitions: for Revolutionary War retribution, 23
Phillips, Samuel, 88
Pickering, Timothy, 106, 108
Pierson, Vincent, 50, 119–20
Piety, 52
Pike, John C., 99
Pinkind, Ariela, 162, 165, 167, 169, 171, 185
Pinkney, Eliza Lucas, 22
Planters: and yeomen, 11, 12–13; and Revolutionary War losses, 22; and wills, 29; and Panic of 1837, 45–46; and mastery, 48, 104; and banks, 100; and class boundaries, 124, 125
Planter widows: independence of, 1; and geography, 8; and demands of

work, 36, 38, 39; and ladyhood, 40; and slave management, 41–42, 44–45; and corporal punishment, 43, 48, 49–50; and genteel housekeeping, 48–49; and sexual coercion, 54; and commercial transactions, 85, 86, 88, 93, 99, 102; and travel, 96–97; clothing of, 97–98; and household protection, 104; and white men's political alliances, 116, 117; and day laborers, 120; authority of, 122; and Civil War, 178
Political democracy, 3, 11, 124–25
Political disputes, 220 (n. 42)
Political involvement: and public activity, 14; and Revolutionary War, 20–21, 23, 24; and class boundaries, 103, 115, 116, 124; and husband's careers, 103, 105–9; informal, 103; disapproval of, 104–5; and elections, 109; and kinship networks, 109–12; and benefits for political widows, 110; and personal advantage, 111; and widowed mothers, 112–15; and Civil War, 176
Political patronage, 103, 105, 107
Political rights, 1, 3, 6–7, 11, 24. *See also* Voting rights
Pollard, Paulina, 27
Poore, Annie, 51
Poor white widows, 4, 9, 94, 98, 150, 200 (n. 12), 223 (n. 14)
Poor white women, 33, 179
Porter, Annabella, 64–65, 85, 86, 87, 88
Porter, William, 88
Prewett, Harriet N., 129
Print culture: and industrious housewifery, 2; and domestic confinement of women, 24, 25, 82, 84, 90, 93; and white women, 29; and planter widows, 41; and travel, 93; and class boundaries, 100; and sentimentalism, 139
Printed forms, 100

Property disputes: and kinship networks, 62, 70, 73–82

Property management: and legal responsibilities, 16; and non-agricultural businesses, 17–18; and wills, 19, 30, 32–34; and slaveholding wives, 25, 84; and kinship networks, 62, 64, 66; and self-mastery, 139; and children, 140; and remarriage, 150

Property rights: and independence of slaveholding widows, 4–5, 62–63; and class boundaries, 11–12; and planters, 13; responsibilities of, 17; contraction of, 19; and Revolutionary War, 22, 24; and taxation, 24; and remarriage, 38, 153, 154–55; and kinship networks, 70; and commercial transactions, 84; and mastery, 104; and slaveholding widows' wills, 136

Proslavery theorists, 2, 12, 13, 49, 208 (n. 3)

Public and private space: and commercial transactions, 14, 83, 84, 89, 90, 92, 101

Racism, 11, 43, 55, 161, 171, 194, 196

Railroad industry, 45

Randolph, George, 167

Randolph, Mary, 25, 167

Reconstruction, 174, 196

Religious activities, 41, 52, 132, 138, 139, 151, 228 (n. 1)

Religious beliefs, 138–40, 149–50, 151

Representative government, 2, 3

Republican Party, 196

Republicanism and political culture, 3, 11, 115, 124, 145

Republican womanhood, 25

Responsibilities: of slaveholding wives, 25–26, 33; of executors, 37, 91–92, 123, 127, 143, 157; of yeoman farmer widows, 37–38, 39, 208

(n. 5). *See also* Commercial transactions; Management

Revolutionary War: and economic losses, 20, 21, 22, 23, 24; and abuse of women, 21, 173; petitions for retribution, 23; southerners as true heirs of, 129

Richardson, Martha: and slave management, 35, 49; and kinship networks, 65, 68, 76–77, 80; as deputy husband, 69; and travel, 95; and banking, 100; and political involvement, 104; and authority, 128, 157

Richardson, Richard, 155

Richmond, Susie, 179

Robert, Eliza, 160

Rootes, Elizabeth, 63

Rootes, Emily, 144–45, 153

Rootes, Henry, 109

Rootes, Jaquelin, 144

Ruffin, Eliza, 57, 104, 138

Rural widows, 40, 105

Rush, Benjamin, 141

Sargent, Winthrop, 108

Schley, Eliza, 4, 107

Schools. *See* Teaching

Schwarz, Philip, 56

Schweninger, Loren, 56

Screven, James, 69

Screven, John, 68

Screven, Sarah, 100

Self-mastery, 132, 137–42, 143

Self-supporting townswomen, 86

Sentimentalism, 139

Separate estates, 75–76, 84, 134–35, 150, 153

Servitude, 2

Sewing, 36, 63, 146, 165–66, 167

Sex, interracial, 54, 188

Sexual coercion, 36, 48, 53–54

Sheriffs, 51, 57

Sherman, William T., 173, 175, 190

Sickness, 47, 49, 140–41; and healthcare, 47–48, 141–42

Simms, William Gilmore, 121–22, 126, 128–30

Singleton, Martha, 123–24, 126–27, 129, 182

Singleton, Matthew, 123, 155

Slave criminals, 57

Slave distribution, 16–17, 29, 30, 31, 37, 43–44, 53, 55, 134

Slave families, 13, 37, 42, 44, 47, 55, 210 (n. 22)

Slaveholding widows' mastery: and political rights, 6–7; and geographical influence, 8; and gender roles, 12, 48, 59–60; public consequences of, 13–14, 83; and slave relations, 13; Civil War's effects on, 14, 161, 175, 190–91; and slave management, 36, 48; as fictive mastery, 60, 193; and commercial transactions, 84, 87; and travel, 98; and merging of masculine and feminine spheres, 102; defense of, 116, 117; and self-mastery, 132, 137–42, 143; and racism, 171. *See also* Authority; Class boundaries; Dependency of slaveholding widows; Independence of slaveholding widows; Ladyhood; Widowhood

Slaveholding wives: and social order, 2; business education of, 18–19, 26–27; as deputy husbands, 18, 19, 23–24, 25, 26–28, 33; management responsibilities of, 25–26, 33; and commercial transactions, 33, 84; and verbal appropriation of slaves' work, 58, 216 (n. 87); domestic confinement of, 98, 226–27 (n. 50); and kinship networks, 216 (n. 4)

Slave management: and authority, 7, 55; and truancy, 12, 23, 37; and benevolent ideals, 35–36, 41, 43, 48, 51, 59; factors in, 35–36; and corporal punishment, 36, 43, 48, 49–50; and ladyhood, 36, 40, 48, 190; and number of slaves, 36; and

slave resistance, 36–37; and workload, 36, 46, 47, 55; and intestate estates, 37–38; and illness, 39, 47–48, 49, 59, 212 (n. 50); and hiring out of slaves, 40, 45, 67, 172, 214 (n. 68); and planter widows, 41–42, 44–45; and incentives to slave workers, 42–43, 51, 174; and permission to grow/sell garden crops, 42; and provisions, 42–43, 46–47; and inspections, 44; and work assignments, 44–45; and surplus labor, 45; and kinship networks, 67; and commercial transactions, 87; and anger, 140; and gender identity, 148; and remarriage, 155; and Civil War, 161, 172

Slave market, 53, 85, 214 (n. 68)

Slave patrollers, 48, 51, 57, 83, 227 (n. 50)

Slave relations: and perfect control myth, 12; and slaveholding widows' mastery, 13; and balance of power, 22, 43, 50, 52, 54; and deputy husbands, 28; and sexual coercion, 36, 48, 53–54; and Civil War, 172

Slave resistance: methods of, 12; and slaveholding women's management, 13, 36–37; and slaveholding women's mastery, 14, 55; and Revolutionary War, 22–23, 242 (n. 36); and arms, 23; and runaways, 55–56, 57; and Civil War, 57, 161, 168–69; and overseers, 127

Slavery: and construct of mastery, 2, 193; marriage compared to, 3; and political democracy, 3; ideological defense of, 12, 34, 130; and mastery, 12, 13; and Revolutionary War, 22–23, 116, 117; and degradation of dependency, 115; and Civil War, 159, 160, 161, 168, 171–72, 173–75, 189–90; and class boundaries, 194

Slaves, domestic. *See* Domestic slaves

Trust estates, 64, 65, 69–70
Tucker, George, 41, 91, 122, 126
Turberville, Gawin Corbin, 118
Turberville, George Lee, 24, 74, 75, 76, 205 (n. 40)
Turberville, Martha Corbin, 74, 92, 97, 117, 118–19, 219–20 (n. 37), 230 (n. 42)
Tyler, Lizzie, 167

Underemployment, 39
Union troops, 160, 161, 164, 166, 168, 170, 172–74, 176–78
University of North Carolina, 166–67
Upper South, 16–17, 45
Urban widows, 40, 51, 104–5

Van Yeveren, Dorothea, 51
Varick, Colonel, 88
Varick, Richard, 107–8
Vaughan, Archibald, 85, 86
Vaughan, Jessie, 72
Violence: slaveholding widows' use of, 7, 13, 36, 49–53, 128; of Revolutionary War, 20; corporal punishment, 36, 43, 48, 49–50; and planter widows, 48; and slavery, 115; and overseers, 122; fears of slave violence, 170; and Civil War, 179
Virginia, 1, 16, 17, 57, 79, 162, 215 (n. 82)
Virginia Association of Ladies for Erecting a Statue to Henry Clay, 108–9
Voting rights, 3, 24, 83, 109. See also Franchise; Political rights

Wage work, 39, 40, 165–67. See also Needlework; Teaching
Walker and Atkinson (cotton factors), 87–88
Washington, Anne, 20
Washington, George, 1, 106, 107, 112
Washington, James, 153

Washington, Martha, 1, 5, 7, 8, 88, 106–8, 110, 111
Washington, Mary, 112, 229 (n. 31)
Watson, J. H., 112
Watson, Sophia, 27
Wethers, George H., 92
Wheeler, Ann, 63, 145–46
Wheeler, Charlie, 146
Wheeler, Joseph, 174
Whigs, 104–5, 108, 109, 111
White men: as masters, 1, 6, 9, 104; and political rights, 3; legal rights of, 4; and assistance to widows, 10; and class boundaries, 10–11; and deputy husbands, 28–29; slaveholding wives distinguished from, 33; and slave management, 36, 55; and upholding slavery, 57; as artisans, 86; and slaveholding widows' commercial transactions, 86; and democratic culture, 102; and elections, 109; and political involvement, 115; slaveholding widows' conflicts with, 116, 126; and suffrage, 116, 117; and slaveholding women's mastery, 122–23; and Civil War, 159, 161, 168, 170; black men compared to, 196, 198
Whites: and class boundaries, 10–11, 115, 161, 179, 193–94; and republican political culture, 115; and poverty, 120; free blacks as threat to, 196–97
White women: and political rights, 3; poor white widows, 4, 9, 94, 98, 150, 200 (n. 12), 223 (n. 14); and class boundaries, 11, 183; poor white women, 33, 179; and commercial transactions, 83–84, 221 (n. 2); and franchise, 83; and Civil War, 159; and black men, 197
Widowers: and remarriage, 38, 150
Widowhood: effects of, 1; desolation associated with, 3–4, 5, 9, 15, 148; and women's life expectancy, 9; fac-

tors shaping, 13; personal implications of, 14; and female heirs, 135; and sexual propriety of widows, 184–88, 197, 244 (n. 85); and management of husband's assets, 200–201 (n. 13). *See also* Planter widows; Poor white widows; Slaveholding widows' mastery; Yeoman farmer widows

Widows. *See* Dependency of slaveholding widows; Free black widows; Independence of slaveholding widows; Northern farm widows; Planter widows; Poor white widows; Rural widows; Slaveholding widows' mastery; Urban widows; Yeoman farmer widows

Widows' thirds. *See* Dower rights

Wiggins, Elizabeth, 164

Wilcox, Edmund, 75

Wilcox, Susannah: and slave management, 45, 47; and kinship networks, 72, 74–75, 76, 80; and commercial transactions, 85, 92, 99; authority of, 117–18; and overseers, 119

Wilkins, Berkeley, 160

Wilkins, Eliza, 45, 53, 64, 65, 68, 95, 160

Wilkins, Gouverneur, 64

Wilkins, Martin, 64, 160

Willard, Joseph, 107

Williams, Nancy, 37, 57

Wills: and slaveholding widows as household heads, 6; and slaveholding widows' property rights, 15, 16, 29; and authority, 19, 29, 31–32; and children, 29–31, 33, 133, 135;

136, 207 (n. 63); terms of lifetime or widowhood, 30, 56; and debts, 36; and property disputes, 76–80; and estate settlements, 90–91; of slaveholding widows, 132, 133–36, 233 (n. 5)

Wills, James, 47

Wilson, Agnes, 78

Wilson, John, 152

Wilson, Peter, 78

Wilson, Ruth, 64, 78, 152, 153. *See also* Hairston, Ruth

Withers, John M., 89

"Woman's sphere," 64

Women. *See* Free black women; Poor white women; Slave women; White women

Women's education, 98–99, 116

Woodin, C. H. A., 185

Woodin, Mollie, 185–86

Woodruff, Isabella, 165, 166, 171, 185–87

Wragg, Henrietta, 22

Wright, Gavin, 120

Wyatt-Brown, Bertram, 82

Yeoman farmers, 11, 12–13, 37, 104, 125, 231 (n. 59)

Yeoman farmer widows: and migration, 8, 99, 208–9 (n. 6), 227 (n. 52); and slave management, 36; responsibilities of, 37–38, 39, 208 (n. 5); and sexual coercion, 54; and commercial transactions, 86, 93, 102; clothing of, 97–98

Young, Jeffrey R., 43

Younge, Rebecca, 39, 65

GENDER AND AMERICAN CULTURE

Taking Haiti: Military Occupation and the Culture of U.S. Imperialism, 1915–1940, by Mary A. Renda (2001).

Before Jim Crow: The Politics of Race in Postemancipation Virginia, by Jane Dailey (2000).

Captain Ahab Had a Wife: New England Women and the Whalefishery, 1720–1870, by Lisa Norling (2000).

Civilizing Capitalism: The National Consumers' League, Women's Activism, and Labor Standards in the New Deal Era, by Landon R. Y. Storrs (2000).

Rank Ladies: Gender and Cultural Hierarchy in American Vaudeville, by M. Alison Kibler (1999).

Strangers and Pilgrims: Female Preaching in America, 1740–1845, by Catherine A. Brekus (1998).

Sex and Citizenship in Antebellum America, by Nancy Isenberg (1998).

Yours in Sisterhood: Ms. Magazine and the Promise of Popular Feminism, by Amy Erdman Farrell (1998).

We Mean to Be Counted: White Women and Politics in Antebellum Virginia, by Elizabeth R. Varon (1998).

Women Against the Good War: Conscientious Objection and Gender on the American Home Front, 1941–1947, by Rachel Waltner Goossen (1997).

Toward an Intellectual History of Women: Essays by Linda K. Kerber (1997).

Gender and Jim Crow: Women and the Politics of White Supremacy in North Carolina, 1896–1920, by Glenda Elizabeth Gilmore (1996).

Delinquent Daughters: Protecting and Policing Adolescent Female Sexuality in the United States, 1885–1920, by Mary E. Odem (1995).

U.S. History as Women's History: New Feminist Essays, edited by Linda K. Kerber, Alice Kessler-Harris, and Kathryn Kish Sklar (1995).

Common Sense and a Little Fire: Women and Working-Class Politics in the United States, 1900–1965, by Annelise Orleck (1995).

How Am I to Be Heard?: Letters of Lillian Smith, edited by Margaret Rose Gladney (1993).

Entitled to Power: Farm Women and Technology, 1913–1963, by Katherine Jellison (1993).

Revising Life: Sylvia Plath's Ariel Poems, by Susan R. Van Dyne (1993).

Made From This Earth: American Women and Nature, by Vera Norwood (1993).

Unruly Women: The Politics of Social and Sexual Control in the Old South, by Victoria E. Bynum (1992).

The Work of Self-Representation: Lyric Poetry in Colonial New England, by Ivy Schweitzer (1991).

Labor and Desire: Women's Revolutionary Fiction in Depression America, by Paula Rabinowitz (1991).

Community of Suffering and Struggle: Women, Men, and the Labor Movement in Minneapolis, 1915–1945, by Elizabeth Faue (1991).

All That Hollywood Allows: Re-reading Gender in 1950s Melodrama, by Jackie Byars (1991).

Doing Literary Business: American Women Writers in the Nineteenth Century, by Susan Coultrap-McQuin (1990).

Ladies, Women, and Wenches: Choice and Constraint in Antebellum Charleston and Boston, by Jane H. Pease and William H. Pease (1990).

The Secret Eye: The Journal of Ella Gertrude Clanton Thomas, 1848–1889, edited by Virginia Ingraham Burr, with an introduction by Nell Irvin Painter (1990).

Second Stories: The Politics of Language, Form, and Gender in Early American Fictions, by Cynthia S. Jordan (1989).

Within the Plantation Household: Black and White Women of the Old South, by Elizabeth Fox-Genovese (1988).

The Limits of Sisterhood: The Beecher Sisters on Women's Rights and Woman's Sphere, by Jeanne Boydston, Mary Kelley, and Anne Margolis (1988).